The Centered Mind

The Centered Mind offers a new view of the nature and causal determinants of both reflective thinking and, more generally, the stream of consciousness. Peter Carruthers argues that conscious thought is always sensory-based, relying on the resources of the working-memory system. This system has been much studied by cognitive scientists. It enables sensory images to be sustained and manipulated through attentional signals directed at midlevel sensory areas of the brain. When abstract conceptual representations are bound into these images, we consciously experience ourselves as making judgments or arriving at decisions. Thus one might hear oneself as judging, in inner speech, that it is time to go home, for example. However, our amodal (non-sensory) propositional attitudes are never actually among the contents of this stream of conscious reflection. Our beliefs, goals, and decisions are only ever active in the background of consciousness, working behind the scenes to select the sensory-based imagery that occurs in working memory. They are never themselves conscious.

Drawing on extensive knowledge of the scientific literature on working memory and related topics, Carruthers builds an argument that challenges the central assumptions of many philosophers. In addition to arguing that non-sensory propositional attitudes are never conscious, he also shows that they are never under direct intentional control. Written with his usual clarity and directness, *The Centered Mind* will be essential reading for all philosophers and cognitive scientists interested in the nature of human thought processes.

The Centered Mind

*What the Science of Working
Memory Shows Us About the
Nature of Human Thought*

Peter Carruthers

OXFORD
UNIVERSITY PRESS

OXFORD

UNIVERSITY PRESS

Great Clarendon Street, Oxford, OX2 6DP,
United Kingdom

Oxford University Press is a department of the University of Oxford.
It furthers the University's objective of excellence in research, scholarship,
and education by publishing worldwide. Oxford is a registered trade mark of
Oxford University Press in the UK and in certain other countries

Published in the United States of America by Oxford University Press
198 Madison Avenue, New York, NY 10016, United States of America

British Library Cataloguing in Publication Data

Data available

Library of Congress Control Number: 2014960130

ISBN 978-0-19-873882-4

Printed and bound by
CPI Group (UK) Ltd, Croydon, CR0 4YY

for Daniel Dennett

—whose work awoke me from my Wittgensteinian slumber—

Contents

Preface

The project of this book developed out of an aspect of my last one. In *The Opacity of Mind* (Carruthers, 2011a), I defended the claim that our knowledge of our own thoughts (our beliefs, goals, decisions, and intentions) is always indirect and interpretive, no different in principle from our access to the thoughts of other people. In order to know our own minds, I argued, we have to turn our mind-reading capacities on ourselves, drawing inferences from sensorily accessible cues (including not only our own overt behavior and circumstances, but also such things as our own inner speech and visual imagery). I argued that this account is supported by a wide range of data from across cognitive science. But I also critiqued a number of competing theories proposed by philosophers. One account that I considered briefly is that we have a special-purpose working-memory system that enables our thoughts to be conscious and widely available to many different faculties of the mind. Since the latter include the mindreading system, we are thereby given direct access to the nature and occurrence of those thoughts—our judgments, goals, decisions, and the rest. It only occurred to me later that views similar to this one are quite widespread in philosophy (albeit using different terminology), as well as having considerable intuitive appeal. Moreover, what is really at stake in this aspect of the debate goes well beyond the topic of self-knowledge. Rather, it concerns the very nature of the cognitive architecture that underlies conscious thinking and reasoning, as well as our explanation of the so-called "stream of consciousness" more generally. In consequence, the topic is important enough to be worthy of a book in its own right.

I rely on an extensive scientific literature on working memory and surrounding issues to make my case.[1] Since working memory is the cognitive system that we employ when we engage in conscious forms of thinking and reasoning, and since (I shall argue) the contents of working memory are always sensory based (depending upon visual, auditory, and other forms of sensory imagery), it seems to follow that conscious thinking, too, is sensory based. In that case non-sensory (or "amodal") thoughts (including goals, decisions, intentions, and many

---

[1] The contents of working memory are generally believed to be conscious, drawing from many different unconscious regions of the mind. Moreover, those contents are likewise made available to many different unconscious mental systems that consume and respond to them. So working memory is, as it were, the place where "everything comes together" in the mind. Hence my title, *The Centered Mind*.

forms of judgment, I shall suggest) are incapable of being conscious. Rather, on the account that I provide, they "pull the strings" in the background, selecting, maintaining, and manipulating the sensory-based contents that *do* figure consciously in working memory. Somewhat surprisingly, then, it turns out that the conscious mind is much like a marionette that is controlled and made to dance by off-stage actors, who do their work unseen. But the main focus of this book is as much about developing a positive theory of reflection and the stream of consciousness as it is about overturning natural philosophical ideas about the nature of reflection. For while there is a wealth of work in cognitive science that bears on the topic, no one has, in my view, successfully woven it all together into a unified account. As a result, the book should be of broad interest to cognitive scientists as well as to philosophers.

The genre of this book is a kind of theoretical psychology, and I count myself (for present purposes, at least) as a theoretical psychologist. Consider an analogy with theoretical physics. Theoretical physicists generally do not conduct experiments. Rather, they take the data provided by experimental physicists and use those data to build general models and theories. The training for the two fields is different, and there is mostly no overlap between the two groups of scientists. In psychology, likewise, there is room for people who attempt to unify and explain the evidence collected by others.[2] This is especially likely to be useful where the data in question cut across disciplinary boundaries (as they do here), or derive from traditions of inquiry whose participants rarely interact with one another. Sometimes theoretical psychologists will also engage in experimental work. This would be true of Steven Pinker, for example. But sometimes they do not. Here Daniel Dennett provides an obvious instance. In this book (even more than in my previous one) I try to emulate the latter's example (albeit without attempting to match his inimitable writing style, and without sharing many of his views).

The initial work for this book was supported by a Research and Scholarship Award from the University of Maryland Graduate School, for which I am grateful. In addition, I wish to thank the following friends, colleagues, and students for their comments on some or all of an earlier draft: Heather Adair, Felipe De Brigard, Mark Engelbert, Peter Godfrey-Smith, Andrew Knoll, Neil Levy, Ryan Ogilvie, Georges Rey, Lizzie Schechter, Julius Schoenherr, Chandra Sripada, Xuan Wang, Evan Westra, Wayne Wu, and two anonymous readers for Oxford University Press. I am grateful to Susan Levi for her help in producing Figures 1, 2, 3, and 4; and to Mark Fox for permission to reproduce Figure 6.

---

[2] Similarly in philosophy, some would say there is room for people who pursue philosophical questions experimentally—hence the nascent field of experimental philosophy. This book is definitely not of that ilk.

Figures

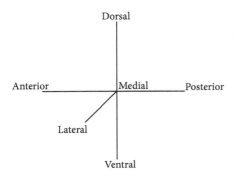

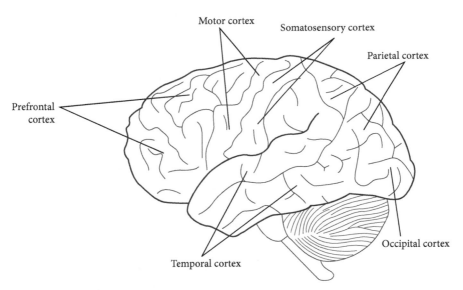

Figure 1. Major regions of the brain together with directional naming conventions. (Left hemisphere, outside view.)

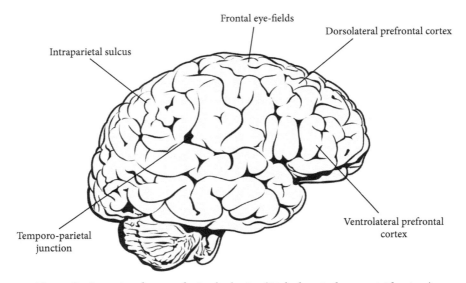

Figure 2. Attentional networks in the brain. (Right hemisphere, outside view.)

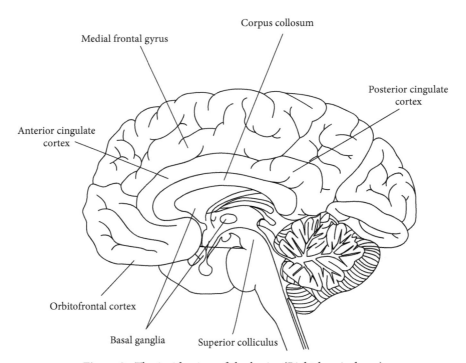

Figure 3. The inside view of the brain. (Right hemisphere.)

Figure 4. The hidden Dalmatian.

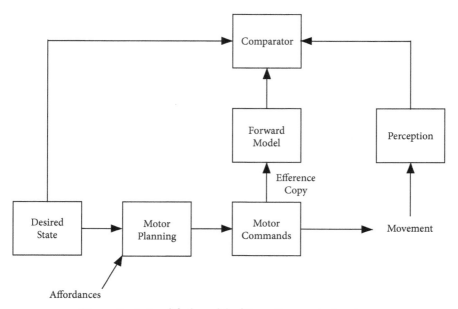

Figure 5. A simplified model of the action-control system.

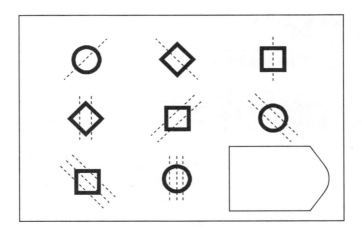

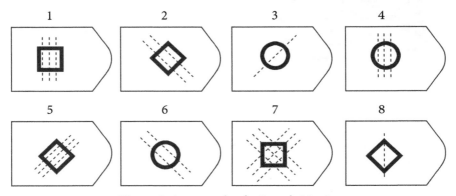

Figure 6. An example of a Raven's Matrix.

One's task is to select the object missing from the bottom right of the topmost set of boxes, choosing from among the eight alternatives provided below.

1

Introduction

This initial chapter will introduce the questions that concern us and say something about their significance. It will introduce the scientific concept of working
memory, and will sketch the account of human thought processes that builds
around that concept. Finally, the chapter will provide an outline of the argument
to be pursued in the chapters that follow.

1. On Reflection

This section introduces the phenomena (reflection and the stream of consciousness) that constitute the primary topics of this book. A number of distinctions are
drawn, and some initial theses are laid out for later discussion.

1.1. The target phenomena

This book is about the nature of the so-called "stream of consciousness" which
occupies our minds with sequences of thinking and imagining through much of
the waking day. My goal is to understand, at least in outline, the processes that
determine the content of that stream, together with the nature of those contents
themselves (specifically, whether those contents include propositional attitudes
as well as feelings and images).[1] But the book is also, and more narrowly, about
the nature of reflective thinking, where we actively organize the stream of
consciousness toward the achievement of a goal of some sort, such as arriving
at a judgment or a decision.

---

[1] Let me emphasize for readers who are psychologists—especially those who are social
psychologists—that I use the term "attitude" throughout in the broad philosophical sense, which
includes all forms of propositional thought. Hence judgments, goals, and decisions, as well as events
of wondering whether something is the case, or supposing that something is so, are all attitudes.
Psychologists, in contrast, often use the term in a highly restrictive sense, to include only evaluative
dispositions. In this narrow sense, *being in favor of affirmative action* and *disapproving of abortion*
are both attitudes; but *believing that one was born in June*, *wondering what one's mother might like
for her birthday*, and *deciding to set one's alarm for 6 am tomorrow* are not. All of these propositional
thoughts are attitudes in the sense I intend here, however.

What happens when we reflect? More broadly, in what does the stream of consciousness consist? Some answers seem obvious. When we reflect, we entertain thoughts: we examine possibilities, consider options, make inferences, arrive at judgments, and take decisions. And the stream of consciousness can also include visual images, fragments of song, episodic memories, inner speech, and many other forms of sensory-like event. But reflection can likewise be a conscious process. So the stream of consciousness can include, as a subset, the kinds of sequence of thought that constitute reflection. If one then believes (as I think one should, and as I will argue in Chapter 2) that many of our thoughts are abstract and amodal (non-sensory) in nature, then one will think that the stream of consciousness is constituted by two kinds of event: a set of sensory-like events of imagining, episodically remembering, and so on; and a set of amodal propositional-attitude events of supposing, judging, deciding, and the like.

1.2. On consciousness

Before continuing, we need to pause for a moment to say something about how consciousness is here understood. (The topic will be considered in more detail in Chapter 3.) Much of the debate within philosophy concerns the nature of so-called "phenomenal" consciousness. This is the sort of consciousness that has a subjective *feel* to it, or that is *like* something to undergo (Chalmers, 1996). Some claim that phenomenal consciousness can be explained in physical terms while others deny it. This is not our concern here. Rather, our focus is on *access* consciousness (Block, 1995), which almost everyone maintains is not nearly so problematic. Indeed, there is now substantial agreement in the literature that access-conscious states are those that have a sort of "global availability" to a wide range of other mental states and processes. This idea is not only scientifically well established, as we will see in Chapter 3, but it fits nicely with our everyday experience. For we know that the events we describe as conscious are ones that we can report, that can issue in new memories, give rise to emotional responses, issue in new goals, and help guide our decisions. They must therefore be accessible to a wide range of different mental states, systems, and faculties. Hence to say that reflection is a conscious process is to say that its contents are globally accessible in this sense.

It is worth noting, too, that conscious states can be roughly divided into two classes: those that are exogenously caused, and perceptual in character; and those that are endogenously caused, brought about through the mind's own operations. Events of seeing a sunset, smelling a rose, or hearing an oboe fall into the former category, whereas the corresponding imaginative acts fall into the latter. When people talk about the stream of consciousness, I think they generally have in mind the set of endogenously caused conscious events. It is the stream of conscious thinking and imagining created through the mind's own activity that constitutes the stream of consciousness, not the conscious perceptions and experiences that result from attending to the external world (or to one's own body). At any rate this is how I propose to understand the notion for our purposes. The distinction is not a sharp one, however. For we know that perception is influenced by top-down endogenous processes, including the direction of attention. And events that are paradigmatic elements of the stream of consciousness, such as episodic memories, can be sparked by externally perceived stimuli, which trigger the memory in question. Moreover, the distinction is not always manifest to subjects themselves. A vivid hallucination, for example (which is endogenously caused), might be indistinguishable from the real (externally caused) thing from the point of view of the person who experiences it.

1.3. Reflection revisited

With these points of clarification behind us, let us return to consider the nature of reflection. Plainly it is largely an endogenous, rather than an exogenously caused, process. And we have already noted that reflection can seemingly include propositional-attitude events such as judgments and decisions, as well as processes like reasoning, and considering possible options when decision making. But is day-dreaming also a form of reflection? When one drifts in a fantasy with one's stream of consciousness populated by images of palm trees, blue skies, cold beers, and golden beaches, is one engaging in reflection? My own intuition is to say "No." I think the term "reflection" would normally be reserved for forms of thinking that are in some more obvious sense *purposeful*, directed toward solving a problem of some sort, arriving at a judgment, or at reaching a decision.

Conversely one can ask: do processes of reflection *always* fall within the stream of consciousness? Plainly reflection is *often* a conscious process. But is it always? My own intuition is to say "Yes." While one might allow that there are unconscious reasoning and decision-making processes of various sorts, one should decline to call these forms of reflection. The upshot is then that reflection is a proper subset of the stream of consciousness. While reflection is always conscious, not everything that can be found in one's stream of consciousness constitutes a form of reflection. Again, this is how I propose to understand these notions for present purposes. Although reflection can include sensory-like events of imagining as well as propositional attitude events of judging and deciding, only those sequences of conscious event that seem to their subjects to be purposeful in nature will qualify as forms of reflection.

Philosophers, too, often make a distinction between active and passive forms of endogenously caused mental activity (Peacocke, 2008; O'Brien & Soteriou, 2009), and one might wonder whether this coincides with the distinction we have drawn between reflection and the other events that constitute the stream of consciousness. It is natural to think that reasoning, judging, imagining, and deciding are mental actions: they are things that one *does*, and does for reasons. In contrast, the thoughts that appear in one's mind unbidden, the snatches of song that reverberate in one's head, and the images that occur to one while one drifts in reverie, are all passive in nature: they are things that happen to one, not things that one does. It seems that this latter class of passive mental events consists of things that *disrupt* reflection, or replace reflection, rather than being constitutive of it. So it may well be that the distinction between reflection, on the one hand, and the remainder of the stream of consciousness, on the other, is grounded in the same intuitive active–passive distinction that is emphasized by philosophers.

1.4. Summary and goals

Let me summarize the three main points that have emerged from our discussion so far:

(1) Among conscious mental events one can distinguish between those that are exogenously caused and those that are endogenously caused; I propose to reserve the term "stream of consciousness" for the latter.

The main goal of this book is to develop an empirically grounded theory of the contents and causes of the stream of consciousness.

(2) Intuitively, the stream of consciousness contains both amodal attitude events of supposing, judging, deciding, and so on, as well as sensory-like events of imagined seeing, imagined hearing, and so forth.

I will argue that our best theory of the stream of consciousness challenges the correctness of this intuition. On the contrary, the stream of consciousness is entirely sensory based.

(3) Intuitively, the stream of consciousness includes both purposeful (or active) and purposeless (or passive) forms of mental activity, with many amodal attitude events falling into the former category; I propose to use the term "reflection" to refer to this sort of apparently purposeful conscious mental activity.

I will argue that our best theory of the stream of consciousness challenges the correctness of the intuitive distinction between active and passive forms of conscious mentality. On the contrary, all components of the stream of consciousness are actively produced.

My main goal, then, is to develop an empirically grounded theory of the stream of consciousness. More specifically, I will attempt to answer the following questions: (a) How are stream-of-consciousness events endogenously caused? (b) What explains how they become conscious (that is, globally available)? And (c) does the stream of consciousness contain amodal attitude events as well as sensory-like ones? There is a great deal of data in cognitive science relevant to answering these questions, spread out over a number of different disciplines. But no one has succeeded in weaving it all together into a unified account. (Or rather, no one has woven it into a story that satisfies all of the constraints that I will argue *should* be satisfied, in this domain.) Much of our focus, however, will be on the processes that constitute reflection more narrowly. For it is here that the account that I provide has especially revisionary implications. In effect, providing an adequate account of the processes that create the stream of consciousness will lead me to deny the reality of the intuitive claims made in points (2) and (3) above, as I now explain.

1.5. Amodal attitudes in reflection?

Suppose one believes (as I will argue in Chapter 2 that one should) that there are propositional attitudes that are amodal, or non-sensory, in character. And suppose one thinks that such attitudes include events of supposing something to be the case, judging that something is the case, and deciding to do something. Then one will naturally think that reflection is, at least partly, constituted by amodal attitudes. For recall the belief that when one reflects, among the contents of reflection are that one supposes things, reasons about things, and arrives at judgments and decisions. If these attitudes are amodal ones, then one must believe that such attitudes are capable of being conscious, and of figuring in the stream of consciousness.

Consider how one might describe to someone a sequence of reflection in which one has just engaged: "I was wondering what to do on Saturday. I thought I might either go to the art museum or go hiking. I remembered that the forecast was good, which made the hike seem attractive. And then I recalled that there would be delays on the metro red-line downtown. So that settled it: I decided to go hiking." Here a reflective process is described as consisting in a series of attitude events: an initial event of wondering (implicit in the description of which is the goal of doing something interesting on Saturday); then a "thinking I might," which should probably be classified as a type of supposition; then an activated memory, which results in an affective (emotional) response; then another activated memory, followed by a decision.

If asked to detail everything that the process of reflection had consisted in, one would list these events together with some others (such as the occurrence of visual imagery of portions of the hike, as well as the goal of doing something interesting on Saturday).

This example could be supplemented by many others in which attitudes of other types would figure: hoping, pretending, and intending; emotional events of anger, disgust, and fear; as well as desires, goals, and more. Hence we seem to assume that attitudes of all different types can be activated and conscious within a process of reflection. Now, *some* propositional attitudes are no doubt partly sensory-like in character. This is true of episodic memories, for example, which can include visual, auditory, or olfactory imagery. It is also true of many affective attitudes, which will include distinctive states of bodily arousal. But many attitudes, it seems, are not at all sensory-like. Judging that 17 is a prime number, for example, seems to be entirely amodal, both in its content and the attitude that one takes toward that content. Likewise, I would say, for a decision to go hiking and for recalling the goal of losing weight. Hence we seem committed to thinking that reflection is partly constituted by amodal attitude events.

If one believes that reflection can contain both amodal attitude events and sensory-like feelings and images, then one can ask how the two sorts of component are related to one another. One possibility is that they are caused independently of one another. But this seems highly implausible. Recalling that the forecast is good, for example (which seems like a good candidate for an amodal attitude event), might be accompanied by a visual image of sunshine and blue skies. The correspondence in content between one's thoughts and one's imagery is often too close to be coincidental. Another possibility is that the relationship is associative. Perhaps one's thoughts associatively evoke related images of various kinds. This idea is plausible, in many cases. But it runs into trouble with reflective uses of inner speech. If one expresses a decision to oneself in words ("So, I'll go hiking then"), the connection between the sensory-like features of the sounds that one thereby imagines and the thought that one thinks seems much too close to be merely associative. A third possibility is that while sensory-like events *can* occur passively in the stream of consciousness (caused by who-knows-what), when one reflects the reflective process itself actively recruits sensory-like representations as an aid to its own operations. (Think how repeating a series of numerals to oneself in inner speech can help one remember the corresponding number.)

1.6. *The sensory-based nature of reflection*

The possibilities canvassed in the previous paragraph will be examined in due course (in Chapters 4 and 5). I will show that they confront considerable obstacles. At the same time I will be amassing evidence that events that are among the contents of reflection (and the stream of consciousness more generally) always constitutively involve, while being causally dependent on, sensory-like components. (I will hereafter express this idea by saying that reflection and the stream of consciousness are "sensory based." The phrase is awkward but concise.) For example, consider an episodic memory of a dinner one once ate at a Moroccan restaurant in the French city of Avignon. Besides conceptual information about the location and type of food, it includes distinctive images of sights, sounds, smells, and tastes. These sensory-like elements are constitutive *parts* of the memory, and don't merely serve to evoke it. Moreover (I will argue), any conceptual components of the episodic memory in question are causally dependent on these sensory-like ones. For if the latter are removed or cease to be attended to, then the conceptual components of the memory will likewise cease to be conscious.

If all reflection is sensory based, then it will follow that amodal (non-sensory) attitudes are incapable of figuring in reflection. Rather, according to the theory I develop, they do their work unconsciously, operating behind the scenes to determine the sensory-based contents that *do* figure in reflection. I will try to show how reflection utilizes the much-studied working-memory system to sustain, rehearse, and manipulate sensory-based representations in visual, proprioceptive, or auditory imagery (including inner speech). Since the contents of working memory are always sensory based, there is no place among them for amodal attitudes. Nor is there any other manner in which such attitudes can be activated and interact in ways that would render them conscious and widely accessible within the mind. So the reflective mind will turn out to be quite other than many of us are apt to think.

I should emphasize that the position I defend is that reflection is always sensory *based*, not that it is purely sensory in character. The latter is the view of Jackendoff (2007, 2012), who claims that *only* sensory representations are ever conscious. So when we hear speech, for example, we experience the sounds, and we have the impression that they are meaningful, but we do not experience the meaning. My view is different. I will argue (in Chapter 3) that amodal conceptual representations are often bound into the contents of sensory experience. This happens when we see something *as* a dog, for example, or when we hear someone *as* asking for directions to the metro station. And something similar is true in connection with endogenously produced imagery, as when one *imagines* a dog. So I allow that certain *kinds* of propositional attitude can figure consciously in reflection. These are ones that have a mixed sensory–conceptual character, such as episodic memories and judgments that are embedded in sensory-like states.

What I will deny is that *purely* amodal attitudes (such as decisions, goals, and intentions, as well as non-perceptual judgments or beliefs) can ever figure consciously in reflection. Such attitudes are real, and can function as parts of the executive component underlying working-memory activity, but they cannot figure among the *contents* of working memory. This is because those contents are always sensory based.

In effect, then, I will be suggesting that our best empirically grounded theory of the stream of consciousness should lead us to deny that streams of consciousness ever contain amodal events of supposing, judging, deciding, and so on. On the contrary, I will argue that amodal attitudes are never conscious. Instead, the contents of the stream of consciousness are exclusively sensory based. Thus the stream of consciousness consists entirely of sensory-like events of imagined seeing, imagined hearing, and so on.

1.7. Passive imagining?

I will also argue that our best theory of the stream of consciousness should lead us to deny the claim made as point (3) in Section 1.4 above, namely that the stream includes both purposeful (or active) and purposeless (or passive) forms of mental activity. It is certainly intuitive that the contents of the stream are sometimes under our control. When one works toward the solution of a problem, or reasons about what to do on Saturday, it seems that one's reflections are actively undertaken in pursuit of the goals in question. But it is equally intuitive that the stream of consciousness can consist in mere happenings, neither undertaken in pursuit of a goal nor comprising any mental actions. When one cannot get a snatch of song out of one's head, for example, it seems as if one is the *victim* of one's imagination, rather than the agent. Likewise when ideas—sometimes creative ones—emerge unheralded in consciousness: one feels that one is not the *producer* of those ideas, but the recipient.

I will suggest in Chapter 6, however, that this distinction is merely epistemic. Rather, all contents in the stream of consciousness are equally active, involving either mental rehearsals of bodily action or decisions to redirect attention toward a novel mental representation (or both). But in some cases we think we know *why* those contents are produced, and hence we deem these cases to be active, whereas in others we don't, and so classify them as passive.

1.8. Sources of error

In effect, I will be developing an *error-theory* of reflection and the stream of consciousness: their nature is other than we are intuitively inclined to think. I have already suggested that the active–passive distinction could arise from differences in our epistemic access to the underlying causes. But where does the temptation to think that attitudes of all kinds can figure consciously in reflection come from? Why is it so easy for us to believe it? At least part of the answer is that this is the way in which our experience presents itself to us when we reflect. When we reflectively generate and manipulate visual imagery (perhaps imagining the negative outcome of some action that is open to us), or when we engage in inner speech, we experience ourselves as supposing, deciding, judging, or whatever. This is (I claim) because the sensory-based contents that figure in working memory when we reflect are available as input to the mindreading faculty, which automatically interprets them (when it has sufficient cues to do so) as expressions of suitable propositional attitudes. Moreover, the same faculty makes a tacit assumption that our minds are transparently available to us. So we take ourselves to be experiencing our attitude events themselves, which figure consciously as *parts* of the process of reflection (rather than as underlying causal determinants of it, as I will argue).

For a full defense of the claims involved in this explanation the reader is directed to Carruthers (2011a), where it is also argued that the transparency-assumption is universal to all historical eras and human cultures. The simplest and most plausible explanation of this finding is that a tacit assumption that people's thoughts are transparently available to them (and thereby access-conscious) is innately channeled in development. Moreover, reverse-engineering considerations applied to a well-designed mindreading faculty predict that it should contain just such an assumption (perhaps embodied as a rule of process-ing rather than an explicit belief). This would greatly simplify the task of interpreting other people's behavior, especially their verbal behavior when they report their own mental states. In addition, it would do so without any loss of reliability, and perhaps with some gains. The same mindreading faculty, then, when directed toward the self and when ascribing attitudes to the self on the basis of visual imagery, inner speech, and other sensory cues, will issue in the impres-sion that one is directly introspecting those attitudes. So it will seem to us that our attitudes figure in our reflections in ways that are both conscious and mutually accessible.

2. The Importance of the Issues

Why do these questions matter? First and foremost, because what is at stake is the very nature of human thought processes, as well as the cognitive mechanisms that underlie and shape the stream of consciousness. Assuming that there are such things as amodal propositional attitudes, are any of them ever conscious? When we reflect and reason about things consciously, are those conscious thought processes constituted, in part, by amodal attitude events, such as goals, decisions, and non-sensory judgments? Or do such events operate beneath the surface of our reflections, selecting, maintaining, and transforming sensory-based representations within a sort of "global workspace" (working memory), thereby making the contents of those representations widely available for processing by different subsystems of the mind? More fundamentally, how are the events that figure in the stream of consciousness selected, and how do they get to be globally broadcast?

There is a wealth of findings in cognitive science that bears on these questions. Some derive from the study of conscious perception and the attentional mechanisms that underlie the global broadcast of sensory representations. Some derive from the study of working memory, which increasingly seems to share many of the same mechanisms as perception. There are also numerous studies of the importance of working memory for human fluid general intelligence, or fluid *g*. And then there is a large body of literature on human reasoning and decision-making abilities, and their relationship to working memory. Although the connections among some of these literatures are often noted, no one has, to the best of my knowledge, attempted to weave them all together into a single integrated account of human conscious thought processes (the stream of consciousness). Doing so is the primary goal of the present book.

These issues also have a bearing on the account one might give of the differences between human minds and the minds of nonhuman animals. For many philosophers have thought that what is distinctive of human propositional attitudes is their "inferential promiscuity" (Evans, 1982; Brewer, 1999; Hurley, 2006). Philosophers have believed that all types of attitude can figure consciously in our reflections, where both the attitudes and the reasoning processes into which they enter fall under our rational control. This is held to underlie the distinctively open-ended and flexible character of human thought and behavior.

Indeed, many philosophers insist that only concepts and attitudes that are, as one might say, "reflection sensitive" can genuinely count as such. Thus both McDowell (1994) and Brandom (1994, 2000) think that human thought is distinguished by its *spontaneity*, distinctively taking place in a "space of reasons."[2] And Korsgaard (1996, 2009) maintains that only beliefs and decisions

---

[2] It might be objected against this reading of McDowell (1994) that he thinks the human capacity for spontaneity is language-dependent. And if the form of reflection that takes place in "the space of reasons" is linguistically constituted, then it would seem that it is not our attitudes, as such, that figure in reflection, but rather visual imagery, episodes of sensory-based inner speech, and so on, much as I claim in this book. However, the dependence in question is intended to be developmental

that result from processes of conscious deliberation are ones for which we have *reasons*. Having reasons for our beliefs and actions is said to depend on the existence of a certain sort of "reflective distance" between the potential grounds for belief or action and those beliefs and actions themselves. On this kind of account our minds (unlike the minds of nonhuman animals, it is said) do not remain passive with respect to our circumstances and experiences. Rather, we are capable of actively weighing reasons for belief and for action, and any thought of ours can spark an open-ended process of reflection and inference in which attitudes of all kinds can actively figure.

Not surprisingly in the light of such beliefs, when philosophers have turned their attention to the minds of nonhuman animals many have denied that the latter are capable of thought at all, in the full sense of the term. Rather, at best animals have *proto*-thoughts composed of *proto*-concepts (Dummett, 1991; Brandom, 1994; McDowell, 1994; Bermúdez, 2003; Hurley, 2006). It is undeniable, of course, that human reasoning and decision-making processes vastly outstrip the powers of nonhuman animals in flexibility and sophistication. But what is at stake is whether the difference in question has an architectural basis (with humans alone possessing a central workspace in which conscious reflection takes place and where amodal attitudes of all kinds can be activated in a controlled manner), or whether the difference is only one of degree. I will argue, in Chapter 8, for the latter view. The evidence suggests that all mammals and birds share essentially the same sensory-based working-memory system in which representations can be consciously activated, sustained, and manipulated. Humans are distinctive only in the kinds of use that they can make of that system.

The idea that propositional attitudes of all kinds can be entertained consciously, in ways that can be both reflected on and actively controlled by their subjects, is deeply embedded in a good deal of philosophical theorizing. Arguably it lies at the heart of the conception of human rational agency sketched above (McDowell, 1994; Korsgaard, 1996, 2009). And it is taken for granted in a number of other philosophical projects. Burge (1996), for example, just assumes without argument that our attitudes can occur consciously, available to be rationally reflected on and controlled, as part of his analysis of our entitlement to claim self-knowledge of them. Many philosophical debates and theories might

---

rather than constitutive. McDowell says (quite plausibly) that it is by being inducted into a community of language users that we acquire the capacity to consider reasons and to reflect on the evidence for our beliefs and the reasons for our decisions. But thought and reflection are not themselves supposed to be linguistic in nature, according to McDowell, even if they are often linguistically expressed.

therefore need to be revisited if the thesis of this book is correct, and amodal attitudes are incapable of being conscious. Some further remarks along these lines will be made in the concluding chapter.

3. Working Memory

One thesis defended in this book is that working memory is the system within which reflective thinking takes place, and in which the stream of consciousness occurs more generally. So understanding the nature of working memory is the key to understanding the nature of both reflection and the stream of consciousness. The present section will therefore provide a brief introduction to the scientific conception of working memory.

Working memory is generally thought to be a central domain-general resource that enables representations to be actively sustained, rehearsed, and manipulated for purposes of reasoning and problem solving. (Examples would include: sustaining a representation of an object that has disappeared behind a screen so that one knows what to expect when the screen is removed; rehearsing a phone number that one has just been given, while hunting for a pad and pencil with which to write it down; imagining some different ways in which a set of boxes might be packed into the trunk of a car; and adding or subtracting numbers in one's head.) The contents of working memory are widely thought to be conscious.

Working memory should not be confused with long-term memory. The latter consists of stored representations that are no longer in an activated state. Working memory, in contrast, consists of representations that are actively sustained by the subject. Moreover, the contents of working memory are always conscious, as we will see, whereas the contents of long-term memory only *become* conscious when recalled into working memory. Empirically, working memory can be distinguished from all forms of long-term memory through its sensitivity to attentional interference. Information sustained in working memory will be lost if subjects are distracted and turn their attention fully to other matters. Long-term memories, in contrast, will merely decay at the normal rate in such circumstances.

Working memory should also be distinguished from sensory short-term memory. The latter can retain information in sensory cortices for around two seconds in the absence of attention, provided that the representations aren't overwritten by subsequent stimuli. Such representations can give rise to priming effects without ever being conscious (Dehaene et al., 2006). They can *become* conscious, however, if attention is directed toward them before they expire

3. WORKING MEMORY   13

(Sergent et al., 2013).[3] They can also be used for online guidance of action in the absence of attention (Milner & Goodale, 1995). The contents of working memory, in contrast, are attention-dependent and conscious. Moreover, they can be held in an activated state for as long as attention is directed at them, and can be retained despite the impact of subsequent stimuli that overwrite the representations in sensory short-term memory.[4]

For purposes of illustration, and to emphasize the ubiquity of working memory in our mental lives, it is worth mentioning some of the kinds of task that can be used to investigate its nature, as well as some of the mental activities that utilize it. Researchers often require participants to engage in mental arithmetic, where the result of one component of a calculation needs to be held in mind while another is executed. Also heavily used are so-called "n-back" tasks, in which a series of numbers, letters, shapes, or sounds is presented, and participants are required to judge whether the currently presented item is the same as the one presented n items back in the series (three, say). To do this, people need to remember the most recent few items and their position in the sequence, while resisting potential interference from their memories of the $n+1$ and $n-1$ items, in order to make the required judgment. Somewhat similar are complex memory-span tasks, in which people are required to remember, in sequence, a serially presented list of words or other items while conducting a demanding secondary activity. For example, while each target word is presented one is required to judge the truth or falsity of an arithmetic equation. Here, too, people need to remember the target items and their position in the sequence while resisting interference from the parallel distractor task.

The everyday mental activities that utilize working memory should certainly include discursive thinking conducted in so-called "inner speech." As with outer speech, one needs to keep in mind what was said recently in order to construct and entertain a suitable sequel. Also included would be episodic remembering, where one activates and sustains an experience-like representation of some past event. And equally important (if not more so) would be prospective reasoning, where one evaluates potential future scenarios. Here one has to construct and sustain in working memory a representation of a target future action or event, elaborating it to consider likely consequences, and responding affectively to the result. As should be clear from these examples, use of working memory is well-

---

[3] Consider the famous example of only noticing the clock strike at the third chime, while at the same time recalling the previous two strokes.

[4] Note, however, that attention is quite sensitive to interference. So sustaining a representation in working memory for an extended period of time is by no means easy.

neigh ubiquitous in our mental lives. What I will suggest is that understanding its nature is the key to understanding the nature of reflection and the stream of consciousness. And that nature turns out to be sensory based.

4. The Sensory-Based Account

Some aspects of the sensory-based model of reflection have already been outlined briefly above. The salient points are summarized here. Further elucidation, together with both experimental and theoretical support, will be provided in later chapters.

According to the sensory-based account, conscious reflection is grounded in the use of working memory, which in turn depends on attentional signals directed at midlevel sensory areas of the brain.[5] The latter results in the global broadcast of the attended-to sensory-based representations, which are thereby made available to a wide range of systems set up to consume globally broadcast perceptual representations generally. These consumer systems draw inferences from the input and give rise to new memories, as well as evaluating and producing affective responses to the represented objects or events. Some of these changes may result in shifts of attention, involving representations that are activated from long-term memory or generated through active rehearsal processes. When attended to, these enter working memory in turn, replacing or modifying the previous ones. The upshot is a kind of "virtual global workspace" in which representations that are grounded in any sensory modality can be activated and manipulated.

While the contents of working memory are sensory based, they often contain abstract, amodal, conceptual information bound into them. It should be stressed that these amodal representations are not merely *associated with* or *causally linked to* the sensory ones, but are bound into them as a result of the same kind of interactive processing that takes place in perception. As a result, not only

---

[5] Midlevel visual areas receive input from V1 and process the motion, color, and form of a stimulus, but without yet conceptualizing or categorizing it (which is regarded as high-level vision). Similar distinctions are applicable in respect of other sensory modalities. There is some dispute about whether attentional signals directly impact *primary* sensory areas, such as V1 in the case of vision (Posner & Gilbert, 1999; Kastner & Pinsk, 2004; Pinsk et al., 2004). I suggest that the impact of attention on V1 is largely indirect, mediated by back-and-forth processing with midlevel sensory areas that are the primary direct targets of attentional signals (Prinz, 2012). At any rate, we know that attentionally modulated V1 activity is not necessary for global broadcasting of visual representations to occur, since people with complete destruction of V1 can nevertheless have intact visual imagery (Goldenberg et al., 1995; Bridge et al., 2012). Moreover, we know that deficits in visual imagery are caused by cortical damage further along in the visual processing stream (Moro et al., 2008).

can one see something *as* a dog in a single integrated percept, but one can likewise sustain such a representation in working memory, thereby *imagining* or *remembering* a dog. And not only can one hear someone *as* asking the way to the metro station, with the content of the request integrated with one's perception of the sounds, but one can likewise hear *oneself* as wondering about the location of the metro station, in so-called inner speech. Moreover, I will argue that the *only* way in which one can think consciously about dogs or metro stations is by tokening some suitable imagistic representation in working memory, into which the relevant concepts can be bound.

Since working memory is sensory based, purely amodal attitudes are incapable of figuring among its contents. So activated beliefs that are entirely amodal in content, as well as goals, judgments, decisions, and intentions, are incapable of figuring directly in our conscious reflections. Such attitudes operate instead within the executive component of working memory, causing and directing the shifts of attention and the mental rehearsals of action that sustain or issue in changes in the contents of working memory. Hence our amodal attitudes *influence* our reflections without ever figuring among the contents of reflection. It should be clear that this model is in direct conflict with some of the intuitive views outlined in Section 1, and with the views of many philosophers. Specifically, the model denies that all types of propositional attitude are capable of being conscious, or of figuring in reflection.

5. The Road Ahead

The overall form of the argument of this book is an inference to the best explanation of the preponderance of scientific data. Many of the individual chapters, likewise, are constructed around an inference to the best explanation of the data in a particular domain.

Chapter 2 is about the nature of propositional attitudes. After discussing some distinctions among kinds of attitude, it reasons by inference to the best explanation to the existence of a set of amodal attitudes. These attitudes possess internal structure, and are built out of component amodal concepts. The chapter rejects the view that human thought is entirely sensorimotor in nature, and argues in favor of a weak form of the language of thought hypothesis (Fodor, 1975). It also uncovers a puzzling implication of the intuitive view that some amodal attitudes not only figure in reflection but are under the active control of the agent. This is that these kinds of attitude must admit of two fundamentally different types: those that are actions, which are under the control of other attitudes, and those that are passive, which do the controlling.

Chapter 3 considers the cognitive and neural mechanisms involved in the global broadcasting of conscious experience. It argues that attentional signals directed at midlevel sensory areas of cortex are a necessary condition for global broadcasting to occur. (Since it will be suggested in Chapter 4 that the *same* attentional mechanisms are responsible for maintaining contents in working memory, this will then provide some reason for believing that working memory is sensory based.) The chapter also argues (again by inference to the best explanation) that amodal concepts are often bound into the contents of perception in the course of normal processing. In consequence, the contents of perceptual experience (and of working memory) are generally mixed sensory–amodal representations, as when we see a colored moving object *as* a car, or hear the sounds someone is making *as* a request for information.

Chapter 4 builds on the foundation of Chapter 3 to argue that the contents of working memory are always conscious, and that they result from the same attentional mechanisms that are responsible for conscious forms of perception. The chapter also considers the relationship between imagery and perception, arguing that concepts are bound into the contents of working memory images using the same sorts of interactive processing that occur in perception. The chapter then argues by inference to the best explanation that the contents of working memory are always sensory based (and hence cannot contain any amodal propositional attitudes), while responding to some initial objections.

Chapter 5 takes up a challenge to the argument of Chapter 4. This is that the data are consistent with the following suggestion: there might be *two* forms of global workspace, one amodal and one sensory dependent. Specifically, it might be claimed that there is a distinct or partly distinct conscious system in which amodal attitudes can figure, which makes strategic use of the sensory-based working-memory system to support its own operations. (This would then explain why content-related sensory activity should always be found, even in abstract reasoning tasks.) But if such a system exists, then one would expect that variance in its properties across individuals should be responsible for much of the variance in people's fluid general intelligence. It is argued, however, that the latter variance is best explained by properties of the sensory-based working-memory system (and especially by people's differential capacities for attentional control), together with other low-level factors, such as speed of neural processing.

Chapter 6 continues and extends the positive task of using the sensory-based framework to explain some of the properties of the stream of consciousness. Specifically, it argues that all working-memory contents are actively produced, either through motivated shifts of attention or mental rehearsals of bodily action. The intuitive distinction between active and passive contents of working memory is illusory. Rather, contents that we intuit as active in nature are ones that occur while we take ourselves to know *why* we entertain them, whereas contents intuited to be passive occur in the absence of any such understanding. In reality, however, both kinds are just as much under intentional control. These ideas are then built on to provide an explanation (at least in outline) of the intentional nature of creativity and mind wandering. The conclusion is that the stream of consciousness is well explained by the sensory-based framework.

Chapter 7 discusses the empirical literature on human reasoning, and specifically the distinction often drawn between System 1 (intuitive) and System 2 (reflective) forms of reasoning. One would think that if evidence of amodal attitudes figuring in conscious forms of reflection existed anywhere, it should be found here. For reasoning is one of the central uses of reflection. In fact, however, the chapter suggests that System 2 reasoning is best explained as making use of the sensory-based working-memory system, relying on a general disposition to engage that system when confronted with problems, together with explicit beliefs about the appropriate norms to employ when reasoning. Since working memory is an active system, and is under intentional control, people are capable of constraining the contents that figure within it to accord with the norms they believe they should employ.[6]

Chapter 8 takes up what may be the central challenge to the sensory-based account, which is to explain *why* reflection should be sensory based. The challenge arises because much of the time, when we reflect, our thoughts concern abstract non-sensory properties, such as kinship and friendship relations, hidden essences, and the mental states of other people. Artificial intelligence researchers who have created reasoning systems for dealing with such matters have not thought to build them in ways that are sensory based. So why should evolution have done so? In reply I suggest that this fundamental feature of human cognitive architecture results from constraints provided by ancestral designs. We could not have evolved an amodal reasoning system for much the same reason that we could not have evolved a third arm. In support of this suggestion the chapter reviews what is known about attention and working memory in mammals and birds, suggesting that the sensory-based system is of quite ancient provenance. Some potential differences between the human working-memory system and those possessed by nonhuman animals are also discussed.

---

[6] This is one of the ways in which human minds can come to differ so dramatically from the minds of animals, since culturally formulated norms of reasoning can be learned and actively implemented, with transformative results.

Chapter 9 pulls together the threads of the argument of the book and provides a summary of the main points at stake. It concludes with a brief discussion of some potential philosophical implications and notes some questions for future research.

6. Conclusion

The goal of this book is to provide an empirically grounded theory of the ways in which the stream of consciousness is endogenously produced, while arguing that the stream is always sensory based (as is reflection). The book will argue that although there are, indeed, amodal (non-sensory) propositional attitudes, such attitudes are never conscious. Rather, in addition to their other roles they are active in the background of the stream of consciousness, causing and controlling the latter's contents.

2

Propositional Attitudes

This chapter discusses a number of questions that are, in one way or another, important for what follows. This is because the topics addressed in this book turn crucially on the properties that propositional attitudes possess. Sections 1 and 2 characterize and draw distinctions among beliefs, desires, goals, decisions, and intentions, describing the functional roles of these states in ways that will prove important for some of the later arguments (especially in Chapters 3, 6, and 7). Section 3 raises a problem for the intuitively plausible view that some propositional attitudes are both conscious and active in nature, and replies to an argument intended to provide support for such a thesis. Then Sections 4 and 5 lay out the case for believing in the existence of a set of compositionally structured, amodal (non-sensory), propositional attitudes. With this thesis in place we can then begin to ask whether such attitudes are ever conscious.

1. Beliefs and Desires

It is often said that common-sense psychology is founded on the twin pillars of *belief* and *desire*. Indeed, some philosophers have thought that all other attitudes can be reduced to these two, while others have confined themselves to arguing that we need to recognize a distinct category of *intention* (Bratman, 1987, 1999). The present section will discuss how these two key kinds of state should be distinguished and individuated, while showing that each fragments into a number of distinct types.

1.1. Functional role versus direction of fit

Searle (1983) argues that we can use the concept of *direction of fit* to characterize attitudes as either belief-like or desire-like (or some combination of the two). Beliefs have a mind-to-world direction of fit. They are *supposed* to match the world, and if there is a mismatch, it is the belief that has gone wrong (is false), rather than the world. Desires, in contrast, have a world-to-mind direction of fit. They are (from the perspective of the agent) *supposed* to get the world to match *them*, and if there is a mismatch, it is the world that has gone wrong. If the world fails to match the mind, then that is because the desire has (as yet) failed to bring about the relevant change in the world.

These ideas have been built upon by others to argue that propositional attitudes are essentially normative in nature (Brandom, 1994; Boghossian, 2003). It is said to be essential to beliefs, in particular, that they are *supposed* to be true or that they *aim at* the truth. But such views are by no means mandatory (Glüer & Wikforss, 2009). Instead, the attitudes can be characterized by their distinctive functional roles. Beliefs guide actions, whereas desires motivate them. Roughly speaking, desires get us to move, and beliefs tell us *how* to move. In fact both kinds of attitude can be partly characterized through their respective roles in the so-called "practical reasoning syllogism" (Lewis, 1970): If someone desires that P, and believes that if Q then P, then that person will (other things being equal) act so as to bring it about that Q.

Beliefs *are* true or false, of course. But this need not be construed normatively. If we take for granted the representational content of belief, then we can say that a true belief that P is a belief that P when P; and a false belief that P is a belief that P when not-P. Of course this leaves open the question of how the notion of content should be characterized in turn. This has been much debated in the philosophical literature, and a variety of different proposals have been made (Field, 1977; Loar, 1981; McGinn, 1982; Millikan, 1984; Block, 1986; Papineau, 1987; Dretske, 1988; Fodor, 1990; Botterill & Carruthers, 1999). Discussion of them would take us too far afield. For present purposes I propose to treat the notion of representational content as a conceptual primitive (just as much work in cognitive science does).

1.2. Kinds of belief

Many people with some knowledge of cognitive science will now accept that the common-sense category of *belief* really fractionates into a number of distinct kinds of state. For among information-bearing propositional states, we know that episodic memory is different in kind from semantic memory. Knowing (in the sense of episodically remembering) what took place on one's last birthday is very different from knowing (based on the reports of one's parents) what happened on one's *first* birthday. The two forms of knowledge are at least partly dissociable, since it is possible to lose episodic memory while one's semantic memory is largely intact, and only episodic memory depends specifically on the hippocampus (which is an ancient structure shaped like a seahorse buried beneath the inside of the temporal lobe; see Vargha-Khadem et al., 1997; Tulving & Markowitsch, 1998).

Moreover, we know that recognition is distinct from recollection. Knowing which items were presented as part of a previous list, for example, admits of two different forms. It is generally much easier to *recognize* items from the list than it is to *recall* or *generate* the items in the list when asked to do so. In addition, each of these kinds of belief is distinct from what might be called "rote belief," such as one's knowledge of one's phone number or of the multiplication tables. For this is really a form of *motor* memory, stored in the form of abstract motor schemata. Rote memory can be left undamaged even in cases of severe retrograde amnesia.

Furthermore, all of these sorts of state are different from the *commitments* that one has to the truth of various propositions (Frankish, 2004). Someone who decides, after reflection, that the Democrats are best qualified to govern probably lacks any semantic memory to that effect (and may soon lose any episodic recall of the process of reflection itself). Rather, what she has is a commitment to think and act on the assumption that the Democrats are best qualified. Such states will be discussed in Chapter 7, where we will consider whether they have the right sort of functional profile to qualify as a kind of belief (arguing that they do not).

We should also distinguish between two different kinds of judgment-like event. One comprises activations of existing belief (of any of the various sorts noted above). The activation of a belief is an event that makes the content of the belief available to play a role in various forms of reasoning and decision making, whereas its merely stored, dormant counterpart is causally inert. In addition, however, there are judgments properly so-called, which are events that tend to give rise to *new* beliefs. Judgments can play a role just like that of activated beliefs, in that they are available to enter into inferences of various sorts and to guide decision making, but their etiology is different. They are caused not by activating an existing memory, but rather by accepting what one is told, accepting the correctness of what one sees or infers, and so forth. They are also apt to give rise to new standing-state (stored) beliefs of the appropriate sort, and when they do, they do so immediately, without any need for further reasoning or decision making.

Finally, we should note the distinction between *implicit* and *explicit* beliefs, which has attracted a good deal of attention recently (Greenwald et al., 2002). People can harbor an unconscious bias against members of other races, for example, which can have significant effects on their behavior, but which they consciously (and sincerely) disavow. In this connection it is important to distinguish between implicit *values* and implicit *stereotypes*, however, since only the latter are a kind of belief. These dissociate from one another, and issue in distinct forms of behavior (Amodio & Devine, 2006). Associating black faces with bad things, and white faces with good things, is different from associating black people with stereotypical properties. For stereotypes can include features that are evaluated as good (including *athletic*), as well as those (such as *criminal*) that are experienced as bad. Since implicit stereotypes can generally be recognized at a conscious level, however (even if they would not be consciously endorsed), it is unclear that they constitute a distinct *kind* of belief. Rather, it may be that one and the same stored structure underlies recognition when the stereotype is explicitly considered, but can also be activated unconsciously, with subsequent effects on thought and behavior.

1.3. Kinds of desire

The common-sense category of *desire* likewise fractionates into distinct kinds. Among activated (as opposed to standing-state or dormant) desire-like states one can distinguish a number of different sorts. One is an affective state of *positive or negative valence* that influences choice and decision making. (This manifests itself as a form of *felt desire* in cases where it is conscious.) Another is a form of core unconscious *motivation* that is apt to issue in action directly unless inhibited by top-down signals. In addition, both are distinct from active *goals* that likewise work unconsciously, especially to sustain activity on a task, to direct attention, and to influence the contents of working memory. (Moreover, there is also a desire-like form of commitment, as we will see in Chapter 7.) The differences among the first two of these kinds of desire will be elaborated here. Discussion of goals will be held over to Section 2, given their similarity to intentions.

The kind of activated desire that is most familiar to common-sense psychology is a form of experienced affective state. It is the pleasure that we feel when we entertain the thought of getting what we want, and the displeasure that we feel when the thing seems out of reach. It is also the pleasure that we feel when we consume, or bask in the achievement of, what we want. As with all other affective states, it has two primary dimensions (Russell, 1980; Barrett, 1998). One is a bodily and arousal dimension, which can manifest itself in different forms in different cases (awareness of one's mouth beginning to flood with saliva as one looks at a slice of chocolate cake, or awareness of one's heart beginning to pound when one approaches a desired partner at a dance). The other is a valence dimension, which can be either positive or negative. This is at the core of the motivational and decision-making role of the affective form of desire, and is best thought of as a nonconceptual representation of the goodness or badness of whatever one is attending to at the time (Carruthers, 2011a).

It is the affective form of desire (and especially, in my view, its valence dimension) that plays a critical role in conscious forms of prospective thinking and reasoning (Gilbert & Wilson, 2007). When one faces a decision (and often when one does not, but is engaged in prospective mind wandering, ruminating over possible future options), one imagines the actions or outcomes at stake, and responds affectively to them. To the extent that they seem good or bad (have positive or negative valence), they seem attractive or repulsive, and one decides accordingly. The arousal component of the affective states that one experiences in prospection may also play a role, of course (Damasio, 1994). If one's heart begins to pound while imagining one's spouse finding out about a potential infidelity, one may take this as a signal that such an outcome would be especially bad. But for the most part it is the seeming badness of that outcome (its overall negative valence) that is apt to influence one's decision.

Note that prospective reasoning of this sort crucially implicates the resources of working memory. When examining an option for action one mentally rehearses it or constructs a representation of the action using components drawn from episodic memory (or, more commonly, both). As we will see, attending to the sensory aspects of these representations causes those representations to be globally broadcast. This leads them to interact with the mechanisms that process reward and punishment, which are for the most part buried deep in subcortical parts of the brain in the basal ganglia (see Figure 3), including the amygdala, nucleus accumbens, and ventral pallidum. The latter set in train bodily changes appropriate for the kinds of value they compute (this is the arousal component of affect). If attended to, some of these changes, too, can be globally broadcast. But the reward mechanisms also project signals of positive or negative value (that is, valence) to multiple cortical sites, but including orbitofrontal cortex where they become a component of the conscious experience of whatever is at the focus of one's attention at the time (see Figure 3).

While valence plays a critical role in conscious forms of prospective reasoning, we also know that representations of value have an unconscious impact at many different levels of cognition. During the course of visual processing of a stimulus or scene, for example, valence is simultaneously computed and influences the extent and manner of processing at quite early stages, as well as at later ones (Barrett & Bar, 2009; Pessoa, 2013). For example, it is possible to discern the effects of the learned values of various stimuli as early as primary visual cortex (Shuler & Bear, 2006; Thompson-Schill, 2013), presumably resulting from the fact that stimuli of known positive or negative value are processed more deeply than those that are evaluatively neutral.

The reward and punishment systems that create affect also often activate motor representations of various sorts, which may need to be suppressed if the action is not to be performed. This is most obvious in connection with emotional forms of affective state, where different basic emotions tend to cause emotion-specific behavioral reactions (smiling, in the case of happiness; frowning, in the case of anger; withdrawing, in the case of fear; and so on). But positive and negative affective desires, too, are accompanied by a disposition to approach or retreat from the object of desire (Centerbar & Clore, 2006). There is evidence that this behavior-causing role of the reward and punishment systems can come apart from the affect-causing one (Berridge & Kringelbach, 2008). Thus certain sorts of direct stimulation of those systems can produce urges to act in the absence of pleasure or any anticipation of pleasure. And the same is true of some addictions and various kinds of compulsive behavior. Hence we should probably regard affect, on the one hand, and direct behavioral motivation, on the other, as distinct forms of activated desire (albeit caused by the same underlying evaluative mechanisms).

What matters more for our purposes, however, is that there is a third kind of desire-like state that is distinct from either of the other two. These are *goals*, which are formed as a result of evaluative and decision-making processes, both conscious and unconscious. For example, when a participant in an experiment is asked to write a persuasive essay on a counter-attitudinal topic, this request is evaluated in the light of various background values (to be cooperative, to do what one has already agreed to, to avoid confrontation, and so on). As a result, the person forms the goal of writing such an essay. This remains activated and operative throughout the experiment, continuing to exist despite distraction or interruption, motivating choices and actions in pursuit of the goal. Moreover, it does so without the need for further evaluative or affective processing. As we will see, it is goals, especially, that control and direct the attentional processes that keep one focused on a task in the face of distractions. Whereas affective forms of desire involve orbitofrontal cortex as well as other regions down the midline of the brain, goals depend on activity in dorsolateral prefrontal cortex, especially those regions that routinely show up in working-memory tasks. (See Figure 2.)

Many of the various distinctions drawn here in Section 1 will be relied on at later stages in the book. But one point that is especially important concerns the functional role of novel judgments. This is that such judgments normally give rise to standing beliefs (long-term memories) *immediately*, without any need for further inferences or decision making of any sort. This point will prove important when discussing what I call "sensorily embedded judgments" in Chapters 3 and 4, and again when discussing so-called "System 2 judgments" in Chapter 7.

2. Goals, Decisions, and Intentions

While goals are like desires in some respects, they also share much of the functional profile of intentions. For the latter, too, motivate action without any need for evaluative or affective processing (Bratman, 1987, 1999). Indeed, goals could plausibly be thought of as a *kind* of intention. But they can be much more abstract and indeterminate than intentions generally are. One can have the goal of *succeeding*, for example, or of *being creative*, without there being any action or task in particular that is targeted for success or creativity. I will discuss intentions first, before returning to consider the nature of goals.

2.1. On intention

Intentions are the immediate products of decisions (although I will argue that some intentions cause decisions in turn). First we reason about what to do, then we decide. For example, having thought about what to do on Saturday, one takes a decision to go hiking. The decision itself is a momentary event. Yet it gives rise to a standing intention to go hiking on Saturday. This motivates the correspond-ing action, but it can also motivate further reasoning about the best way to *implement* the intention. (Where to go? When to set out? And so forth.) As Bratman (1987) argues, however, the intention *can* issue in hiking-behavior without any further evaluative or affective reasoning needing to take place (if, for example, the time and place for one's hikes is habitual).

One should distinguish between decisions (and the corresponding intentions) for the here-and-now and decisions (and intentions) for the future. Suppose the room is hot, and one decides to open a window. The decision will normally give rise to an intention that issues in action immediately. But the intention (unlike the decision) continues to exist throughout the process of acting, flexibly guiding its implementation as one walks toward the window, avoiding obstacles along the way, and grasps the handles in some appropriate way. Here the intention should probably be thought of as an abstract motor plan of some sort, which is both created and activated by the decision in question.[1]

Intentions for the future work somewhat differently. Suppose one reasons that the house will get too hot if the windows remain open throughout the day, and one decides to close them later in the morning. Here again the decision creates an intention (probably in the form of an abstract motor plan), but this time the intention is stored in memory. As is familiar to all of us, it is easy for such intentions to be forgotten, and so never implemented. Moreover, even when something jogs one's memory and the intention becomes activated, initiation of action is by no means automatic. This is because the conditions for the execution of the intention have been left vague or unspecified. As a result, one first needs to

---

[1] This point about decisions for the here-and-now will prove important in Chapter 7, when we discuss so-called "System 2 decisions."

reason that the time for doing what one intends is now, issuing in a *decision* to do it now. This is, of course, the root of the familiar problem of procrastination: one fully intends to do something, but whenever one recalls the intention one judges that the time for acting is not now (generally because of countervailing motivations, such as that the action in question requires effort). Notice, however, that one's reasoning in such cases doesn't generally challenge the original decision. That, and the corresponding intention, can remain untouched. What one reasons about is only whether or not to do what one intends *now*, or in *these* circumstances.[2]

It is possible, however, to form intentions for the future that are fully specific about the time or circumstances for action. One might, for example, decide that one will close the windows when one hears the clock strike twelve, or immediately before one sits down to lunch. In the empirical literature these are referred to as "implementation intentions" (Gollwitzer & Sheeran, 2006). Forming intentions of this sort makes it much more likely that one will act in the way that one has decided. This is because if the intention becomes activated by a recognition that the implementing condition now obtains (for example, one hears the clock strike twelve), it thereby becomes transformed into an intention for the here-and-now. In consequence, the resulting intention will generally lead to action automatically, unless something happens to make one reconsider one's original decision. (For example, one sees that the day has clouded over and the weather remains cool.)

2.2. Goals

In much of the scientific literature the language of "goal" and "intention" is used inter-changeably. (In cases where the distinction isn't relevant, I will do the same.) Thus one could be said to have the *goal* of opening the window as well as the *intention* of opening the window. But among the class of states that are created by decisions and that motivate action independently of further affective or evaluative reasoning, it is possible to distinguish between those whose contents specify an *action* of some sort, and those that specify objects or states of affairs. It can sound strange to say that someone has the intention of being wealthy, or the intention of being a property-owner. For being wealthy or owning a house are not things that one *does*. One can, however, have the *goal* of being wealthy, or the *goal* of being a home-owner. Such states operate at a more abstract level than normal intentions. Although they do not motivate any specific form of action, they can motivate reasoning and decision making designed to achieve the goal. Given the

---

[2] This point, too, will prove important in Chapter 7.

goal of being a home-owner, for example, one might decide to open a savings account to accumulate the necessary deposit, or decide to check on one's credit rating.

In this respect goals are desire-like. Just as one can have the goal of being a home-owner, so one can *want* to be a home-owner. Moreover, unlike intentions, goals are not stored and activated in the form of abstract motor plans. But unlike desires, they generally result from prior decisions. Moreover, even when activated they need not involve affective states of any sort, unlike paradigmatic cases of activated desire. In these respects goals are more intention-like. Often, however, goals can be deeply embedded among one's values and evaluative dispositions, in such a way that any perceived threat to one's goals will issue in an affective reaction. If one is told that one's credit rating is too poor for one to qualify for a mortgage, for example, the threat to one's goal of being a home-owner is likely to result in one experiencing disappointment. In this respect goals are like desires (obviously), but are also similar to intentions. For if one learns that the park where one had intended to go hiking is closed because of wildfires then this, too, will be apt to cause one some distress.

With these distinctions now behind us, we will turn, in Section 3, to consider another contrast among kinds of propositional attitude. This is the distinction between active and passive components of the stream of consciousness, which is often made by philosophers when analyzing our common-sense view of conscious reflection. Before doing so, however, it is worth emphasizing that nothing in our characterization of the various types of propositional attitude discussed in Sections 1 and 2 requires that instances of those types be conscious. Indeed, most people will now accept that there can be unconscious beliefs, desires, decisions, goals, and intentions. In fact, given our earlier characterizations, it can be an open question whether propositional attitudes are *ever* conscious. I propose to argue that (in the case of amodal attitudes) they are not.[3]

3. Active versus Passive: A Problem

Intuitively, reflection seems to contain both active and passive attitude events. It seems that judging and deciding are things that we *do* in reflection, whereas we are passive in the face of the memory of a popular jingle that keeps interrupting our thoughts. The present section will outline some difficulties with this idea,

---

[3] Notice that if one were to insist that amodal propositional attitudes like decisions are *necessarily* conscious, then my conclusion would need to become more radical. It would have to be that there are *no such things as* amodal attitudes, so understood.

before criticizing an argument that might be supposed to support it. Chapter 6 will argue, in contrast, that all forms of reflection are active in nature. Yet all of the events that occur in the stream of consciousness are sensory based. And while some of our propositional attitudes can be *influenced* or *caused* by the activity of reflection, they are not themselves active in nature. Put differently: I will argue that any control that we exert over our attitudes is indirect and mediated by other mental events. In fact the sensory-based mental actions that constitute reflection stand to our attitudes, at best, somewhat like the action of strangling someone stands to his death. Although the strangling is an action (and although the entire sequence can be described as an action of killing), the person's death is not an action; it is not something we *do*, but is the result of what we do.

3.1. Two kinds of amodal attitude

People committed to some version of the idea of an amodal (non-sensory) central workspace in which attitudes of all sorts can be activated will generally endorse the common-sense distinction between active and passive forms of reflection, as do McDowell (1994) and Peacocke (2008).[4] While sometimes the stream of consciousness seems to us to be active and under our control, at other times contents enter our minds unbidden, and our thoughts can meander aimlessly. But both sets of attitudes are conscious, however, figuring in the stream of consciousness. It is important to see that anyone endorsing this distinction will also need to postulate a set of attitudes that are both passive and *un*conscious. For by being committed to a set of reflective attitudes that are active in nature, one must also think that there is a second set of attitudes that exists in the background, outside of reflection, while serving to control and motivate the active attitudes. On pain of vicious regress, if some reflective attitudes are under one's intentional control, then there must also be attitudes (namely, the ones that exert that control) that are *not* themselves controlled (Arpaly & Schroeder, 2012; Kornblith, 2012).

   The intuitive account of the stream of consciousness thus requires three types of amodal attitude: (1) those that are active in nature and conscious; (2) those that are passive and conscious; and (3) those that are passive and *un*conscious (needed to explain the active status of those in the first group). The distinction between types (2) and (3) is easy enough to explain, at least in outline. These can

---

[4] Note that there are two distinct contrasts in play here. For an attitude to be *activated* means that it is now playing a causal role of some sort in ongoing cognitive processes (in contrast with *standing* attitudes, or *stored* attitudes, which are not). For an attitude to be an active one, on the other hand, means that it is an *action* of some sort. It is a product of practical reasoning and results from a *decision* (in contrast with attitudes that are passive, which are not so caused).

be the very same kinds of attitude, distinguished only by their relationship to whatever is required by one's favored theory of access-consciousness. The distinction between type (1) and the others is much more problematic, however. For it needs to be explained how the same kinds of propositional attitude (judgments, say, or decisions) can admit of both active and passive varieties. The problem is that the causal etiology of those attitudes in the two cases will be quite different. Why, then, should we regard them as being of the same kind? For attitudes are generally thought to be distinguished from one another (at least in part) by their functional roles.

Consider what happens when one judges (passively) the truth of a new proposition and forms a new belief in consequence. Various kinds of information are integrated, and the proposition in question may be checked for consistency with the most relevant among one's existing beliefs, before it is accepted and stored in long-term memory. For example, suppose that one reads in a newspaper article that the pace of global temperature rise has slowed over the last decade. Given one's tacit belief in the authority of the source and the fact that no conflicting beliefs are activated as one reads, one unreflectively accepts what one has read, and thereafter believes that global warming is slowing. The event in question (judging the truth of a proposition) has a distinctive functional role. Its causal etiology includes information from the world (and from memory, where relevant). And its normal causal consequence is storage in long-term memory, as well as availability of the proposition in question to guide action (such as answering a question about the pace of global warming).

Now consider what supposedly happens when one makes the same judgment actively and reflectively, on the assumption that the event in question is an amodal one. If the judgment is an action, then it must result from a process of practical reasoning (presumably unconscious). This will involve interactions among incoming information, existing beliefs, and desires or goals. Reading the newspaper article must unconsciously activate a motivating state of some sort, such as the goal of believing only what is true. This interacts unconsciously with the belief that the writer is a trustworthy source to issue in an unconscious *decision* to believe that the pace of global warming has slowed. This decision, in turn, issues in a conscious *action* of judging the proposition to be true, which is apt to cause it to be stored in long-term memory and become available to inform future action.[5] (Note that all that need happen at a conscious level in a case of this

---

[5] It is controversial whether or not one can believe at will (in the absence of evidence, or contrary to the evidence), and some have argued that this is impossible (Williams, 1973). It is much less controversial that one can decide to believe something based on one's evaluation of the evidence.

sort is that one thinks to oneself, "Hmm... should I believe this?" and then judges—apparently actively—that one should. The underlying reasoning that is necessary to secure the active status of the concluding judgment remains unconscious.)

Notice that the causal etiology of what are (allegedly) two types of judgment are quite different in these two cases. In the passive case, information from the world that meets some set of standards issues in belief directly. In the active case it only does so indirectly, interacting with some or other motivational state and entering into a process of practical reasoning, before issuing in a decision to undertake the act of judging. Given these differences, there is a strong case for thinking that we are dealing here with two different *types* of attitude, rather than with passive and active varieties of the *same* attitude.

It might be replied that despite the differences in etiology, it is sufficient for the two states to count as kinds of judgment that they both issue in long-term memories and in the availability of the information in question for future planning. In fact, however, it is quite unclear why one should prioritize the *effects* of a state over its causes when individuating functional kinds, especially if one is asked to ignore differences in causes altogether. But in any case the *ways* in which the two states issue in long-term storage are also different. It is surely one thing for information to be received and stored (the passive case). And it is quite another thing for an *action* to issue in the same result. The processes in question must be distinct, even if the upshot is the same.

There are two separable problems for the standard account of reflection that arise out of these points. One is conceptual. It is a challenge to justify classifying both passive and active attitudes as belonging to the same kinds, despite their differences in functional role. The other is more empirical. It is that we are required to postulate two quite different sets of processes involving amodal attitudes, underlain, presumably, by distinct mechanisms. The sensory-based account of reflection to be developed in this book, in contrast, will treat all of the sensory-based contents of reflection as equally under active control, created by motivated shifts of attention or mental rehearsals of action. The attitudes that do the controlling, on the other hand, are all equally passive in nature. This point will be developed at length in Chapter 6.

3.2. Knowledge of active attitudes

It is sometimes thought that by accepting that some or all of the amodal attitudes that figure in reflection are active in nature, we can at the same time explain how such attitudes can be known. For philosophers often suppose that we have direct non-inferential knowledge of our own actions (Anscombe, 1957). If amodal attitudes *are* actions, then it can be argued that the benefit will be a unifying account of self-knowledge that embraces both. And this might then be a reason for believing in the active status of the amodal attitudes that figure in reflection, invoking an inference to the best explanation.

Notice, first, that there will be no particular gain, here, if one also accepts that some of the attitudes that figure in the stream of consciousness can be passive in nature. For that would still leave us needing to appeal to two distinct mechanisms of self-knowledge—one for actions, and one for passive attitudes. But let us set this point to one side. For it would always be possible for someone to claim that the passive events that figure in the stream of consciousness (such as ideas that seemingly appear out of nowhere, or thoughts that seem to force themselves on us unwillingly) are not really attitudes, but mere sensory-based phenomena of one sort or another (visual and auditory imagery, and so on).

Peacocke (2008) mounts just such an argument for the active status of amodal attitudes. He argues, first, that we do have direct non-inferential knowledge of our bodily actions. And he argues, second, that we have knowledge of our active attitudes in the same way, via the "corollary discharge" that all actions produce. Carruthers (2009a, 2011a) provides an extended critique of both claims. The evidence Peacocke adduces for thinking that we have direct knowledge of our own actions does not really support this view. Rather, it can equally well be explained in terms of the afferent feedback produced by our actions together with the motor images (sensory "forward models") that our motor instructions create. Moreover, the claim that we are aware of our active attitudes via their corollary discharge makes little sense. For the latter is a copy of the motor instructions sent to the muscles to initiate movement. And whatever else might be true of events of judging or deciding, they surely involve no such thing.

For arguments in defense of these claims, readers are directed to Carruthers (2009a, 2011a). Here I want only to emphasize the conclusion they support: namely, that there is no sound argument for believing in the active nature of (some or all) amodal attitudes from the benefits thereby provided for a theory of self-knowledge.

4. The Case for Amodal Attitudes

It is implicit in the discussion of this chapter so far that most attitudes are not, themselves, sensory or sensory-involving states or events. If this is true, and yet it is also true that reflection is sensory based (as this book will argue), then the idea that all kinds of attitude can figure in reflection will have been decisively undermined. The present section will elaborate and defend the assumption that most attitudes are amodal, drawing on the relevant empirical literature. It will at the same time argue against so-called "sensorimotor" accounts of cognition, which maintain that all representation in the brain is modality specific (Barsalou, 1999; Prinz, 2002).

It is certainly intuitive that many types of attitude are amodal, without sensory components.[6] We think that suppositions, semantic memories, judgments, goals, hopes, decisions, and intentions are amodal attitude events. Each might some-times be *accompanied* by sensory activity of one sort or another, such as visual imagery or inner speech. But we think that this activity is either associated with or expresses the attitude events that accompany them. Even when a decision-like sentence such as, "I'll leave for the bus now" is tokened in inner speech, this is experienced as *expressing* a decision that is distinct from the speech event itself. It is not experienced as *constituting*, or even partially constituting, such an event. We no more think (nor should we think) that the words that figure in inner speech are constitutive of judging, deciding, and the rest, than we think such words spoken aloud (by oneself or by another person) constitute such attitudes.

These intuitive views are correct, in my view. I will argue that concepts and most of the attitudes they compose are amodal representational states that can be in one way or another *associated* with sensory activity without being even partially constituted by such activity. Indeed, I will argue that amodal forms of representation are a long-standing evolutionary adaptation, widespread in the animal kingdom, which may have evolved initially to facilitate cross-modal forms of learning and flexible types of inference.

4.1. Sensorimotor concepts?

It might seem that the hardest cases for sensorimotor theories to explain are abstract concepts like *justice*, *democracy*, and so on; and no doubt many philo-sophers dismiss such accounts on this basis. But these are uniquely human concepts. So it is open to sensorimotor theorists to claim that they are constituted by links among linguistic *words* (which are themselves sensorimotor representa-tions, on this view). Hence the word "democracy" is linked to "vote," which in turn might evoke sensorimotor images of voting or of a polling booth, and so on. Accordingly, I will focus on concepts that humans share with other animals.[7]

---

[6] Exceptions would include episodic memories, which are generally partly sensory in nature, and felt desires and emotions, which have an experiential component. Moreover, one can distinguish two different varieties of the attitude of imagining, one of which is propositional, but the other of which is sensory, involving visual or other forms of imagery.

[7] Some philosophers will object that animals lack concepts altogether, on the grounds that their representations fail to satisfy the "generality constraint" (Dummett, 1991; Brandom, 1994;

Consider concepts that designate individual agents. Humans and many other social animals (including all other species of primate) can recognize familiar individuals through more than one sense modality. We might recognize someone visually from her facial appearance or distinctive gait; or we might recognize her voice or the sound of her steps. (Occasionally we might recognize someone by smell; this will be much more common among other animals, whose sense of smell is by no means as weak as ours.) And of course, information about an individual acquired through one sense modality is immediately available when the person is identified through the other. If someone describes to me over the phone where she lives (auditory presentation), then I will not be surprised to see her face when I knock on the door of that house some days later (visual presentation). It is natural to model this in terms of individual folders or files of information, headed by an amodal file-locator. That is, one has an amodal concept containing links to all the information we possess about the person. This concept can be activated by either visual or auditory representations of the individual, and can be retrieved from memory for purposes of inference.

It might be replied that an amodal concept of the individual isn't necessary. Rather, information acquired about a person when visually presented will be stored linked to that visual representation, and information acquired when the person is identified through hearing will be stored linked to the sound of her voice. But because the visual and auditory representations of her are linked to one another, stored information that is attached to the one can be activated by activation of the other, by means of a sort of transitive inference (Barsalou, 1999). Note that on this account there is no single representation of an individual. Rather, the individual is represented by the entire network of sensorimotor information about her.[8]

McDowell, 1994; Bermúdez, 2003; Hurley, 2006; Beck, 2012). This maintains that genuine concept-users should be capable of understanding all possible combinations of the concepts they possess (Evans, 1982). I have argued elsewhere that this constraint is ill-conceived (Carruthers, 2009b). All that really matters is that concepts should be capable of combining with *some* others in compositionally structured thoughts. But even if one were to insist that representations meeting only this weaker constraint are mere *proto*-concepts, rather than concepts proper, the strategy of the present section need not be affected. Whether the representations in question are concepts or proto-concepts, what matters for our purposes is that many of them are amodal in nature.

[8] Notice that one could express this view by saying that one's concept of the individual is a *multi*-modal one (rather than either modal or amodal), with that concept being realized in a distributed manner across a number of different modality-specific representations together with the causal links between them. An *a*modal concept of the individual, in contrast, will be a unitary representation, which may *have* causal links to modality-specific representations and processes without being constituted by such links.

But now the account faces the problem that this entire network needs to be activated every time one entertains a thought about that individual. Not only would a cognitive system that operated in this way be extraordinarily inefficient, but it is quite hard to see how an entire active network of this sort could enter into inferences. This is a problem that Prinz (2002) recognizes. In response, he proposes that on each occasion when one thinks about someone, one employs a sensory *proxy* for the entire network of information that represents her. On one occasion, for example, it might be a memory image of the sound of her voice, on another occasion a visual image of her house, and on yet another a visual image of her dog. But now this suggestion faces problems of its own: what makes a sensory proxy a representation of *the person*, rather than simply an image of her voice, or house, or dog? Indeed, most of the information contained in the network that represents a given individual will also figure in other networks. The person's house, for example, may be linked not just to other information about that person, but might also be a useful landmark on one's way to a rarely used bus stop. If one entertains an image of that house, then what determines that one is thinking of the person rather than thinking of the bus stop?

This is, in fact, a long-standing problem for concept-empiricists who try to account for concepts in terms of sensorimotor images. Thus Berkeley (1710) famously noted the problem of using an image to think about triangles in general, given that any image one might form would be an image of a particular type of triangle. Berkeley's own solution was that one is thinking about triangles in general if one *uses* the image of a particular triangle in the right way, so that nothing in the inferences one draws from it depends upon its specific properties, but only on the fact that it is a triangle. But of course this could only work if the inferential mechanisms involved could somehow "know" that the image in question was supposed to be an image of triangles in general rather than an image of (say) an isosceles triangle. Seen from the perspective of contemporary cognitive science, this looks very much like an appeal to magic.

Moreover, Mahon & Caramazza (2008) review the empirical evidence that is thought to support sensorimotor accounts of concepts, and conclude that it can equally well be explained by supposing that concepts have a central amodal representation, but that activation flows associatively between amodal concepts and linked sensory and motor representations. (Note that something like this is what one might predict from the "object file" account of concepts sketched above.) They also point out that the neuropsychological evidence supports the latter view. For there are patients with apraxia who are impaired in their use of common tools like a hammer, which cannot be explained in terms of any general motor impairment, but who are nevertheless normal in recognizing and describing the function of those tools, as well as in recognizing their pantomimed use. There are also patients with the reverse impairment: who can pantomime the use of a hammer, but who cannot recognize one. Intuitively, both sets of patients still retain the concept HAMMER,[9] in which case that concept cannot be constituted by sensorimotor links.

4.2. Social concepts

Additional limitations of the sensorimotor account of concepts emerge when we consider cases where *inferences* are drawn about an individual. For many of the inferences that humans and other primates make concern abstract relationships that would be hard to represent and reason about in sensory terms. I will illustrate the point using inferences about dominance hierarchies in baboons. Cheney & Seyfarth (2007) show that baboons have rich social knowledge of the individuals in their group and the relationships among them. In particular, they know the dominance hierarchy of all the female members of the group, which is organized by matrilines. All the females in family A (mother, daughters, and sometimes granddaughters) will be ranked relative to one another, and all are ranked above the females in family B, who in turn rank above the females in family C, and so on. These rankings are generally quite stable, but occasionally reversals of rank occur. When they do, all members of a family shift up or down together (maintaining their relative rank), even if the reversal initially only concerned one individual from each family. For example, if female number 3 from family B defeats female number 5 from family A, thereafter all the members of group B will rank above all the members of group A. We know experimentally, using spliced-together auditory recordings of the members of the troop, that if a baboon overhears such a reversal (for example, a threat-scream from a member of group B followed by a submissive shriek from a member of group A), then she will expect a female from A to give way to a baboon from B when she next encounters any members of groups A and B together.

It is quite hard to see how baboons could make these inferences if they had access only to modality-specific representations. For then each individual's knowledge of the social structure would consist in a complex web of sensory memories and expectations, linking all the females in the troop on a pair-wise basis in visual, auditory, and olfactory modalities. Yet the observed reversal of rank would somehow have to bring about a systematic shift in these expectations. Hearing female 3 from family B defeat female 5 from family A, she would then

---

[9] Throughout I use small capitals when designating mental representations that are the primary bearers of content, and italic to designate those contents themselves.

need to erase her previous expectation that if female 2 from family A issues a threat-grunt, female 4 from family B will move aside, replacing it with an expectation (represented separately in all three modalities) of the reverse. It is puzzling what principles of inference could lead to such a change, and even more puzzling how a great many pair-wise sensory-based expectations could alter likewise, and following just a single exposure.

Cheney & Seyfarth (2007) argue for a much more plausible view. They suggest that each baboon's knowledge of social relationships is stored in the form of an amodal hierarchically organized tree-structure, which on one level represents the dominance rank of each individual in the troupe, but on another level represents the dominance rank of each family. Then when a female from a lower-ranking group defeats one from a higher-ranking one, the nodes representing those two families are reversed, with the resulting change in the dominance rank of each individual following automatically from that shift. Here we see displayed one of the major advantages of abstract, amodal, representations: they simplify and facilitate inference.

Note that a dominance hierarchy is not itself directly observable. One would also expect to find amodal representations in any other domain that deals with unobservables. Consider the mindreading capacities of human one-year-old infants, for example. There is now robust evidence that infants represent the goals, beliefs, and intentions of other agents, and form expectations about the behavior of other people accordingly (Carruthers, 2013a). Some theorists have tried to argue that they might instead be relying on a distributed multimodal system linking visual, auditory, and other sensory representations of the behavior and circumstances of other agents with sensory representations of expected outcomes (Povinelli & Vonk, 2004; Perner, 2010). But on closer examination it is quite implausible that such a system could achieve the flexibility that we already observe in human infants (Carruthers, 2013a). Rather, the evidence suggests that humans possess amodal representations of the mental states of other agents, which are computed on the basis of observations of behavior and circumstances. Moreover, these representations serve as the basis for generating novel predictions, as we will see in Section 5. Furthermore, the evidence suggests that a simpler version of such a system, at least, is likewise present in other species of primate (Fletcher & Carruthers, 2013).

4.3. Number concepts

Perhaps the clearest, and most heavily studied, domain of amodal representation concerns number (Dehaene, 1997). We now know that there are representations of approximate numerosity in human adults, infants, and many other species of animal. For example, Jordan et al. (2008) show that monkeys can match the numerosity of sets across modalities, judging that an array of squares contains approximately the same number of items as a previously presented sequence of tones, for instance. This suggests quite strongly that monkeys have amodal representations of numerosity onto which are mapped representations received from the various sense modalities. Izard et al. (2009) demonstrate essentially the same result with newborn human infants. Similarly, Barth et al. (2003) show that human adults are no slower, and no less accurate, when comparing the numerosity of large swiftly presented sets across stimulus modalities than they are when judging numerosity within a single sense modality. Again this suggests that numerical stimuli in different sense modalities are mapped to amodal representations of number for judgment and comparison, rather than compared in modality-specific format.

As before, the benefits of amodal representations of numerosity can be seen most clearly when they are employed in inference. We know experimentally that many species can add and subtract approximate numbers, for example (Jordan et al., 2008). And although we don't yet have the same sort of controlled experimental data to demonstrate multiplication and division, the evidence suggests quite strongly that many species are capable of these manipulations also. We know that rats and other animals, for instance, are excellent at judging rates of return from differing food sources (Gallistel et al., 2001), and a *rate* is quantity per unit of time—that is to say, total quantity received *divided by* time elapsed. Moreover, we also know that mice are excellent at judging risk (Balci et al., 2009), and one might think that the natural way to estimate risk in an ongoing sequence of events would be to periodically divide the total number of negative outcomes in an interval of time by the total number of trials. It is quite hard to imagine how any of these calculations could be effected using modality-specific representations.

4.4. Action concepts

Thus far the empirical case in support of amodal concepts and attitudes has been mostly presumptive. It has taken the form: how *else* could humans and other animals do what they are manifestly capable of doing? But there is also direct evidence against sensorimotor views, drawn especially from the domain of action concepts. In fact, even action concepts seem to be realized abstractly outside of sensorimotor cortices, despite the fact that they would be ideal for sensorimotor representation (or so one might think).

Bedny & Caramazza (2011) review the evidence of sensorimotor involvement in action-verb understanding and find little that is convincing. They note that some studies have seemed to show activity in motion-processing visual area MT when people comprehend motion verbs, suggesting that visual representations are constitutive of our understanding of motion concepts. However, later, more fine-grained investigations have shown that it is actually a region just anterior to MT called the medial temporal gyrus that is activated. In fact primary visual motion areas like MT and the superior temporal sulcus fail to respond specifically to action verbs (compared with nouns). And likewise, neither premotor nor primary motor cortex seems to play any role in action-verb understanding.[10] Indeed, the one region of cortex that *does* seem to be specifically involved in action-verb understanding is an amodal area, rather than a sensory or motor one, which is equally strongly activated by amodal action verbs like "think" or "decide." This is the left medial temporal gyrus.

Moreover, sensorimotor accounts of concepts (including action concepts) make a clear prediction with respect to people who are congenitally blind. Since such people lack visual access to actions, their action concepts should be differently represented in the brain. And one would expect, too, that there should be differences in the semantic properties of their concepts. But neither prediction turns out to be correct (Bedny et al., 2012). The semantic judgments of blind people are indistinguishable from those of sighted people (even with respect to their understanding of visual verbs like "glance," "peer," "flash," "glow," and so on). And the left medial temporal gyrus responds in just the same way to action verbs in both sighted and congenitally blind people, whether those verbs are high in motion properties (like "jump") or low in such properties (like "think"). Overall, the evidence suggests that action concepts are abstract amodal representations that lack either sensory or motor components.

4.5. The extent of amodal representation

How widespread are amodal forms of representation in the animal kingdom? One might expect to find them wherever animals need to learn about the same phenomena through two or more sense modalities. This is because of the way in which amodal representations can facilitate the inferences that need to be drawn from the acquired information. Bees, for example, need to learn the locations of various items and substances in their environment, doing so both from their own calculations of distance and direction when in flight (using the

---

[10] Admittedly, some regions of premotor cortex seem to respond to sentence-length descriptions of actions. But Bedny & Caramazza (2011) argue that this is best understood in terms of those regions' contribution to the construction of motor imagery that *accompanies* understanding without constituting it.

visual modality) and from observations of the dances of other bees (using their tactile and proprioceptive modalities while on the inner walls of the hive in the dark). Recent experimental work shows that from these sources bees build a map-like representation of the relative locations of places around the hive, and that they are able to calculate novel vectors when navigating, integrating information learned through one sense modality with information acquired from another (Menzel et al., 2005, 2011; Menzel and Giurfa, 2006).

Indeed, it seems that bees, and perhaps many other organisms, often encode information at the most abstract level of representation available to them, presumably to facilitate generalization across different sensory modes of presentation. Thus bees who are trained to turn right at the second gateway of a maze if it displays the same color as was displayed at the first gate (turning left if the colors displayed are different) will spontaneously generalize so as to turn right at the second gateway if it is marked with the same *odor* that also marked the first (Giurfa et al., 2001). They therefore seem to have encoded the initial learning trials in terms of the amodal concepts SAME and DIFFERENT. (See Wallis et al., 2001, for similar findings with monkeys.)

I conclude, then, that one aspect of our intuitive beliefs about the nature of thought is correct. Many attitudes are amodal events, constructed out of amodal concepts. Hence if reflection turns out to be sensory dependent, as the present book will argue, it will follow that the attitudes in question cannot, themselves, figure among the contents of reflection (nor in the stream of consciousness more generally).

5. The Case for Structured Attitudes

Sensorimotor theorists do not deny that propositional attitudes exist; they just maintain that they are structured out of sensorimotor components. Some theorists have denied, however, that propositional attitudes exist at all, on the grounds that the brain does not contain any states with the right kinds of structure to qualify as propositional attitudes (Churchland, 1979, 1993). This view will be addressed briefly here.

This section builds on the arguments of Section 4 to defend the view that the mind contains structured entities composed of component amodal concepts. Intuitively, a decision to leave for the bus involves the concept LEAVE and the concept BUS, as well as the concept MOVING TOWARD, which distinguishes a decision to leave *for* the bus from a decision to leave the bus *behind*. Attitudes with differing contents will either be composed of distinct concepts, or else constructed of the same concepts differently combined (as in the difference between JOHN LOVES MARY and MARY LOVES JOHN). Indeed, consideration of the requirements for flexible forms of learning and inference led Fodor (1975) to postulate a *language of thought*. This is supposed to be an amodal representational system in which inferences can be conducted. The system need not, of course, be similar to a natural language, especially in using representations that are (like speech) linearly ordered. But it would be compositionally structured, with thoughts being built in systematic ways from component concepts.[11]

5.1. Distributed need not mean unstructured

There have, of course, been challenges to the idea of a language of thought, most notably from those espousing radical forms of connectionism (Rumelhart & McClelland, 1986; Smolensky, 1991, 1995). Those defending the idea of a language of thought have replied that while connectionist architectures can *implement* symbolic, rule-based forms of cognition, they cannot replace them altogether (Fodor & Pylyshyn, 1988; Fodor & McLaughlin, 1990; Marcus, 2001). As a result, there have been significant concessions from connectionists, with many now allowing that activation vectors in connectionist networks have the compositional properties of a language (Smolensky & Legendre, 2006). But some remain recalcitrant. Here I will briefly discuss the recent work of Churchland (2012), since he has long been at the forefront of opposition to the idea of a language of thought (Churchland, 1979). As a result, he denies that propositional attitudes exist at all.

Churchland (2012) argues that the mechanism of neural Hebbian plasticity ("neurons that fire together wire together") results in a large set of neural populations, each of which has been sculpted into a high-dimensional feature-map of some domain. In the case of face-recognition, for example, the neural population in question will represent the various dimensions along which faces can differ from one another. Recognition of a particular face will then result from heightened activity in a specific region of this state-space, which lies at the intersection of activation-levels along each of the dimensions of the space that are reliably evoked by the face in question.[12]

---

[11] Note that we have already seen an example of what compositionally structured non-linguistic thought might be like when we discussed baboons' beliefs about dominance hierarchies in Section 4.2. It seems that the information is stored in a form that is more diagram-like than sentence-like (Camp, 2009), using tree-structures to order the various matrilines as well as the individuals within them. Presumably when an animal needs to draw an inference about just two individuals, it can then activate only the relevant components of the entire structure, forming expectations accordingly.

[12] While Churchland (2012) maintains that all neural networks are sculpted slowly by learning, in fact we know that many are innate (unlearned). For example, we know that both human and

The state-space theory of the most basic level of representation in the brain is by no means implausible. Indeed, the idea of distributed-representation neural networks is quite widely accepted in cognitive science. But there is nothing in such an approach itself to rule out the existence of structured representations. Indeed, Churchland's own account needs to be heavily supplemented to explain the full range of human and animal cognition, and the most obvious supplementation available would appeal to compositionally structured representations. For he contrasts the conceptual frameworks that result slowly from learning, and reflect the fixed causal structure of the environment, with ephemeral activations within those networks that locate the organism in the here-and-now, enabling it to know what to expect next or how to effect changes in that environment. But there is a huge space of forms of representation of the environment that is missing from this dichotomy, including both semantic and episodic forms of memory.

The state-space structures that Churchland claims are built slowly by Hebbian learning correspond most closely to what would normally be described as *implicit* forms of knowledge. Our knowledge of the ways in which faces vary from one another is mostly implicit and inarticulable, for example. And then online activity of specific regions in these state-spaces represent the here-and-now, such as the face of a specific individual person whom one is now seeing. Yet humans and other animals possess many forms of knowledge that fall into neither of these categories, since they require interactions *between* neural maps. Indeed, most theories of human memory now maintain that memories bind together neural populations across a number of distinct regions of cortex, each of which represents a specific property or set of properties.

Consider episodic memory, for example. Such memories are not regions in any one state-space. Rather, they seem to involve the creation of long-term linkages between regions of many different state-spaces, corresponding to the various sensory components of the original experience, in such a way that activation of any one of these is likely to cause activation of the others. If one recalls an episode of half-a-dozen brown eggs falling on one's kitchen floor and smashing, for example, then this would seem to require a long-term link between the region of color state-space that represents brown and the region of food-type state-space that represents eggs, together with the region representing a numerosity of six

monkey infants have the capacity to distinguish between faces and non-faces (such as scrambled facial components) at birth (Farroni et al., 2005). Moreover, monkeys who have never had any exposure to faces at all (who were raised by humans wearing opaque gauze masks over their heads) nevertheless show capacities for fine-grained discrimination among both human and monkey faces that are close to normal (Sugita, 2008).

and the region of location-space that corresponds to one's kitchen. Indeed, it is in just such terms that the formation of episodic memory is characterized by many cognitive scientists (Tulving, 2002). It is thought that the hippocampus, in particular, plays a special role in building event-files, using neurally coded spatial and temporal coordinates to bind together the properties of the event that are represented in other cortical state-spaces. But notice that the resulting structure is discrete and distinct from most other episodic memories. It is also compositionally structured out of the state-space regions that represent the various component properties of the original event.

Something similar will surely be true of many forms of semantic (or "factual") memory. Consider what happens when one unexpectedly encounters a colleague while out walking the dog, and she points out the house where she lives nearby. The resulting knowledge is not comfortably assimilated to knowledge of the enduring causal structure of the world represented by state-spaces themselves. (Nor, seemingly, is the knowledge in question natural-language based.) Rather, it would appear to require building a link from the regions of various state-spaces (e.g. of the face-recognition system) that represent one's colleague to the region of spatial state-space that corresponds to the location of her home. And this, too, will be a compositionally structured discrete representation: a sentence in the language of thought, no less! I conclude, therefore, that the idea of distributed neural representation is fully consistent with the claim that many of our beliefs and other attitudes are compositionally structured out of component representations.

5.2. A case study: infant mindreading

The strongest case for a language of thought has always derived from the systematicity of the inferences into which our attitudes can enter (Fodor, 1975; Davies, 1991, 1998). Two baboons observing the very same rank-reversal, for example, and updating their beliefs accordingly, might draw opposite practical conclusions, given their own respective positions in the rank. One of them might now approach and displace an animal who had previously ranked higher than her, thereby gaining access to a valued food resource. The other might move off to avoid confrontation with the same displaced animal, although previously she would have stood her ground. Here I will briefly develop another example, drawing on the extensive recent literature on the mindreading abilities of human infants.

The evidence comes out of many different labs and employs a number of different dependent measures (Onishi & Baillargeon, 2005; Southgate et al., 2007, 2010; Surian et al., 2007; Song & Baillargeon, 2008; Song et al., 2008; Buttelmann et al., 2009; Poulin-Dubois & Chow, 2009; Scott & Baillargeon, 2009; Kovács et al., 2010; Scott et al., 2010; Träuble et al., 2010; Luo, 2011; Knudsen &

Liszkowski, 2012; Yott & Poulin-Dubois, 2012; Baillargeon et al., 2014; Southgate & Vernetti, 2014). Most people in the field now accept that the data show that infants between the ages of six and eighteen months are capable of tracking the goals, perceptual access, and beliefs of other agents, and of drawing inferences accordingly. While it is still disputed whether the infants are representing other people's false beliefs *as such* (Carruthers, 2013a; Butterfill & Apperly, 2013), few now deny that the infants employ structured representations that enable them to track both the attitude types and conceptual components of other people's mental states.

Consider, for example, the inferences that an infant needs to make in the true-belief condition of the active helping studies employed by Buttelmann et al. (2009). The infant watches as an experimenter plays with a toy, before placing it in one of two boxes. The toy is then moved from that box to the other while the experimenter remains present, and both boxes are then locked while the experimenter is absent. The experimenter then returns and attempts (without success) to open the *other* box (not containing the toy). The dependent measure is whether or not the infants help to open that box. In order to succeed in this task, it seems the infant needs to reason as follows:

- [from the experimenter's perceptual access]: She thinks the bunny is in the green box.
- [the bunny is moved while the experimenter is present: belief attributions are updated]: The bunny is in the red box and she thinks the bunny is in the red box.
- [the boxes are locked, the experimenter returns and attempts to open the green box]: She thinks the bunny is in the red box; she is searching in the green box; people search where they think they can get what they want; so she wants something in the green box; I want to help her get what she wants; so I'll open the green box.

Note that the infant here relies upon the experimenter's belief in order to figure out what she wants. Now consider how the infant must reason in the false-belief condition, where the bunny is moved to the other box while the experimenter is *not* present:

- [from the experimenter's perceptual access]: She thinks the bunny is in the green box.
- [the bunny is moved while the experimenter is absent: no updating]: The bunny is in the red box and she thinks the bunny is in the green box.
- [the experimenter returns and attempts to open the green box]: She thinks the bunny is in the green box; she is searching in the green box; people

search where they think they can get what they want; so she wants the bunny; the bunny is actually in the red box; I want to help her get what she wants; so I'll open the red box.

Here again the infant must use information about the experimenter's (false) belief in order to figure out her goal. Notice that both sets of inferences depend crucially not just on the *types* of attitude ascribed to the experimenter, but also on the internal structure of those attitudes: that they are about the bunny being in the red box in the one case, and about the bunny being in the green box in the other. And these contents then have to interact with the infant's own beliefs about the location of the desired toy in order to issue in the conclusion.

It seems likely that infants' (and adults') representations of the attitudes of others are distributed ones. That is, some sort of AGENT X THINKS...operator is used to bind together the infant's own representations of the relevant situation, much as an episodic memory will use spatial and temporal representations to bind together other features of the observed event, distributed over various regions of cortex. This suggestion is consistent with the finding that contents attributed to other agents can prime or interfere with one's own actions, almost as if they were one's own beliefs (Kovács et al., 2010; van der Wel et al., 2014). This could happen in a way that is quite similar to the interference-effects that episodic memories with similar contents can exert on one another, despite the fact that they are bound together by different spatial and/or temporal locations.

It remains as an unsolved challenge for anyone who thinks that humans do *not* employ structured amodal representations in the contents of their attitudes to explain in some other terms how infants can succeed so flexibly in such tasks. Of course explaining any *one* task would be easy enough: one could train up a network for the purpose, or propose an associationist rule linking low-level features of the experimental setup. The challenge is rather to construct a single non-representational framework that can explain the totality of the data, in all its varied detail. Until this challenge has been met, it is reasonable to believe that the contents of our attitudes are compositionally structured out of conceptual components.

6. Conclusion

This chapter has drawn distinctions among a number of types of propositional attitude, arguing that they are best individuated by their functional roles. It has also uncovered a problem for those who think that amodal attitudes can figure consciously in reflection under the active control of the agent. But most importantly for our purposes, the chapter has argued for the existence of a set of amodal compositionally structured attitudes. Given that such attitudes exist, one can then ask whether or not they are ever conscious, and whether or not they ever figure among the contents of our reflections. This is one of the main tasks of the remainder of the book.

3

Perception, Attention, and Consciousness

This chapter argues, first, that the "global broadcasting" of perceptual contents in the brain is what causes those contents to become conscious. It then argues by inference to the best explanation that attentional signals directed toward midlevel sensory areas of the brain are necessary and (with other factors) sufficient for global broadcasting to occur. This conclusion is important because Chapter 4 will argue that it is these same attentional mechanisms that sustain representations in working memory, leading us to conclude (again by inference to the best explanation) that working memory is sensory based. It will then follow either that amodal attitudes are never conscious, or that there is some other global workspace in which such attitudes can interact and do their work. (This suggestion will then be addressed in Chapter 5, before my own positive account is developed in more detail in Chapter 6.) The present chapter also argues, however, that amodal *concepts* can nevertheless be bound into the content of perception and globally broadcast along with it. Since the same is true of endogenously generated imagistic states (as we will see in Chapter 4), it will follow that amodal *content* can figure in the stream of consciousness even though (most)[1] amodal *attitudes* cannot.

1. Kinds of Consciousness

The present section will rehearse some familiar distinctions, separating out the questions and theories that are relevant to our concerns.

---

[1] As we will see in Section 5, sensorily embedded amodal concepts can constitute an attitude of *judging* that something is the case. When we hear someone as saying that there are delays on the metro, this can be thought of as containing a sensory-based judgment with the content, *he is saying that there are delays on the metro*.

1.1. Creature versus state

We can begin with the distinction between *creature* consciousness and *state* consciousness. One can say of an animal or person that she is conscious, or one can say of someone's mental state (a perception of movement, say, or an experience of color) that it is conscious. Moreover, creature consciousness can be either intransitive or transitive. One can say that someone is conscious *simpliciter* (that she has just woken from a nap, for example, or that she has emerged from a general anesthetic). This is intransitive creature consciousness. Alternatively, one can say that she is conscious *of* some object or event. This is transitive creature consciousness.

Transitive creature consciousness seems to entail state consciousness. If Mary is conscious of something moving across a screen, then her perception of movement across the screen is a conscious mental event. Indeed, some have suggested that state consciousness can be reduced to transitive creature consciousness (Dretske, 1995). But this may go too far, and risks begging important questions related to our topic. For propositional attitudes are often described as (state-) conscious, yet in such cases it can be hard to find any equivalent creature-conscious locution. If one says that Mary's hope for recovery is conscious, or that she is consciously wondering what the doctor will recommend, then what is it that she is conscious of? She is not conscious of recovering, or of the doctor's recommendation. It *may* be that she is conscious of hoping, or of wondering. But if this were built into the analysis, it would commit us to a form of higher-order account of consciousness (see Section 1.2). In fact the creature-consciousness locution is most naturally restricted to instances of perception.

1.2. Phenomenal versus access

It seems, then, that we should focus on the broader notion of mental-state consciousness. Here it is common to distinguish between *phenomenal* consciousness and various forms of *access-conscious*ness (Block, 1995).[2] The former is the subjective, felt aspect of our conscious mental events; it is the "what-it-is-likeness" of those events. The latter, in contrast, consists in the availability of the event to other (specified) states or systems. It is phenomenal consciousness that is claimed to give rise to the "hard problem" of consciousness, and which is said to be difficult to reconcile with a physicalist world-view (Chalmers, 1996). While

---

[2] In the first instance the distinction is a conceptual one, representing two different ways of thinking of conscious states, and suggesting distinct explanatory projects. It is another matter whether the distinction corresponds to any real difference among the states represented. The latter question will not be addressed here.

I have well-developed views on this question, this is not the place to review them (Carruthers, 2000, 2005). What is relevant for our purposes (as we will see shortly) is not whether phenomenal consciousness can be reductively explained in terms acceptable to a physicalist about the mind, but rather the nature of the mental architecture that at least *correlates* with, or *co-occurs* with, phenomenally conscious experience (at least in humans).

Access-consciousness, on the other hand, is a functionally defined notion (or notions). As such, there is general agreement that it is not deeply problematic, and raises no threat to physicalism. Some have claimed that access-conscious states are those that are available for verbal report (Dennett, 1978; Kurzban, 2011). Epistemically, this is broadly correct, for we can often only know what conscious states people are undergoing by asking them. But as a constitutive account of the nature of consciousness (or even an invariable correlate of consciousness) it is plainly problematic. It entails, for example, that those suffering from severe aphasia are no longer capable of conscious states, since they are unable to report them. Other theorists have said that conscious states are those that are available to higher-order thought, in such a way that subjects are aware of those states, or know of themselves that they have them (Rosenthal, 2005). This view, too, has implications that are unacceptable to many. For it entails that creatures incapable of higher-order thought (which presumably includes most species of animal) are incapable of undergoing conscious states.

1.3. Global broadcasting

The most widely endorsed notion of access-consciousness, by far, asserts that conscious states are ones that are *generally*, or *globally*, accessible to an extensive set of other cognitive systems, including those for forming memories, issuing in affective reactions, as well as a variety of systems for inference and decision making (Baars, 1988; Tye, 1995; Block, 1995; Dennett, 2001). It is this notion that will form the main focus of our attention here. This is partly because of its widespread acceptance among cognitive scientists. But it is also because it incorporates within itself, as a special case, each of the alternative notions of access-consciousness. For states that are globally accessible will of course be available for verbal report in beings capable of making such reports; and they will likewise be available to higher-order thought in creatures capable of such thoughts. This means that proponents of these alternative views can concede that conscious states are those that correlate with, or co-occur with, global broadcasting in the relevant populations. At any rate, this is so provided there is no *direct* channel of access between conscious states and the language system, or between conscious states and the faculty of higher-order thought, which could enable states to be conscious in the absence of global broadcasting. While some have made claims of this sort, postulating a faculty of "inner sense" that enables direct knowledge of our own mental states, for example (Nichols & Stich, 2003), such views are deeply problematic. Indeed, when all the evidence is considered, they can be decisively rejected (Carruthers, 2011a). As a result, nothing will be lost if we focus exclusively on a notion of access-consciousness that defines it in terms of global availability.

Moreover, there is an important point to note in the context of our current consideration of the nature of human thought processes. This is that theories accounting for the conscious status of thoughts in terms of their availability to higher-order thought will be of little help to those wishing to argue that amodal thoughts can figure consciously in reflection, unless this is also tied to claims about global availability. For the ordinary idea of reflection includes much more than that the thoughts that figure within it are ones that one has knowledge of, as we noted in Chapter 1. Rather, we intuitively think that those thoughts can give rise to explicit memories, evoke affective reactions, and enter with others into a wide range of different forms of inference and decision making. This is tantamount to believing that reflective thoughts are *globally* accessible, and not just available to higher-order thought.[3] So even if there were such a thing as a faculty of inner sense targeted at one's own thoughts and giving us knowledge of them, this would provide little support for the ordinary conception of reflection unless those thoughts were also globally available.

Not only is a global broadcasting account of access-consciousness widely accepted, but it is also widely accepted that *phenomenal* consciousness correlates with, or is co-extensive with, global broadcasting (at least among humans). Many accept that phenomenally conscious states are all and only those that are globally broadcast to a wide range of systems in the brain. This is agreed even by those who think that phenomenal consciousness cannot be physically explained at all, let alone explained in terms of global broadcast (Chalmers, 1996, 1997). One exception to these generalizations is Block (1995, 2002), who thinks that there can be phenomenally conscious states that aren't access-conscious. This view, too, can be left to one side, since it has little bearing on the question of the mental architecture subserving working memory. For even if there are mental states that are phenomenally conscious without being globally accessible, these states don't

---

[3] Likewise, philosophers who emphasize the *inferential promiscuity* of human thoughts and attitudes (Hurley, 2006) seem committed to something like the global accessibility of conscious thoughts.

belong among the contents of working memory (as Block himself concedes). So it can be widely agreed that the contents of working memory are globally broadcast (and hence access-conscious), even if there are some phenomenally conscious states that are *not* access-conscious.

Access-consciousness is often operationalized in terms of availability to verbal report (Dehaene et al., 2006). A mental state is regarded as conscious just in case the person can report its occurrence. This is comparatively harmless where the states in question are sensory or sensory-based ones (perceptual experiences, visual images, episodic memories, and so forth). For we know that such states undergo global broadcasting, and are thus directly available to one's language-production system among many others. In connection with amodal attitudes, however, we know that access-consciousness and availability to verbal report can pull apart. Indeed, on a view such as my own, according to which amodal attitudes are never globally broadcast, it follows that such attitudes are never access-conscious. They can nevertheless be reported. For people are capable of attributing such thoughts to themselves on the basis of a variety of indirect cues (Carruthers, 2011a). In the present context it is therefore question-begging to infer from the fact that someone can *report* the occurrence of some amodal attitude state that the state in question is an access-conscious one.

1.4. Cognitive phenomenology

There is one other debate about the nature of consciousness that should be mentioned here. This concerns the question of *cognitive* phenomenology (Bayne & Montague, 2011). Some philosophers claim that thoughts, as well as experiences, can be phenomenally conscious (Strawson, 1994; Siewert, 1998; Pitt, 2004). On this view some of our attitude states, together with their component concepts, are phenomenally conscious. Others maintain that phenomenal consciousness is restricted to states with fine-grained nonconceptual content, such as perceptual experiences, affective states, and visual and other forms of imagery (Tye, 1995, 2000). Everyone allows, of course, that our attitudes can make a *causal* contribution to phenomenology (issuing in an affective reaction, say, or evoking associated imagery). What is at stake in this debate is whether concepts make a *constitutive* contribution to phenomenology, and are thus phenomenally conscious in their own right (Veillet & Carruthers, 2011).[4]

---

[4] Note that this debate by no means disappears even if one insists, as does McDowell (1994), that perceptual experience is itself constituted by myriad fine-grained indexical concepts, like *that shade of color*. For the claim can then be that only *fine-grained* concepts make a constitutive contribution to the phenomenology of experience.

If the views defended in this book are correct, then it follows that none of our amodal attitudes are constitutively phenomenally conscious (at least, provided that phenomenal consciousness coincides with global broadcasting). For such attitudes are never, themselves, globally broadcast, and cannot figure among the contents of working memory. There are, however, a variety of sensory-involving attitudes, as we will see. These include episodic memories, affective states, and sensory-embedded judgments (seeing *as*, hearing *as*, and so on). These attitudes are, at least partly, phenomenally conscious. However, my own view is that the conceptual components of such attitudes fail to make a constitutive contribution to their phenomenally conscious properties. Rather, such properties are exhausted by the nonconceptual, fine-grained contents of sensory and sensory-involving experience (Veillet & Carruthers, 2011). This is because it is only nonconceptual content that seems ineffable (try to say what Colombian coffee smells like!), and it is this sort of fine-grained content that gives rise to the other puzzling features of phenomenal consciousness (the conceivability of zombies and so forth; see Chalmers, 1996). These are not views that need to be defended here, however. For our focus will be on the question whether attitudes of all types can figure in the stream of consciousness and among the contents of working memory.

This section has argued that *access-consciousness* (understood to involve global broadcasting) is the relevant notion of consciousness for our purposes. In asking whether amodal attitudes can figure consciously in reflection, what we need to consider is whether such attitudes are ever globally available to a range of systems for forming memories, creating affective reactions, and for reasoning and decision making.

2. Global Broadcasting

This section will sketch some of the evidence supporting a global broadcasting account of the correlates of consciousness. Then Section 3 will argue that attention is a necessary condition for global broadcasting to occur. These topics are important because Chapter 4 will argue that working memory relies on the same attentional mechanisms targeted at midlevel sensory areas to create the stream of consciousness. This will serve to ground our initial argument that conscious reflection is sensory based.

2.1. The theory

Baars (1988) was the first to develop in detail a global broadcasting account of the brain-correlates of consciousness. He argued that the difference between conscious mental states and their unconscious counterparts is that the former are made widely available to different mechanisms in the brain, including those for forming memories, for forming new values, for creating affective states, and for reasoning and decision making (the latter systems being located especially in the frontal lobes). Unconscious mental states, in contrast, have more limited effects. They might prime a choice, for example, making selection of that item more likely, but they don't give rise to most of the other effects mentioned.

Baars' global broadcasting theory coheres quite well with proposals made by a number of philosophers. Tye (1995), for example, argues that conscious states are those that are *poised* to have an impact on inferential and decision-making systems, and Block's (1995) account of access-consciousness makes essentially the same claim. Moreover, although Dennett (1978, 1991) had initially developed two different accounts in earlier publications (that differed not only from each other but also from the global broadcasting idea), he subsequently came to argue that consciousness should be understood in terms of "fame in the brain" (2001). This is, in effect, the global broadcasting account, except that it suggests that conscious status might be incremental, or a matter of degree. Baars, in contrast, postulates a kind of sharp "state change" once a certain level of activation is reached, an idea that has since received significant experimental support (Sergent & Dehaene, 2004; Del Cul et al., 2007).

Global broadcasting accounts have been elaborated and confirmed by other cognitive scientists in addition to Baars (Sergent et al., 2005; Dehaene et al., 2006; Bekinschtein et al., 2009; Dehaene & Changeux, 2011). They also seem to converge with a number of other recent suggestions made by neuroscientists, although the language used often differs. For example, although Crick & Koch (1990) initially proposed an account in terms of synchronous neural oscillations in the 40–70 Hz range, even then this was presented as a theory of how the contents of working memory are determined. In more recent work, Crick & Koch (2003) emphasize the role of brain-wide coalitions of activated neurons, while also saying that consciousness can be characterized very roughly in terms of the front of the brain "looking at" activity in the back. Both accounts seem quite close to the idea of global broadcasting. Likewise Lamme (2003) emphasizes the role of recurrent processing in conscious experience, in which a forward sweep of neural activation in sensory areas becomes linked to activity in more frontal regions of the brain. Similar ideas have been proposed by Edelman (2003) and by Tononi (2008).

2.2. Evidence

There is now extensive evidence supporting the global broadcasting account. Much of this looks at differences in brain activity between cases of conscious and unconscious experience, using either fMRI or EEG (Dehaene et al., 2006; Dehaene & Changeux, 2011). Many contrasts have been studied, including contra-lateral neglect (and its absence), binocular rivalry, change blindness, inattentional blindness, and responses to masked versus unmasked stimuli.[5] But perhaps the strongest paradigm involves the so-called "attentional blink," because the stimulus conditions and task demands can be matched exactly between conscious and unconscious trials (Sergent et al., 2005). Participants see a swiftly masked pair of successive stimuli, and their task is to say whether a third stimulus that follows them matches the first. But on some trials they are also asked to report whether they saw the second stimulus. With attention thus directed toward the first stimulus, the second often goes completely unseen. Indeed, if the timing and intensity of the stimuli are set correctly, participants will fail to see the second stimulus on about 50 percent of the trials, despite the fact that everything in the experimental setup remains the same throughout.

What such studies show is that in cases of unconscious perception there is a forward sweep of activity through visual cortex and some local reverberation in regions of the temporal lobes. Although participants say they see nothing, and their performance is no better than chance when they are asked to select the stimulus that had been presented to them, there is nevertheless often robust priming, not just of low-level sensory properties, but also of a semantic sort. In cases of conscious perception, in contrast, the forward sweep of activity through visual cortex is rapidly followed by reverberating activity in frontal, temporal, and parietal cortices. It appears that when activity in visual cortex is targeted by attention (at least, under the right conditions), the information encoded by that neural activity is made widely available to many different brain regions, and especially to frontal cortex, where it can inform reporting, planning, and decision making.

We also know that the brain has a long-distance architecture of the sort predicted by a global broadcasting account of perceptual consciousness. In particular, it has a "small world" architecture consisting of densely locally connected sensory, motor, and association areas linked via midline hubs and long-distance white-matter neural pathways (Sporns, 2011). When these long-distance pathways are differentially damaged, as they are in people suffering from the early stages of multiple sclerosis, conscious perception is correspondingly impacted, while priming effects are left unchanged (Reuter et al., 2007, 2009). In particular, such patients require a longer interval than normal between stimulus

---

[5] Masking can be thought of as a sort of "overwriting" of the sensory activity caused by one stimulus with activations caused by a swiftly succeeding one, which can render the former invisible.

and subsequent mask for the former to be consciously perceived, with the extent of the increased interval correlating with the extent of their white-matter damage. This is just what one would predict if consciousness co-occurs with global broadcasting. For it will require a stronger and/or longer stimulus to insure that the signals are globally transmitted.

Much of the evidence supporting a global broadcasting account of the neural correlates of consciousness derives from the study of vision, which is, by far, the most heavily studied sensory system. But there are similar findings for conscious versus unconscious tactile perception (Boly et al., 2007; Jones et al., 2007). And in the auditory domain, too, conscious and unconscious stimuli differ in the wave of global activity that accompanies only the former (Bekinschtein et al., 2009; Diekhof et al., 2009; Sadaghiani et al., 2009). So it is reasonable to believe that global broadcasting accompanies conscious forms of perception quite generally.

3. Consciousness and Attention

This section will consider the relationships between global broadcasting and attention. It argues that attention to a stimulus is *necessary* for perception of that stimulus to become conscious. (It also argues briefly that attention is not, in contrast, a *sufficient* condition for consciousness to occur.) This point is important because Chapter 4 will argue that working memory is likewise attention based, while making endogenous use of some of the same sensory mechanisms that are responsible for conscious perception. This will give rise to an argument that working memory is sensory dependent.

3.1. Attention is necessary for consciousness

There is a good deal of evidence to suggest that global broadcasting (and hence consciousness) depends upon attention. Consider inattentional blindness, for example (Mack & Rock, 1998). When attention is occupied elsewhere, even highly salient stimuli can remain unseen, and can do so even when occupying foveal vision for a significant period of time. Such results are widely interpreted as showing that attention to a stimulus is necessary for it to become conscious.

It might be objected that the effect of distracted attention in inattentional blindness is not to disrupt conscious perception of the target, as such, but rather to interfere with memory formation. Perhaps stimuli that go unreported are consciously perceived at the time, but fail to be remembered. Perhaps the direction of attention elsewhere means that no memories are formed, even though the perceptions in question are momentarily conscious. Although possible, this interpretation is quite implausible. For in many such experiments the "unseen" event is both unusual and striking (such as a man in a gorilla suit appearing in the middle of basketball practice). It is hard to believe that, if seen, it would not have been remembered.

The attempt to explain inattentional-blindness data by appealing to failures of memory becomes even less likely when other forms of evidence are also considered. For example, instances of change blindness are *not* accompanied by globally broadcast brain activity (Pessoa & Ungerleider, 2004). When subjects successfully detect a change in the stimulus following an interval there is extensive activation in frontal, parietal, and temporal regions of cortex. When subjects fail to detect the change, in contrast, very little differential activity is found. So in this paradigm, at least, there is reason to think that conscious perception of the change does *not* occur, even momentarily. Moreover, in the attentional blink paradigm, questions about visibility are asked just moments following the stimulus presentation. This makes it hard to believe that people's reports of failure to see the target could result from failures of memory. In addition, of course, among people suffering from neglect, stimuli go unreported even when concurrent. This point is worth elaborating.

It has long been known that neglect is an attentional deficit, rather than a purely visual one (Mesulam, 1999). For one thing, all sensory modalities on the left side of the body, and not just vision, are often implicated following damage to regions of the right hemisphere.[6] Moreover, unconscious forms of perception remain intact. For example, a neglect patient asked to copy a drawing of a house whose left side is on fire will draw only the right side of the house, but will say that there is something dangerous about the house, and that he would not want to live in it. We also know that neglect is a deficit especially of bottom-up forms of attention (Bartolomeo & Chokron, 2002; Todd et al., 2005), and that attentional training can reduce the severity of unilateral neglect (Robertson et al., 1995). So it appears that the left side of space fails to issue in conscious perceptions in neglect patients because it fails to attract attention.

In addition (and just as one might predict if attention to a stimulus were necessary for global broadcasting to occur), transcranial magnetic stimulation (TMS) applied over regions of parietal cortex that are known to be parts of the attentional network can make stimuli fade or disappear (Meister et al., 2006; Kanai et al., 2008). And in a separate experiment, TMS applied over right parietal cortex during a change detection task resulted in greater latencies to detect the change and

---

[6] These regions include especially right ventral parietal cortex near the temporo-parietal junction and right ventrolateral prefrontal cortex, which are now known to be parts of the "bottom-up" attentional system (Corbetta & Shulman, 2002). See Figure 2.

a greater rate of change blindness, suggesting that disruption of the attentional mechanism was rendering the changes invisible (Beck et al., 2006). So these findings, too, support the view that attention is necessary for global broadcasting.

Everyone in the field now grants that attention can be an important determinant of conscious experience. But some have denied that it is strictly necessary (Koch & Tsuchiya, 2007; Tononi & Koch, 2008). This is because of data suggesting that background scene perception is independent of attention. For example, Mack & Rock (1998) failed to show inattentional blindness for scenes, and others have shown that in change-blindness experiments people instantly notice if the "gist" of a scene is altered, whereas they fail to notice many other sorts of change (Rensink et al., 1997; Simons & Levin, 1997). However, Cohen et al. (2011) hypothesize that this is because background scene information can be processed with very *little* attention, rather than without attention at all. They suggest that previous studies may have placed insufficient demands on attention, leaving enough remaining for the gist of a scene to be consciously perceived. They were able to test this in a pair of studies. In the first, they found that when people are given a highly demanding attentional task they *do* fail to notice dramatic changes in background scenes. In the second, they used a dual-task method to show that as the difficulty of the primary object-tracking task increases, so participants make many more errors in classifying background scenes, suggesting that both tasks are drawing on a common resource (namely, attention).

Block (2013), too, argues that attention isn't strictly necessary for conscious perception. But what he actually shows is something much weaker, namely that there can be conscious perception of individual objects in the absence of *object-based* attention. He does not argue that perception of individuals can occur without attention at all. On the contrary, in the examples he discusses it is feature-based attention that enables the individual objects to stand out from one another in a crowded display, even though attention doesn't have the fineness of grain required to latch onto each of those individuals independently of their features.

If one were to assume that attention is fundamentally object based or event based, then it might indeed follow that consciousness can occur without attention. And it may be that some such view is adopted (albeit tacitly) in parts of the literature. For it is common to describe the limits on working memory in terms of the number of individuals or events that one can keep in mind at once, and the limits on working memory derive from limited powers of attention, as we will see in Chapter 4. So people might assume that all attention is object based. However, the existence of feature-based attention is also widely accepted (Bisley, 2011). Moreover, recent models suggest that the limits on attention and working memory are informational rather than "slot based," resulting from competition for information-representation among cortical maps (Franconeri et al., 2013). If this is right, then the fact that people can consciously perceive individuals that they cannot pick out in attention doesn't count against the view that attention is necessary for consciousness.

Taken altogether, then, the best explanation of the evidence is that attention is necessary for global broadcasting to occur and that, when certain other conditions are satisfied, it is attention to a stimulus that *produces* conscious experience of it.

3.2. Is attention sufficient for consciousness?

Prinz (2012), however, goes beyond the ideas defended in Section 3.1. He argues that attention is not only necessary, but strictly sufficient, for conscious experience. He claims that in cases where it might seem that we have attention to a stimulus without consciousness, the neural activity caused by the stimulus does not last long enough for attention to have its normal impact. Consider visual masking, for example. Although subjects are trying to attend to the masked stimulus (in order to report it), the neural activity is over-written by the mask too swiftly for attention to have any effect.

Prinz's claim is thus that attention, when timed in such a way as to *interact* with a representation of a stimulus, is always sufficient for consciousness to occur. This can successfully explain away some of the results in the literature that might seem to support the insufficiency of attention for consciousness. For example, McCormick (1997) claims to show that attention can be captured by a briefly presented cue (to the left or right of fixation) that makes participants respond more quickly and accurately when a target appears in the same location, even when the cue is never consciously perceived. Prinz can plausibly reply, however, that in these experiments attention was *attracted* to the *location* of the cue, and so was already targeted at the correct location when the stimulus appeared, but without ever having interacted with a representation of the cue. So this is not a case where attention and perceptual activity interact without being sufficient for consciousness.

There are other results, however, that appear to refute Prinz's (2012) claim that attention is sufficient for consciousness (van Boxtel et al., 2010; De Brigard, 2012). For example, Kentridge et al. (2008) use metacontrast masking to demonstrate that attention modulates the processing of an unperceived target, while also reviewing a number of other results that support the same conclusion.[7]

---

[7] Metacontrast masking occurs when a target such as a colored disk is swiftly replaced with a ring that precisely encloses the space previously occupied by the disc. In these conditions the disk itself can remain invisible.

Participants were first presented with a spatial cue, pointing to one side or the other of their fixation point. Then two differently colored disks were briefly presented (one on each side), followed by two colored rings enclosing the spaces previously occupied by the discs. The participants' task was simply to indicate the color of the rings. The result was that they were swifter to do so when they were cued to a disc that was congruent in color with the subsequent rings, suggesting that the color of the disc had been processed more deeply as a result of the shift in attention caused by the cue. Yet the disc itself remained invisible.

Bressan & Pizzighello (2008) also present findings that challenge the sufficiency of attention for consciousness, using an inattentional blindness experiment. Participants were required to count the number of times that some randomly moving black-and-white shapes touched the sides of the screen. At some point during the trial a colored cross moved across the screen, which was noticed on only about half the trials. The finding was that participants performed *worse* in cases where the cross remained unseen than when it was noticed. This suggests that the cross had attracted (and hence divided) the participants' attention in the unseen condition, leading to poorer performance in the primary task. Yet attention was still insufficient to issue in conscious perception of the cross. In cases where the cross was noticed, however (and even though this might have resulted from a larger initial shift of attention), subjects could recognize that the movement of the cross was irrelevant to their task, to which their attention could then be fully returned.

I conclude, then, that not only are conscious perceptual states those that are globally broadcast to a wide range of states and systems in the brain, but in addition, attention is necessary for global broadcasting to occur. Moreover, it seems that attention is sufficient for global broadcasting in cases where *enough* attention is devoted to a stimulus that is *sufficiently intense and long-lasting*.

4. The Nature of Attention

This section will distinguish a number of different forms of attention, and will outline the brain mechanisms that are thought to underlie them. Some understanding of these mechanisms will be important for the argument of Chapter 4, where it will emerge that it is the very same mechanisms operating in the same way that are required for contents to enter working memory and the stream of consciousness. The best explanation of this and related findings will then be that only sensory-involving representations are capable of being conscious.

4.1. Overt versus covert attention

It is often noted that attention can be either overt or covert. Consider the former first. In the case of vision, one can attend to something by shifting one's gaze and focusing one's eyes on it (thereby enabling maximum information from the object to be processed by the densely packed neurons in the fovea of the retina). In the case of audition, one can attend by shifting the position of one's head relative to the direction of the sound, or by cupping one's hands behind one's ears. With smell, one can attend to the smell of something by sniffing it, and with taste, one can attend by manipulating the substance into closer contact with one's tongue. In the case of touch, one can attend by shifting one's hands to bring the thing into contact with the movements of one's fingertips (where touch sensitivity is greatest).

Not all sensory systems permit overt forms of attention, however. In the case of interoception there is nothing overt one can do to attend to a pain, a contraction of the gut, or one's own heartbeat. Nor, in the case of proprioception, is there anything overt one can do to attend non-visually to one's own bodily position or movements. Moreover, it can be argued that cases of overt attention without covert attention are not properly deserving of the name. As inattentional blindness demonstrates, one can have one's eyes focused on an object or event—thereby overtly "attending" to it—without seeing it at all. And one can, likewise, sniff an object or roll a substance over one's tongue with one's (covert) attention wholly occupied elsewhere, hence neither smelling nor tasting anything in the circumstances. Similar things can happen with touch and sound.

It seems, then, that it is the covert form of attention—hereafter, "attention"—that carries most of the explanatory load, and which should form the target of scientific inquiry (as indeed it does). While attention is often *supported* by various forms of overt activity (shifting one's eyes, turning one's head, moving one's hands, and so on), it is fully capable of operating without such activity. Thus one can attend visually to one thing while having one's eyes focused on another, or one can attend to one of two nearby conversations at a party without altering the orientation of one's head, and so on. Attention is, fundamentally, a *cognitive* process, enabling the extraction of information about one aspect of the environment or body to the exclusion of others. Indeed, this seems to be its function. The amount of information impacting all of our senses at any given moment is overwhelming. Since much of this is irrelevant to current needs or concerns, it would be hugely wasteful (and probably impossible) to attempt to process it all. In short, attention is what enables the mind to focus its resources on information that is *relevant*.

4.2.   Top–down versus bottom–up attention

It is now known that there are two largely distinct but interacting cortical networks involved in the control of attention (Corbetta & Shulman, 2002; Corbetta et al., 2008). One links together dorsolateral prefrontal cortex, the frontal eye-fields in dorsal motor and premotor cortex (which are also involved in controlling movements of the eyes), and the intraparietal sulcus bilaterally, which is arranged vertically down the center of parietal cortex in each hemisphere. This is the network that controls top-down attention (see Figure 2). It is thought that dorsolateral prefrontal cortex maintains current goals, interacting with the frontal eye-fields to transmit attentional signals to the intraparietal sulcus, which in turn focuses both boosting and suppressing signals on relevant midlevel regions of visual (and other sensory) cortex. The result is that some perceptual representations are globally broadcast whereas others are not.

The second cortical attentional network is located most strongly in the right hemisphere. It links a region of right ventral parietal cortex near the temporoparietal junction (this is the corner where temporal and parietal cortices join) with right ventrolateral prefrontal cortex and right medial frontal gyrus (see Figures 2 and 3).[8] This is the network responsible for some kinds of bottom-up attention. It is thought that right ventral parietal cortex continually monitors unattended sensory representations (such as surrounding conversations at a party), interacting with ventrolateral prefrontal cortex and subcortical value systems to determine the relevance of those representations to both current goals and standing values. When relevant signals are detected (such as the sound of one's own name), the ventral network interacts with the dorsal attentional system via the medial frontal gyrus and the anterior cingulate (see Figure 3). The result is either that the previous focus of attention is maintained in the face of a potential distracter, or the dorsal network shifts its focus to the novel stimulus, which is then consciously experienced as a result.

In addition to these two cortical networks there are a variety of subcortical systems in the basal ganglia (see Figure 3), involving portions of the amygdala, thalamus, superior colliculus, and other structures, which can be involved in bottom-up forms of attention (Vuilleumier, 2005). The superior colliculus, in particular, constructs a salience map of visual and auditory space, modulated in part by top-down signals from the two cortical systems (Knudsen, 2011; Mysore

---

[8]   Right ventrolateral prefrontal cortex seems also to play a crucial role in a variety of forms of self-control (Aron et al., 2004; Cohen & Lieberman, 2010).

& Knudsen, 2013). These subcortical mechanisms can interrupt the processing of each of the cortical networks (seizing control of the dorsal attentional system in particular), responding to loud noises, bright flashes, and other high-intensity stimuli, as well as to stimuli of innate or learned emotional significance (a snake in the grass; bared teeth; an angry face; the face of a loved one; and so on). The result is that the dorsal system shifts its focus to the novel stimulus, at least temporarily until further appraisal can assess the latter's real significance (for example, on closer examination the snake-like shape turns out to be a piece of rope).

It seems likely that these attentional systems are an amodal, domain-general resource. At any rate, there is direct evidence that the systems described above underlie both visual and auditory forms of attention. This provides some reason to think that the finding might generalize to all sensory systems.[9] Thus Schönwiesner et al. (2007) map a cortical network for bottom-up forms of auditory attention that is remarkably close, at any rate, to the system described above for vision. Moreover, the same dorsal network that controls top-down attention to visual stimuli is also what controls endogenous attention in the auditory domain (Shomstein & Yantis, 2006; Wu et al., 2007; Cowan et al., 2011; Li et al., 2014). In addition, just as this account would predict, Saults & Cowan (2007) show that visual and auditory forms of working memory share the same attentional resources, with the maximum number of items that can be retained in each sensory domain being the same, while also matching what can be retained in cross-modal tasks.

4.3. How attention works

Attention is thought to operate by biasing sensory processing, enhancing the sensitivity of selected groups of neurons and suppressing the activity of others, seemingly by increasing or decreasing the extent to which those neurons fire in phase with one another (Jensen et al., 2007). Thus Gazzaley et al. (2005) show that when people are directed to remember faces in a mixed presentation of faces and scenes, activity in the fusiform face area is enhanced relative to baseline, while activity in the parahippocampal place area is correspondingly suppressed. The reverse occurs when people are directed to remember the scenes and ignore the faces.[10] Moreover, the primary locus of influence is on midlevel sensory areas.

---

[9] In addition, the executive component of working memory is a domain-general resource that is common to working memory in all sensory domains, as we will see in Chapter 4.

[10] In addition, these regions are *faster* to respond when attended. See also Carrasco & McElree (2001) for evidence that attention speeds up perceptual processing.

For example, spatial attention enhances the activity of specific groups of neurons in area V4 (which processes both color and form information), and attention to motion alters the activity of groups of neurons in area MT (Treue & Maunsell, 1996; Reynolds & Chelazzi, 2004). When attention is directed at a location that falls within the receptive field of a neuron in V4, the latter's sensitivity is enhanced, enabling it to respond to stimuli that would otherwise be too faint to elicit a response.

Moreover, attention alone, in the absence of sensory input, causes activity in the relevant regions of sensory cortex, presumably because baseline levels of neural activity have been increased. For example, Voisin et al. (2006) show in a dichotic listening task that when people are expecting a sound to be heard in just one ear there is enhanced activity in primary auditory cortex and surrounding areas on the contralateral side. They argue that this is unlikely to result from auditory *imagery*, since the sounds are never repeated, and participants have no idea of what sort of sound they might hear in a given trial. Rather, it appears that attention alone increases baseline neural activity in sensory areas, thereby preparing for the global broadcast of any stimulus-caused representation when it occurs.

It should also be stressed that attention doesn't merely boost overall levels of activity in selected visual areas while repressing others. Rather, it also enhances *contrasts* within attended items, with consequent effects on visual phenomenology (Störmer et al., 2009). This was elegantly demonstrated by Carrasco et al. (2004). They presented participants with pairs of Gabor patches (which are low-contrast objects, vaguely striped and bordered) at varying orientations. Participants were asked to judge the orientation of the higher-contrast patch. On trials when subjects had their attention drawn to a particular patch by a briefly presented spatial cue, they perceived its contrast to be higher (even though it wasn't), and judged accordingly. Attention also has a variety of other neural effects in the regions targeted (Bisley, 2011).

4.4. Is attention a natural kind?

Some have argued that attention is not a natural kind, but rather a heterogeneous collection of processes and behaviors (Mole, 2010; Wu, 2011). What is certainly true is that the *term* "attention" in ordinary speech does not pick out a natural kind. For we have already noted in Section 4.1 that both overt and covert processes are described as forms of attention, whereas from a scientific perspective only the latter should qualify. Moreover, the bottom-up and top-down systems described in Section 4.2 have distinct neural realizations and perform different functions. Chun et al. (2011) suggest that there are many distinct forms of attentional mechanism, which are differentiated from one another by the content-domains with which they deal. They propose a main overarching division between *external* (perceptual) and *internal* (mnemonic) forms of attention. Nevertheless, Chun et al. think that these mechanisms can all be unified at a functional–computational level, since all have the functions of *selecting* some things (whether items of information or different forms of behavior) while *filtering out* or *suppressing* others, and while *modulating* (generally by enhancing) the selected items.

Mechanisms that select, filter, and modulate are probably ubiquitous in cognition. Indeed, as a number of authors have pointed out (Chun et al., 2011; Wu, 2011), they are also involved in action-selection, where competition among the multiple things one could do or say at any one time is resolved by selecting and modulating one while suppressing the others. But the causal roles of the action-selection mechanism are very different from those of the attentional mechanisms involved in perception. In particular, action-schemata, once selected, are *implemented*, not globally broadcast. (On the contrary, they remain unconscious; Jeannerod, 2006.) Indeed, when seen from this perspective, it is probably a mistake to regard the bottom-up attentional system as genuinely attentional, too. For it, too, is not charged with causing the global broadcast of attended representations. Rather, it sifts among incoming representations for relevance to current goals and values, and competes for control of the top-down system. Only the latter results in the global broadcasting of the representations at which it is directed.

But what of the contrast between internal and external forms of attention? We will see in Chapter 6 that it is actually the same top-down attentional system centered on the intraparietal sulcus (which is involved in conscious perception) that is also implicated in the retrieval of episodic memories (resulting in the global broadcast of sensory-involving memory representations). Distinct ancillary processes are involved in each, of course. In particular, memory search uses conceptual and other cues to activate stored representations that are processed and evaluated for relevance through the bottom-up system. But top-down attention is employed in each case to render the selected representations conscious (De Brigard, 2012). There is a case for saying, then, that there *is* a single natural kind at the heart of the phenomena that are often described as involving attention. This is the top-down attentional network involving especially the frontal eye-fields and intraparietal sulcus.[11]

---

[11] I will continue to use the phrase "bottom-up attention," however (largely because it is so entrenched in the literature), even if, as I have suggested, it is not strictly a form of attention at all.

Overall, then, one can say that the mechanisms underlying attention, together with the roles that attention plays in causing global broadcasting of perceptual representations, are increasingly well understood. We will see in Chapter 4 that it is these same mechanisms that are responsible for maintaining representations of previously perceived stimuli in working memory, and also for the global broadcasting of visual, auditory, and other images, thereby contributing to the contents of working memory. This will give rise to an argument that the stream of consciousness is intrinsically sensory based, which implies (if true) that amodal attitudes are incapable of being conscious.

5. Amodal Content in Perception

The present section will argue that concepts and other amodal representations (such as scalar representations of numerosity) are bound into the content of perceptual experience, and are globally broadcast along with the latter. This will set the stage for an explanation in Chapter 4 of how a working-memory system that is sensory based can at the same time traffic in amodal, conceptual representations. We will also see in the present section how the application of concepts to experience can change the character of the latter. This might help us to understand how thoughts and attention can work together to generate sensory-based contents for working memory, as we will see in Chapter 6.

5.1. Phenomenological considerations

Philosophers sometimes suggest that there is a sharp divide between perception and cognition (Dretske, 1979; Fodor, 1983; Tye, 1995). The idea is that perceptual systems do their work independently of conceptual ones, in such a way that the former are encapsulated from the latter. *First* there is seeing and *then* there is believing, and what one believes doesn't influence what one sees. But such views seem belied by the phenomenology of perception. When one looks out on a scene one does not first see uncategorized patterns, colors, and shapes, thereafter coming to believe that there is a red car going past, a person walking, and so on. Rather, it seems that one sees the first moving object *as* a red car and the other *as* a person walking. It seems that conceptual contents such as *car* and *person* are right there in the content of conscious perception, not added later in thought. Admittedly, there are cases that fit the latter description. When one views an ambiguous figure one might first see it just as surfaces and shapes, only later realizing that it is an old lady seen in profile, or a Dalmatian dog in dappled light. But this is by no means the normal case.

There are also cases, of course, where one withholds assent from what one sees, or only comes to believe what one sees after further reflection. Although one sees a performer in a magic show *as* plucking a coin out of a volunteer's ear, one might decline to believe that he really did so. And although it looks just as if he has pulled a real rabbit out of a tiny box, one might doubt that it is a live animal until one sees the rabbit begin to wriggle and squirm. Nevertheless, we believe what we see by default. What we see things *as* will (if salient enough) automatically give rise to an episodic memory, and will be reported as fact. Moreover, after observing just a single episode of a cat scratching someone, one will be apt, thereafter, to believe the generic *cats scratch* (Leslie et al., 2011). For these reasons, episodes of seeing-*as* can be thought of as forms of perceptually embedded *judgment*, since they have much of the distinctive functional role of judgment. (See Chapter 1.1.) Cases where one doesn't believe what one sees are best thought of as involving a *clash* of judgments, one of which is perceptually embedded and the other of which is formed by inference from background knowledge.

Of course one can, if one prefers, insist on reserving the term "judgment" for episodes of *reflective* belief formation. This would preserve a sharp distinction between perception and judgment. But it would leave untouched the claim that in episodes of seeing-*as* concepts are bound into the contents of vision. And it would also leave intact the claim that there is no sharp divide between perception and cognition generally. Moreover, it would remain true that in many respects episodes of seeing-*as* are judgment-*like*, since by default they issue in new beliefs and are immediately available to inform our decisions. In what follows, therefore, I will continue to describe these as perceptually embedded judgments.

Similar points can be made in connection with perceptions of sound, especially heard speech. One does not first hear patterns of phonemes, thereafter coming to believe that the speaker is saying that a line of storms is approaching. Rather, one *hears* her *as* saying that a line of storms is approaching. It seems that the content of a speech act (as well as the intent behind the act—assertion, question, command, and so on) is right there in the experience of speech itself, not added later. Within the auditory–linguistic system itself, of course, there may well be a stage at which phonemes are represented in the absence of conceptual content. (Although in fact the evidence suggests that speech processing proceeds in parallel throughout, with phonology, syntax, and semantics all being processed at the same time in an interactive way; Hickok & Poeppel, 2007.) But by the time the attended products of the system are globally broadcast, it seems that concepts are thoroughly embedded in one's conscious experience of speech.

5.2. The case from cognitive science

Introspective appearances can be deceiving, of course (Carruthers, 2011a). It might be said that our impression of undergoing hybrid sensory–conceptual states results merely from the regular coincidence in time between two separate conscious events: a sensory experience and an indexical belief grounded in the content of that experience. When one sees someone walking past in the street, for example, it may be that two distinct mental states are globally broadcast. One is a nonconceptual sensory experience of moving colors and shapes, and the other is a belief with the content, *That is a person walking* (where the indexical *that* refers to the moving colored thing represented in the perceptual state).

In this instance, however, cognitive science and introspection are largely in agreement. Building on more than twenty years of detailed research conducted in multiple labs, Kosslyn (1994) develops a model of high-level visual processing that involves continual back-and-forth questioning between midlevel visual areas and regions of association cortex (especially in the temporal lobes) that store conceptual information about objects and events. (See Vetter & Newen, 2014, for a recent review along the same lines.) Information from conceptual regions is projected back to earlier stages of processing, influencing the latter, and becoming a component in the perceptual state that follows visual recognition. It seems that a conscious percept is a hybrid conceptual–nonconceptual representation, just as our introspective access to states of seeing *as* and hearing *as* suggests.

Moreover, notice that the attempt to keep cognition separate from perception sketched above makes use of indexicals to link the two together. But in fact such indexicals are needed in midlevel vision as well, to enable the binding of perceptual properties that are processed in separate parts of the visual system. Numerous vision researchers make use of the idea of *object files*, in particular, which can be thought of as location-based indexicals that latch on to particular entities (Kahneman & Triesman, 1984; Kahneman et al., 1992; Pylyshyn, 2003). But as the name suggests, these indexicals come with folders attached, into which are placed various forms of property-information about the individual. Using boldface type to indicate that a representation is a nonconceptual one (and small capitals, as usual, to represent concepts), an object file produced by perception of a falling tomato might have the content: THAT: **red, round, smooth, moving down**. Then given that indexicals need to be employed anyway to anchor visual percepts themselves, it seems otiose to postulate yet another set of indexicals to anchor the perceptually based thoughts that are (it is said) globally broadcast alongside perception. And indeed, object files are generally understood by vision scientists to include conceptual as well as nonconceptual representations of an object's properties. So the full conceptual–nonconceptual content of the above perceptual state might be: THAT: **red**, RED, **round**, ROUND, **smooth**, SMOOTH, **moving down**, FALLING, TOMATO.[12] One sees the thing *as* a falling tomato, in addition to seeing its fine-grained properties.

It should be stressed that in order to see something *as* an instance of a kind it is not enough that one be entertaining a thought (even a thought that is seemingly conscious) of the kind while perceiving the thing in question. Rather, the two components need to be bound together in a single integrated representation, resulting from the back-and-forth processing that underlies object recognition. Turn back to examine Figure 4, in the knowledge that the picture contains, somehow, a representation of a Dalmatian dog. If you have not seen this picture before, it is likely that it will take you a little while to see a subset of the patterns of dark splotches *as* a Dalmatian. In the intervening time you were consciously experiencing the dots, of course, while also entertaining the concept DALMATIAN. But it is only when recognition occurs that a subset of the dots configures into a familiar Dalmatian shape. A plausible interpretation is that binding the concept DALMATIAN into your perception of the dots is necessary for you to see them *as* parts of a Dalmatian.

Similar considerations apply in the auditory domain. One can know what someone is saying, and hear the sounds that they are making, without hearing the person *as* saying that. For example, you are traveling with a guide in a country where you don't know the language, and are about to stop at a small country inn. Your guide tells you that the first thing your host will say to you is that you are very welcome in his home. When your host opens the door he does, indeed, say that. Although you *know* that he is saying that you are welcome, and although you hear him quite clearly, you don't hear him *as* saying that you are welcome in his home. This is because (since you don't know the language) the back-and-forth interpretive process that is a necessary condition for meaning-recognition fails to issue in a single integrated event-file into which both the sounds and their intended meaning are bound. On the contrary, although the two components are both present, they remain separate.

Notice, too, that in both of these examples one might be entertaining a thought that is linked indexically to the content of one's experience, prior to or in the absence of recognition. While listening to one's host speak, for instance, one

---

[12] Note that on this account event-files are implicitly conjunctive in nature, listing a conjunction of properties of the event. It may well be that event-files possess additional internal structure, with slots for agent and patient roles, for example. This idea is consistent with the work of Pietroski (2010), who suggests that conjunctive event-representations are the fundamental form of the semantic representations that underlie linguistic meaning.

might have a thought with the content, *That is him saying that I am very welcome in his home.* Yet one still does not *hear* him *as* saying that. This is because the conceptual content isn't linked to the sounds at the level of detail required for hearing *as*, where one experiences certain aspects of the sound-sequence as expressing specific aspects of the meaning. Something similar is true in the example of the hidden Dalmatian. When one eventually sees some of the splotches *as* a Dalmatian, one sees a subset of them as the head, others as the back left leg, and so on. In short, when one experiences something under a concept, the conceptual and sensory forms of information are *integrated* into a single sensory–conceptual conscious event.

Another consideration in favor of the construal of perceptual content being outlined here is its economy. Relying on only a single set of attentional mechanisms targeted at midlevel perceptual regions, together with mechanisms for interactively identifying and classifying the objects of perception, the brain can insure the global broadcast of a wide range of both conceptual and nonconceptual information. As a result, stored semantic knowledge or episodic memories can be evoked by either form of information, affective responses can be caused, and so forth. One can then understand how a cascade of cognitive and affective reactions can issue from a single conscious perceptual state (Barrett, 2005). If cognition and perception are kept separate, in contrast, then one will need to postulate a second set of mechanisms for making perceptually grounded thoughts globally accessible, as well as a second set of indexical mechanisms to link thoughts to perception (in addition to the object-file mechanisms already present in the latter).

5.3. Jackendoff

A prominent dissenting voice in cognitive science to the picture sketched here is that of Jackendoff (2007, 2012). He claims that *only* the midlevel, nonconceptual contents of vision and hearing are conscious.[13] When we hear people speak, for example, we are conscious of the phonological properties of their utterances, and we are conscious of a *feeling of meaningfulness* that accompanies meaningful speech; but we are *not* conscious of the meaning itself. Unfortunately, however, Jackendoff persistently conflates together *access-conscious*ness and *phenomenal*

---

[13] Prinz (2012) makes a very similar claim when defending his AIR theory of consciousness, while citing Jackendoff's work. ("AIR" stands for "Attended Intermediate-level Representations.") But Prinz is more clear-headed, I think, in offering a theory of *phenomenal* consciousness. He does not deny that concepts can figure in the globally broadcast contents of working memory. (Note, however, that he is an empiricist about concepts, denying that any are genuinely amodal in character.)

consciousness. Construed as a theory of the latter, I can (and do) agree with him. But there are also passages where he plainly intends to be offering a theory of the former. Yet he provides no evidence for the claim that meanings are never access-conscious, whereas there is ample reason to think that this claim is false. Let me elaborate.

It seems that Jackendoff's primary intention is to provide a theory of phenomenal consciousness. So construed, his "intermediate-level theory" amounts to the claim that it is the fine-grained, nonconceptual contents of one's experiences that constitute the latter's phenomenal properties. This is a thesis that I agree with (Carruthers, 2000; Veillet & Carruthers, 2011). But notice that this view is entirely consistent with the claim that amodal conceptual representations are bound into the contents of one's perceptual experiences at higher levels of processing and globally broadcast along with them. (It is also entirely consistent with claiming that the concepts that one deploys in the course of one's experience can make a significant causal difference to the phenomenal properties of that experience, as we will see in some detail in Section 5.4.) From the fact that only nonconceptual content is phenomenally conscious it does not begin to follow that only nonconceptual content is *access*-conscious. Yet this is an inference that Jackendoff (2007, 2012) persistently slips into making.

In fact, Jackendoff frequently uses language characteristic of access-consciousness when characterizing his "unconscious meaning hypothesis." He says that we do not *perceive* the meaning of someone's utterances, that we are not *aware* of the meaning of those utterances, that meanings are "hidden from awareness," and so on. In support of such claims he points out that we cannot be aware of meanings *on their own*. This, too, is something I agree with. Indeed, it is one of the theses defended at length in Carruthers (2011a). But it doesn't follow that one cannot be aware of meanings *at all* (as Jackendoff seems to think). On the contrary, one might be aware of them when bound into the content of a globally broadcast sensory-based representation. This is the view that I have been defending here.

The claim that meanings cannot be access-conscious is obviously false, I suggest. Indeed, in normal circumstances the heard meaning of people's utterances meet all of the criteria for access-consciousness. One can report what they have said (and not just the sounds that they used to say it). One can generally later recall at least the gist of what they said. One can respond emotionally to the content of what was said. One can plan an appropriate response to the content of what was said. And so on. The interpreted meaning of the utterance is, plainly, just as globally accessible as are the sounds of the utterance. So the meaning is access-conscious. The only real question is whether the meaning is a constitutive *part* of a single auditory experience that also represents the phonological properties of the utterance, or whether it is globally broadcast separately as a bare amodal belief. I have been arguing that the former of these two options is correct. The claim that meanings and concepts are not access-conscious at all is, quite simply, a non-starter.

5.4. How concepts and perception interact online

We now know that concepts interact with visual processing at early (pre-attentive) stages to alter the resulting perceptual contents and perceptual phenomenology. It has long been known that concept-learning has an impact on perception (Goldstone, 1994; Goldstone et al., 2001). Acquiring concepts that classify a set of arbitrary similar-seeming shapes into two distinct categories, for example, transforms the perceived similarity spaces among the shapes. Those that seemed similar before now seem distinctively different as a result of category acquisition. Until recently, however, it was unclear to what extent these effects reflect a late decision-like stage in processing, or whether sensory experience is altered by concepts in an online manner. But there is now ample evidence of the latter.

Thierry et al. (2009), for example, tested speakers of English and Greek on a simple task in which they had to detect the presence of a different shape (a square) in a sequence of briefly presented colored circles. Greek differs from English in having two distinct terms for blue: "ghalazio" for light blue and "ble" for dark blue. All participants watched a series of blue circles (in the experimental condition) on the lookout for an occasional blue square, or watched a series of green circles (in the control condition) on the lookout for a green square. The blue circles were either mostly light blue, with an occasional dark-blue one inserted into the sequence, or were mostly dark blue with an occasional light-blue circle. The experimenters recorded the participants' brain waves throughout. What they measured was the pulse of so-called "visual mismatch negativity" over visual cortex that occurs about 200 milliseconds following presentation of an oddball stimulus (e.g. a square following a series of circles). This is thought to reflect a preattentive and unconscious stage of visual processing, which occurs when an unexpected difference is detected in the course of one's experience.

All participants in this experiment showed a mismatch negativity response for all color contrasts. Among the English speakers there was no difference between their response to a light-green/dark-green contrast and their response to a light-blue/dark-blue contrast. Among Greek speakers, on the other hand, the negativity response to the latter contrast was significantly larger. This suggests that the two blues were seen as more unlike one another than the two greens. It seems that because Greek speakers have distinct *concepts* for light blue and dark blue, they see the two colors as more unlike one another. And they do so from quite early stages in visual processing, prior to the impact of attention or judgment.

Mo et al. (2011), too, looked at the visual mismatch negativity response (this time among native speakers of Mandarin). As in the experiment described above, the changes in color were irrelevant to the participants' task. Subjects were required to fixate on a central cross flanked by two colored squares, and were asked to respond as swiftly as possible whenever the cross changed to a circle. The squares were positioned so that the one on the left would be represented initially in the right hemisphere whereas the one on the right would be represented initially in the left (linguistic) hemisphere. As expected, both hemispheres showed a mismatch negativity response to changes in the presented color. But in the right hemisphere there was no difference in the amplitude of the response to changes of color within a category (one shade of green changed to another shade of green) versus across categories (a shade of green changed to a shade of blue). However, in the left (linguistic/conceptual) hemisphere there was a significant difference, with a much larger effect for cross-category changes. Again the early (150-millisecond) nature of these effects suggests an influence of concepts at quite an early stage of visual processing.

One possible explanation of such results is that concept acquisition permanently "warps" the processing that takes place in midlevel visual areas. This would be consistent with maintaining that in online tasks a sharp division is maintained between perception and cognition. However, Lupyan (2012) reviews a number of studies suggesting that the influence of cognition on perception is an online one, and can be eliminated in individual trials through simple manipulations. Consistent with the views of Kosslyn (1994), he argues that concepts and nonconceptual feature-representations interact in an online manner at early stages of visual processing, with the former exerting a causal influence on the latter.

For example, Winawer et al. (2007) tested both English and Russian speakers in an experiment that required participants to judge, on each trial, whether the top color presented exactly matched the shade of one or other of the two colors presented simultaneously below it. All the colors were shades of blue. Russian (like Greek) has two different names for light blue and dark blue. On some trials the two comparator shades belonged to the same Russian category, whereas on others they belonged to different categories. There was no difference in reaction times among English speakers in these circumstances. But Russian speakers were significantly faster in the cross-category trials. However, this effect was easily reversed. Under conditions of verbal interference the effect went away, suggesting that it depends on an online interaction between concepts and the visual system, rather than a permanent language-caused reconfiguration of the latter.

Consistent with this view, Lupyan and Spivey (2010a) show that a verbal cue that is completely redundant in the circumstances (but which would nevertheless activate the corresponding concept) assists participants in a visual discrimination task. Throughout the forty-five-minute experiment people had to attend to arrays of intermixed "2"s and "5"s, pressing a button as swiftly as possible if a ring appeared around one of the "5"s. In randomly intermixed trials in which participants heard the word "five" just before they were presented with the stimulus array, they responded more quickly and accurately; and they did so even for stimulus presentations as brief as 100 milliseconds. The authors suggest that activations of the concept FIVE send anticipatory signals to visual cortex, temporarily pulling the features distinctive of "2"s and "5"s further apart from one another, while rendering the "5"s more perceptually similar (and therefore easier to attend to).

In the same spirit, Lupyan and Spivey (2010b) show that an auditory cue can render briefly presented masked stimuli visible that would otherwise remain invisible. On each trial a letter was presented on the screen for just 53 milliseconds, followed immediately by a 700-millisecond masking pattern. Participants had to respond "seen" or "unseen" to each trial. Under these conditions the letters often remained invisible. But in conditions where they heard the name of the to-be-presented letter just prior to the stimulus presentation, discrimination improved significantly. It seems that activation of the relevant concept feeds back into visual cortex, boosting baseline neural activity related to features of the corresponding letter, thereby rendering the appearance of that letter more visible.

Of course it would be possible to maintain, in the face of all these data, that although concepts *interact* with visual processing at quite early stages, visual and conceptual contents are nevertheless globally broadcast independently of one another. Although the data force us to relinquish any claimed independence of perception and cognition at the level of online perceptual processing, such independence can still be insisted on at the level of output. But such a view now seems quite unmotivated. Given that conceptual and nonconceptual representations interact so deeply and pervasively in perceptual processing, it makes more sense that both should be integrated into the results of that processing, and bound into object-files and event-files that incorporate both forms of representation.

5.5. Two caveats

Before concluding this section, let me stress that in arguing that concepts are bound into the contents of globally broadcast perceptual states I should not be taken as committing myself to the idea that concepts make a constitutive contribution to the phenomenal properties of those perceptual states. That they make an important *causal* contribution to phenomenology should be obvious from the data reviewed in Section 5.4. Deploying one or another (or no) concept can make a large difference to the way an object seems to us, or to the way it is phenomenally experienced. But it does not follow that concepts themselves make a *constitutive* contribution to the resulting phenomenal experience. Concepts can be constitutive components of globally broadcast perceptual states while making only a causal contribution to the phenomenal properties of those states. (See Veillet & Carruthers, 2011, for a defense of this combination of views.)

Let me also stress before concluding that concepts are not the only amodal representations that can be bound into the contents of perception. On the contrary, when one looks at a large group of objects, or listens to a swift series of taps, a nonconceptual, amodal representation of numerosity will be bound into the content of what one sees or hears. One thus has an *impression* of a number of some approximate quantity without employing any numerical concept. Similarly, in my view, when one looks at or imagines something attractive, a nonconceptual, amodal representation of value will form part of the content of the state (this is the valence component of one's affective response to the thing), resulting in a degree of *seeming goodness* or *seeming badness* attributed to the object in question (Jackendoff, 2007; Carruthers, 2011a). It may be, too, that the spatial representations that are added to the content of what one sees (or hears or feels) are intrinsically amodal in nature, albeit bound into the output of a particular sense modality.

When I suggest in Chapter 4 that working memory and the stream of consciousness are sensory *based*, then, this should certainly not be construed as claiming that the contents of working memory are always and exclusively modality specific. Rather, the claim will be that working-memory contents generally involve a mixture of amodal and modality-specific representations, with the presence of the former depending causally on the effects of attention directed toward the latter.

6. Conclusion

This chapter has reviewed some of the extensive evidence supporting a global broadcasting account of the neural correlates of conscious experience, as well as evidence demonstrating that global broadcasting depends on attentional signals directed toward activity in midlevel sensory areas of the brain. This chapter has also argued that globally broadcast perceptual representations are generally integrated conceptual–nonconceptual hybrids, and that episodes of seeing *as*, hearing *as*, and so on should be thought of as forms of perceptually embedded judgment. These claims will form an important part of the foundation for the account of working memory to be presented in Chapter 4. For working memory uses the same attentional apparatus to generate and sustain globally broadcast sensory-based representations in the absence of a stimulus. The result is the creation of a "global workspace" within which partly conceptual sensorily embedded representations can be entertained and manipulated in an offline manner, thereby creating the stream of consciousness.

4

The Nature of Working Memory

This chapter builds on the conclusions of Chapter 3. It reviews what is known about the nature of working memory, and argues that the contents of working memory are not only conscious but always sensory based (while also generally including amodal conceptual information). Note that there is widespread agreement that working memory provides a conscious workspace in which information can be sustained, rehearsed, and manipulated for purposes of reasoning and decision making. That is to say, it is a system in which conscious reflection can happen. Indeed, many hold, more generally, that working memory is the system within which the stream of consciousness plays out. Understanding its nature may then provide the key to understanding the nature of the stream of consciousness in general, and conscious reflection in particular.

The upshot of the argument of this chapter is to set a dilemma for traditional accounts of reflective thinking: either those accounts are mistaken, and attitudes that are wholly amodal never figure in the stream of consciousness; or there is some other global workspace in which conscious reflection can take place, in addition to the working-memory system that has been studied by cognitive scientists hitherto. The latter idea will then be examined (under a number of separate guises) in Chapters 5 and 7.

1. Working Memory, Imagery, and Perception

Working memory has been studied by psychologists since at least the early 1970s (Baddeley & Hitch, 1974). Early models of working memory suggested that it consisted of a number of subsystems, comprising a central executive and two distinct "slave systems." One of these latter systems was called the "phonological loop" and was thought to be the resource underlying rehearsal of verbal information, such as occurs when one repeats a phone number to oneself while searching for a notepad to write it down. The other was called the "visuo-spatial sketchpad" and was thought to underlie one's capacity to manipulate visually based information, such as might occur when one's normal route home is blocked by an accident and one needs to plan out a novel alternative in one's head. These two subsystems are known to be independent of one another, since interfering with the activities of either one can leave untouched working-memory tasks that involve the other. We will begin by discussing how these subsystems are realized in the human brain.

1.1. Locating the systems

The executive component of working memory controls and directs the others, and has long been known to be situated in the frontal lobes (Baddeley, 1986). The two slave subsystems were also thought initially to be frontally based. But this turns out to be an error. It is now known that working memory utilizes the resources of perceptual systems, and does so in all different sense modalities, not just two (Postle, 2006). Thus, in addition to visual and auditory forms of working memory, there are also forms of working memory for smell, touch, proprioception, and affect, all of which implicate the resources of the relevant sensory areas of the brain (Dade et al., 2001; Harris et al., 2002; Jeannerod, 2006; Mikels et al., 2008). We can conclude that working memory (or at any rate the forms of working memory that are involved in the kinds of tasks employed by psychologists) is sensory *involving*, at least. Indeed, whenever brain imaging has been used to investigate the networks involved in working-memory tasks, activity in some or other sensory area has been found that is distinctive of the involvement of working memory, appropriate for the task demands (Postle, 2006; D'Esposito, 2007; Jonides et al., 2008; Serences et al., 2009; Sreenivasan et al., 2011).

A similar conclusion can also be reached indirectly, arising from what is known about the nature of visual (and presumably other forms of) imagery (Kosslyn, 1994; Pylyshyn, 2003; Kosslyn et al., 2006). Relying on an extensive range of experimental, neuropsychological, and imaging data, Kosslyn (1994) argues that visual imagery co-opts and utilizes the processing resources of the visual system itself. The same top-down mechanisms that are used during online processing of visual input to categorize and conceptualize a stimulus (described in Chapter 3.5) are used offline to *create* neural activity in midlevel visual areas similar to what would occur if an object of the appropriate kind were being perceived. Indeed, the same category-specific patterns of activity occur in both midlevel and higher-level areas of the temporal-cortex visual-processing stream, no matter whether instances of those categories are perceived or imagined (Reddy et al., 2010; Vetter et al., 2014). These patterns of activity (when attended) are globally broadcast in the same manner as perception, entering consciousness in the usual way (Mechelli et al., 2004). Since visual images can be equated with the contents of the visuo-spatial sketchpad of the working-memory system, we can conclude that the visually based component of working memory depends upon the activity of midlevel sensory mechanisms.

It is important to realize that these claims about visual imagery are independent of the debate between Kosslyn (1994) and Pylyshyn (2003) about the *imagistic*, pictorial nature of imagery. For both authors accept that vision and visual imagery share mechanisms. This is all that matters for our purposes. But Kosslyn goes on to argue, in addition, that the representational vehicles of visual imagery (and of visual perception) are image-like, in the sense that they represent space by using spatial relations among the representations themselves (somewhat as a picture does). This claim is premised on the well-known finding that neurons in visual cortex are laid out spatially across the back of the brain in a retinotopic map, in such a way that neurons that are close to one another in the cortex receive their input from similarly related regions of the retina and distal scene. Pylyshyn, in contrast, thinks that this finding is irrelevant to the question of how space is represented in the visual system, which he maintains is fully symbolic (or language-like). In Pylyshyn's view, the retinotopic organization of visual cortex plays no role in explaining its representational properties.

In this debate I am inclined to side with Kosslyn. The map-like organization of the visual system is by no means unique. As is well known, the same is true of the organization of somatosensory cortex, the spatial arrangement of which maps a little "homunculus" across the top of the brain. And it has been suggested that map-like cortical systems are a central organizing principle of representation in the brain (Riquimaroux et al., 1991; Churchland, 1993; Kaas, 1997). If so, it makes sense that this principle should automatically be "known" by down-stream consumer systems, in such a way that activity deriving from one portion of the map is interpreted as deriving from the corresponding region of the world, without this needing to be learned or explicitly signaled. However, I don't need to take a stand on this issue here. All that matters for our purposes is that the *same* sensory mechanisms are employed in both perception and imagery. Whether visual representation is map-like or purely symbolic, mental images still possess their representational properties in the same way, using top-down activation of the very same mechanisms.

1.2. Working memory and episodic memory

A line of converging argument can be gleaned from the literature on episodic memory. This is the sort of memory that involves "re-living" an event from one's past. Such memories have a significant sensory component. When remembering an event, one re-experiences (images of) the sights, sounds, smells, and emotional feelings involved. These images are globally broadcast and hence conscious, and they can be sustained in working memory to be contemplated or elaborated if one so wishes. It is widely agreed that the hippocampus plays a key role in the storage and activation of episodic memories. In particular, it is thought to store the spatial and temporal coordinates of the event, binding them together with sensory (and conceptual) representations involved in the experience of the event, located especially in midlevel regions of the various sensory cortices (Eichenbaum et al., 2012). Indeed, a widely accepted generalization in cognitive neuroscience is that memories are stored where they are processed, within the same systems that gave rise to the information in the first place (Mayes & Roberts, 2002). Hence the experiential components of episodic memory are stored in the relevant sensory cortices, and activating and sustaining this episodic information within working memory will depend on the same sensory regions.

It may be worth noting that the present perspective (which unites together into a single framework of working memory, episodic memory, and the global broadcast of attended sensory representations) has the resources to explain one of the most well-established findings about episodic memory. This is its *constructive* nature (Cowan, 1995; Schacter, 2001). Such memories tend to get elaborated each time they are activated, relying on tacit inferences to embellish the memory with extra properties and components (which sometimes really did figure in the original event, but often did not). These are then stored as part of the episodic memory and re-activated with it on the next occasion the memory is recalled. Why this should happen is easy to understand if we accept that episodic memories are globally broadcast in the same manner as perception. For they will then be accessed by all of the conceptual and inferential systems that normally form expectations in an online manner from perceptual input. So whatever these systems produce as output when receiving an activated episodic memory as input will tend to get linked to the latter, and stored with it thereafter.

There is another benefit of understanding the working-memory system as involving the same mechanisms as are used in episodic remembering and in the global broadcast of attended sensory representations. This is that it enables us to provide a unifying account of the mechanisms that *sustain* a representation in working memory and (one of) the mechanisms that *generates* content for working memory. (The role of mental rehearsals of action in creating content will be discussed in Section 4.) From this perspective, when one is required to keep in mind one or more perceptually presented items, one uses a combination of conceptual and contextual cues to identify those items and to guide the focus of attention onto them, thereby keeping active (and globally broadcasting) the neural patterns that represent them. The same thing happens when one activates a long-term memory into working memory: contextually relevant cues are used to activate a set of representations in long-term memory, which are then targeted by attention and become globally accessible. Likewise, too, when one needs to create content for working memory de novo (as when one is asked to imagine some unusual things one could do with a brick): weakly associatively linked conceptual cues are used to activate representations of actions or events involving bricks, which are targeted by attention and globally broadcast for consideration. These ideas will be elaborated in Chapter 6.

1.3. Conceptual involvement in working memory

It is important to stress that although the contents of working memory are sensory based (or at least sensory *involving*—the stronger conclusion will be defended in due course) they generally also have conceptual information bound into them. I will emphasize this point in connection with inner speech (the "phonological loop") in Section 4. Here I will focus on visual imagery (the "visuo-spatial sketchpad").

We described in Chapter 3.5 how conceptual representations are generally bound into the contents of perception, resulting from the back-and-forth processing between conceptual and midlevel sensory areas that issues in perceptual identification and categorization. The same is true of visual imagery, just as one might predict from the fact that perception and imagery share mechanisms. The difference is just that activated concepts are often the top-down causes of the sensory components of imagery. Cued to recall an image of one's mother's face, for example, it will be the concept of one's mother that guides the search for stored visual representations, and which helps to target attention onto them when found. The resulting globally broadcast representation will then have the concept MOTHER bound into it. Likewise when cued to recall one's college graduation, conceptual information will be used to target a search for episodic memories that are then activated, sustained, and elaborated in working memory. The resulting images will be *experienced as* being about one's graduation, generally with a good deal of additional conceptual information (relating to people, places, and times) bound into them.

There is every reason to think, however, that in order for amodal conceptual information to be globally broadcast along with a visual image it needs to be bound into the content of that image, using the same kind of back-and-forth processing that binds concepts into the content of perception. Recall that it is not sufficient for one to see the pattern represented in Figure 4 *as* a Dalmatian that one should have the concept DALMATIAN activated while perceiving the figure. It is only when the process of visual search is resolved and the concept is *matched* or *fitted* with the stimulus that one sees the figure as a Dalmatian, and the concept DALMATIAN then becomes bound into the globally broadcast object-file. The same holds for visual imagery. Entertaining the concept DALMATIAN while imagining some black-and-white splotches is by no means sufficient for one to have a conscious image of a Dalmatian dog. This point is familiar from failures of visual memory search. When trying to recall what Mary looks like one generates a variety of face-like or face-involving images. So one's concept MARY will be activated while one entertains various facial images. But it is only when one retrieves an image of a face that is sufficiently Mary-like to ground recognition that one experiences the result *as* an image of Mary's face.

A converging body of evidence demonstrates, then, that working memory (at least frequently, or in the kinds of task standardly employed by psychologists) is sensory *involving*. The contents of working memory always or often include sensory images as well as conceptual information, where the former can be drawn from any sensory modality. These images are caused by attentional signals directed at content-appropriate neural activity in midlevel sensory areas, much as if an object or event of the relevant kind were being perceived. In due course we will consider whether such sensory images are a mere by-product of the normal operation of working memory, or whether they are integral to its functioning.

1.4. Attitudes in working memory

Chapter 3.5 argued that perception can contain a limited class of sensorily embedded attitudes, especially sensorily embedded judgments and desires. To what extent is the same true of working memory? I will continue to focus here on the visual domain, holding back any discussion of inner speech to Section 4.

Since concepts can be bound into the contents of visual imagery, it is plain that such imagery can embed attitudes of propositional imagining. If one forms a visual image of a tropical beach, including images of golden sand, blue sea, and palm trees, then one is at the same time imagining *that* there is a beach of golden sand containing palm trees next to a blue sea. The image itself contains both conceptual and nonconceptual representations, just as does one's perception of a tropical beach. And here, too, the conceptual components can be thought of as amounting to a sensorily embedded propositional attitude—in this case the attitude of imagining.

Visual imagination of a tropical beach, when attended to and globally broadcast, will be received as input by one's valuation systems, often giving rise to an affective reaction of some sort. This, too, can become a component of one's conscious experience, leading one to see the imagined beach as *good*, for example. (Recall that this is the valence dimension of affect.) The resulting state can be thought of as a kind of sensorily embedded propositional *desire*. (In Carruthers, 2011a, I characterize such states as *momentary felt desires*.) For we know from the literature on prospective reasoning that such states are intrinsically motivating (Gilbert & Wilson, 2007), and they can be thought of as directed toward the conceptual content of the image.

Episodic memories, too, when activated into working memory, can embed the propositional attitude of *remembering* the conceptual contents of the memory. An episodic memory of one's college graduation, for example, might contain a range of nonconceptual details relating to the event, such as the distinctive accent of the main speaker. But it will also generally embed quite a bit of conceptual information. It seems likely that such states will automatically, by default, assume the causal roles of memory—guiding inference and planning on the assumption of truth—without needing to be interpreted and classified as such. Although one might create the very same set of images as part of a fantasy of some sort, the swiftness and effortlessness with which episodic memories are generally evoked is probably a cue that leads them to be relied on as true by default.

What of semantic memories? Can they, too, enter the stream of consciousness by being embedded in the content of a visual image? It certainly seems plausible that semantic information that is stored in visual or spatial format can do so. For example, one might recall that New York City is north-east of Washington by calling to mind an image of a map of the United States, on which distinct locations are seen as New York and Washington respectively. In such cases, however, I am much less confident that the images can acquire the causal roles of memory without being interpreted and classified as such. This is because visual imagery is a ubiquitous component of many people's stream of consciousness (Heavey & Hurlburt, 2008). How, then, are the consumer systems that feed off globally broadcast working-memory contents to know which ones should be treated as fact, and which as fantasy? (In the case of episodic memory, in contrast, the effortlessness of image formation combined with approximate past-tense content might provide sufficient cues to trigger a default setting of *treat-as-true*.)

It seems very likely that representations *of* attitudes of many different kinds can be bound into the content of visual imagery as a result of the interpretive work of the mindreading faculty, using the same back-and-forth processing that is responsible for other forms of sensorily embedded conceptual content. When entertaining an image of a Caribbean beach, for example, one might experience oneself as *wondering* whether to go there on vacation. The resulting state would comprise mixed sensory–conceptual representations somewhat as follows: THAT: **golden**, BEACH WITH PALM TREES, THIS IS A WONDERING WHETHER [GO THERE]. Likewise if the image is followed by a visual image of one's nearby airport, one might interpret oneself as *deciding* to fly to the Caribbean, and experience the episode accordingly. Notice, though, that the states in question are sensorily embedded (higher-order) *judgments*, rather than events of the represented kinds.[1] (In the first case the embedded judgment is that one is wondering, in the second case the judgment is that one is deciding.) As we remarked in Chapter 1.1, this might explain why we so naturally take our reflections to include attitude events of all kinds within them (including attitudes that are amodal in nature). The explanation is that this is how our stream of consciousness often presents itself to us.

I conclude that only a limited range of propositional attitudes can be embedded in the content of visual working memory. Attitudes of imagining, wanting, and remembering can do so, as can sensorily embedded higher-order judgments about the presence of any of a much larger range of attitudes. But it seems unlikely that goals, decisions, or intentions (among others) can ever figure in the contents of working memory. For these events are purely amodal.

2. Working Memory and Consciousness

This section will consider the relationship between working memory and consciousness. It will argue that the contents of working memory are always conscious, just as might be predicted if working memory relies on the same attentional mechanisms as does conscious perception. (It will also consider whether the contents of working memory *exhaust* the contents of consciousness.) The section will thus establish that working memory is a sort of *global workspace*, enabling us to identify it as the system (or at least *a* system) that realizes the stream of consciousness. Understanding how the contents of working memory are determined (to be discussed later in this and subsequent chapters) will then enable us to understand the stream of consciousness and the nature of conscious reflection (or at least important aspects thereof).

2.1. Are conscious states always contained in working memory?

Baars (1988) suggests that conscious states are a subset of the contents of working memory. Mental states are conscious, he thinks, only when they are in the spotlight of attention, and thus when they are currently being globally broadcast. But working memory can apparently include a good deal more than this. In

---

[1] As we will see in Chapter 7, sensorily embedded attitude representations can assume causal roles *a bit like those* of the represented attitudes. *Interpreting* oneself as having decided, one then might regard oneself as obliged to do what one takes oneself to have decided to do, and therefore does it (even if no decision has ever really been made). I will argue in Chapter 7, however, that the causal roles of such events are too different for them to qualify as attitudes of the relevant kinds.

conversation, or when reading text, for example, one needs to keep in mind what was recently said (or written) in order to understand and interpret what is currently being said, or what is currently being read. While this information is not conscious at that moment, it remains readily accessible to consciousness, and thus belongs among the contents of working memory, in Baars' view.

The basic finding appealed to here—the ready accessibility of memories of recently experienced items—is correct. It is well established that language comprehension depends fundamentally on the comparative *accessibility* of various sorts of representation—syntactic, semantic, pragmatic, and so forth (Sperber & Wilson, 1995). But it is doubtful whether it is the working-memory system that is involved. For if it were, the result would far exceed the limit of around four chunks of information that is characteristic of working memory (Cowan, 2001). Some use the term "long-term working memory" in this connection, suggesting that it is a separate system (Ericsson & Kintsch, 1995). But it is more likely that what is involved is just regular long-term memory, subject to the fast initial decay rates that characterize such memory in the absence of special emotional significance, on the one hand, or rehearsal and consolidation, on the other (Schacter, 2001). A great deal can be recalled from the long-term memory system over the time-frames that govern a normal conversation, but most of this will be lost thereafter. Hence long-term working memory is really just activated (or recently activated) long-term memory (Cowan, 1988).

It is important to realize that although they are intimately related, working memory and global availability are conceptually distinct. For working memory involves globally broadcast sensory-involving representations that are not just experienced but *sustained*. That then leaves open the possibility that some of what is globally broadcast never enters working memory because it is never held in place by top-down attention. Put differently: since working memory is a form of actively sustained *memory*, much of what is consciously experienced may never enter working memory because no steps are taken to keep it actively in mind. Such experiences are, rather, purely ephemeral, decaying swiftly in the absence of sustained attention. This is, I think, the position of Prinz (2012): conscious states are ones that are *available* to working memory rather than *in* working memory. This is because conscious states are those that are globally broadcast as a result of initial attention, but may or may not be sustained in place thereafter, which is what is required for them to belong among the contents of working memory. Anything globally broadcast is *available* to be kept active in working memory, but much may not be.

If Prinz (2012) is correct, then all working-memory contents are thereby conscious, but much may be conscious without ever being sustained in working memory. Note that the asymmetry envisaged here is diachronic. The amount that can be conscious over a given period of time may far exceed what enters working memory over the same period. Consistently with this, one might nevertheless claim that the amount of information that can be globally broadcast at any *one* time is no more or less than can be held in memory at that time. Since both depend on the limited resources of top-down attention (as we will see in Section 3), such a claim might make sense. But equally, since the role of attention is to boost neural activity in midlevel sensory areas beyond a threshold for global broadcast (as we saw in Chapter 3.4), it may be that the amount of *perceptual* information that can be broadcast exceeds what can be sustained in working memory. This is because neural activity in the former case will already be high, driven by external stimuli in a bottom-up manner. Fewer attentional resources should therefore be required for global broadcasting to occur.

A famous experiment by Sperling (1960) is often thought to support the latter position. If a random array of letters and shapes is flashed briefly in a three-by-four grid, and thereafter backward-masked, subjects will report that they *saw* all twelve items clearly; but when asked to report the nature of those items (which letters? which numbers?) they can describe only about four. From these data alone one might conclude that the extent of conscious experience is quite limited, with people's own claims about the richness of their initial experience dismissed as a pervasive error. However, what Sperling found was that if subjects are cued, post-presentation, to report just one line in the grid, then they can report all four items. This suggests that people did, indeed, experience all twelve items in enough detail to identify them, with their later failures to report many of those items resulting from the limits in their capacity to sustain representations in working memory for long enough to formulate a report.

These early findings have since been consolidated and extended. Using a change-blindness paradigm, Landman et al. (2003) show that recall is near ceiling for an eight-item display of patterned shapes across a 1500-millisecond interval when the location of the item to be recalled is cued during the interval. This, too, suggests that the contents of conscious experience are richer than those that can be retained in working memory, since the limit on the latter is known to be about four items (Cowan, 2001). Moreover, in an experiment in which changes in the size and orientation of the items are randomly mixed, a post-presentation cue still proves effective (Landman et al., 2003), suggesting that size and orientation properties had already been bound together across all items in the array. Similar results are reported by Sligte et al. (2008), also using change-blindness. When cued post-presentation to the location of an item in a thirty-two-item or sixteen-item display, people can then determine whether change has taken place in that item in the display presented shortly thereafter. While performance is by no means at ceiling for this number of items, across a variety of control conditions it remains at least twice as good as the four-item limit in equivalent working-memory tasks.

While it is natural to interpret such results as supporting people's subjective sense that they are conscious of more than they can subsequently report, other possibilities remain. One is that the richer body of information reverberates in some sort of visual short-term memory store without yet being globally broadcast, only becoming so when attention is drawn to particular items by the post-presentation cue. It is possible that only the gist of a complex scene is initially conscious, with conscious awareness thereafter being subject to the same attentional limits as those that constrain working memory. So it has not yet been established that the richness and detail contained in experience at any one time can outstrip the amount of information that can be sustained in working memory at that time.

This debate is somewhat peripheral to the main topic of this book, however. What matters for our purposes is that the contents of working memory depend on the same attentional and global broadcasting mechanisms as do conscious forms of perception, not whether the contents of the latter can outstrip the former. So the important claim, here, is just that the contents of working memory are always conscious (that is, globally broadcast or globally available). While this claim is widely accepted by cognitive scientists, it has been denied by some. We will consider their arguments next.[2]

2.2. Unconscious working memory?

We turn now to the question whether the contents of working memory are *always* conscious. Hassin et al. (2009) develop a novel experimental paradigm intended to test for the presence of unconscious working memory. Circles are presented sequentially at the intersections of the lines in a large rectangular grid.

---

[2] It is worth noting that the richness attributed to conscious experience, in comparison to the paucity of working memory, would only be modest, even if we took the results of the studies considered above at face value. They certainly should not lead us to endorse the common-sense view that one's entire visual field is experienced in rich detail at every moment. On the contrary, such strong claims are known to be false, as demonstrated by a raft of inattentional blindness and change-blindness experiments, as well as the known paucity of discrimination in the periphery of the visual field. What is consciously experienced depends on the direction of attention, and attention *is* a limited resource. The claim considered above is only that this resource can generate a richer set of globally broadcast representations when it impacts neural activity that is externally caused, in perception, than when attention is used endogenously to *sustain* the broadcast of such representations in working memory.

Circles are either filled or empty, and the participants' task is simply to press a button as swiftly and accurately as possible to indicate which. Each trial consists of a sequence of five presented circles. In one sort of condition the sequence forms a simple spatial pattern (such as a zigzag), with the final instance in the sequence conforming to the pattern. In another condition the first four instances in the sequence conform to a pattern but the fifth deviates from it. (There is also a control condition in which there is no pattern.) People are significantly faster to judge the fifth item in the series in the predictable condition than in the counter-prediction one. But they are generally unaware of the pattern itself, whether measured by verbal report, or recognition immediately afterward. Moreover, there is no improvement in performance when people are made aware of the existence of the patterns and asked to look for them.

In order to explain these differences in performance we need to suppose that some sort of memory of the position of each circle in the sequence is retained long enough for the pattern to be computed, thereby generating an expectation regarding the location of the fifth circle in the series. But it is far from clear that this is a form of *working* memory, with the representations in question sustained through some kind of executive control. Sensory short-term memory may be sufficient to explain the effect. For people's reaction times in this experiment are, on average, around half a second, and the interval between each response and the presentation of the next item is only 150 milliseconds. So the first four items within each series will have been responded to in less than two and a half seconds, with the first three items completed in less than two seconds. (Recall from Chapter 1.3 that the limit of sensory short-term memory is thought to be about two seconds.) And just as with priming effects generally, it is possible that the mechanisms that extract patterns from sequential data operate automatically, outside of executive control.

Moreover, even if records of the initial items in the sequence *are* sustained in working memory by top-down attention, it still does not follow from these data that there is such a thing as unconscious working memory. All that follows is that the computed pattern, and the expectation that results from it regarding the position of the fifth item in the series, are not among the *contents* of working memory. But this should not be surprising. In general, multiple inferences will be drawn from any given set of globally broadcast representations, generated by numerous different consumer systems. The results of these computations will need to compete with one another, and with ongoing input from perception, to gain entry into working memory, thereby becoming globally accessible in their own right. Yet even when they are unsuccessful, they may still exert an influence on subsequent cognition and behavior.

Soto et al. (2011) also claim to show the existence of unconscious working memory. People are briefly presented with Gabor patches of one orientation or another, which are then masked and often remain invisible. But they are told to attempt to identify the orientation of the patches (whether seen or not), and their task is to judge whether a consciously perceived patch presented shortly thereafter is rotated clockwise or counterclockwise relative to the initial stimulus. Since people perform significantly better than they would by chance in trials in which the initial patch remains completely invisible, the experimenters argue that people must be able to sustain an unconscious working-memory representation of the unseen stimulus to guide their explicit response. Indeed, people are also above chance even when an intervening (and consciously perceived) distractor pattern is presented between the initial stimulus and the required judgment, which should overwrite any sensory short-term memory that remains.

This last finding *suggests* that people's performance in the experiment depends on attention directed at the unseen stimulus, but does not demonstrate it. And unfortunately, the experiment failed to include an unattended control condition to demonstrate that the effect goes away if people fail to attend. However, even if we grant the point, these data do nothing to challenge the basic picture of working memory as dependent on attention directed at midlevel sensory areas, which then issues in the global broadcast of the attended representations. For we have already allowed in Chapter 3.3 that attention can boost the processing of a stimulus without rendering it conscious. There we reviewed the results of Kentridge et al. (2008), which show that attention can modulate the processing of an unconsciously perceived target. Hence attention directed at an unseen stimulus might have an effect on later choice-behavior without a representation of the stimulus ever becoming globally broadcast or entering working memory. Consistent with this interpretation, it should be noted that people's gains in performance in the experiments conducted by Soto et al. (2011) were quite minor. On average, people correctly guessed the orientation of the unseen patch on around 56 percent of trials, only slightly (albeit significantly) better than chance.

It might be replied that even a small effect of attention in sustaining a representation in the face of distraction should count as a kind of working memory. I won't quibble over the label. But the main function of working memory appears to lie in its capacity to globally broadcast representations to many different regions of the brain, thereby providing a central workspace that can coordinate the activities of different components. That is missing here. And in any case there is nothing in the data to challenge the idea that the contents of working memory are always sensory dependent, which is the main conclusion toward which this chapter is working.

Finally, Hassin (2013) reviews the results of a number of experiments while arguing for fully unconscious forms of working memory. But in addition to data like those reviewed above, all of his points concern unconscious inferences and unconscious kinds of executive function or decision making. But these should not be in dispute. It is the *contents* of working memory that are globally broadcast and conscious, not the executive processes that direct attention and issue in mental rehearsals of action. (For more on the latter, see Section 4.) Moreover, many of the inferences that are drawn from globally broadcast contents take place unconsciously, and their results are often themselves not globally broadcast.

Hassin (2013) cites a study by Lau & Passingham (2007), for example, as showing that control mechanisms can operate unconsciously. Participants switched back and forth between two simple tasks, with the task that they should perform on a given trial being signaled by a consciously accessible cue. On some trials participants also received a subliminal cue, which could either be congruent or incongruent with the explicit one. The behavioral results (confirmed by fMRI data) showed that task-setting control mechanisms were activated by the subliminal cues: when the two forms of cue were incongruent, people were slower and less accurate in their responses. Such data are entirely in line with the perspective being developed in this book: control processes take place outside of awareness, helping to determine the contents of working memory without ever figuring among those contents themselves. There is nothing here to challenge the claim that the contents of working memory are always conscious.

3. Working Memory and Attention

This section will argue that the contents of working memory depend on the operation of the very same attentional mechanisms that determine the content of conscious perception. This will be an important step toward the conclusion that working memory is not just sensory *involving* but sensory *dependent*. We will also point out that there is no evidence that attentional signals can be directed toward brain regions outside of sensory processing areas.

3.1. Evidence that working memory depends on attention

The groundwork for our discussion has already been laid in Chapter 3.3, where it was argued that conscious experience is dependent upon attention, and in Chapter 3.4, where the nature of the attentional mechanisms in the brain was discussed. We have already noted, in Section 2, that there is widespread agreement that the contents of working memory are conscious, and also that the few counter-arguments against this claim are unsound. This suggests that the contents of working memory may be attention dependent. And indeed, there is now wide-spread agreement that this is so (Awh & Jonides, 2001; Engle, 2002; Cowan et al., 2005; Lepsien & Nobre, 2006; Knudsen, 2007; Mayer et al., 2007; Unsworth & Engle, 2007; Berryhill et al., 2011; Lepsien et al., 2011; Zanto et al., 2011; Gazzaley & Nobre, 2012; Rottschy et al., 2012). At the very least it can be said that working memory is attention *involving*, since the same brain regions that are involved in the control of top-down attention (specifically dorsolateral prefrontal cortex, the frontal eye-fields, and the intraparietal sulcus; see Figure 2) seem always to be differentially active in working-memory tasks.

One reason for thinking that working memory is attention *dependent*, and not just attention involving, is that the limits on working-memory capacity appear to be closely tied to the limits of attentional capacity. One strand of evidence that this is so comes from studies showing that activity in the intraparietal sulcus (and only the intraparietal sulcus) increases as the number of items to be remembered also increases, but then levels off at the working-memory limit of about four items (Todd & Marois, 2004; Ikkai et al., 2010). A natural construal of this finding is that more attention is required as additional items need to be held active in memory, but that attention is a limited resource whose limits are the *cause* of working-memory limits. Another strand of evidence is that people's working-memory abilities correlate well with measures of attentional capacity (Cowan et al., 2005). For example, individual working-memory span correlates with success in an antisaccade task, in which people are required to look in the opposite direction to a cue (Kane et al., 2001), and also with performance in a variety of other attention-requiring tasks (Engle, 2002; Unsworth & Spillers, 2010; Shipstead et al., 2012).

Additional evidence that working memory is attention dependent comes from lesion studies conducted with both humans and monkeys (Curtis, 2006). In particular, lesions in either the frontal eye-fields or around the intraparietal sulcus produce impaired performance in working-memory tasks. (Note that these are crucial components of the top-down attentional network.) In humans, however, it may be preferable to rely on evidence from transcranial magnetic stimulation (TMS), because of its greater site-specificity. (Brain lesions caused by injury, as opposed to the targeted surgery employed with monkeys, will generally also impact a range of nearby areas.) TMS is known to disrupt neural activity in brain regions to which it is applied, thereby adding noise to whatever processing is being conducted in those regions, in effect inducing a temporary lesion. Hence impairments in working memory induced by TMS applied to elements of the attention network provide strong evidence that attention is necessary for normal working-memory operation.

Numerous TMS studies have demonstrated the importance of dorsolateral prefrontal cortex for working memory, and especially for the latter's executive component (Mottaghy, 2006). As we noted in Chapter 3.4, this is also the main executive region for top-down forms of attention. Other TMS studies have demonstrated an important role for regions around the intraparietal sulcus (Koch et al., 2005), including one showing that disruptions to this region interfere with tasks involving verbal working memory (Mottaghy et al., 2002). This is consistent with the evidence reviewed in Chapter 3.4 that the intraparietal sulcus is part of a multimodal attentional system, and is not just restricted to vision.[3]

If working memory is dependent on the same attentional network that under-lies conscious perception, then one would predict that improvements in working-memory capacity, resulting from intensive working-memory training, should result in improvements in attentional tasks. (A number of recent studies have demonstrated that working-memory abilities can be improved by training. See Jaeggi et al., 2008, 2011; Chein & Morrison, 2010; Brehmer et al., 2012.) This prediction is confirmed by Kundu et al. (2013). They used intensive training on an *n*-back task (which has been found to cause improvements in working-memory abilities generally, as we will see in Chapter 5), combined with measures of functional connectivity among the regions of the fronto-parietal-visual atten-tional network, as well as a behavioral measure of visual attention ability. They found that working-memory training induced improved functional connectivity in all regions of the network, combined with improved visual retention and visual search abilities.

3.2. Dissociating working memory and attention?

In contrast with the evidence reviewed above that working memory depends on attentional mechanisms, Lewis-Peacock et al. (2012) claim to find a dissociation between working memory and attention. Their work builds on the finding that different brain regions are used to process faces, natural scenes, and everyday objects respectively. They combined this with multivariate pattern analysis of fMRI data to determine, for each person, the extent to which the relevant brain region is active. In their first experiment participants initially learned a set of paired associates from these three categories, such as a face paired with a scene, or a scene paired with a household item. (Their second experiment was designed to

---

[3] A further study used TMS to show that distinct regions of the dorsolateral prefrontal cortex are involved in working-memory *retention* (keeping in mind a list of words) and in working-memory *manipulation* (alphabetizing a recalled list of words) respectively, but failed to find such a dissocia-tion (while continuing to find disruption of working memory) from TMS applied to the intrapar-ietal sulcus (Postle et al., 2006).

control for alternative explanations of the data obtained from the first, and used words, pronounceable pseudo-words, and line drawings, with similar results.) Participants were then placed in the scanner and presented (for one second) with an item from each learned pair. After a delay of eleven seconds they were then presented with a putative paired associate for the initial item, and required to judge whether it was, indeed, the appropriate member of the pair. The crucial feature of the experiment, which enabled the effects of attention to be pulled apart from working memory, was that on some trials four distractor items drawn from the third irrelevant category were swiftly presented over a two-second period (for half a second each) during the retention interval. By assumption, this would draw attention away from the task-relevant item that was being retained in working memory.

Lewis-Peacock et al. (2012) were able to construct a continuous mapping of activity in the three content-related brain areas during the retention interval. What they observed was sustained activity in the relevant area while an item was in the focus of attention. However, activity dropped to baseline when attention was withdrawn; yet this had no effect on working-memory performance. Hence (the experimenters reason) items can remain in working memory to guide successful performance even when they are not in the focus of attention. In which case working memory is not entirely attention dependent.

This conclusion is by no means forced on us, however. For we noted in Section 2 that some scientists have introduced a concept of *long-term working memory*, precisely to cover cases where information is no longer maintained in an active state, but where it nevertheless remains readily accessible (Ericsson & Kintsch, 1995). Indeed, Lewis-Peacock et al. (2012) themselves indicate that the mechanisms involved in the two cases are likely to be quite different. In one (working memory properly so-called), neural activity corresponding to the target item is sustained through top-down attention. In the other, temporary synaptic bindings have been created (presumably as a result of prior attention), in such a way that contextual cues can easily *re-activate* just such a pattern. Since they are so different, it would only invite confusion to describe these both as forms of working memory. Hence there is nothing here to challenge the claim that working memory, properly so-called, depends upon the same attentional mechanisms that issue in conscious forms of perception.

3.3. Attention outside of sensory areas?

In Chapter 3.4 we noted that attentional signals appear to be directed especially at midlevel sensory areas. It is important to stress that there is no evidence that they can be directed toward association areas of temporal and parietal cortex, or toward prefrontal cortex. While the intraparietal sulcus, in particular, has recip-rocal functional connections with many of these areas, there is no evidence to suggest that these enable a corresponding direction of attention (Uddin et al., 2010; Bisley, 2011). Such connections may serve to carry signals from frontal and temporal cortex to guide the direction of attention (as well as signaling back that such direction is taking place). But it appears that attention itself has an exclu-sively sensory focus.

To illustrate, Cristescu et al. (2006) devised an experiment in which partici-pants were either cued to the spatial location of an upcoming target word (which would need to be sustained in working memory until the word arrived), or they were cued to the semantic category (tools versus animals) of an upcoming word. As one might predict, people were faster at identifying real words versus pro-nounceable pseudo-words when given a valid advance cue (whether spatial or semantic). Using fMRI, regions of frontal and temporal cortex in the left hemi-sphere that are associated with semantic analysis of words were found to be differentially active in the semantic-cue condition. But the important point for our purposes is that *both* conditions activated the same fronto-parietal network centered on the frontal eye-fields and intraparietal sulcus, together with midlevel regions of visual cortex. Taken together with the other findings reviewed earlier, the most plausible interpretation of these data is that while regions of cortex associated with semantic processing were activated by the semantic cues, those regions were used to inform and direct the sensory-based attentional system, rather than being a target of attention in their own right.

The overall conclusion of this section, then, is that the contents of working memory depend upon the same attentional mechanisms that issue in the global broadcast of perceptual information. This provides important support for the view being proposed here, that working memory is sensory dependent.

4. Mental Rehearsal

Our focus so far in this chapter has been on the role of attention in activating and sustaining sensory-involving representations (especially visual ones) in working memory, thereby rendering them conscious. But the functions of working mem-ory are said to include not only capacities to *activate* and *sustain*, but also to *rehearse* and *manipulate* mental representations. Only the sustaining function is strictly a form of memory. But we noted in Section 1 that the same mechanisms that are used to sustain an already-existing globally broadcast representation can also be used to activate such representations in the first place, thereby creating, and not just sustaining, contents for working memory. Rehearsal is the other main mechanism that can generate content for working memory (as well as refreshing it thereafter, successively re-activating the representations involved and thereby approximating or simulating the role of memory). Rehearsal will form the topic of the present section. Manipulation, on the other hand, refers to capacities to transform and sequence working-memory representations (generally in the service of some goal or goals). This will be discussed in Chapter 6.

4.1. Mental rehearsal and motor imagery

Mental rehearsal can be equated with the processes that generate motor imagery, including, but by no means restricted to, the contents of the phonological loop.[4] Motor imagery has been much studied in recent decades, and its nature is now well understood, at least in outline (Jeannerod, 2006). Interestingly, the core architecture underlying it probably evolved initially for other purposes, specifically for the control and swift online correction of overt actions. That story needs to be told first.

People with some knowledge of vision science will be familiar with the concept of *corollary discharge* or *efference copy* (Palmer, 1999). Each time one moves one's eyes a copy of the motor instruction involved is sent to visual centers of the brain to correct for the resulting movement of stimuli across the retina. When the two sources of information are integrated, one can see the world as remaining still despite a sideways shift of its representation on the retina, and one can see moving objects as moving more slowly (or faster, given an eye movement in the same direction) than the movement of their images across the retina would otherwise suggest. It turns out, however, that similar phenomena are by no means restricted to vision, and that efference copies are in fact employed, not just in sensory processing, but in the control of action.

Whenever actions are initiated, efference copies of the motor instructions involved are sent to one or more emulator systems containing an implicit model of the kinematics of the body. There they are used to generate so-called "forward models" of the expected sensory consequences of the movement. These models, in turn, are received by one or more comparator systems, where they are matched against the afferent sensory feedback resulting from the movement as it unfolds (Wolpert & Kawato, 1998; Wolpert & Ghahramani, 2000; Grush, 2004; Jeannerod, 2006). Adjustments in the movement can thus be made as the action

---

[4] The term "motor image" is something of a misnomer, however, as we will see. Motor images are images that are *caused* by offline motor instructions, but they are nevertheless in sensory format. Understood narrowly, motor images are restricted to proprioceptive representations. But understood more broadly, they can include motor-caused visual and auditory images.

proceeds, for example when a grasped object turns out to be heavier or lighter than expected. Note that these forward models, although caused by sets of motor instructions, are in sensory format for comparison with the afferent feedback. The format can be auditory (especially in the case of speech), visual, tactile, or proprioceptive. For the most part forward models remain unconscious, and they do their work unconsciously (Jeannerod, 2006).

Motor images result when motor instructions are activated in an off-line fashion, with output to the muscles suppressed. The efference copies of those instructions are still generated and transformed into sensory forward models. (Note that only proprioceptive forward models are generally referred to as "motor images," although visual and auditory images can be produced in the very same way.) When attended, these images can become conscious. Moreover, proprioceptive imagery appears to be realized in somatosensory cortex (Pfurtscheller & Neuper, 1997; Stippich et al., 2002; Szameitat et al., 2007), although forward models may initially be produced in the cerebellum (Blakemore et al., 2001; Kawato et al., 2003). Interestingly, proprioceptive imagery has been shown to assist in the acquisition and maintenance of bodily skills (Jeannerod, 2006). For example, people wanting to improve at weightlifting can significantly increase how much weight they can bench-press merely by repeatedly *imagining* the movements involved; and skiers who have broken a leg can preserve much more of their skill during their forced inactivity in similar fashion.

Motor-produced imagery in other sensory formats is mostly used for other purposes. Visual images produced in this way are especially important for prospective reasoning. When one is unsure which of a number of potential future actions one should perform, people often mentally rehearse those actions, issuing in conscious visual imagery of each action together with its likely consequences. These representations are received by one's affective and evaluative systems among others, which respond by generating positive or negative affective responses. These can become conscious in turn, and can be monitored to guide one's selection (Damasio, 1994; Gilbert & Wilson, 2007). Note that motor-produced visual imagery—for example, of rotations of pictures of hands and tools—involves activity in midlevel visual areas of cortex, just as one might predict (Vingerhoets et al., 2002).

Auditory imagery that is produced by mental rehearsal can play a variety of roles. A composer might rehearse the actions necessary to produce a series of notes (either singing, or on the piano, say), thereby "hearing" in his or her head what such a tune might sound like. And of course one can (in imagination) repeat a word to oneself while trying to learn it, or repeat the digits in a phone number while searching for a piece of paper to write it down. Note also that one can *continue* to repeat such rehearsed actions in a cycle, thereby continually refreshing the resulting auditory representations in working memory, and thus constituting the "phonological loop" of classical models (Baddeley, 1986). In doing so, one in effect uses (unconscious) *motor* memory of the actions in the sequence to issue in repeated conscious awareness of the corresponding sounds, thereby approximating to a form of auditory memory. Consistent with this account, we know that transcranial magnetic stimulation (TMS) applied to left premotor cortex significantly disrupts verbal working memory (Herwig et al., 2003).

4.2. *Mental rehearsal and inner speech*

Mental rehearsal of *speech* actions plays an especially important role in many people's lives, occupying at least some of the resources of their working memory for much of the waking day (Heavey & Hurlburt, 2008). By rehearsing the motor instructions for a given spoken sentence, with output to the articulatory systems suppressed, one creates from the efference copy of those instructions a forward model of the intended sounds, thereby "hearing" the sentence in question in auditory imagination (Tian & Poeppel, 2012; Scott et al., 2013). As a result, one can argue with oneself, exhort oneself, try out and evaluate hypotheses, and so on, all without engaging in any relevant overt behavior, as we will see in more detail in Chapters 6 and 7. Additional support of this account of inner speech comes from the finding that both speech-production and speech-comprehension areas of the brain are active during inner speech (Paulesu et al., 1993; Shergill et al., 2001). Moreover, Wilson & Fox (2007) show that working memory for language depends on a *general* capacity for mental rehearsal of actions, rather than being specific to language.

It is important to note that efference copies are generally agreed to be low-level, nonconceptual representations of sets of motor instructions (Jeannerod, 2006). In effect, all records of the concept-involving intentions that issued in those instructions are left behind, and the resulting forward models are (initially) purely sensory in character. Indeed, this makes possible one of the functions of the system in the online control of action, which is to enable a comparison of the forward model with one's prior intention, making corrections in one's motor plan even as overt movements are just being initiated (at which point there is, as yet, no sensory afferent feedback). For if the forward model somehow had the content of the original intention already embedded within it, then no meaningful comparison would be possible. In fact, models of motor control generally include at least two comparator systems (see Figure 5). One of these compares the forward model with the afferent sensory feedback, and one compares it with the content of the originating intention (Frith et al., 2000). In the case of speech, for example, it would completely subvert early forms of semantic monitoring, correction, and repair if the intended content of the speech act could somehow be preserved intact into the forward model (Levelt, 1983, 1989). For that would mean that there would be an automatic match between one's intention and the predicted result, leaving no possibility for early detection of errors.

We emphasized in Section 1 that visually based contents in working memory generally have conceptual representations bound into them. A similar point needs to be made here. For in the case of motor-produced imagery, in particular, once sensory forward models are attended to they will be globally broadcast, and they will be processed and become conceptualized in the normal way. As a result, one imaginatively sees oneself, not just as making a certain physical movement with a rigid object in one's hand, but as signing a check with a pen, and so forth. And one imaginatively hears oneself, not just as entertaining certain speech sounds, but as saying to oneself that it is time to prepare dinner, for example. Hence motor-produced images can be concept involving, even if the efference copies that cause them are not. Notice, however, that since the relevant concepts will have been active in the content of one's intention just moments before, it is especially likely that they will thereafter become bound into the content of the resulting image, resulting from their ready accessibility.

In the case of inner speech these points pan out as follows. First there is a concept-involving intention to generate a sentence with a certain content. This is used to create an appropriate set of motor instructions, which in turn issues in an efference copy while output to the musculature is blocked. The efference copy is transformed by the speech emulator system to create a sensory forward model of the expected sounds (Scott et al., 2013), proceeding via an intermediate proprioceptive representation (Tian & Poeppel, 2012). At this point in the process the forward model is purely nonconceptual, but when attended to it is both globally broadcast and processed by the language comprehension system in something resembling the normal way. The language system attaches both a syntactic structure and a semantic interpretation to the "heard" sentence, utilizing normal interpretive principles. But because the latter relies heavily on the comparative *accessibility* of concepts (Sperber & Wilson, 1995), in the absence of articulatory errors it is very likely that the output of the interpretation process will match the original semantic intention (even setting aside the normal contextual cues that will generally be available). For all of the relevant concepts will have been active just moments before, and will thus be especially readily accessible. The account of inner speech sketched here will prove especially important in Chapters 6 and 7.

Notice that motor plans can be more or less abstract or concrete. Indeed, most models of motor cognition assume that the production process involves an implementational cascade from an abstract motor intention (PICK UP THAT CUP WITH THIS HAND) through progressively more fine-grained motor instructions (specifying the speed and trajectory of the reach, the precise manner and strength of grip, and so forth), all the way down to patterns of activation and innervation of specific muscle groups (Rosenbaum, 2010). One might thus predict that forward models would be generated at multiple levels in this hierarchy, thereby providing for smooth online correction at all different levels of implementation as well. It is therefore to be expected that motor-produced imagery can be more or less concrete, depending on the level at which efference copies are generated (or put differently: the level beyond which further motor instructions are suppressed). This is consistent with the finding that inner speech can vary in its abstractness, either being confined to phonological representations of sound, or also including phonetic (articulatory) detail (Oppenheim & Dell, 2010).

Our discussion of the mental rehearsal function of working memory has further confirmed the main finding of earlier sections of this chapter: the contents of working memory are always at least sensory *involving*, and there is good reason to think that they are sensory *dependent*. Indeed, in connection with mental rehearsal the case for the sensory-dependent character of working memory is especially powerful, as we will see in Section 5.

4.3. Attitudes in inner speech

Can propositional attitudes be bound into the contents of inner speech, and if so, which ones? Most obviously, inner speech, like outer speech, can embed judgments of meaning and intending. Just as one can hear someone as saying that a line of storms is approaching, or as asking the way to the church, so can one hear one's own inner speech as embedding the corresponding attitudes. Indeed, there seems no limit to the range of attitudes that one can hear oneself as having. Under interpretation, an episode of inner speech might be heard as *wondering* whether something is the case, as *wanting* something to be the case, as *hoping* for something, as *deciding* on something, and so on. But let me stress that these are sensorily embedded second-order judgments *about* the relevant attitudes, not embeddings of the attitudes themselves. When combined with an implicit model of the mind as transparent to itself, however, the result will be the familiar intuition that attitudes of all kinds themselves figure in our reflections (Carruthers, 2011a).

Imagine a case where one unconsciously takes a decision to leave for the bus (without involving working memory). And suppose that this decision causes one (when combined with other factors) to rehearse in inner speech the sentence, "I'll leave for the bus now."[5] This is globally broadcast and received as input by language-comprehension and mindreading systems, leading it to be heard *as* a decision to leave for the bus now. Does this mean that the original decision has somehow become bound into the content of a sentence in inner speech, thereby insuring its own conscious status? It does not, for at least two reasons. The first is that hearing the sentence *as* a decision means that it actually embeds, not a *decision*, but a higher-order *judgment* to the effect that one is taking a decision. Indeed, it is unclear what it would even *mean* for an utterance in (inner or outer) speech to *be* a decision. (Some possible suggestions will be considered and rejected in Chapter 7.)

The second reason why the originating decision in the above scenario remains unconscious emerges when we focus just on the content of the decision. For it is not the very same (token) propositional content of the decision that is globally broadcast, but another token of the same type. Hence the originating event (a decision with a specific type of content) does not itself figure in working memory. Let me explain.

Deciding to leave for the bus initiates a sequence of verbal action planning. Words and syntactic structures are selected, and used to create a set of motor instructions for generating a specific English utterance. Note that by this point the content of the original decision has been left behind. The only content possessed by the resulting representations concerns movements of the mouth and larynx. These instructions are activated, but before being implemented the instructions to the muscles are suppressed. Nevertheless, an efference copy of the motor instructions has been generated, and is used to create a sensory forward model of the expected speech utterance. When attended to, this is globally broadcast and received as input by the language-comprehension and mindreading systems, which set to work interpreting the sensory input received, attaching semantic and pragmatic properties to it. As a result, the representation LEAVE FOR THE BUS NOW may get bound into the representation of the sounds and globally broadcast along with them, thereby entering working memory. Notice, however, that it cannot be the same *token* representations that figured in the original decision that are now active in working memory. For those were left behind at the point where the decision was used to construct a motor plan. Rather, they are

---

[5] Note that I am discussing here a best-case scenario, in which the underlying attitude and the attitude expressed in speech coincide. In fact the social science literature is rife with cases where there is a mismatch between one's true attitudes and the attitudes one expresses verbally. See Carruthers (2011a) for extended discussion.

tokens of the same type, constructed via the process of interpretation. So it is not the very same (token) content from the original decision that figures in the content of inner speech, but only a token of the same type. In which case the original decision (which was, notice, an individual token event) is not *itself* made globally available.

Can *any* other attitudes besides sensorily embedded judgments figure in working memory through our use of inner speech? One obvious candidate would be rote memories of the sort mentioned in Chapter 2.1. When children learn their multiplication tables the corresponding numerical information becomes stored in the form of well-rehearsed motor plans. One's belief that $7 \times 7 = 49$, for example, is stored as a motor plan for generating the spoken utterance, "Seven sevens are forty-nine." When one tokens that sentence in inner speech in the course of solving some problem, the result is that the belief itself has been tokened in working memory. Or so one might think. But even here there is a distinction between the stored belief itself (which is a motor plan, representing a set of movements) and the sentence in inner speech, which is a representation of the utterance that normally results from the execution of that plan.

Similar points can be made in connection with most other forms of memory. If one's belief that New York is north-east of Washington is used as the basis for tokening in inner speech the sentence, "New York is north-east of Washington," for example, this only insures that information with the same *type* of content is globally broadcast following interpretation, rather than the token belief itself. The one exception would be episodic memories of one's own or someone else's utterances. For these can be evoked and added to the contents of working memory without needing to proceed through speech motor processes (assuming that they are stored in auditory rather than motor form). When one recalls the last words one's father uttered on his death-bed, for example, then it is that episodic memory itself that is made globally available.

The only other kinds of attitude that can enter working memory through inner speech are felt desires. For of course speech, like other forms of experience, can evoke affective responses. What someone says can make one angry or sad, for example. The same will hold for inner speech, since the representations in question will be made available to evaluative mechanisms through global broadcasting. Recalling one's father's last words, for instance, may evoke feelings of grief, or shame, or admiration.

This section has shown how mentally rehearsed actions result in working-memory contents, generally involving visual, auditory, or proprioceptive imagery. As with imagery generally, amodal concepts can be bound into the contents of the resulting images and globally broadcast along with them. As a result, when the contents of working memory include inner speech we often hear ourselves *as* entertaining attitudes of various kinds, with specific propositional contents. But the "distance" between the attitudes that cause the rehearsed action and the subsequent contents of the resulting images means that there are fewer kinds of sensorily embedded attitude in this domain than are found in the case of visual imagery.

5. The Sensory Basis of Working Memory

The present section will pull together the strands of our discussion so far and will defend the claim that working memory is always sensory *based*, and not just sensory involving. A number of competing suggestions will be considered and excluded. One is that the data seemingly supporting a sensory-based view are merely an experimental artifact, resulting from cognitive scientists' exclusive focus on sensory *tasks*. Another is that the sensory activity produced during working-memory tasks results from activation that spreads associatively from an amodal, attitude-involving, working-memory system (where it is the latter that does the real work). A third idea is that our amodal attitudes strategically activate sensory representations to insure their own conscious status. With these three alternatives shown to be highly implausible, that will leave in play a final possibility. This is that sensory activation is often or always used strategically as a supporting *aid* to an amodal working-memory system that is already conscious in some other way. This alternative will be evaluated in Chapter 5.

5.1. Drawing conclusions

Over the course of this chapter we have seen that imagery of all kinds (including the contents of the phonological loop and visuo-spatial sketchpad) share mechanisms with perception, and that sensory activity of an appropriate sort is always present during the performance of working-memory tasks. We have seen, too, that the contents of working memory are always conscious, being widely accessible to many different subsystems in the brain. Moreover, working memory tasks utilize the same attentional mechanisms that are responsible for the global broadcast of sensory representations in general, and working memory itself is attention dependent, with performance collapsing if attention is withdrawn. The best explanation of this set of findings is that working memory is sensory dependent. That is to say, global broadcasting of sensory representations, resulting from attentional signals directed at midlevel sensory areas, is a necessary condition for contents to enter working memory. Nevertheless, we have also seen how amodal conceptual representations can be bound into these sensory representations, and how a limited range of sensorily embedded propositional attitudes can figure in the contents of working memory (and be conscious) as a result. If working memory is the system that makes possible the stream of consciousness, however, then it must follow that amodal attitudes are incapable of being conscious, and hence that they are incapable of figuring in our conscious reflections.

Some challenges to this line of argument will be considered shortly. But one obvious question concerns the *scope* of working memory. Granting that working memory itself is sensory dependent, it does not follow that there is no *other* global workspace in which amodal attitudes can be activated and can figure consciously in reflection. Such an amodal workspace might either make use of the same attentional mechanisms that are employed in working memory, or it might rely on some other mechanism to insure that the attitudes in question are made globally available. This suggestion will be evaluated at length in Chapter 5. But notice that we have already argued, in Section 3.3, that there is no evidence that attentional signals can be directed toward regions of the brain that realize our amodal attitudes. Nor is there evidence of any other mechanism that can issue in the global broadcasting of amodal information.

Absence of evidence is not the same thing as evidence of absence, of course. That we lack any evidence of mechanisms that could insure the global availability of our amodal attitudes is not, itself, direct evidence that we lack such mechanisms. Notice, however, that when it comes to choosing among competing theories, a theory that provides *some* explanation always trumps one that gives *no* explanation. And our goal is to explain how the stream of consciousness is generated. Since we know nothing about the supposed mechanisms that might undergird an amodal workspace, we cannot yet explain how this (alleged) aspect of the stream of consciousness is created and sustained. In contrast, if the stream of consciousness is identified with the sensory-based contents of working memory, as I suggest, then we have in hand a full explanation of how it works (at least in outline). Other things being equal, therefore, the latter theory is the better of the two.

If this argument is to be convincing, then it needs to be shown that a sensory-based working-memory system can do all of the things that we know reflection can do. In particular, we need to show how it can make possible forms of inference and decision making that are indefinitely flexible and creative. This positive task will be begun in Chapter 5 and will continue through the chapters that follow. At this point we will confine ourselves to considering some challenges to the argument for the sensory-based character of working memory.

5.2. An experimental artifact?

One way in which traditional models of reflection could be defended against the argument of this chapter would be to claim that sensory involvement in working-memory tasks is merely an artifact of task design. If participants are asked to remember sensory properties, then of course one might expect sensory areas of the brain to remain active, and to do so as a result of attention directed toward the relevant midlevel sensory regions. But this would not show that working-memory deployment of conceptual and amodal information requires activity in sensory regions. Hence it might be claimed that cognitive scientists have been misled into thinking that working memory is sensory based because of their exclusive focus on sensory tasks.

There is a small grain of truth underlying this challenge. This is that *some* of the working-memory tasks employed by researchers have been exclusively sensory in character. Sometimes *n*-back working-memory tasks might require people to recall arbitrary shapes or patterns, for instance, for which the participants lack any concept. Or people might be asked to recall fine-grained colors or textures, for which they likewise lack concepts. There would be no way of succeeding in such a task *except* by using top-down attention to keep active the original sensory representations of the properties in question, even if people did possess a distinct amodal working-memory system.

It is simply false that all, or even most, working-memory tasks have this sort of sensory character, however. For it will often suffice to recall the *category* to which presented instances belong (dog, cat, or whatever). This could be done amodally and purely conceptually, if such a thing were really possible. Moreover, one sort of frequently used working-memory task involves temporary recall of words (either in an *n*-back experiment, say, or in a complex memory-span task). Although words are presented in sensory format (normally either visual or auditory), linguists regard words as amodal entities onto which these alternative sensory representations are mapped. So if there were such a thing as an amodal working-memory system there would be nothing to prevent it being employed in such tasks, keeping a representation of the presented word active while allowing the initial representation of its sensory properties to decay. (Indeed, since it is rare for language-involving working-memory tasks to employ distractor synonyms, participants could just recall the associated *concepts*, and drop the linguistic presentation of those concepts altogether.) Notice, too, that it is generally made quite clear to participants that it is the *word* they are required to recall, rather than the sensory properties involved in its presentation.

Other frequently employed working-memory tasks involve numbers. These might need to be recalled in a memory-span task, for example, or they might need to be manipulated in a task requiring mental arithmetic. And of course concepts of number are the very archetype of abstract, amodal entities. So if purely amodal thinking and reasoning of a reflective sort were really possible, one might expect it to be employed for explicit numerical tasks of these sorts. Yet sensory activity seems always to accompany both the recall and manipulation components of numerical working-memory tasks. It seems that people always rehearse and manipulate sensory representations of *numerals*, rather than operating directly with amodal representations of number. This would be quite puzzling if there were really such a thing as an amodal workspace in which one could engage in non-sensory reflective reasoning about numbers.

5.3. *Spreading association?*

There are other ways in which someone might attempt to defend the traditional account of reflection in the face of the evidence that working memory is sensory dependent. One would be to claim that the findings result merely from associatively spreading activation of related sensory representations, caused by the activation in working memory of amodal concepts and attitudes. It would be the latter that carry the real functional burden in working-memory tasks, and which can, in principle at least, operate in the absence of relevant sensory activity. But this view, too, is highly implausible in light of everything we know about working memory.

One problem for the spreading-activation account of sensory involvement in working memory is that a variety of kinds of evidence suggest that damage or disruption to midlevel sensory areas has a corresponding impact on working-memory function (Pasternak & Greenlee, 2005). For example, brain damage to these areas impairs working-memory abilities in the corresponding domain (Levine et al., 1985; Gathercole, 1994; Müller & Knight, 2006). Moreover, transcranial magnetic stimulation (TMS) applied to midlevel sensory areas disrupts working-memory tasks that would normally involve imagery of the relevant sort. Thus TMS applied to the lower regions of parietal cortex during the retention interval disrupts working memory for spatial layouts (Oliveri et al., 2001), whereas TMS applied to area V5/MT disrupts working memory for direction of motion (Campana et al., 2002). In addition, presentation of distracter stimuli during the retention interval in working-memory tasks only has a disruptive effect on those tasks if the stimuli are perceptually similar to the target. For example, location distracters interfere with memory for location but not color, whereas color distracters interfere with working memory for color but not location (Vuontela et al., 1999).

It might be objected that such results are not really surprising, given that the working-memory tasks in question themselves involve sensory properties. Hence it would be consistent with such results that working memory of a semantic sort, or involving abstract properties, should *not* depend on the activity of midlevel sensory areas. But this objection seems not to be sustainable. For notice that many of the results reported above involve spatial working memory (e.g. concerning direction or position). Yet space is an abstract property that can be represented in many different sense modalities. So if working memory were ever able to operate in the absence of related sensory activity, one would expect that spatial working memory would be a good candidate. But as we have seen, the experimental data seem to rule this out.

It might be possible to explain at least some of the results mentioned above from the perspective of a spreading-activation account of sensory-area involvement in working memory. For if activation can spread associatively in one direction, it can presumably also spread in the other. Hence the noise introduced by applying TMS to sensory areas may spread upwards to interfere with the maintenance of more abstract information, and likewise content-relevant sensory distractor stimuli may more readily introduce interference at a conceptual level.

There are other powerful reasons to reject a spreading-activation account, however. Recall that working memory uses the same top-down attentional mechanisms directed at midlevel sensory areas that are implicated in conscious forms of perception. These mechanisms are executively controlled in light of one's currently active goals and values, so their operations are certainly not associative. And recall, too, that working memory is attention *dependent*. Under conditions of distraction, working-memory performance collapses. This enables us to conclude that the sensory-area activity in working-memory tasks both depends on attention and plays an important role, at least, in working-memory performance. It is almost certainly not a mere side-effect resulting from associative spreading of neural activation.

The spreading-activation idea is even less plausible in connection with forms of working memory that involve mental rehearsal. For the sensory activity that populates working memory in such cases is two steps removed from the amodal concepts and attitudes that allegedly form the essential core of the working-memory system. The latter would have to select and activate some suitable set of motor instructions while suppressing any output to the motor system, and it would also have to direct attention to the sensory forward models of the actions that would otherwise have resulted. It is barely conceivable that all this complex and executively directed activity could result from mere spreading activation caused in an associative way by the amodal thoughts in question.

5.4. Co-opting sensory resources?

Someone might concede that working memory is sensory dependent while insisting that amodal attitudes can nevertheless figure among its contents. For perhaps such attitudes strategically evoke content-relevant sensory activity that becomes a target of attention, thereby insuring those attitudes themselves are made globally accessible as well. In effect, the idea is that our amodal attitudes can co-opt the resources of the sensory-based working-memory system in order to render themselves conscious.

This suggestion is mysterious, however. We have been given no indication as to how the proposal might work. We know how sensory representations get globally broadcast through the direction of attention, and there is good reason to think that amodal conceptual information can likewise be globally broadcast when bound into the content of the sensory representations in question. And on this basis we have seen how the stream of consciousness can contain a number of different kinds of sensorily embedded propositional attitudes that are created in this manner. But it is quite another matter to claim that already-existing amodal attitudes can likewise be globally broadcast. Indeed, nothing in the data suggests that it is possible.

In fact there is direct evidence against this proposal. For we have already seen that the mere fact that an amodal concept is activated and co-occurs with content-relevant sensory activity is *not* sufficient for that concept to become conscious. Merely thinking of a Dalmatian while consciously experiencing the pattern of splotches represented in Figure 4 is not sufficient for *seeing* those splotches *as* a Dalmatian. It is only when recognition occurs as a result of back-and-forth perceptual processing, and the concept gets bound into one's representation of the image, that one becomes conscious of the presence of a Dalmatian. It seems that only *sensorily embedded* amodal concepts can become conscious by utilizing the global-broadcasting properties of sensory attentional networks.

Quite a different version of the "co-opting sensory resources" idea is also available, however. One might claim, in particular, that there is an amodal global workspace whose contents are made conscious in some other unknown manner. But in order to explain why attention-dependent sensory activity is always present in working-memory tasks, and why performance in such tasks should be quite poor in the absence of attention, it might be proposed that content-relevant sensory activation is a *strategy* that people adopt to help them keep amodal information actively in mind. On one level this is correct, of course. Given that amodal conceptual information is bound into the sensory contents of working memory (as we have seen), and is often the intended target of recall or manipulation, then that *is* what the sensory activity is for. The difference on this view, however, would be the claim that amodal concepts and attitudes can be globally accessible in the absence of such activity. Sensory activity gets strategically added as an *aid* to working memory, rather than forming its basis. This idea will be evaluated in some detail in Chapter 5.

5.5. An ambiguity?

A final concern is that there is a fallacy of ambiguity in the argument for the sensory-based character of working memory. For the conclusion is supposed to be that the stream of consciousness is always grounded in modality-specific *experiences* of one sort or another, including conscious visual imagery, conscious auditory representations in inner speech, and so on. But much of the evidence has had to do with the distinctive presence of activity in sensory regions *of the brain* in working memory tasks. These are surely not the same thing.

Indeed, they are not. But they can be connected through an inference to the best explanation. For we have reviewed evidence that working memory is attention dependent. And we have seen that the best explanation for the activity observed in sensory regions during working-memory tasks is that it is caused by attentional signals being directed at those regions. We have also seen that the effect of sustained attention targeted at specific sensory regions when guided by contextual cues or conceptual templates is to issue in the global broadcasting of the relevant sensory representations, thus resulting in a conscious experience. So there is good reason to think that the dependence of working memory on both attention and activity in sensory regions of the brain results in working memory being dependent on sensory experience. Moreover, it is the conscious status of those experiences that enables working memory to perform the functions of a *global* workspace.

We can draw a number of conclusions from the arguments of Section 5. One is that the sensory-area activity that is distinctive of working-memory tasks is not merely an experimental artifact. Another is that such activity is executively caused and controlled, and thus doesn't involve activation that spreads associatively from the workings of an amodal workspace. A third is that amodal attitudes do not themselves become conscious through association with conscious sensory activity. For the present, therefore (pending further consideration in Chapter 5), it remains the case that an inference to the best explanation supports the sensory-dependent nature of working memory, and hence the sensory-dependent character of the stream of consciousness.

6. Conclusion

This chapter has reviewed some of what is currently known about the nature of working memory. There is widespread agreement that the sustaining function of working memory co-opts the resources of sensory regions of the brain. It is also known that it employs the same top-down attentional mechanisms that are responsible for the global broadcasting of perceptual representations, thereby insuring that the contents of working memory are always conscious. Mental rehearsal, in contrast, uses the forward-modeling functions of the systems that control and correct our motor actions to create, offline, sensory forward models of potential actions. When these are attended to they, too, are globally accessible and conscious. All of this adds up to a powerful case in support of the sensory-dependent nature of working memory. Additional arguments for this conclusion will be presented in Chapter 5.

If working memory is sensory dependent, then it must follow that it is not a system in which amodal, non-sensory attitudes can be active and do their work. If traditional ideas about reflection are to be defended, then it must be claimed that there is an additional central workspace in which reflection takes place. Perhaps this system strategically recruits the resources of the sensory-dependent working-memory system. But it might be said that the latter is not strictly necessary for conscious forms of reflection to take place. This remaining possibility will be evaluated in Chapter 5.

5

The Unity of Working Memory

This chapter will evaluate the suggestion raised at the end of Chapter 4. This is that conscious reflection can take place in an amodal system that operates alongside, and often or always co-opts the resources of, the sensory-based working-memory system. Given the strength of the evidence that working memory itself is sensory based (discussed in Chapter 4), this appears to be the only way in which traditional accounts of reflection can be defended. It will be shown, however, that the proposal faces a number of important difficulties. This chapter will also embark on the positive task of showing that a sensory-based working-memory system can explain known properties of human problem-solving abilities. Here our focus will be on the question whether variations in sensory-based working-memory abilities can explain all of the variance in people's fluid general intelligence.

1. An Amodal Workspace?

The present section will outline and explore the idea that there is an amodal global workspace in which propositional attitudes of all sorts can be activated. It will also present some initial reasons to be skeptical of such a suggestion.

1.1. The multiple-modes model

One can envisage two possible variants of the idea of an amodal workspace, depending on whether or not it is the same attentional mechanisms that result in the global availability of both sensory-based representations and amodal attitudes. Let us first consider the suggestion that the mechanisms are the same. We can refer to this as the "multiple-modes model" of working memory. The idea would be that working memory is a single system that can operate in a number of different modes. It contains an executive system that can employ attentional resources in a flexible manner. The latter can be directed at sensory-based representations alone, or (perhaps rarely) amodal propositional attitude representations alone, or (most commonly) attention can be divided in such a way that suitable sensory-based contents for working memory are used strategically to support amodal functions of remembering, thinking, and reasoning.

The multiple-modes model can explain one of the findings of Chapter 4. This is that performance in working-memory tasks seems always to depend on sensory activity of a content-relevant sort. At least, it can do so provided one assumes that the strategy of seeking sensory support is almost always in effect. (Why this should be so is perhaps puzzling, as we will see shortly.) The model can also explain why working memory should display the same signature limits, no matter whether the materials to be retained are abstract, sensory, or a combination of the two (such as words and shades of color). This is because the account postulates a single resource—attention—that is employed in all three modes. It can be supposed (consistent with the beliefs of most cognitive scientists) that it is this resource that is responsible for those limits.

The multiple-modes account also faces a number of difficulties, however. One is that there is no evidence that attention can be directed outside of midlevel sensory areas. As we noted in Chapter 4.3, the top-down attentional system appears to comprise regions of dorsolateral prefrontal cortex, the frontal eye-fields, and the intraparietal sulcus, with the latter constituting the "business end" of the system. It is signals emanating from the intraparietal sulcus that are responsible for the sustaining and repressing functions of attention when directed at populations of neurons in sensory cortices. Yet there is no evidence that signals from the intraparietal sulcus directed toward temporal or prefrontal cortex can play such a role. This objection is not necessarily devastating, of course. For it can be maintained that the relevant evidence has not yet been found. As we noted in Chapter 4.5, however, this does mean that the multiple-modes model of working memory cannot (at present) *explain* how the stream of consciousness is endogenously generated, since it cannot specify the mechanisms involved.

There is an additional problem for the multiple-modes account. This is that it becomes difficult to understand why the strategy of employing sensory support for abstract working-memory tasks should be so strongly entrenched. (Recall that such a claim is necessary to explain why content-relevant sensory activation should always be found in working-memory tasks.) For notice that the account postulates a single attentional resource that needs to be *divided* to secure such support. So it is quite unclear why there should always be a gain in working-memory capacity or efficiency from activating sensory-based representations as well as amodal ones. Why would this be a sensible strategy to adopt? Given that there is a single attentional resource to be deployed, why would it always be beneficial to direct it toward both sensory and amodal representations, rather than devoting it entirely to the latter whenever the task itself is an amodal one?

Additional ad hoc assumptions will need to be added to the multiple-modes account at this point, thereby significantly weakening the appeal of the view. For example, it might be claimed that there is a "multiplier effect" of dividing attention between amodal and modal representations, in such a way that the capacity of the divided system is somehow greater than its purely modal or amodal uses alone. However, we already know that the capacity of the divided system is *not* greater that its purely sensory use. For the same signature limits are found in both concept-involving and purely sensory tasks. (The latter might involve complex shapes for which one lacks any concepts, for example.) At least, this is true provided that care is taken to avoid conceptual "chunking" of stimuli in the concept-involving tasks (Cowan, 2001). So if there is a multiplier effect, for some reason it only improves the recall of purely amodal contents by combining them with sensory ones, rather than vice versa. It is hard to imagine what this reason might be.[1]

1.2. The two-systems model

We can now consider the possibility that the mechanisms underlying global broadcasting are not the same in the amodal case. Suppose that the central attitude workspace relies on some resource other than attention in order to insure the global availability of the attitudes that are activated within it. This would be tantamount to claiming that there are two distinct working-memory systems, one sensory based and the other amodal. So let us refer to it as the "two-systems model" of working memory. On this account it is immediately clear why people should almost always employ the strategy of activating the sensory-based system, even when engaged in abstract tasks. This is because one can thereby increase the total resources devoted to the undertaking.

The two-systems model faces a corresponding problem, however: how is it to explain why the same signature working-memory limit should obtain whether one is engaged in a sensory task, a purely abstract one, or a mixture of the two? One might expect that when the two systems are both engaged (that is, in a mixed case), working-memory capacity would be roughly twice what it is when either is used alone. This puzzle can be answered in the case of abstract tasks, provided

---

[1] In addition, the phenomenon of *masked semantic priming* provides some evidence that attentional signals cannot render an amodal representation conscious in the absence of conscious sensory experience (Dehaene et al., 1998). For the semantic effects of an unconscious visual stimulus themselves also remain unconscious. It would be puzzling why this should be so, if the multiple-modes model of working memory were correct.

that people always adopt the strategy of activating the sensory-based system in support of the amodal one. But it remains puzzling why working-memory capacity should not be significantly lower in tasks that are purely sensory. Since there is nothing that the amodal system can do to assist in recalling shapes or patterns for which one possesses no concepts, one would expect that such tasks would exhibit a more stringent working-memory limit. But the evidence suggests that they do not (Cowan, 2001).

This argument moves a little too swiftly, perhaps. For we know that working memory benefits from *chunking*. Whenever some (but not all) of the items to be remembered fall under a single category, some of those items can then be recalled as a single unit, and working-memory limits are thereby increased. But this does not yet support the idea of an amodal (conceptual) working-memory system in addition to a sensory-based one. For there is good reason to think that concepts can be bound into the contents of perceptual and imagistic representations, as we saw in Chapter 3.5. Rather, the idea would have to be that the amodal and sensory-based systems can support one another by deploying concepts twice over: once in the amodal system and again in the sensory-based one. And the problem still remains that one would expect that retaining sensory items in working memory for which one lacks any concepts should be significantly harder than concept-involving tasks where chunking strategies are carefully excluded. But this seems not to be the case.

Someone might attempt to reply to this objection by claiming that the limits on working memory derive, not from limits on attention, but rather from the limits of the executive systems that direct attention. Since these can be assumed to be held in common to both the amodal and sensory-based working-memory systems, we can now explain why the same signature limits should obtain across all combinations of task. There is direct evidence against this suggestion, however. For recall that activity in the intraparietal sulcus increases linearly with increasing memory load, leveling off when working-memory limits are reached. In contrast, activity in the frontal lobes (the presumed seat of executive functions) continues to increase beyond those limits (Todd & Marois, 2004; Ikkai et al., 2010). This suggests quite strongly that it is the attentional system that is responsible for the limits on working-memory capacity, rather than the executive. (See also Berryhill et al., 2011, for additional evidence for the same conclusion.)

Moreover, recall from Chapter 4.3 that people's working-memory capacities correlate quite well with measures of attentional capacity (Cowan et al., 2005). This, too, suggests that the putative amodal working-memory system utilizes the resources of attention in some way. Indeed, the two-systems model appears not to be consistent with one of the claims defended in Chapter 4.3, that working memory is attention dependent. For this latter claim would not be true if there were an amodal working-memory system that doesn't require attention to insure the global availability (and hence conscious status) of its contents.

1.3. An empirical prediction

Both the multiple-modes and two-systems views face significant problems, then. It should also be noted that each appears to make the same empirical prediction. This is that working memory should admit of three discrete levels of performance whenever the target to be recalled is something amodal, like a sequence of numbers. There should be a baseline level (in cases of full distraction, or where no attempt is made to keep the target information active) where unaided long-term memory will be the only contributor to performance. There should then be an improved level of performance when people attempt to remember the conceptual information involved but *without* adopting the strategy of seeking additional sensory support, or when that strategy is disrupted. And then the best performance should result when people attend *both* to the conceptual information (the sequence of numbers) *and* employ a sensory-involving strategy (such as repeating the sequence of numerals to oneself in inner speech). Articulatory interference combined with sensory masking of stimuli, for example, should undermine the third level of performance while leaving the second intact. In such circumstances we should see levels of recall significantly higher than when people are completely distracted after presentation of the numbers, and are thus unable to make any attempt to remember them. I am aware of no evidence of any such distinction in the empirical literature, however. (But again, note that absence of evidence is not evidence of absence.)

Both versions of the amodal workspace idea face initial problems, then. The remainder of this chapter will develop a number of further difficulties that apply equally to each.

2. The Problem of Self-Knowledge

This section will explore another prediction made by both versions of the amodal workspace account. This is that people's knowledge of their own propositional attitudes that are currently activated in the workspace should be direct and immediate (albeit not infallible). The section will then argue that this prediction is false, drawing on points developed at length in Carruthers (2011a).[2]

---

[2] Note that my earlier book likewise rejects the idea of an amodal workspace. So there might seem to be a vicious circularity in appealing to the conclusions of that work in support of the present

2.1. Self-knowledge of the amodal workspace

Recall from Chapter 3.2 what global broadcasting is: it is a mechanism that makes attended perceptual contents widely available to many different systems in the brain, for forming memories, issuing in affective reactions, engaging in inferences, and informing decisions. If there is an amodal workspace that likewise makes activated propositional attitudes globally accessible, then those attitudes should be available as input to a wide variety of different systems. Among the latter would presumably be whatever system is responsible for knowledge of our own current thoughts. This will be true whether that system is some sort of introspective self-attribution mechanism (Nichols & Stich, 2003; Goldman, 2006), or the same mindreading mechanism that is responsible for attributing mental states to other people (Carruthers, 2011a). Attributing current thoughts to oneself should therefore be trivially easy (especially in respect of the contents of those thoughts). Receiving as input an activated goal or decision, say, the system would just need to identify the features of the state that confer on it its distinctive causal role (goal-like or decision-like) and then embed the content of the state into the content of an appropriate higher-order judgment (I HAVE JUST DECIDED: I WILL SET OUT FOR HOME, for instance). Self-knowledge should not need to be *interpretive*, on this account (certainly not in respect of the content of the state), and it should not depend on the same sorts of cues that one relies on when attributing thoughts to other people.

As Carruthers (2011a) demonstrates at length, however, there is voluminous evidence that these predictions are false, much of it collected by social psychologists over many decades. On the contrary, there are many circumstances in which people will confabulate about their current thoughts, and their self-attributions seem to be guided by just the sorts of contextual and behavioral cues that influence their attributions of thoughts to others. These data could be explained, of course, if the mindreading system were unusual among conceptual systems in lacking access to the contents of the global attitudinal workspace. But such a suggestion seems quite ad hoc. Indeed worse, if it were true, then it would be hard to see how the mindreading system could contribute to reflective reasoning about the mental states of others, of the sort that manifestly occurs quite often. For this would seem to require the system to have access to the contents of those reflections.

argument against such a workspace. But what will actually be relied upon here are just those portions of the earlier book that present evidence against direct and immediate knowledge of our own currently active attitudes. So there is no circularity involved.

Nichols & Stich (2003) attempt to accommodate the evidence of confabulation, while maintaining that self-attribution can be direct and immediate, by drawing a distinction between *explaining* and merely *reporting*. They suggest that requests for explanations of one's behavior will cue the third-person mindreading system into operation (often issuing in confabulation). And they note that many of the results in the social-psychology literature derive from experiments in which people are asked to explain their choices, not just to report their thoughts. Moreover, even when people are asked merely to report a mental state, often those states are some seconds or minutes in the past. If we suppose (quite plausibly) that no records of the contents of the amodal workspace are generally kept, then people will have no alternative but to engage in self-interpretation in such cases. Nichols & Stich (2003) suggest that whenever people are asked just to report on their *current* (or very recently past) mental states, on the other hand, their knowledge is direct and immediate.

This position is untenable, however. For there are numerous experiments in which people confabulate when asked to make reports about their current or recent thoughts, and they do so in circumstances where one might expect the thoughts in question to be active in the amodal global workspace, if such a thing really existed. I will sketch just two examples. For further instances, and for more extensive discussion, see Carruthers (2011a).

2.2. Two data-points

Wegner & Wheatley (1999) asked participants to jointly control a large computer mouse with another person (who was actually a confederate of the experimenters). Participants were told that the experiment was to test how feelings of control over an outcome can come and go. Both people wore headphones (so that the participant could hear a "distractor word" in some conditions, and so that the confederate could receive instructions from the experimenters). Participants were told to move the cursor around the screen jointly with the other person for about thirty seconds, and then to bring it to a stop at a point of their choosing thereafter. They were then immediately to record their sense of control over the stop on a scale ranging from zero ("I allowed the stop to happen") to 100 ("I intended to make the stop"). Note that they were asked just to *report* their intention, and that the reports were given within moments of it being active. Note, too, that since the whole point of the experiment was to get people to track their own intentions, and since they knew from the outset that they would be required to make a report on each trial, one would expect the relevant intention to be not only activated but attended to within the amodal workspace.

The results of this experiment belie such predictions, however. In some conditions participants actually had complete control over the cursor and its stopping-point. (Here the confederate was told just to rest her hands passively on the mouse, and to take no part in moving it.) Yet participants scored their sense of having intended the stop at just 56, only marginally above the mid-point. It seems that they assumed from the experimental instructions that control would be shared, and so anchored on the mid-point of the scale, only adjusting their score upwards slightly in conditions where they actually had full control. (Presumably in these conditions they were somewhat sensitive to the lack of resistance on the mouse, and to the smoothness of its movements.) In other conditions, in contrast, it was the confederate who actually had full control over the stop. (She was guided throughout by instructions from the experimenter.) Yet participants scored their sense of having intended the stop only slightly lower than the mid-point, at 45. (Presumably in these circumstances they were somewhat sensitive to the resistance they experienced to their own intended movements.) Yet in the same conditions, if participants heard over their headphones the name of the object pictured among many on the screen (such as an umbrella) that the confederate brought the cursor to a halt over, their sense of intention was scored much higher, above 60. It seems that they interpreted themselves thus: "I was thinking about an umbrella, so I must have (partly) intended to stop on the umbrella."

These results suggest quite strongly that there is no global workspace in which activated intentions can figure. Admittedly, they derive from just a single experiment. My other example, however, has to do with confabulations of current belief in the so-called "dissonance" paradigm (Festinger, 1957), where one can draw on converging results from hundreds of experiments. The basic finding is that if people are induced to write an essay arguing for the contrary of what they believe, while nevertheless having the sense that they did so freely, they will thereafter shift their reported belief on the topic very significantly. But they have not really changed that belief (or at least, not prior to the moment of report). For we know that the action of writing the essay makes people feel bad, presumably because they have the sense that they are responsible for doing something bad (Elliot & Devine, 1994). And we know that they feel better as soon as they have had the chance to express a shifted attitude thereafter. Moreover, we know that they will take whatever opportunity is offered to them first to present their own action in a better light, such as denying responsibility for it, or denying the importance of the issue, as well as expressing a congruent belief, with whatever attitudes are queried next being expressed unchanged (Simon et al., 1995). It seems that participants are using their expressions of belief strategically, making themselves feel better about what they have done by presenting it to themselves in a better light.

For a full discussion of these experiments readers are directed to Carruthers (2011a). But notice that the participants are asked a direct question about what they believe. (For example: "How bad do you think it would be if tuition were raised by $1000 next semester?") One would expect that this would activate the belief that we know they possess (from answers to the same question on a supposedly unrelated questionnaire completed some weeks before, say). So if there were a global attitudinal workspace, one would expect the participants' beliefs to be activated within it. One would also expect that a direct question about their beliefs should lead them to attend to the contents of the attitudinal workspace. But instead of reporting the belief that they find there, they say that a rise in tuition would be neutral or mildly positive. Yet participants surely cannot *both* be aware of their belief *and* be using their answers to manage their own negative feelings. For they would then be aware that they are lying, and that should make them feel worse, not better.

These and other data make a powerful case against the view that people ever have direct, non-interpretive access to their own amodal attitudes (Carruthers, 2011a). And by the same token they provide strong reasons to reject the proposed amodal global workspace, in either of its two guises. An opponent might suggest that one can accommodate the data, however, by claiming that people rely *both* on the contents of the amodal workspace *and* on behavioral, contextual, and other sensorily accessible cues when attributing thoughts to themselves. It might be said that in most cases where confabulation occurs, it is the sensory cues that have dominated; but in other cases people may enjoy direct non-interpretive knowledge of the contents of the workspace (Rey, 2013). Notice, however, that *accommodating* the data is not the same as *explaining* it. For the latter, one would need to be able to predict when confabulation will occur. But a mixed-methods view makes no such predictions. Rather, it seems to be merely an ad hoc maneuver designed to preserve the standard philosophical model of reflection in the face of contrary evidence.

Notice, moreover, that even this sort of mixed view cannot really accommodate the dissonance data. For in these cases confabulation results not from interpretation of sensory cues, but rather from unconsciously undertaken emotional self-manipulation. So not only is the suggestion ad hoc and non-explanatory, but it cannot even *accommodate* a large swath of the relevant data.

2.3. Evidence of introspection of attitudes?

There is only one body of data that lends some indirect support for the idea of an amodal attitudinal workspace.[3] This is the finding that some people (but note: only some people) participating in introspection-sampling studies will sometimes report experiencing amodal, purely propositional thoughts at the moment when cued by the beep (Heavey & Hurlburt, 2008; Hurlburt & Akhter, 2008). Moreover, in a subset of these cases there seem to be no contextual or other sensorily available cues that might provide a basis for ascribing such a thought to oneself through self-interpretation. If these reports are taken at face value, then they can be appealed to in support of an amodal attitudinal workspace (at least when combined with other assumptions, such as a critique of the inner-sense idea).

There are a number of ways in which these data can be alternatively explained, however. (These are discussed in some detail in Carruthers, 2011a.) Perhaps the simplest is to postulate that there *were* sufficient sensory cues available, either at or shortly before the moment of the beep. But these were forgotten when participants complied with the requirements of the introspection-sampling protocol and recorded only what was at the *focus* of their attention at the moment of the beep. (This suggestion is tentatively endorsed by Hurlburt himself. See Hurlburt, 2009.) Moreover, the data are, in any case, just as problematic as supportive for the idea of a central attitudinal workspace. For recall that only *some* people report entertaining amodal thoughts. This would be quite puzzling if such a workspace existed, since it would presumably be present in all normal humans. Are we to suppose that a large portion of the population possess an amodal workspace that they never use? This seems about as plausible as the suggestion that many people could have a capacity for episodic memory without ever actually employing it.

In response to this challenge, amodal-workspace theorists might appeal to the same idea utilized by their opponents. That is, it might be suggested that all memory of the contents of the amodal workspace is wiped out in such people following the moment of the beep. This could be because it is the sensory accompaniments to those thoughts that are at the center of the person's attention at the time. This explanation might be testable if one could develop an independent measure of people's overall focus along the cognitive–sensory dimension. If those who regularly pay more attention to sensory experience

---

[3] The support is indirect because the data are equally consistent with other theories that make no commitment to an amodal attitude workspace, such as that we possess an "inner sense" for detecting our own propositional attitudes (Goldman, 2006). For the introspectability of attitudes provides no guarantee of their global availability.

never report amodal thoughts, while those who have a more cognitive focus do, then this would render the divergence in introspective reports consistent with the amodal workspace idea, in either of the two guises discussed in Section 1. But at present such evidence is lacking. And in any case, those using this strategy effectively concede that failures to report items in working memory can result merely from the fact that those items aren't currently at the *focus* of attention. This admission also undercuts the introspective evidence of purely amodal thought, as we have seen.

Overall, it seems that the extensive data collected by cognitive scientists concerning people's knowledge (and lack thereof) of their own current thoughts counts strongly against the suggestion that there is an amodal global workspace in which activated attitudes can be entertained, inferences drawn, and decisions made. Nor are there any data that unequivocally support the existence of such a workspace.

3. The Importance of Working Memory

The present section will emphasize how fundamental working memory is for many aspects of our lives. This will serve two purposes. One is to build a foundation for another argument against the amodal workspace idea, to be presented in Section 4. The other is to demonstrate that working memory is not merely an arcane scientific construct but a vital component of human intellectual functioning. Indeed, as we will see, many have suggested that it is the primary resource underlying fluid general intelligence, or *g*. This is fully consistent with one of the main theses of this book, that working memory provides the workspace in which reflective forms of thinking, reasoning, and decision making take place.

3.1. Working memory and reasoning

Consider, first, the relationship between working memory and reasoning. Using very large samples in a number of different experiments (over 400 participants in each), Kyllonen & Christal (1990) used a battery of tests of reasoning ability, as well as a variety of tests of working-memory capacity. They found quite high correlations between the two, of between 0.8 and 0.9. Likewise, Capon et al. (2003) found moderate to strong correlations (varying from 0.3 to 0.6) between a number of different measures of working-memory capacity and both spatial and syllogistic reasoning ability; and Süß et al. (2002) found that measures of both working-memory storage and processing correlated with reasoning ability to a degree of 0.7. Moreover, Prabhakaran et al. (1997) showed using fMRI that brain regions associated with working memory are differentially active when people solve reasoning problems. In particular, regions associated with the phonological loop are active during analytic reasoning tasks, whereas those linked to the visuo-spatial sketchpad are active during spatial reasoning tasks.

Although correlations can't demonstrate causation, these findings suggest quite strongly that reasoning abilities rely heavily on the use of the working-memory system.[4] Moreover, just as might be predicted if successful reasoning performance depends on the resources of working memory, dual-task studies, which require people to reason under working-memory load, show that reasoning capacities are directly impacted by load (De Neys, 2006a). Similarly, De Neys (2006b) shows that reasoning tasks that require people to reflect before generating a correct response are interfered with by secondary tasks placing demands on working memory, whereas reasoning tasks that can be answered more intuitively are not. This is consistent with the dual-systems account of human reasoning capacities, which will form a major topic of discussion in Chapter 7. For it is common for those working in this framework to argue that so-called "System 2" (the reflective system) depends distinctively on the resources of working memory.

Note that many reasoning tasks are entirely abstract, such as evaluating the logical relationship between premises and conclusion. The finding that performance in such tasks depends heavily on working-memory capacities (which are in turn measured using tasks that regularly demonstrate sensory involvement) is nevertheless consistent with the claim outlined in Section 1, that there is, in addition, an amodal global workspace that strategically recruits the sensory-based working-memory system. It is deeply problematic for an idea mooted in Chapter 4.5, however, that sensory involvement in working-memory tasks is merely an artifact of the use of sensory-based experiments. For it seems plain that whatever is measured in such experiments is doing important cognitive work, and is doing it in abstract tasks as well.

Mathematics is also highly abstract, of course. Raghubar et al. (2010) review a wide range of studies of the relationship between working-memory capacity and mathematical abilities. Although the account they present is nuanced, with different forms of working memory being implicated in distinct mathematical tasks, in general they conclude that working memory has an important role to play in mathematical thinking and reasoning. For example, dual-task studies that

---

[4] In any case it is unclear what it would mean for there to be a causal relation in the reverse direction. How could working memory depend upon reasoning? It is likewise unclear what third factor could underlie both.

place a simultaneous load on the working-memory system have been used in conjunction with mathematical tasks, and they demonstrate that the latter depend significantly on the resources of working memory. Moreover, differences in working-memory ability predict a significant portion of the variance in children's mathematical skills, even when controlling for age, intelligence, language ability, and other cognitive factors. Interestingly, however, mathematics does have an important domain-specific component. Halberda et al. (2008) show that children's approximate number acuity (measured by requiring them to make swift comparative judgments of *more* or *less* when presented with large numbers of dots) predicts mathematical ability even when controlling for multiple domain-general factors (including working memory). Similarly, Kroesbergen et al. (2009) show that both working memory and approximate number acuity make significant and independent contributions to mathematical ability, controlling for language and intelligence.

The kinds of finding reviewed above for reasoning and mathematical ability are just the tip of a rather large iceberg. For there have been, in addition, studies demonstrating that working-memory capacity overlaps significantly with people's abilities for reading comprehension (Daneman & Carpenter, 1980, 1983), for language comprehension (King & Just, 1991; MacDonald et al., 1992), for learning to spell (Ormrod & Cochran, 1988), for following directions (Engle et al., 1991), for vocabulary learning (Daneman & Green, 1986), for note-taking (Kiewra & Benton, 1988), and for writing (Benton et al., 1984), among others. What has attracted most attention recently, however, have been a series of studies suggesting that working-memory capacity constitutes much of the basis of fluid general intelligence, or fluid *g*. Some of this work will be discussed next.

3.2. Working memory and fluid general intelligence

General intelligence has been heavily investigated for more than a century. It is not itself a cognitive system, but is rather an inferred common factor (or "latent variable") extracted by statistical factor-analysis from people's performance on a great many cognitive and real-life tasks. It is generally now divided into two components. One is crystalized intelligence, which roughly corresponds to measures of general knowledge. The other is fluid intelligence, which corresponds to what one might think of as mental quickness, or being smart. (Indeed, measures of fluid *g* correlate quite well with people's intuitive judgments of how smart someone is.) Fluid *g* turns out to be a good predictor of many real-life outcomes, including educational attainment and lifetime earnings. For example, when measures of fluid *g* are taken within single families (to control for socioeconomic and parenting differences), it turns out that siblings with high fluid *g* earn three times as much as those with low g (Nisbett, 2009). Small wonder, then, that psychologists have wanted to discover the mechanisms that underlie differences in general intelligence.

There is a growing consensus that differences in working-memory capacity account for at least a large portion of people's variance in fluid g (Conway et al., 2003; Cowan et al., 2005; Colom et al., 2004, 2008; Kane et al., 2005; Unsworth & Spillers, 2010; Redick et al., 2012b; Shipstead et al., 2014). Engle et al. (1999), for example, found that individual abilities in complex-span tasks (such as retaining a list of words while also judging the truth of arithmetic statements) correlate with g fairly highly, at 0.6. Correlations at least this strong have been obtained in numerous studies since then. Indeed, in a large study conducted with nearly 600 participants, Colom et al. (2004) were able to obtain a near-perfect correlation between the two. And in a series of tests using running-memory tasks, Broadway & Engle (2010) found correlations with fluid g of 0.8.[5] Moreover, brain imaging studies suggest that there is heavy overlap between the attentional network employed in working-memory tasks and the brain regions whose activity tracks differences in general intelligence (Gray & Thompson, 2004; Jung & Haier, 2007; Deary et al., 2010; Tang et al., 2010).

It is less clear what aspects or components of working memory are most relevant for explaining differences in fluid g. Some have said that it is the capacity to sustain information in the face of interference that is especially important. Thus Engle et al. (1999) found that measures of simple retention (such as remembering a list of words or numbers) fail to correlate significantly with g at all, while also finding that complex-span tasks (which place a premium on capacities to resist attentional interference) correlate strongly with g. In contrast, Colom et al. (2008) found that simple memory-span abilities account for most of the variance in fluid g, while differences in performance using complex working-memory tasks explain somewhat less.

While the literature on this topic is still somewhat tangled, two recent studies have been especially illuminating. Following Unsworth & Engle (2007), Unsworth & Spillers (2010) suggest that within working memory one can differentiate between the use of attention to *sustain* a representation (often in the face of interference) and the use of attentional strategies to activate task-relevant representations from long-term memory. They devised separate batteries of tests for

---

[5] In such tasks participants are presented serially with a number of items, knowing that they need to recall the final n items presented, but without knowing the length of the total list.

each. They used tests like the Stroop[6] and the anti-saccade task (in which one has to look away from a sudden cue, rather than toward it) to measure simple attentional control; they used a variety of tests of long-term memory ability, such as delayed free recall of a list of items; and they used a variety of complex-span tasks to measure working memory itself. In addition, they administered three separate tests of fluid g. They found that attentional control and memory abilities each contributed independently to working-memory capacity, while also making independent contributions to g.

Likewise, Shipstead et al. (2012) set out to disentangle the contributions made to general intelligence by simple working-memory retention, on the one hand, and attentional control (operationalized using complex-span tasks), on the other. They were able to show that these are separate components of working memory, and that each makes a significant contribution to fluid g. However, they also used structural equation modeling to show that the contribution made by simple working-memory retention to fluid g is mostly explained by processes closely related to the controlled use of attention. It seems that attention and attentional control lie at the heart of working-memory capacities (just as we argued in Chapter 4.3), and are also what explain much of people's variance in fluid general intelligence.

Now recall that fluid g is a statistical construction arrived at by factor analysis across a varied battery of cognitive tasks. If working memory is the cognitive system that constitutes that common factor, then one would predict that improvements in working-memory ability should cause improvements in general intelligence. There have now been a flurry of studies designed to test this prediction. Some have returned negative results, as did Colom et al. (2010) and Redick et al. (2012a). But these findings may have been caused by the experimenters' failure to examine those who benefited from working-memory training separately from those who showed little or no improvement in working memory. In contrast, Jaeggi et al. (2008) used extensive training with an n-back task (which puts a premium on capacities to control working-memory interference), and were able to demonstrate transfer to measures of fluid g. Moreover, the extent of the benefit in the latter was found to correlate with the length of the training period. These results were replicated and extended by Jaeggi et al. (2010). Then Jaeggi et al. (2011) extended their previous findings to children. They used a video game-like n-back working-memory task to engage the children's interest,

---

[6] In the Stroop test one has to name the color of typeface in which words are printed as swiftly as possible. Some of these words are themselves names of colors, however. Reaction times are slower when the colors and semantic properties of the words are inconsistent (such as the word "red" printed in green, to which the correct response is "green").

and carefully titrated the difficulty of the task so that children remained challenged but not overwhelmed. Among children who showed significant improvements in the task, there was transfer to measures of fluid *g*. Moreover, these children continued to show the benefits of working-memory training on general intelligence three months later. These findings are also consistent with those reported by Klingberg (2010).

There have been methodological criticisms of some of these studies using working-memory training (Shipstead et al., 2010). Specifically, the need for an active control group has been emphasized (who are trained on some set of tasks unrelated to working memory), as has the need for multiple measures of general intelligence. These challenges are taken up by Jaušovec & Jaušovec (2012), who find improvements in all of a number of measures of fluid *g* following thirty hours of training on working-memory tasks, while a control group (who underwent thirty hours of communication training) showed no improvement. In addition, the authors found changes in brain activity, suggesting that working-memory training had effects on both attentional (parietal) and executive (frontal) regions of the brain. The methodological challenges are also taken up by Jaeggi et al. (2014), who find improvements in a composite measure of fluid *g* using two sorts of working-memory training. They also uncover a number of individual differences contributing to training success that might explain why some researchers have failed to find transfer-effects.

3.3. *Working memory and temporal discounting*

While the field is still subject to controversy then, there is reason to think that working memory is, indeed, the mechanism responsible for at least a large portion of people's variance in fluid general intelligence. This conclusion can be further supported by considering the relationships among intelligence, working memory, and temporal discounting. The latter consists in the ability to resist current rewards in order to achieve larger future ones. Low temporal discounting scores (like high intelligence) predict a great many types of real-world success (Tangney et al., 2004). Moreover, there is also a moderate negative correlation (of around –0.25) between temporal discounting and intelligence (Shamosh & Gray, 2008). It is natural to wonder, then, whether the correlation between the two might be mediated by working-memory capacity, and whether working-memory training might lead to improvements in temporal discounting rates.

Shamosh et al. (2009) conducted a study that related performance in working-memory tasks, in temporal discounting, and in measures of general intelligence. They found a strong correlation between working memory and intelligence (of about 0.6), as well as a moderately large negative correlation between intelligence and temporal discounting (of –0.4). They also found a moderate negative correlation between working memory and temporal discounting (of around –0.25). Statistical analysis suggested that the contribution of working memory to temporal discounting was the same as whatever mediates the connection between working memory and intelligence. Moreover, the causal nature of the relationship is confirmed by Bickel et al. (2011), who show that working-memory training using n-back tasks reduces temporal discounting in addicts. They also suggest that the reason for the relationship may be that those with strong working-memory abilities are better able to envisage the benefits of waiting for future rewards, as well as to direct attention away from current temptations.

These findings of a connection between working-memory abilities and capacities to delay gratification are consistent with a robust body of work suggesting that one important determinant of self-control is a capacity to deploy one's attentional resources intelligently. In a groundbreaking series of studies conducted with children in the 1970s, Mischel & Mischel (1983) tested children's ability to resist the temptation of one marshmallow now in order to get two marshmallows a few minutes later. They found that differences in this ability predicted many positive outcomes through the school years and beyond into adulthood, including school grades, truancy (or its lack), college graduation, rates of divorce, and much more. But they also found that the proximate cause of the children's success or failure lay mostly in how they directed their attention. Successful children turned their back on the marshmallow, looked at the ceiling, sang songs to themselves, and so forth (Metcalfe & Mischel, 1999). Unsuccessful children looked longingly at the marshmallow itself. And attentional control, of course, lies at the heart of people's working-memory abilities, as we saw in Chapter 4.3.[7]

Overall, then, we can conclude that working memory is a vital component of many important human capacities. This is fully consistent with the suggestion that working memory is the system in which conscious forms of reflective reasoning and decision making take place.

4. The Case of the Missing Variance

This section will build on the findings of Section 3 to argue against the amodal-workspace idea sketched in Section 1 (in either of its two variants). Specifically, it will argue that such a workspace should, if it existed, contribute an independent

---

[7] Note that the studies described here involve the intelligent use of overt, as opposed to covert, attention. But as we will see in Chapter 6, the same executive and control mechanisms govern both.

source of variance to people's reasoning and decision-making abilities, as well as to their fluid general intelligence. Evidence will then be reviewed that there is no such variance remaining, at least once other factors are accounted for. So a central prediction made by the amodal-workspace idea fails to hold up.

4.1. Predictions of the amodal-workspace theory

Recall from Section 1 that there is seemingly only one way for traditional models of reflection to be defended against the evidence of the sensory-based nature of working memory discussed in Chapter 4. This is to claim that there is an additional amodal global workspace that operates alongside, and generally recruits the resources of, the sensory-based working-memory system. In one version, it could be claimed that the amodal workspace relies on some of the same attentional resources as working memory, only directed toward amodal activated attitudes. In another version, it could be claimed that there is some other mechanism that can make activated attitudes globally available, thereby constituting an amodal workspace. But on either account, use of the amodal workspace should be something that people can be better or worse at independently of their other abilities, and specifically, independently of their sensory-based working-memory abilities.

This point is easiest to see on a two-systems account, where the amodal workspace is thought to depend on some resource other than attention. For whatever that resource is, people should vary in how much they have of it, just as they vary in almost every other measurable property. Just as some people have hands that are bigger than others, or legs that are longer than those of others, or a greater facility to pick up new languages, so we should predict that people will differ in their abilities to activate, sustain, and deploy their attitudes in the amodal global workspace. Moreover, everyone acknowledges that reflection is important for many real-world activities and outcomes. So we should expect that if reflection is underpinned, even in part, by such an amodal workspace, then this should show up as an independent source of variance in people's performance of those activities, as well as in their relative achievement of those outcomes. Indeed, given the importance traditionally attached to amodal forms of reflection and reflective reasoning, we should expect that the amodal workspace's contribution to performance (especially in abstract domains) would be quite large.

It might be replied that the contributions made by the amodal and sensory-based workspaces cannot be wholly independent, given the hypothesis that the amodal system strategically recruits the resources of the sensory-based one on a regular basis. This might lead one to expect that a better sensory-based system would correlate with better use of the amodal one, and that a weak sensory-based system would correlate with weaker performance in amodal thinking and reasoning. The point is correct so far as it goes. But since the attentional and sensory resources that underlie working-memory capacity fall outside of the amodal system (on a two-systems account), there should still be significant independent variance in the contributions of the two systems to people's performance.

The same case is still valid, but a little more complex to make, if a multiple-modes model is assumed, and the amodal workspace shares the same attentional resources as the sensory-based working-memory system. Recall that on this account there is only one system involved, but with two modes of activity. Given this, it might be thought that the system would show up as just a single source of variance in people's performance in the sorts of tasks that require reflection. This is a mistake, however. For even if we allow that reflection is underpinned by a single system, its distinct modes depend on the engagement of different component parts. Hence even if attentional mechanisms are engaged in both modes (perhaps centered on the intraparietal sulcus in each case), the two would surely involve distinct neural pathways. In sensory-based mode these will focus attentional signals on regions of sensory cortices, whereas in amodal mode a distinct set of fibers would focus such signals on regions of prefrontal and temporal cortex, where amodal attitudes are realized. These two sets of neural pathways can of course differ in the thickness of the fiber bundles involved, as well as in the depth of myelination of the neuronal axons, each of which is known to have an impact on processing speed and efficiency. Moreover, the principles according to which the amodal workspace operates would surely be different. And one might also expect that people would differ in their habits of use of the two modes, with some relying more on one mode and others more on the other. Over time this, too, would be expected to generate differences in the capacities of the two.

Notice that analyses of variance across tasks enable the working-memory system to be fractionated into components, with the various parts contributing differentially to different sorts of tasks or in different contexts. Thus Kane et al. (2004) administered a range of both simple and complex working-memory tasks to people, as well as tests of reasoning and general intelligence. Factor analysis then enabled them to test different models of the contributors to performance, with the result comprising an executive that was implicated to some degree in all tasks (especially in complex memory-span tasks), together with two modality-specific components (one for vision, one for verbal material) which were partly independent of one another and of the central executive. Similar analyses should then be capable of differentiating the amodal from sensory-based uses of the global workspace, if they both exist.

Someone might suggest that the known component structure of working memory itself can be mapped onto the distinction between an amodal and a sensory-based workspace, with the executive component comprising the former and the attentional and sensory components constituting the latter. It should be granted that the frontal executive is amodal in nature, of course. But it is a far cry from this to claiming that the frontal lobes realize a globally accessible amodal workspace in which reflection can take place, and in which it can do so independently of sensory-based working memory (at least in principle, absent a strong tendency to make strategic use of the resources of the latter). If this were true, then it should be possible for factor analysis to isolate two components of the executive: one that directs attention and resists interference while controlling the sensory-based system, and another that makes amodal attitudes (which are realized in the frontal and temporal lobes) globally accessible throughout the brain.

While many component-factor analyses of executive function have been conducted, and while the field is still somewhat murky, no one has proposed any such distinction. For example, Miyake et al. (2000) used a battery of executive function tasks to demonstrate the partial separation between functions of mental-set shifting, information updating and monitoring, and inhibition of prepotent responses. In contrast, Nee et al. (2013) argue that much of the work purporting to distinguish functional components of the executive is subject to experimental confounds of various sorts. Rather, they defend a version of the content-based division initially proposed by Levy & Goldman-Rakic (2000) on the basis of neurophysiological evidence. Their meta-analysis shows a division in the frontal lobes between spatial content and object-based content, with the regions involved forming the terminus of the "where" and "what" visual streams established by Ungerleider & Mishkin (1982). (For convergent findings, see the meta-analysis by Rottschy et al., 2012.) But I have been able to find nothing in the field to support the claim that one component of executive function amounts to an amodal global workspace.

We can conclude that if there were an amodal global workspace for reflection in addition to a sensory-based working-memory system, then this should show up as an independent source of variance in people's intellectual performance. The question, now, is how this prediction stacks up against the empirical evidence. There are two extensive literatures that bear on the issue. One concerns reasoning performance, and the other fluid general intelligence. We will consider the latter first.

4.2. Explaining variance in fluid g

We have already noted in Section 3 that variance in working-memory explains a large portion of people's variations in fluid general intelligence. Note, however, that even if working memory were *the* cognitive system or capacity underlying the range of abilities we identify as general intelligence, we should not expect measures of the two to be perfectly correlated. For there will be factors that influence performance in specific working-memory tests that have less influence on the outcome of intelligence tests, and vice versa. In particular, content-relevant knowledge and skills will vary in the subject population in ways that impact some tests but not others. In a group of participants drawn from among undergraduates, for example, some might have strong mathematical skills whereas others are much weaker. One would expect that a complex span-task requiring participants to judge the truth of an arithmetic proposition while recalling a list of words would be much less demanding of the attentional resources of the former group than the latter. Given the inevitability of this sort of noise in the data, a correlation of 0.8 or 0.9 (together with evidence of tight causal relatedness) might be considered close enough to amount to an identity.

In any case, however, we know that there are additional sources of variance in fluid g that are at least partly independent of working memory, but which provide no support for an amodal global workspace. One is *speed of processing*. This is likely to reflect low-level brain-wiring efficiency and the extent of neural myelination, and is generally measured using tasks that require speed of perceptual discrimination. Speed of processing is known to increase through childhood and adolescence, and declines in older age. One can then examine how changes in speed relate to changes in working memory and fluid g. Clay et al. (2009) show, for example, that most of the decline in working memory and fluid g with age can be attributed to a decline in speed of processing, together with sensory decline more generally. However, they also note that working memory and speed of processing are partly independent of one another. This suggests that speed of processing may be another factor alongside working-memory ability that explains some of the variance in fluid g.

Similarly, Schretlen et al. (2000) examined the causes of normal age-related decline in fluid g. They administered tests of speed of processing (using speed of perceptual matching), working memory, and executive function, while also obtaining measures of frontal-lobe volume. The important finding for our purposes is that 97 percent of age-related declines in g were accounted for by changes in simple comparison speed and working memory, which were at least partly independent of one another. However, the contribution of working memory to the decline in g was wholly explained by the decline in executive function and frontal lobe volume.[8]

Others have investigated the relationship between speed of processing, working memory, and g in development and among young adults (Coyle et al., 2011; Redick et al., 2012b). For example, Demetriou et al. (2013) conducted three longitudinal studies with children and adolescents to examine the relations between speed of processing, working memory, and fluid g (as well as correlations between each and age). They found that speed of processing co-varied strongly with age (with correlations of between 0.6 and 0.7) up to age thirteen, declining rapidly thereafter (to about 0.2). Working memory was moderately related to speed throughout the entire span of ages. But by adolescence, with speed and age controlled for, working memory overlapped almost fully with fluid g (at around 0.9).

In addition to speed of processing and working memory (where the latter includes an executive function component, of course), are there any other factors that are known to contribute to fluid general intelligence? Until recently there were none that were well established. However, Kaufman et al. (2009) investigated whether associative learning might also be important for general intelligence. (This is learning of the sort that might occur when one sees two words paired together for a brief time, later using the one as a cue to recall the other.) They found that working memory and associative learning are weakly related, but that all three of working memory, associative learning, and processing speed make statistically independent contributions to fluid g. Yet there is nothing about associative learning ability, of course, to suggest the existence of an amodal workspace in which propositional attitudes of all sorts can be activated and globally accessible.

We can conclude that fluid general intelligence is best explained by some combination of working memory capacity, speed of processing, and perhaps associative learning ability. In most studies working memory overlaps quite strongly with fluid g, generally explaining between 0.6 and 0.9 of people's variance in the latter.

---

[8] Executive function was measured using the Wisconsin Card Sorting Task. This is generally thought to test hypothesis formation and outcome monitoring, perhaps suggesting that an amodal attitude system might be involved. But in fact there is evidence that the processes that mediate performance on the Wisconsin Card Sorting Task are sensory based, and make heavy use of the same attentional resources that underlie working memory (Monchi et al., 2001; Buchsbaum et al., 2005).

4.3. Sensory attention and fluid g

It doesn't follow from these findings that there is no amodal workspace in which propositional attitudes can be activated and conscious, of course. For some of the variance in people's working memory capacities may be due to the properties of just such a workspace. However, we have already noted that there is no hint in the literature of a partition within working memory between modal and amodal content, which is what the existence of an amodal workspace should predict. And we have also noted that low-level attentional capacities of the kind that are measured using anti-saccade tasks and flanker tasks correlate quite strongly with fluid g in their own right (Unsworth & Spillers, 2010; Shipstead et al., 2014). So we can at least conclude that the sensory-based working-memory system is responsible for a significant portion of people's variance in fluid general intelligence.

The most direct test of the involvement of an amodal global workspace in fluid g would be to administer a series of well-validated measures of working-memory ability that vary in the extent to which they involve amodal content (such as tasks involving words or numbers) in addition to nonconceptual sensory information (such as patterns and shapes for which we possess no concepts). If such a workspace exists, then one would expect to find decreasing overlap between working memory and fluid g when one moves from tasks that are more abstract in nature to those that are purely sensory. Put differently, if the hypothesis of an amodal workspace is correct, then one would expect to find stronger correlations with fluid g using abstract measures of working memory, since these will benefit from both modal and amodal involvement. To the best of my knowledge, no one has conducted such a test. But one can look across studies in which both conceptual and nonconceptual measures of working memory are employed and correlated with fluid g on an individual basis. Initial indications are that the prediction does not pan out.

To test the prediction, I searched for papers correlating working memory with fluid g, looking especially for those that utilize both concept-involving and nonconceptual tests of working memory, and which also provide details of correlations among individual tests. This search turned up five recent papers: Unsworth & Spillers (2010), Burgess et al. (2011), Redick et al. (2012b), Shipstead et al. (2012), and Shipstead et al. (2014). All five employed two types of working-memory test that should unambiguously benefit from the involvement of an amodal workspace, if such a thing exists. Thus all used *operation-span* tests, which require one to recall lists of words, letters, or numbers while undertaking a secondary mathematical task. Four also used *reading-span* tests, which have the same format except that the secondary task involves responding to sentences. The fifth instead used two *running-memory* tests (Shipstead et al., 2014), which require one to keep in mind serial lists of letters or numbers without any secondary task. All five studies also used a type of test that seems to be largely nonconceptual in nature. These are *symmetry-span* tests, which require one to keep a running memory of illuminated positions in a 4 × 4 grid interleaved with judgments of the symmetry of unnameable geometric figures.[9] Moreover, all five used a number of different tests of fluid general intelligence. Averaging across these five studies, the correlation between the concept-involving measures of working memory and the tests of fluid *g* is 0.35, whereas the correlation between the nonconceptual measure and the tests of fluid *g* is 0.40, somewhat *higher*, not lower.[10]

This finding is problematic for the idea of an amodal global workspace. For if such a thing existed, then it would surely make *some* contribution to individual differences in fluid general intelligence. The putatively distinct sensory-based system surely could not account for all variance in fluid *g* on its own. We therefore ought to see lower correlations with fluid *g* using working-memory tasks that are purely sensory in nature than are found using tasks of a mixed modal–amodal sort. But this seems not to be the case. Of course, the studies in question all happened to employ the same nonconceptual measure of working memory, which might turn out to be anomalous in some way. Nor were those studies specifically designed to test the prediction under consideration here. So the present argument cannot be regarded as definitive.

In addition, however, there is direct evidence that low-level sensory and attentional factors correlate with fluid intelligence about as closely as working memory itself does, thus providing further support for the claim that the latter is entirely sensory-based. Melnick et al. (2013), in particular, used a test that combined speed of sensory processing with automatic sensory suppression of large (as opposed to small) moving stimuli.[11] They found high correlations (of 0.65 and 0.71 in two experiments) between their low-level sensory measures and

---

[9] Even if symmetry-span tests are not fully nonconceptual, they are certainly *less* conceptual in nature than the operation-span, reading-span, and memory-span tests, which use words, letters, or numbers. This is enough for our purposes. If there is a separate amodal working-memory system, the latter tests should correlate with fluid *g* more strongly than does the symmetry-span test.

[10] Note that these are correlations between tests of working memory and *tests* of fluid *g*, not fluid *g* itself (which is the underlying common factor extracted from a number of such tests). This might explain why the correlations reported here are lower than those generally found between working-memory capacity and *g*.

[11] The suppression effect is thought to be an innate bias in the mechanisms that guide attention to ignore and suppress stimuli that are generally less likely to be relevant.

a variety of different measures of fluid general intelligence. Since we know that executively controlled attention is also a vital component of working memory (as well as for tasks that measure fluid *g*), it appears from this study that there might be no variance in the latter remaining to be explained by a postulated amodal system.

Converging evidence is provided by a number of further studies, which have examined the relationship between capacities for sensory discrimination and fluid general intelligence in both children and adults (Acton & Schroeder, 2001; Deary et al., 2004; Meyer et al., 2010). The tests of sensory discrimination in question require people to order a series of color-chips by shade of color, to order a series of lines by length, to order a series of objects by weight, to order a series of tones by pitch, and so on. The tests are not time-limited, so speed of processing is unlikely to play much of a role. From these measures one can use statistical analysis to extract an underlying common factor that is shared by them all (much as one can extract *g* itself as a common factor underlying a number of measures of intelligence). Variance in sensory acuity across sensory modalities is thus washed out in this analysis. One can then examine the correlations between this common factor and fluid *g*. These range between 0.68 and 0.92 across studies—that is, between *very strong* and *almost identical*.[12]

It is not yet clear what cognitive mechanisms constitute the common factor involved in sensory-discrimination tasks. But it is plausible that attentional control and sensory working memory are the main components. When one makes a judgment of the comparative pitch of two tones, for example, one has to hold in place a working-memory representation of the tone one has just heard, comparing it for pitch against the current stimulus, while resisting interference from memories of other recent tones. Even where one makes a simultaneous judgment of color or comparative length one needs to look back and forth between pairs for comparison, holding in working memory a representation of the one that has just been examined and comparing it with the object of current attention. What is surely quite clear, however, is that the underlying common factor in sensory-discrimination tasks cannot have anything to do with the properties of the postulated amodal global workspace.

Those seeking to defend the idea of an amodal workspace in which attitudes of all types can be activated might respond that it hasn't yet been demonstrated that there is *no* variance remaining that is unaccounted for by low-level sensory factors. So there is still a possibility that this additional variance is explained by

---

[12] Note, too, that this is essentially the same range of correlations as is generally found between working-memory capacities themselves and fluid *g*, which tend to fall between 0.6 and 0.9.

properties of the amodal workspace. Such claims are hard to refute. But we can say with some confidence that there is no *need* to appeal to such a workspace in order to explain variations in fluid intelligence. Variance in the controlling executive system combined with variations in attentional capacities, speed of processing, and perhaps associative ability are fully sufficient to explain the data. Moreover, recall that fluid *g* is highly predictive of success in the modern world, which sets a premium on abstract and decontextualized forms of reasoning and decision making. One might have expected, then, that variance in the properties of the supposed amodal workspace (in which most of the real work of thinking and reasoning takes place, according to adherents) should be responsible for a *large* portion of people's variance in fluid *g*. But plainly it is not.

It is possible for the hypothesis of an amodal workspace to be saved, of course, by postulating that there are no variations in its structure or properties across individuals. For if that were so, then of course all of the variance in fluid *g* would need to be explained by other factors. But such a claim is entirely arbitrary, and quite implausible. Since there is variance in virtually every other measurable property of human beings, it would be extraordinary if none were found here. We can conclude, therefore, that an inference to the best explanation strongly favors the claim that there is just one working-memory system that is sensory based.

4.4. *Explaining variance in reasoning*

In addition to the work on fluid *g* discussed above, there is also an extensive literature on the factors that underlie variations in reasoning ability. Indeed, human reasoning has been heavily researched over the last half century and more. We know that people often fall prey to a variety of fallacies and biases, and that they do so in predictable ways (Kahneman et al., 1982). But we also know that it is possible for people to avoid such errors, and that there are large individual differences in how reliably they do so (Stanovich, 1999). This literature has given rise to "dual systems" models of human reasoning, which will be a central focus of our discussion in Chapter 7. (At this point it is worth noting only that so-called "System 2" is widely agreed to depend heavily on the resources of working memory.) There is dispute about whether the reasoning methods that people generally employ are really erroneous, however, or are rather "quick and dirty" heuristics that are both computationally frugal and reliable enough to be useful (Gigerenzer et al., 1999). While I am sympathetic toward the latter position, it is undeniable that heuristic reasoning can often prove disastrous in our modern world (which places a premium on abstract, de-contextualized, and exact reasoning and decision making). Moreover, capacities for valid non-heuristic reasoning correlate well with many measures of real-world success (Stanovich, 2009).

Our present interest is in the factors that explain individual variance in successful reasoning of this sort.

Stanovich (2009) reviews much of the existing literature, and argues that there are just three components underlying successful performance in reasoning tasks. One is fluid general intelligence. Smarter people are more likely to spot the tempting but fallacious option, and to see their way to a correct solution. But we have already concluded that fluid *g* is largely constituted by strong sensory-based working-memory abilities, supported by speed of processing and perhaps associative learning. The second component underlying successful reasoning is a feature of personality. It is a disposition to be reflective, which is related to what psychologists sometimes call "need for cognition." While a reflective disposition *could* be used to activate an amodal global workspace, if such a thing existed, it provides no evidence for the existence of such a workspace. The final component in reasoning success is explicit knowledge of norms of reasoning, which Stanovich (2009) refers to as "mindware." Not surprisingly, people who have benefited from instruction in methods of reasoning tend to do better in reasoning tasks (provided that they reflect long enough to deploy their knowledge). Again, there is nothing here to suggest an amodal global workspace. In Chapter 7, in contrast, we will show how the sensory-based account of reflection can explain the key findings in this area.

We can conclude that the literature on individual differences in cognition provides a powerful empirical case against traditional models of reflection. If an amodal workspace existed in which propositional attitudes of all sorts could be activated and globally available, then we would expect it to contribute a significant source of variance to people's cognitive performance. But there is not even a hint in the data that this is the case. Moreover, enough is known about the factors that do underlie success to suggest quite strongly that it is *not* the case.

5. The Default Network

This section will consider a body of data deriving from brain-imaging studies of the so-called "default network" in the human brain (Raichle et al., 2001; Mason et al., 2007; Buckner et al., 2008). These might seem, on the face of it, to support the existence of an amodal global workspace.

The default network is differentially active when people are *not* involved in any specific task, but when they nevertheless report that they are engaged in conscious thought, with their minds wandering freely over matters not directly related to the present. The regions involved include medial prefrontal cortex and posterior cingulate cortex along the midline of the brain, together with ventral parietal cortex (including the temporo-parietal junction), lateral temporal cortex, and the hippocampus together with nearby structures in the medial temporal lobe. (See Figures 1–3.) Importantly for our purposes, regions *not* included in this network are midlevel sensory cortices together with the intraparietal sulcus and dorsolateral prefrontal cortex, which form central components of the working-memory system. (See Figure 2.) Since the default network is active when people engage in conscious stimulus-independent thought, but without apparently employing sensory-based forms of working memory, then this might be taken to provide evidence of an amodal global workspace.

5.1. Subtraction methodology

There are numerous reasons why this conclusion should be resisted, however. One is that there exist alternative explanations for why brain-imaging studies of the default network should fail to show activity in the attentional system and modality-specific sensory areas. In this connection it is an important point to note that *all* regions of the brain are *always* active. Brain imaging produces maps of *differential* activity by using a subtraction method: brain activations in a control task of some sort are subtracted from activity that occurs during the target experimental condition. So what one sees are the regions of the brain that were *more* active in the target condition than in the control condition. When maps of the default network are produced, the control condition is generally an attention-demanding visual or auditory task of some sort. It is hardly surprising, then, that sensory regions should appear to be suppressed by comparison in the target "mind wandering" condition. For in the latter condition there is no bottom-up sensory stimulus to be attended to. Rather, any imagery produced during mind wandering will be caused and sustained by top-down signals. Small wonder, then, that modality-specific sensory activity is lesser by comparison.

Moreover, we know that mind wandering frequently involves episodic memories, which generally contain sensory-specific components (visual, auditory, olfactory, and so on). And we know that regions of visual and auditory cortex *are* differentially activated during retrieval of memories of pictures and sounds respectively (Wheeler et al., 2000). Indeed, when visual and auditory imagery are contrasted with one another, and with perception in the relevant sense modality, not only is modality-specific activity in midlevel sensory areas found, but so also is activity in core regions of the default network (Daselaar et al., 2010). These include medial prefrontal cortex, posterior cingulate, and ventral parietal cortex. Moreover, as well as modality-specific activity in midlevel sensory areas there is modality-specific *suppression* in primary sensory cortices (Daselaar et al., 2010).

Similar considerations relating to the subtraction methodology can explain why activity in dorsolateral prefrontal cortex, the frontal eye-fields, and the intraparietal sulcus (that is, the core regions of attentional and working-memory systems) is not observed during periods of mind wandering. This is because mind wandering involves a form of *defocused* attention (Smallwood et al., 2011), whereas the comparison tasks that are used for purposes of subtraction will generally involve an attentionally demanding assignment of some sort. That there is *lesser* involvement of the top-down attentional network in the former condition is exactly what one might expect. But it does not follow that top-down attention is not involved at all.

5.2. The content of default-network activity

In addition, the involvement of most of the regions that make up the default network is explicable in term of the normal contents of mind wandering and stimulus-independent thought. The involvement of the hippocampus and nearby regions of medial temporal cortex is easy to explain, for example. For these structures are known to be critically involved in the storage and activation of episodic memories (Tulving & Markowitsch, 1998). Moreover, evidence continues to accumulate that those same memory systems are heavily involved in *prospection*, where one constructs, elaborates, and evaluates future events and scenarios, often for purposes of decision making (Addis et al., 2007; Buckner et al., 2008; Spreng et al., 2009). For we know that much of the time when people's minds are wandering they are reliving episodes from their past or imagining potential future actions or events. In contrast, when engaged in the control tasks used for subtraction, people will be focused on the here-and-now.

Similar content-related considerations can explain the involvement of medial prefrontal cortex, posterior cingulate, and lateral temporal cortex. Consider the latter first. This is known to be one of the main brain regions involved in the storage and activation of concepts (Binder et al., 2005; Martin, 2007). And mind wandering will generally involve thoughts that are much more heavily and richly conceptualized than are the thoughts evoked by the relatively simple sensory decision-tasks that tend to be used for purposes of subtraction. Likewise, medial prefrontal cortex and posterior cingulate are known to be among the main regions underlying social cognition of all sorts (Frith & Frith, 2003; Saxe, 2009; Saxe et al., 2009; Lieberman, 2013), and mind wandering will frequently involve contents that are at least partly social in nature. For we spend much of our time when not on task thinking about ourselves and our relationships with other people, real or potential. The control tasks, in contrast, are hardly ever of this sort. It is hardly surprising, then, that these regions should reliably show up as belonging to the default network that is active when one engages in stimulus-independent thought.[13]

What, then, explains the involvement of ventral parietal cortex in default-network activity? It might be tempting to look for an explanation in terms of the involvement of the bottom-up attentional system, given that this likewise implicates ventral parietal cortex, as we saw in Chapter 3.4. But in fact the region of ventral parietal cortex that forms part of the default network is *anti*-correlated with what some have called the "salience network" (Menon, 2011; Yeo et al., 2011). Rather, the region in question embraces the temporo-parietal junction, which is known to be a critical component of the mentalizing system (Saxe, 2009). So once again the explanation is likely to be content based: when our minds wander, much of the time we are thinking about and evaluating the mental states of ourselves and others.

5.3. *The involvement of working memory in default activity*

The most important point for our purposes, however, is that there is no reason to think that sensory-based working memory is *not* involved during mind wandering and stimulus-independent thought. On the contrary, people's introspective reports of the kinds of thought in which they engage while the default network is active routinely involve visual and auditory imagery, as well as richly sensory episodic memories of the past together with imagery of potential future events (Mazoyer et al., 2001; Buckner et al., 2008; Andrews-Hanna et al., 2014). Thoughts of this sort are known to involve activations of midlevel regions of the relevant sensory modalities, as does imagery generally, as we saw in Chapter 3.1.

In addition, a number of carefully controlled studies have revealed activity in sensory cortical areas under such conditions (Addis et al., 2007; Spreng et al., 2009; Daselaar et al., 2010). Indeed, Hassabis et al. (2007) argue that the common function supported by all forms of default-network activity is that of sensory-based *scene construction*. Drawing, in part, on the well-known finding that episodic memory is always partly constructive in nature (Schacter, 2001), they argue that the core function that is common to both episodic remembering and imagining of fictitious or future scenes is the generation and maintenance of complex visual representations, especially of the spatial context of objects and

---

[13] Another hypothesis, however, is that medial prefrontal cortex and the posterior cingulate are among the primary network *hubs* of the brain, causing it to show up more in conditions where people engage in varied forms of stimulus-independent thought than in circumstances where they are focused on a specific task (Sporns, 2011). We will return to this point in Chapter 8.

events. Summerfield et al. (2010) then devised a task that enabled them to "slow down" the construction process, observing which brain areas are especially active at different stages of construction. These include many default-network regions, but also dorsolateral prefrontal cortex and the intraparietal sulcus, which are core components of the top-down attentional system that underlies sensory-based working memory.

There is good reason to think, then, that the seeming absence of activity in attentional and working-memory networks in many studies of mind wandering is an artifact of the subtraction methodology employed. Moreover, since we know that the thoughts that occupy people's minds in such circumstances generally have rich sensory-based imagistic contents, there is every reason to believe that the working-memory system is involved. In addition, a number of studies suggest directly that this is, indeed, the case.

6. Conclusion

This chapter has shown that there are a number of deep problems confronting the idea of a central amodal workspace in which our propositional attitudes can be activated and globally accessible. One is that if there were such a workspace, then knowledge of our own current attitudes should often be direct and non-interpretive. But it is not. Another is that if there were such a workspace, then one would expect that variance in its properties should make a substantial contribution to variations among people in general intelligence and abstract reasoning abilities. But it seems that such variation is adequately explained by variance in sensory-based working-memory capacities combined with a number of low-level factors such as speed of processing. Moreover, we have shown that there is no reason to think that the default network is a viable candidate to realize an amodal workspace. In contrast, the sensory-based account of reflection and the stream of consciousness being developed in this book can explain all of the well-established properties of the human mind that we have discussed so far.

6

Working Memory in Action

This chapter will describe in more detail the positive alternative to the amodal model of reflection critiqued in previous chapters. (This work will continue through Chapter 7.) On the proposed account, the contents of the stream of consciousness in general (and reflection in particular) are constituted by the sensory-based contents of working memory. Our amodal attitudes, in contrast, operate unconsciously in the background, activating, sustaining, and manipulating the contents of working memory. One goal of the present chapter is to provide a sketch of an empirically supported theory of how this system works. Another is to vindicate our intuitive belief that reflective thinking is a form of action (at least in the sense that it is under direct intentional control). The chapter also argues, more controversially, that the seemingly passive nature of much of the stream of consciousness is actually active in nature.

1. Unconscious Goal Pursuit

This section will consider some of the evidence suggesting that goals can be activated, and can guide action, without being conscious. Thereafter the chapter will show how unconscious goals control mental actions of attending and rehearsing, thereby determining the contents of working memory and giving rise to the stream of consciousness.

1.1. Some goals are unconscious

There is a burgeoning literature showing not only that goals can be created in people without their awareness, but also that such goals can motivate action outside of awareness (Dijksterhuis & Aarts, 2010). These findings are important because they demonstrate the reality and efficacy of unconscious goals. The latter play a crucial role in the sensory-based model of reflection and the stream of consciousness, as we will see. Moreover, it should be stressed that the experimental studies in question work with the most demanding possible conception of what it takes for goals to be unconscious; namely, that subjects should have no knowledge of them. If we equate consciousness with the results of global broad-casting, in contrast (as we have been assuming since Chapter 3), then there will be many mental events that are not globally broadcast (and are hence unconscious) although subjects know, by interpretation, that they occur. Put differently: from the fact that one knows that one has a certain goal one cannot conclude that the goal is a conscious one. For the knowledge in question might be grounded in unconscious inferences from one's own behavior or circumstances, or derived indirectly from sensory-based cues of one sort or another (Carruthers, 2011a). With the bar for unconscious goal pursuit set so high, it is not surprising that it has required extensive experimentation to establish the reality of the phenom-enon. But by the same token, once established, we can be confident that it is really quite widespread.

It has been known for some time that unconscious priming can increase the strength of a goal, thereby impacting how someone will act. For example, Bargh et al. (2001) primed the goal of succeeding or doing well by having people complete word puzzles in which terms like "success" figured, whereas a control group completed puzzles in which these terms did not occur. The people primed for success subsequently worked harder and longer at an unrelated task. Likewise, people playing the role of a fishing company who were primed for cooperation did more to replenish the fish stocks than did people who were not so primed. However, this research does not demonstrate the existence of unconscious goals. It only shows that goals can be *influenced* unconsciously. For people in the control groups, too, presumably had the goal of succeeding at the task they had agreed to do, or of cooperating to some degree, and there is no reason to think that these goals were unconscious. (Or none that is provided in these experiments, at any rate. In fact it follows from the sensory-based model of reflection that *all* goals are *always* unconscious, as we will see.) Priming merely increased the *strength* of these goals outside of people's awareness.

There is now, however, an extensive body of evidence showing that goals can be activated, and can influence behavior, outside of people's awareness (Dijksterhuis & Aarts, 2010; Huang & Bargh, 2014). For example, Lau & Passingham (2007) were able to demonstrate that subliminal priming can activate goals that would otherwise not be present. Participants engaged in a task where they either had to make a semantic judgment (indicating whether a word was concrete or abstract) or a phonological one (indicating whether the word was bisyllabic). The judgment that they were to make on each trial was signaled by a prior visible cue (a square or a diamond respectively). Shortly before presentation of the cue, participants were presented with a smaller square or diamond shape, in conditions where it was rendered either visible or invisible through the timing of a backward mask. They were told to ignore these initial shapes, which could be either congruent or incongruent with the target cues. What the experiment found was that when the prime was both subliminal and incongruent with the target cue, people made more errors and were slower to respond, suggesting that the prime had activated the opposite goal, which then conflicted with the cued goal. (There was no effect when the prime was visible.) Moreover, brain imaging revealed increased activity in cortical areas associated with semantic and phonological judgments respectively that was consistent with the subliminal prime, as well as increased activity in dorsolateral prefrontal cortex in cases where the subliminal prime and target cue were in conflict. These findings strongly suggest that the goal of making a semantic judgment, for example, was unconsciously activated by the subliminal prime and that it interfered with the operation of the consciously caused goal of making a phonological judgment.

Similarly, Marien et al. (2012) designed a number of experiments to investigate the question whether subliminally primed goals would interfere with tasks that require significant executive-function resources. For unconscious goals, if they exist, should compete for control of attentional resources in the service of their own achievement, just as do consciously caused ones. This would then reduce the resources available to serve other goals, such as the ones that participants are pursuing consciously. In some of the experiments the participants' primary task was, in effect, a working-memory one. They were shown a display of four letters and then, after a delay of a few seconds, were presented with a probe letter and required to judge whether or not it belonged to the initial set. Tasks of this sort are known to require inhibition of memories deriving from immediately preceding displays, which would otherwise interfere with judgments relating to the target. In one experiment participants were subliminally primed with the goal of socializing, whereas in another they were primed with a goal known to be important to them individually from a previous questionnaire. Reaction times in trials where the working-memory task required inhibition of previous memories were significantly slower among subliminally primed participants than in controls, suggesting that their newly active unconscious goal had hijacked some of the attentional resources required for the task. Marien et al. were able to show, moreover, that this did not just result from a decrease in motivation toward the primary task, since the effect was not moderated when people were paid to succeed in that task. The finding also generalized to other tasks requiring attentional control, such as detecting errors in text.

1.2. All goals are unconscious

These and voluminous other data demonstrate that goals *can* (and sometimes do) operate unconsciously. This secures one of the main assumptions required for the truth of the sensory-based accounts of reflection and the stream of consciousness to be presented in this and the following chapter. But of course such data cannot demonstrate that goals *always* operate unconsciously. Nevertheless, this stronger conclusion is warranted, I suggest, by combining the claim that goals *can* operate unconsciously with three additional assumptions. The first is that goals themselves are amodal states, as discussed in Chapter 2.2. (Recall that goals are non-affective intention-like states, which have propositional contents structured out of amodal concepts.) The second assumption is the global broadcasting account of consciousness, discussed in Chapter 3.2. (Recall that access-conscious states are those that are made widely available to other states and faculties of the mind. Moreover, since one can know through swift self-interpretation that a mental state is occurring, it is not sufficient for a state to be conscious that one should know intuitively that it exists.) And the third assumption is the denial of an amodal global workspace, defended in Chapters 4 and 5. (Recall that the evidence suggests that amodal attitudes cannot be globally broadcast, and that amodal concepts can only be conscious when bound into the contents of globally broadcast sensory-like states.) When taken together, these claims entail that no goals are ever conscious. Hence they can *only* operate unconsciously.

This argument is not conclusive, of course. In part this is because it depends on a number of inferences to the best explanation. But it is also because we have yet to consider the possibility that some kinds of conscious sensory-based event (such as saying to oneself, in inner or outer speech, "I will be a home-owner one day") can be, or can *constitute*, a sort of goal-state. Some versions of this idea will be considered in Chapter 7.

2. Attention as Action

Recall from Chapter 1.1 that conscious reflection is the subset of the stream of consciousness that strikes people as being under their control. One can, to a significant degree, *direct* the course of one's reflections in the service of one's goals. One can focus on thinking about the solution to a particular problem, or one can choose to replay a familiar fantasy in order to relax before falling asleep. The active nature of reflection is something that I endorse. But if reflection is sensory based, as I suggest, and involves rehearsal and manipulation of sensory-based information in working memory, then attention, too, must be under intentional control. For as we have seen, attention is the primary cause of global broadcasting, and is a major determinant of the contents of working memory. The present section will elaborate and begin to defend this idea.

2.1. What are actions?

Before discussing the active nature of attention, a prior question to consider is what actions, in general, are. From a common-sense perspective, the paradigm case of an action is a bodily movement that is caused and controlled by an immediately preceding decision to act. First we engage in practical reasoning in light of our beliefs and desires; then we decide; and the decision (if the decision is for the here-and-now) creates an intention that causes and controls the motor processes that issue in the movements decided upon. But of course practical reasoning often concerns what to do in the future, rather than the here-and-now. In this case the result of a decision is the formation of a standing intention, or intention for the future, which is later activated when the circumstances required for the execution of the action obtain.

It seems plausible, however, that these two cases follow essentially the same pattern. That is, in the second case the activated intention interacts with judgments about the current circumstances to issue in a *decision* to act *now* (but without any need for further practical reasoning about whether or not to act at all; Bratman, 1987), which leads the intention to initiate and control the resulting bodily movements. So the suggestion that actions are bodily movements caused by immediately preceding decisions can be allowed to stand. If the idea of *mental* action is to make any sense, then this analysis needs to be made more abstract, of course. One could say, perhaps, that an action is any *event* (whether involving bodily movements or not) that is directly caused and controlled by an immediately preceding decision.

Although intuitive, we now know that not all bodily actions fit this pattern. This is because many movements are caused and controlled directly by perceptions of affordances in the environment in the *absence* of a decision *not* to act. Perceptions of familiar tools, for example, automatically activate the motor plans for their use, which need to be inhibited by top-down executive signals if they are not to be carried through to completion (Frith et al., 2000; Negri et al., 2007). As a result, people with certain forms of frontal-lobe damage can suffer from *utilization syndrome*, meaning that they cannot inhibit themselves from grasping and using things in accordance with those things' affordances (Lhermitte, 1983, 1986). For example, if a glass is placed on the desk, the patient will reach for it; and if a pitcher of water is placed on the desk as well, he will pour water into the glass and drink, irrespective of the context. Intuitively these are nevertheless forms of action. They are controlled and apparently goal-directed, and lack the ballistic quality of obvious non-actions like the knee-jerk reflex.

One option would be to say that there are two distinct kinds of action. There are movements that are caused and controlled by immediately prior decisions. (These might be called "intentional actions.") And there are movements that are caused and controlled by motor plans in the absence of a decision not to act. (These might be called "automatic actions.") Another option, however, would be to extract the common core from the two kinds, and say that an action is a bodily movement that is caused and controlled by a motor plan. For in the case of intentional actions, too, the result of a decision to act is presumably the activation and execution of an appropriate set of motor schemata. If this latter option were to be adopted, then that would probably restrict the range of potential mental actions to the set of mental events (such as inner speech) that are caused and controlled by mental *rehearsals* of action, which likewise activate an appropriate set of motor schemata. Attentional processes would thus likely be excluded.

It is unclear which of these alternatives better reflects the underlying reality of the mind, or which will prove more theoretically fruitful for cognitive science. But even if it should turn out that the motor-plan conception of action is more scientifically robust, we can still say that mental events that are caused and controlled by an immediately preceding decision are at least action *like*. That will be sufficient for our purposes.

2.2. The control of attention

Attention is a form of basic action (or is at least an action-like event), I suggest. Attending is something one can "just do," without knowing how one does it, just as lifting one's arm is something one can do without knowing how. Attention is not, of course, a physical action. Rather, it is a mental action. What makes it active is that it is (generally) caused by *decisions* to attend, where these decisions are informed by knowledge of the context together with current goals and standing values. This account will be supported in due course, in part through its capacity to explain familiar features of conscious reflection and the stream of consciousness more generally. (Sections 3 and 4 of this chapter will focus on reflection, while Section 5 discusses mind wandering.) It is also supported by recent models that see the role of anterior cingulate cortex as mediating between bottom-up and top-down forms of attention, making cost–benefit calculations about the allocation of top-down executive resources (Shenhav et al., 2013). But at least a limited version of the idea comports quite well with aspects of common-sense belief. For we know that one can, at will, comply with a request to attend to one thing rather than another (just as one can comply with a request to raise an arm), and we know that one can *try*, but fail, to attend to something (just as one can try, but fail, to raise an arm). In these respects, at least, attending seems thoroughly action-like.

Often, of course, things just seem to *grab* one's attention. In such cases attending seems passive rather than active. It seems to be something that happens to one rather than something that one does. But most instances of bottom-up attentional capture are really active in nature. Or so I will initially suggest here, and then defend more fully in Section 5. (Exceptions might include the impact of highly salient stimuli like loud noises, bright flashes, or sudden dramatic movements, which can redirect attention without much involvement from frontal decision-making systems.) As we noted in Chapter 3.4, the bottom-up cortical attentional system continually monitors unattended aspects of the input, checking those representations for relevance to ongoing goals and existing values, and competing to redirect the top-down attentional system accordingly (Corbetta & Shulman, 2002; Corbetta et al., 2008). When it succeeds, and attention is captured, this is best seen as resulting from a *decision* to attend to the novel stimulus because of its apparent relevance. The difference is just that in such cases one is generally unaware of the rationale underlying the decision. Hence such cases do not strike one intuitively as agentive in nature, in contrast with cases where, for example, one knows that one is actively complying with an experimenter's request to attend to one thing rather than another.

We noted in Chapter 2.1 that value-processing interacts with perceptual processes at many different levels within perceptual networks (Barrett & Bar, 2009). One way of understanding why this should be so is that it drives the competition for attentional resources. One cannot attend to everything, of course. Indeed, quite the contrary: attention is a highly limited resource (Cowan, 2001). Hence it is important that it should be allocated wisely, directed toward those stimuli that matter most. And just as one might then expect, the bottom-up attentional or "salience" network is partly defined through the involvement of sub-cortical valuational systems (Menon, 2011; Yeo et al., 2011). Perceptual processing thus involves a hierarchy of increasingly fine-grained, context-sensitive value judgments, with the eventual winners becoming the targets of the sort of top-down attention that is needed for them to be globally broadcast, and thus to become widely accessible to numerous systems throughout the brain. Just as actions are generally initiated by decisions made in the light of value judgments together with current circumstances, so, too, are allocations of top-down attention, I will suggest.

2.3. Unconscious decisions

Why should we regard the events that issue in the control and redirection of attention as *decisions*, however? Primarily, this is because those events fit much of the functional profile of decisions, and so are at least decision-*like*. We noted in Chapter 2.2 that decisions are events that conclude an episode of practical reasoning about what to do, immediately issuing in intentions that cause and control the decided-upon actions. And it seems that attentional shifts, likewise, are caused by events that conclude episodes of (unconscious) reasoning about which of the representations competing for attentional resources are the most relevant. If we assume that such shifts are themselves actions, then the event that concludes the process of reasoning about what to attend to, which causes such a shift, looks much like a decision. And indeed, it seems to be the very same sorts of computation of the expected value of cognitive control, taking place in anterior cingulate cortex (which also serves as the primary mediator between bottom-up and top-down forms of attention), that issue not only in actions of a physical sort but also in redirections of attention (Shenhav et al., 2013). So there are theoretical gains to be had from treating both sorts of conflict-resolving event as kinds of decision. We can thereby unify two sets of phenomena under the same explanatory umbrella, constituting a single natural kind.

It might be objected that the events that shift or maintain attention are not (or not generally) *personal-level* decisions. It is not *the person* who decides to shift attention to the sound of his own name, and away from a current conversation at a party, thereby giving rise to the so-called "cocktail party effect." Rather, it is a subcomponent or module within the person that does so. Now, sometimes the language of "personal" versus "subpersonal" is used just to mean "conscious" versus "unconscious." But in that case an argument exactly parallel to the one presented in Section 1.2 for the case of goals will establish that there are no such things as personal-level (conscious) decisions. At other times personal-level mental events are understood to be those that the entire agent controls, or that all (or most) of the mental states of the agent can contribute to. This idea can still be made good sense of, as we will see in Chapter 9. But it does nothing to challenge the claim that the events that determine shifts of attention are a species of decision. Let me elaborate.

In denying that decisions themselves are ever conscious one need not deny that any of the processes that *issue in* decisions are ever conscious, of course. Nor need one deny that there are any personal-level decisions in the above whole-agent sense. So consider a case where one reasons, consciously, about whether to shift attention for a while to another conversation. When the sound of one's own name pops out, one might say to oneself in inner speech, "She is talking about me. Should I listen in?" The resulting contents are globally broadcast to many different regions of the mind, giving all of them a chance to contribute to the decision-making process. (The process that shifted attention to the sound of one's own name in the first place, in contrast, was a much more local affair.) But any representations evoked by one's conscious reflections will still need to compete with one another to influence one's attentional control processes. And it is still likely to be cost–benefit analyses conducted in anterior cingulate that determine the result. I suggest, in fact, that both conscious and unconscious decision-making processes issue in events of the same kind: unconscious decisions.

2.4. How remembering works

The idea that attending is action-like can be put to work in understanding how, in outline at least, memory-search operates. (Recall from Chapter 4.1 that episodic memory is heavily attention dependent.) And note that memory-search, too, is intuitively active in nature, at least on many occasions. (Exceptions will include cases where memories seem to spring to mind unbidden, perhaps evoked by a spoken phrase or a familiar scent. But again I will argue that even these seemingly passive instances of remembering are really action-like in nature.) One can try but fail to remember something. And one engages in active, motivated, memory-search every time one tries to answer a question. Moreover, remembering can unfold over time in accordance with one's goals, as one gradually builds and elaborates a memory of some important event. Yet we know that conscious remembering results from targeted attention (De Brigard, 2012). So if remembering is active in nature, this reinforces the claim that attending is too.

It has been known for some time that parietal cortex plays important roles in episodic remembering (Wagner et al., 2005). Indeed, damage to ventral parietal cortex causes a form of *memory neglect* (Berryhill, 2012). People with damage to this region have trouble spontaneously activating relevant details into memory, whereas they can still recover those details when directly questioned (Berryhill et al., 2007). These findings make sense once we realize that episodic memory involves both top-down and bottom-up attentional networks, which are centered on the intraparietal sulcus and areas of ventral parietal cortex respectively (Cabeza, 2008; Ciaramelli et al., 2008). When searching for a memory one uses the cues provided to evoke activity in those sensory-involving regions where the information is stored, utilizing the back-projecting conceptual-to-perceptual networks discussed in Chapter 3.5, and using the top-down attentional system to target and globally broadcast the results.

A prediction of this account is that activity around the intraparietal sulcus should be highest when memory-search is most effortful and attentionally demanding, and thus when memory performance and memory confidence are both low. That is, indeed, what we find (Kim & Cabeza, 2007). When memories are *evoked*, in contrast, the bottom-up attentional system monitors the representations produced and evaluates their relevance to one another and to the probe, attracting top-down attention when there is a good enough fit. This predicts that activity in ventral parietal cortex should be highest when memories are rich in detail, and when both confidence and accuracy are highest. This, too, is what we find (Kim & Cabeza, 2007).

This model of the involvement of the two attentional systems in episodic memory is also consistent with the finding of strong neural connections between ventral parietal cortex and the hippocampal formation, which is known to play a vital role in memory storage and retrieval (Vincent et al., 2006). It makes sense that evoked information should be received by ventral parietal cortex in the first instance (just as bottom-up perceptual contents are), so that they can be evaluated for relevance, attracting top-down attention (and hence becoming globally broadcast) if they should pass muster.

While evidence of the involvement of top-down attention in episodic remembering is robust (Hutchinson et al., 2009; Cabeza et al., 2010; De Brigard, 2012), there may be less overlap in the bottom-up saliency mechanisms involved in perception and episodic memory respectively. Specifically, while the bottom-up perceptual-attention system is largely lateralized to the right hemisphere, the bottom-up memory system is mostly lateralized to the left (Ciaramelli et al., 2008; Hutchinson et al., 2009). Moreover, the regions of ventral parietal cortex that are involved are only partly overlapping, with the perceptual-saliency system being located around and above the temporo-parietal junction, whereas the mnemonic-saliency system is lower, overlapping parts of the temporal lobe (Sestieri et al., 2010; Cabeza et al., 2012). It makes sense that the mechanisms that process the relevance of perceptual and mnemonic representations should be to some degree specialized, and also that they should be partly segregated so that both processes can continue in parallel. For one needs to monitor the environment for relevance while engaged in stimulus-independent thought, of course. And we have reason to think that activated memories, too, are continually monitored while one focuses on an external task, causing one's mind to wander when some of those memories are deemed to be sufficiently relevant.

On the account sketched here, evoked memories are likely to be just as active as memories that are searched for, although they are less obviously so from the perspective of the person doing the remembering. (In the former case a memory just appears in consciousness, seemingly unbidden, whereas in the latter case the memory will have been preceded by a question of some sort that one is aware of.) Consider a case where a waft of cinnamon when passing a shop evokes a sudden vivid memory of a dinner eaten in the Moroccan quarter of the French city of Avignon some years before. The smell in question activates associated representations that are linked both to it and to one another as a result of the original event. These are received in ventral parietal cortex where they are processed, and from where messages are exchanged with ventrolateral prefrontal cortex and subcortical value systems, assessing their relevance to one's goals and values. Since the Avignon dinner is linked to a number of important values (a shared experience with one's spouse, love of all things French, and so on), it is found relevant enough to enter into competition (via the anterior cingulate) with the goals controlling the current focus of attention. By hypothesis, it wins this competition, resulting in a decision to redirect top-down attention to the memory representations in question, rendering them conscious. The experience of the memory thus results from an action or action-like event (a redirecting of attention), although it doesn't seem like that to the agent.

2.5. Memory-search and spatial search

Not only is attention action-like in the ways discussed above, but it also plausibly evolved from related forms of *physical* action. Recall from Chapter 3.4 that the frontal eye-fields are an important component of the top-down attentional network. These regions of the dorsal prefrontal cortex are parts of premotor and motor cortex, and play a central role in the control of eye movements (as does the intraparietal sulcus). And we know that eye movements are generally under intentional control, even in infancy (Kidd et al., 2012). Often, of course, one's eyes and one's covert attention will shift together, and generally one attends to what one is overtly looking at. But we know that this is not strictly necessary. One can look in one direction while attending elsewhere. And many eye movements are best thought of as exploring a single object of attention, without being accompanied by any shifts in attention. Moreover, attention can zoom in or out even when one's eyes and one's attention are both focused in the same direction (Kosslyn, 1994). So the frontal eye-fields appear to form a common component in two partially distinct controllers: one for overt eye movements and one for covert attention.

As we will see in Chapter 8, attentional systems are highly conserved across species. And we know that overt and covert visual attention can be deployed separately in both birds and mammals (Mysore & Knudsen, 2013). Moreover, it is plausible that capacities for covert attention evolved from earlier capacities for the control of eye movements. This would explain why they are subserved, in part, by the same brain regions. But in any case what surely follows is that the mechanisms that control top-down covert attention are ideally positioned to be intentionally controlled by one's goals and decisions. For eye movements, like most other forms of movement, are under intentional control. So the neural wiring necessary to exert that control would already have been in place when the frontal eye-fields (or their evolutionary precursors) began also to direct covert forms of attention.

Interestingly, a number of recent studies support both the active nature of attending and the suggestion that covert attentional control may have evolved from earlier mechanisms for controlling overt movement. These studies demonstrate commonalities among spatial search, attentional search of the environment, and attentional search of memory, together with evidence of a phylogenetic progression from the former to the latter (Hills, 2006). Not only is there evidence of common search strategies in the three domains, but also evidence that the neural mechanisms underlying these strategies in all three domains are similar, involving reward-processing doperminergic networks (Hills & Dukas, 2012).[1]

All animals confront the problem of searching for valued resources, which involves a trade-off between exploration and exploitation. Often such resources are patchily distributed in the environment, and patches differ in their size and value. The problem for any animal is then: when to stay and when to go? Time spent exploring is time that is not spent exploiting whatever valuable resource is at stake. But on the other hand, if one spends too long extracting value from any given patch, one may lose out on more valuable patches nearby. In the context of foraging, this problem has been extensively studied, and many of the search heuristics employed by animals in different environments—most of which approximate to an optimal foraging strategy—are known (Stephens & Krebs, 1987).

More recently, people have realized that *cognitive* search shares much of the same structure. Not everything in one's immediate environment is equally interesting, and features of interest are often patchily distributed. The same holds for regions of one's visual field. Both overt and covert attention thus face the same exploration–exploitation trade-off (Hills & Dukas, 2012). Moreover,

---

[1] Moreover—and highly relevant to the topic of the present book—variations in capacities for dopermine synthesis in an important part of this network in humans—the ventral striatum—correlate with individual differences in working-memory capacity (Cools et al., 2008). It makes good sense that well-applied strategies for when and why to shift one's attention should be an important component of people's working-memory abilities.

many forms of memory, too, are patchily distributed. Words are linked to one another in clusters, for example, with names of common farm animals being semantically linked to one another while only being distantly linked to names of common African animals, which are in turn strongly linked to one another. Experiments suggest that when people are asked to generate names of animals they follow essentially the same strategy that creatures use when exploiting a patchy environment: they stick with farm animals until names are no longer easy to retrieve, then switch to African animals, and so on (Hills et al., 2012).

These commonalities among spatial search, attentional search, and memory-search do not demonstrate that the same mechanisms are involved in each, of course. But they do suggest that each is equally active in nature, at least to the extent that each can be controlled by the same heuristics that control behavioral search of the physical environment. And as we also noted, this conclusion is further supported by the existence of shared decision-sensitive neural mechanisms (especially the frontal eye-fields).

2.6. Habits of attention and cross-cultural differences

If attention is a form of action, as I have been suggesting, then it should be controllable in any of the ways that overt action can be controlled. My focus in this section so far has been on *intentional* control, arguing that attention, too, is controlled by (unconscious) decisions taken in the light of one's goals and standing values. But actions can also be *habitual*, of course. In such cases features of the context will trigger a motor schema directly unless inhibited, without the need for evaluation or decision making (Lisman & Sternberg, 2013).

It is certainly intuitive that patterns of attention can become habitual, although I know of no direct scientific work on the topic. Someone might say, for example, "Whenever I enter a new place, I find myself scanning for the exits." Cases like this could just as well be explained in terms of intentional attention-allocation, however, caused by persisting motivational states (in this case, anxiety). More promising, perhaps, are cases of habitual *thought*, given that these are caused by the way in which one directs one's attention. Someone who habitually calls up the same set of images when lying down to sleep at night may well exhibit patterns of attention that are genuinely habitual and non-intentional.

Indirect evidence of habitual use of attention can be gleaned from the literature on cross-cultural differences in cognition, however, particularly the finding of systematic use of "holistic" versus "analytical" processing styles in Eastern versus Western cultures (Nisbett, 2003). Among these differences are variations in the way that members of the two cultures attend to, and hence recall, visual scenes

(Ji et al., 2000; Masuda & Nisbett, 2001). For example, when presented with a picture of some fish swimming, Japanese people might pay as much attention to the background of reeds and rocks as they do to the fish themselves. As a result, when shown a picture of a lone fish and asked to recall whether it was in the original picture, they are helped if contextual cues are provided. In contrast, Americans shown the same picture will attend mostly to the focal fish, paying little attention to the background. As a result, contextual details fail to aid them when asked to recall an individual fish. Indeed, they are *better* able to recognize an individual fish in the *absence* of any background.

How are these findings to be explained? We know that the differences don't result from long-term structural cognitive–perceptual differences between Easterners and Westerners. In part this is because the effects are reversible using simple forms of priming (Oyserman & Lee, 2008). A Westerner who is asked to read a passage containing repeated use of the terms "we," "us," and "our" (emphasizing collections of people) will thereafter perceive and recall the pictures in a manner normal for an Easterner. Likewise, Japanese people who read the same passage only with the words "I," "me," and "mine" substituted throughout (emphasizing the individual) will thereafter perceive and recall the pictures in the manner of a Westerner. It also seems unlikely that these patterns of attention are *motivated* ones, with Easterners frequently taking (unconscious) *decisions* to attend to the background while Westerners often decide to ignore the background. Rather, what seems most plausible is that while both patterns of attending remain easily *available* to members of both groups, differences in cultural norms and expectations give rise to an *habitual* tendency on the part of Easterners to pay attention to contexts and situational factors, as well as to a corresponding habitual tendency on the part of Westerners to direct attention toward focal individuals. If this is true, then it provides an additional reason to think that attending is genuinely action-like.

3. Mental Rehearsal and Mental Manipulation

Recall from Chapter 4.4 that the functions of working memory are normally thought to include capacities to *activate*, *sustain*, *rehearse*, and *manipulate* representations. The first two functions depend directly on the allocation of attention. Section 2 has argued that this is an active process, and is generally directed by decisions taken in the light of one's goals and values. The present section will argue that rehearsal and manipulation are also forms of action. In addition, it will begin to demonstrate how the present framework can explain familiar features of reflection.

3.1. *Mental rehearsal as off-line action*

As we saw in Chapter 4.4, mental rehearsal is really just off-line action, with the predicted sensory consequences of action attended to and globally broadcast while movements of the muscles are suppressed (see Figure 5). So mental rehearsal can be guided and influenced by anything that can guide and influence action generally (with the exception of afferent sensory feedback from the body or world, of course, since no movements are really made). In particular, like overt action, mental rehearsal can be guided by current goals and values, as well as other items of information that are active in one's mind at the time. Our focus in this section will be on rehearsal of non-speech actions, together with their role in prospection and future decision making. Inner speech will form the topic of Section 4.

Mentally rehearsed actions cannot be motivated in exactly the same way that overt actions are, of course, if only because something must lead to the suppression of overt movement in the former cases. Indeed, part of what it means to be a reflective (as opposed to an unreflective) person is that one frequently inhibits one's initial overt response to a situation or question and mentally rehearses it instead, evaluating the imagined result. Such inhibition might be habitual, or it might be motivated by chronic caution or some other goal or value. In effect, one thinks, "I am tempted to say/do X. But is that really the best response?" In such cases the goals and values that underlie the mental rehearsal can be just the same as those that would motivate the overt action, but perhaps with the added goal of not acting prematurely. (If the person's reflectiveness is *habitual*, in contrast, then the motivational factors involved can be exactly the same.) The result is that the decision is a decision to activate-and-suppress (that is, mentally rehearse), rather than to act.

Not all mental rehearsal is externally prompted, of course. Indeed, quite the contrary. Since so-called "stimulus-independent thought" occupies much of our waking lives, and since a good deal of this involves mental rehearsals of action of one sort or another, much mental rehearsal must involve more than mere inhibition of an externally prompted action. (This is a topic we will return to in Section 5.) But one plausible possibility is that what it *is* to be engaged in, or to switch into, stimulus-independent thought is that one has (or that one activates) the standing goal of inhibiting the execution of any intentionally controlled action.[2]

---

[2] Of course one can engage in stimulus-independent thought while walking or driving, say. But these actions are very likely habitual ones, involving interactions between perception and the motor system, without the intervention of goals or decisions.

Consider, for simplicity, some cases where reflection is already ongoing. Suppose a practiced skier is engaged in a fantasy ski-run down a mountain she will visit that weekend. In the course of this she imagines a tree straight ahead with some rocks to its left. (This might be thrown up by attention directed at memories of the mountain, or by quasi-random activation and attention to things that one might confront while skiing. See Section 5.) As a result, she immediately activates the motor schemata for a right-hand turn, and her imagined ski-run unfolds accordingly. Here the rehearsed action is likely to be habitual, prompted by the imagined scene alone.

Alternatively, think of someone engaged in a fantasy about a Caribbean holiday. He is sitting at a bar with a bottle of his favorite beer in front of him and with the beach behind him. The beer is seen as positively valenced, which activates the motor schemata for reaching out to grasp, lift, and drink it. Accordingly, that is what he imagines himself doing. Here what motivates the imagined action is just what might motivate the real action: the seeming-goodness of drinking the beer, combined with a perceptual representation of it as being within reach.

No doubt there is much more that might be said. (And some of it *will* be said in what follows.) But enough should have been done to support the thesis of this subsection. This is that mentally rehearsed actions are actions in pretty much the same sense as overt ones. They involve activations of motor schemata that are either immediately prompted as part of a habit, or that result from the same sorts of decision-making processes that issue in overt action.

3.2. Three kinds of dynamic imagery

The imagery that results from mental rehearsal of action is, of course, dynamic in character. It will be imagery of perceived or felt movements, together with their likely consequences. But there are other ways of generating dynamic imagery. One is from memory of perceived movements. Creating an image of a horse galloping across the landscape, for example, will require a guided search of memory, using top-down projections of the concept HORSE GALLOPING in coordination with targeted attention. It probably works somewhat as follows. Activation of the concept HORSE GALLOPING triggers associated representations stored in a distributed manner across regions of visual cortex. Those that match the concept sufficiently well become targets of attention, and the resulting dynamic image is thereby made globally accessible.

A similar distinction can be made in connection with dynamic auditory imagery. Imagery of musical melodies, for example, can be created through off-line rehearsal of the actions that would issue in those melodies, by either singing or playing a musical instrument. If the melody is a familiar one, it will be recalled by activating a well-rehearsed sequence of motor schemata. In this case memory for the sound-sequence is really a form of motor-memory, with mental rehearsal of the actions that would produce that sequence being used to create appropriate auditory images. If the melody is a novel one, it will be generated by constrained quasi-random activations of a sequence of component motor schemata. (See Section 5.) On the other hand, a melody can be imagined by directing attention at a memory of the relevant sequence of sounds, perhaps using some sort of conceptual trigger. ("The opening bars of Beethoven's Ninth.") And it may well be possible to create a novel melody in imagination in similar fashion, by targeting memories of short phrases or individual notes in a constrained but quasi-random manner. (Again, see Section 5.) In the first sort of case the active nature of auditory imagery is obvious, since it results from mental rehearsals of sound-producing actions. But even the second sort of case is no less active in nature, given that directing and shifting attention qualify as forms of mental action, as was suggested in Section 2.

There is, in addition, a third way in which dynamic imagery can be produced. This is by directing rehearsed motor movements at an existing perceived object, thereby transforming one's image of the latter in the manner that might be predicted if one were really acting in that way on the object represented. This sort of mental manipulation of imagery has been extensively studied, especially using mental rotation experiments. As a result, we know that activity in motor and premotor cortex is reliably observed during mental rotation (Richter et al., 2000; Vingerhoets et al., 2002). Moreover, mental rotation is impacted by con-current movement. For example, if one moves one's hands to rotate a real object while mentally rotating an image in the same direction, then the latter is speeded up, whereas overt rotation in the contrary direction slows it down (Wexler et al., 1998). In addition, applying transcranial magnetic stimulation (TMS) to the hand region of primary motor cortex interferes with mental rotation (Ganis et al., 2000).[3]

In all of these cases it should be emphasized that dynamic imagery is import-antly predictive in nature. For as representations of the target movements or changes are globally broadcast, they activate both memories and predictive

---

[3] There are other data that suggest, however, that mental rotation can be conducted by infants who as yet lack the physical coordination to really rotate anything. Thus Moore & Johnson (2011) found that three-month-old male—but not female—infants could recognize the completion of a previously habituated partial rotation, in contrast with its mirror-image rotation. One possibility is that there are innate linkages between structures in motor cortex and visual cortex, which mature in males in advance of capacities for overt motor control.

inference-mechanisms to create representations of the likely immediate consequences of those movements or changes. If attended to these, too, will be globally broadcast. Thus when one visually imagines a galloping horse one will be apt also to hear the sound of its hoof-beats in auditory imagination. And when one rehearses the action of throwing a stone at a window, one will likely form an image of the trajectory of the stone and the subsequent shattered glass. As we will see in due course, the predictive character of imagery is one of the things that makes it useful, enabling us to discern and evaluate the likely consequences of our actions in advance.

3.3. Mental manipulation

In the literature on working memory, "manipulation" has both a narrower and a wider meaning. In the narrower sense it refers to the capacity to bring about changes in one's imagery by activating manual motor schemata, as in the mental rotation experiments described above. But in the wider sense, it refers to the capacity to construct ordered sequences of images in the service of one's goals. Examples would include mental arithmetic, spatial planning, and prospective reasoning. (The latter will be discussed in Section 3.4.) In this wider sense mental manipulation is a form of skillful, knowledgeable, intelligent action, and is motivated accordingly. It is this that will be our focus here.

Consider someone tasked with subtracting 17 from 32 in her head, for example. What ensues will be a controlled sequence of auditory imagery, visual imagery, or both combined, implementing well-rehearsed procedures. She might picture the two numerals one above the other, for instance, as if written on the page, and then imagine removing a unit from the "3" and placing it in front of the "2," before saying to herself, "Seven from twelve is five," thereafter mentally inscribing "5" beneath the "7." She then transfers her attention to focus on the left column, which now contains a "2" inscribed above the "1." This immediately enables her to construct the answer: 15. This sequence is plainly active, involving mental rehearsals of familiar actions and action-sequences, combined in a flexible way in response to the initial problem or goal.

Now consider someone driving home after work, who hears on the radio that her normal route has been blocked by an accident. Supposing that an alternative route does not immediately come to mind following a search of memory, she now needs to engage in a sequence of spatial planning. She might call to mind a memory of a road map of the area, for example, or some memory images of major nearby landmarks or roads, which come already flagged as "places I could get to from here" (perhaps by swiftly entertained imagery of the intervening route). She might then say to herself, "From Georgia I could go down Wayne," but this prompts a memory image of long queues at the traffic lights at the junction of Wayne and Flower. This motivates an additional search of memory. Returning to the initial partial map of the nearby roads, for example, she might imagine herself driving up New Hampshire Avenue. As the predicted sequence of sights (drawn from memory) flips by, she says to herself, "Then I could go up Sligo." The resulting image of the initial part of Sligo Parkway feels highly familiar, or issues in a swift sequence of images that terminates at home. So she turns toward a road she knows will lead her to New Hampshire Avenue.

Notice the close parallels between this sequence of working-memory contents and what might happen in a case of real, overt, spatial exploration.[4] The same goal in each case motivates searches of memory, and selects and activates action schemata guided by those memories. In a case of real travel, of course, a sequence of perceptions is caused by one's real movement through the world, whereas in the case of spatial planning the images are called up predictively from memory following each rehearsed action-schema. But both are equally active and intentionally controlled.

Notice, too, how there is a place for something resembling real discovery in cases where one manipulates working-memory contents for purposes of planning. Had our agent *really* driven up Georgia and down Wayne, she might really have encountered a long line of traffic as a result. This is a new (although perhaps predictable) item of information about the world. When rehearsing the route, in contrast, she cannot discover anything that she doesn't already know (albeit implicitly), of course. But what she *can* do is evoke knowledge that would otherwise have remained inaccessible. It is only by imagining herself driving toward the junction of Wayne and Flower that she activates the knowledge that the approach roads are often snarled with traffic. She thereby discovers (in the sense of bringing to consciousness) that this is not a good route to take.

What we have found in these examples extends to mental manipulation of contents in working memory quite generally. Goals motivate both searches of memory and mental rehearsals of action. The resulting contents then evoke yet other memories, or predictions grounded in existing knowledge or procedures. And at each stage (if the account sketched in Section 2 is on the right lines) a multitude of evoked contents will compete with one another through bottom-up attentional networks to attract the spotlight of top-down attention and enter the stream of consciousness. Generally the contents deemed to be most relevant to

---

[4] The main difference is that had she really driven up Georgia and then down Wayne, only to find her route blocked, she would probably not have needed to return to her point of origin in order to find her way home.

the overall goal or goals will win. The result is that not only are the individual stages of the working-memory sequence active in nature, but so too is the sequence as a whole.

3.4. Prospection

Prospective reasoning, in the most general sense, is reasoning about the future. But in the recent literature it has come to acquire a narrower meaning, restricted to cases where one *imagines* or envisages oneself performing one or more future actions, generally for purposes of decision making (Gilbert & Wilson, 2007). It is now widely accepted that capacities for prospection and episodic memory are tightly linked (Schacter et al., 2007; Buckner, 2010). The hippocampus, in particular, is heavily implicated in both, and amnesic patients turn out to have mirroring difficulties in envisaging their own futures. Moreover, some have claimed that the resulting capacity for "mental time-travel" is uniquely human—indeed, that it is perhaps *the* major cognitive factor that distinguishes humans from other animals (Suddendorf & Corballis, 2007; Suddendorf et al., 2009). These claims about human uniqueness will be examined—and critiqued—in Chapter 8.

Episodes of prospective reasoning are often prompted by an externally presented question or choice, as when one is asked whether one would rather do A or B, or when one receives a job offer and has to decide whether or not to accept. But they are also frequently self-initiated during mind wandering. Someone entertaining a job offer, for example, will probably revisit the choice on a number of occasions each day for multiple days or weeks before reaching a decision, often breaking off from other attentionally demanding activities to do so. Internally prompted forms of prospection will be considered in Section 5. Here we can focus on cases where the initial stimulus comes from outside.

Sometimes prospective reasoning will start from mental rehearsals of the actions being considered. In such cases the process is quite obviously active in nature. If asked, "Would you rather climb that fence or walk around to the gate?," one may rehearse the two actions involved. In the one case this issues in imagery of one approaching the fence, clambering up it and then down the other side. As a result one experiences, predictively, some of the effort likely to be involved, and one's imagination may also become elaborated with likely side-effects, such as a painful fall to the ground if one catches one's leg on the top rung. (Such elaboration is especially likely to occur if episodic memories of oneself or others suffering similar falls are evoked.) In the other case mental rehearsal will issue in imagery of walking some distance up the hill to the gate that can be seen in the distance (or that is known to be there), again resulting in a prediction of the effort involved. As we will see shortly, the decision that one takes between the two options will often be grounded in one's overall affective reaction to each scenario.

On other occasions prospection can start from imagery of some of the known consequences of the action being considered. Confronted with a job offer that would require relocating to Chicago, for example, one may imagine being in Chicago. This is likely to build from episodic memories of visits one has made to the city (where available), or from images that one has of it from movies or the TV news. One might imagine walking along the lake shore with the city skyline alongside; or one might imagine taking a boat ride on one of the canals. Or one might simply imagine oneself being in one of Chicago's streets. Again, what one imagines is likely to become predictively enriched as further knowledge of the city or the job opportunity is evoked. One might imagine oneself huddled in a winter coat against the bitter winter winds, with one's face going numb from the cold. Or one might imagine oneself working alongside future colleagues whom one has already met at interview. The overall sequence of reflection will result from a complex amalgam of mentally rehearsed actions together with images called into working memory from searches of long-term memory using targeted attention. In any case, here, too, the process is thoroughly action-like, with the overall sequence intentionally controlled by the goal of reaching a decision.

When one engages in prospective forms of reflection, the images that one entertains in working memory will be made available to affective and evaluative networks, among others, as a result of being globally broadcast. These systems respond with some degree of positive or negative affect. This might include some of the bodily changes constitutive of the affective states in question (some visceral, some motor), or swift "as-if" predictions thereof, which can be monitored and used as cues for decision making (Damasio, 1994). But much more important, in my view, is the valence component of affect, which will lead the represented scenarios to seem good or bad to one as one reflects (Carruthers, 2011a). The result is that one option will come to strike one as intuitively better than the other, leading one to choose it.

Orbitofrontal cortex is known to be the main terminus of affective processing in the brain, and damage to this region is known to result in greatly impoverished decision making (Damasio, 1994; Rolls, 1999). Strikingly, patients with orbitofrontal damage can still reason perfectly sensibly about the options open to them, and can offer well-articulated reasons for and against each. Indeed, in many cases their theoretical judgments of which option would be better are quite normal. But their actual decisions fail to reflect those judgments. It seems that there is an immense difference between explicitly *judging* that an option is good and *seeing it as such*. The latter is constituted by the valence component of affective processing, and seems to depend especially on the normal functioning of orbitofrontal cortex. It appears that valence is needed to provide the motivation for making one decision rather than another.

We also know that when explicit forms of decision making, involving articulated reasons, are pitted against the intuitive affective results of prospection, the latter will often prove superior. This is especially likely where the good-making features of a choice are not obvious, or not easy to articulate (Wilson et al., 1993), or when multiple good-making features need to be combined to reach an overall evaluation (Dijksterhuis et al., 2006). It seems that one of the adaptive (but also potentially misleading) features of the affective system is that valence produced by multiple properties of a situation or thing can be summed together into an overall affective intuition, in ways that are hard to mimic through discursive reasoning (Carruthers, 2011a). In such cases one will just *see* one option as better than another while being unable to articulate why.[5]

Another adaptive feature of affect-based prospective decision making can be inferred from the mechanisms governing entry into working memory, discussed briefly in Section 2. We noted that searches of memory (and probably also mental rehearsals of action) issue in bottom-up forms of relevance-competition. Multiple representations will generally become active in response to any specific memory cue (and multiple action schemata will likewise become active as one searches for actions that might realize a goal). These will compete with one another through the bottom-up attentional mechanism to attract the spotlight of top-down attention and thus enter working memory. As we noted earlier, these competitive processes will involve tacit judgments of value and of relevance to current goals. The images that enter working memory when one engages reflectively in prospection will thus already have been pre-selected as especially relevant to the task or decision at hand.

The upshot of our discussion in this section is that the sensory-based model of reflection has the resources to explain many familiar facts about the nature of reflection, together with a number of less familiar ones as well. Moreover, all of the processes we have considered turn out to be action-like in nature, resulting from intentionally controlled forms of mental rehearsal and attention-allocation.

---

[5] Or rather, one's attempts at articulation will often fail to track the actual adaptive value of the decision. One can always confabulate an answer, of course, and people in such circumstances often do.

4. Generating Inner Speech

Much of the time, when we reflect, our reflections involve inner speech.[6] The active character of inner speech has already been discussed in Chapter 4.4. We noted that it depends on the mental rehearsal of speech actions, issuing in forward models of the likely sensory consequences of those actions (normally, heard speech). When attended, these sensory predictions are globally broadcast and processed by the language comprehension system. The result is that one *hears oneself as* wondering or asserting some specific content in inner speech. It seems plain, then, that this form of reflection is not only active in nature but sensory based.

On the account of reflective thinking being defended in this book, the contents of working memory (especially when stimulus-independent, as is inner speech) are both controlled and motivated by one's goals and values in the light of current or recently salient information. To be plausible, this should come paired with a mirroring account of the production of overt speech. For it seems quite unlikely that inner speech should be controlled by unconscious forms of decision making whereas overt speech is not. One aim of the present section is to determine whether this commitment to parallelism between inner and outer speech is plausible. Another is to provide a sketch of how covert uses of speech can constitute familiar forms of reflection.

4.1. Speech as a form of unconscious goal pursuit

Standard models of speech production take their start from a communicative intention, or a *thought to be expressed* (Levelt, 1989). But of course speech is generally in the service of wider goals. One may be attempting to persuade someone of something, attempting to establish a rapport with a potential business collaborator, or attempting to impress a potential employer. So at the very least, one's communicative intention is always to express a given thought in the service of some further goal or goals. Sometimes these goals are ones that the speaker knows about, and could articulate if asked.[7] But often they are not. The literature in social psychology is rife with effects on people's speech behavior of goals that speakers are presumably unaware of at the time. These include self-presentation effects, desires to fulfill (or frustrate) the goals that they tacitly

---

[6] Note, however, that proportions of inner speech, visual imagery, and other forms of stimulus-independent thought vary significantly between people (Heavey & Hurlburt, 2008).

[7] Let me stress again that this does not mean that those goals are conscious. For consciousness requires global broadcasting, rather than knowledge grounded in inferences from ancillary cues.

attribute to their interlocutor, and so on (Kunda, 1999; Moskowitz, 2005; Fiske & Taylor, 2008). For example, people who expect to have their opinions on a topic challenged will modify the views that they express in the direction of those of their audience, presumably with the goal of avoiding confrontation (Cialdini & Petty, 1981).

For a clear example of the effects of unconscious (and competing) goals on speech behavior, we can return to the well-validated findings of the counterattitudinal essay paradigm, discussed in Chapter 5.2. Recall that after writing an essay arguing for the contrary of what they really believe people will (if their freedom of choice in writing the essay is made salient to them) thereafter express a belief that is much closer to the view they have been defending. We know that they do this in order to make themselves feel better about what they have done, or to present their actions in a better light. Yet it is quite unlikely that this goal is a conscious one. For if it were, and people were aware of saying something other than they believe, then one would expect them to feel *worse* as a result, not better. But notice that the goal of saying what is true (or saying what one believes) does not cease to have any influence at all. If it did, then one would expect people to report the *opposite* of what they believe (that is, the same as the belief they have been arguing for). For that would present their behavior in the *best* light. Rather, people's expressed beliefs are generally somewhere around the middle of the scale between what they really believe and the view they have just been defending. This is best understood as resulting from an unconscious *compromise* between two incompatible goals.

Items of information, too, can compete for expression outside of one's awareness. And sometimes distinct and incompatible items of information can be expressed simultaneously (in different modalities) in the service of the very same goal. This is nicely illustrated by the work of Goldin-Meadow (2005) on gesture. Children who are trying to explain how to solve a math problem will sometimes *say* that the numbers should be combined in a certain order (incorrectly) while at the same time their hand gestures reveal knowledge of the correct groupings. This is especially likely to happen among children who are on the cusp of being able to answer correctly. It seems that the goal of saying how the numbers should be grouped can lead one to express incompatible beliefs in different modalities simultaneously.

Speech is, of course, a form of action. And like other forms of action it can be undertaken in the service of multiple goals influenced by multiple forms of information, often outside of the awareness of the speaker. These points can nevertheless be rendered consistent with the standard model (Levelt, 1989), provided that all of this decision making takes place prior to the formation of a communicative intention (that is, prior to selection of a thought to be expressed). But it seems much more likely that speech production (like speech comprehension; Hickok & Poeppel, 2007) proceeds in parallel (or at least interactively; Nozari et al., 2011) with decisions about *what* to say being taken while one is in the process of saying it (Dennett, 1991; Lind et al., 2014).

This suggestion is consistent with the findings reported by Novick et al. (2010), that patients with damage to Broca's area (leading to a form of production aphasia) also show much wider deficits, especially in their capacity to inhibit prepotent actions. (For example, they perform quite poorly in the Stroop test.) For such people's expressive difficulties emerge only in cases where there are many competing things they could say. For example, when asked to generate verbs associated with a given noun, patients with damage to Broca's area may become paralyzed when prompted with "ball," since there are many related verbs to choose from ("throw," "kick," "pass," "catch," and so on), while performing as normal when prompted with "scissors," which is associated with just a single action ("cut"). Similarly, healthy people given the same test show increased activity in Broca's area when selecting a verb out of many alternatives, as well as during conflicting-action trials of the Stroop test. At the very least these findings establish that speech production involves competition among expressive *actions*, as well as competition between thoughts to be expressed.

The competitive processes involved in speech production are generally unconscious, of course. Indeed, just as value is processed unconsciously during bottom-up perceptual processing, often issuing in decisions to shift attention from one thing to another, so too is it processed in competition among motor schemata. Decisions about what to say, what words to use, and so on are generally taken "on the fly," resulting from swift evaluations of the competing alternatives. The same is then presumably true in connection with inner speech, thus meshing quite nicely with the account of reflective thinking being presented here.

4.2. Goals in inner speech

Sometimes the goals that guide and motivate inner speech are precisely those that would guide and motivate overt speech (except that something must motivate suppression of overt speech actions in the former case). For sometimes inner speech takes the form of an imagined conversation, or at least speech directed toward an imagined audience. Sometimes one rehearses (and thereby consciously evaluates) what one could say, or should say, or could *have* said to someone. These cases fit the mold of mental rehearsals of action generally, especially as used in prospection. And the same goals will then be in play as would figure in overt actions of the same sort. It seems unlikely, however, that inner speech is always of this kind. In particular, what goals motivate one's production of inner speech in cases where there is no imagined audience?

Sometimes inner speech is directed toward the solution of some problem. This is supported by the findings of so-called "think aloud" protocols, undertaken while people attempt to solve problems that admit of systematic (uncreative) solutions. (In cases requiring a creative solution, thinking aloud seems actually to impair performance; Schooler et al., 1993.) In these circumstances speech productions turn out to mirror one or another of the objectively determined strategies toward a solution, and the time-course of the sequence maps smoothly onto what happens when people are asked to solve the same problem silently (Ericsson & Simon, 1993). It seems that in such cases one's goal, in producing any given sentence, is to state the next step toward a solution. This issues in a speech act that is globally broadcast, interpreted, and evaluated for relevance and likely success. So there need be no communicative intent, and no goal of producing an effect in an audience. Here the function of inner speech seems comparable to the function of writing that is undertaken for one's own benefit, as when one writes solely to work out one's thoughts. For by providing a sentence that can be consciously perceived, one recruits all of the brain's circuits to evaluate it, and to compete with one another in offering suggestions about what should come next.[8]

It seems that much inner speech meshes nicely with our model of the active, sensory-based nature of reflective thinking. But some inner speech is not so obviously purposeful. Sometimes, especially during episodes of mind wandering, seemingly random sentences and phrases appear suddenly in consciousness, apparently out of nowhere. Such cases will be discussed in Section 5. But it is likely, I will argue, that they reflect unconscious evaluations of the relevance of competing speech motor schemata under conditions of low cognitive control. The result is a seemingly uncontrolled sequence of speech. But in reality, each item is motivated by a momentary unconscious decision.

4.3. Pragmatics in inner speech?

If inner speech is like outer speech, only with the overt motor component suppressed, then we should expect the meaning of utterances in inner speech to have a rich pragmatic component, just as does outer speech. This is almost certainly true of inner speech that occurs in the context of imagined conversations (although I know of no systematic studies of the question). Based on my

---

[8] Whether people *intend* these effects when they engage in inner speech is another question, however. Some considerations relevant to this question will be presented in Section 5.

own introspective evidence, at any rate, not only does one seem to take account of earlier stages of the imagined conversation (when selecting pronouns and so forth), but one's inner speech can be rich in irony, sarcasm, and other prototypically pragmatic communicative devices.

In the case of purposeful, problem-directed speech, too, one would expect to see pragmatic effects. For the processes that generate such speech should be sensitive to the same contextual factors (the perceived layout of the environment, memories of recent utterances, and so on) that operate when one speaks to another person. Admittedly, when there is no audience (real or imagined) there is no need to take into consideration the knowledge or ignorance of the other person, and their differing perspective on the situation. Nor is there any need to build a representation of "common ground" that one is said to draw on when producing utterances for an audience (Stalnaker, 2002). But such representations seem to play a much smaller role in language production than was once thought. For speakers often default to their *own* perspective on the situation when selecting utterances, needing to inhibit this tendency if they are to take account of others' differing perspectives (Horton & Keysar, 1996; Shintel & Keysar, 2009).

It is hard, of course, to undertake direct experimental studies of the role of pragmatics in inner speech. But on the assumption that people engaged in think-aloud protocols make utterances that faithfully reflect what they *would* have said silently to themselves otherwise, one can study transcripts of what people say aloud in such circumstances. And in fact such transcripts are rife with pragmatic effects. Indeed, without knowledge of the exact circumstances, one can frequently not understand what the speaker is referring to at all. Consider, for example, just one episode selected from among the raw data of a think-aloud protocol used while participants solved a set of Raven's Matrices (kindly made available to me by Mark Fox).[9] One person said this: "Oh, um, for each there's a diamond. Um, a diamond. And one going the other way."

Reading this, one has to ask: for each *what*? And one *what* going the other way? Looking at the matrix that this person was solving (see Figure 6), one can figure out that he means each *line* in the matrix contains a diamond. And what "goes the other way" are a set of diagonal lines that bisect each figure on each line, one upright, one slanted to the left, and one slanted to the right. Indeed, when thus interpreted, the two statements strongly suggest a particular solution to the problem. Since he did, indeed, get the answer right, it seems likely that the

---

[9] Raven's Matrices are often used in intelligence tests. They comprise sequences of geometric figures, and the participants' task is to select the next shape in the sequence from a number of alternatives. See Figure 6.

person's speech played a role in enabling him to solve it. Indeed, the episode strongly suggests that one of the functions of inner speech is to fix in working memory some of the components of the solution to a problem while one continues to consider others.

If speakers lack introspective access to their communicative intentions while speaking, as I have argued (Carruthers, 2011a), then how do participants who are thinking aloud (or entertaining the same sentences in inner speech) know how to interpret their own utterances? Many of the same contextual cues are available in the first-person as in the third, of course. And interpretation can also be guided by knowledge of one's own focus of attention. In the episode described above, for example, the person was presumably attending to the rows while saying, "For each there's a diamond," and was attending to the diagonal lines in the figures while saying, "And one going the other way." We, too, would have known how to interpret these utterances had we been aware of what he was attending to at the time.

Overall it appears that the sensory-based model of reflection has the resources to explain some of the familiar properties of inner speech. And the close parallels between inner and outer speech support the view that the former is active in nature, and results from goals and values that do not themselves figure among the contents of working memory.

5. Creativity and Mind Wandering

The topic of the present section is uses of working memory that do not seem, introspectively, to be active in nature. Sometimes one's thoughts change direction for no apparent reason (especially when one's mind is wandering). Sometimes ideas seem to leap to mind unbidden (particularly when those ideas are novel or creative). It seems to us in such cases that we are passive receivers of our own thoughts, rather than agents who actively produce or control them. Indeed, it seems to us that the stream of consciousness when we mind-wander flows according to some unknown set of forces and influences, rather than being actively produced. I will argue that this impression is a mistake. I will also consider what can be said about the nature of creativity, from this perspective, as well as what can be said about why we engage in mind wandering at all.

5.1. The active nature of mind wandering

There are strong negative correlations between working-memory capacity and the extent to which people mind-wander during attentionally demanding tasks. This has been shown using introspection-sampling probes to establish the presence of mind wandering, both during experimental tasks of varying demand-ingness (Kane & Engle, 2003) and during everyday life (Kane et al., 2007). Moreover, the capacity to sustain attention to a task seems to involve two distinct components. One is the ability to maintain a goal in an activated state over stretches of time when it does not need to be acted upon (such as watching out for an "oddball" stimulus in long sequences of predictable stimuli), and the other is the capacity to direct attention in the light of that goal while resisting interference from other factors (McVay & Kane, 2009).

On the face of it, such findings might seem to undermine, rather than to support, the claim that mind wandering is active in nature. For mind wandering seems to occur when controlled attention to a task fails. In fact, however, there is continual competition between the "task positive" (attention-controlled) and the "task negative" (default) networks (Kelly et al., 2008) mediated by the bottom-up attentional system (Yeo et al., 2011). While the latter is probably *always* active, monitoring both peripheral stimuli and partially activated endogenous represen-tations for relevance to one's values and current goals, its influence is especially noticeable during mind wandering. I suggest that during such episodes the bottom-up system is winning the competition for top-down attentional resources, wresting control of that system away from the current task-dependent goal (if there is such a goal).

Consistent with this suggestion, the region of medial prefrontal cortex that constitutes part of the default network is anterior cingulate (Buckner et al., 2008), which is known to play a crucial role in conflict monitoring (Botvinick et al., 2004; Kerns et al., 2004). Indeed, the most recent model of the function of anterior cingulate is that it makes decisions about the allocation of top-down control based on cost–benefit analyses of the conflicting alternatives (Shenhav et al., 2013). Also consistent with the proposed active nature of mind wandering, the executive components of top-down attentional systems are also active during mind wandering (Christoff et al., 2009; Smallwood et al., 2011; Christoff, 2012), especially those located in dorsolateral prefrontal cortex.

We can hypothesize, then, that during mind wandering there is no single goal controlling the direction of top-down attention in a sustained way. Rather, contents that have been partly activated through associative and other uncon-trolled processes are evaluated by the bottom-up attentional system, competing with one another (and with the task goal, if there is one) for control of the top-down attentional system and subsequent entry into the global workspace. Sometimes one of these contents wins the competition and is judged most relevant to one's values or goals, issuing in a decision to redirect top-down attention accordingly. But in the absence of a strong enough sustained goal, that conscious content or series of contents is likely soon to be supplanted by another. As a result, one's thoughts when mind wandering may flit from topic to topic. But each individual content or short sequence of contents nevertheless results from a momentary decision to redirect top-down attention in the light of a judgment of relevance. Each therefore results from a process that is action-like in nature. So while the entire sequence of contents during mind wandering is not goal directed or actively controlled, each individual content is.

Mind wandering is active, I suggest, in much the same sense that someone *physically* wandering around in a garden is active. Such a person's movements are actions governed by momentary decisions—now to walk here, now to walk there—even though there is no overarching goal that governs his actions (beyond, perhaps, the goal of allowing himself to wander at will).

Moreover, recall that mind wandering often involves inner speech. Since the latter results from mental rehearsal of speech actions, it, too, is active in nature, even when not controlled by a sustained overarching goal. It seems likely that just as sensory-based representations compete with one another through the bottom-up attentional network to gain entry into working memory, so is there also competition among potential speech actions for rehearsal and subsequent global broadcast. Current or recent contents of working memory will prime one for speech, and in people who habitually engage in inner speech there will be bottom-up competition among the speech acts one could activate in response. The one deemed most relevant will be rehearsed, and its forward model, when attended, will be consciously experienced. So although it can seem to one during mind wandering that one simply *finds oneself* entertaining sentences in inner speech, in reality the latter are actively caused and controlled.

When our minds wander, we often have the impression that we are passive with respect to our own conscious thought processes. (This is especially likely to be true when our minds wander in ways that strike us as novel, creative, or unexpected, as we will discuss shortly.) It is not *us* who controls the contents of our minds in such circumstances, we think, but some set of forces outside of us. But this impression is an illusion. In these cases, too, decisions are taken about the contents that are most relevant to our goals or concerns, and those decisions control the direction of top-down attention. The difference between cases where our thoughts seem to us to be actively controlled and those where they do not is just the difference between cases where we think we know immediately *why* we entertain the thoughts that we do, and those where we take ourselves to be ignorant of those reasons.

5.2. Explaining creativity

Creative episodes can be divided into two main components or phases, as emphasized by so-called "GENEPLORE" (for "generate and explore") models of creative cognition (Finke et al., 1992; Finke, 1995; Ward et al., 1999). The first is the generation of candidate ideas, and the second is the evaluation and development of those ideas before acceptance or implementation. (In practice, of course, the two phases will be intermixed, as one generates and evaluates one idea while also considering others.) As one might expect, the evaluative, analytical phase of creativity is associated especially with activity in executive and top-down attentional regions of cortex, including dorsolateral prefrontal cortex (Ellamil et al., 2012). Our focus here will be on the generative component of creativity, since it is this that gives rise to the feeling that we are passive with respect to the emergence of new ideas.

Numerous forms of data suggest that the generative phase of creativity results from decreased or defocused top-down attentional control. Thus (and consistent with folk beliefs) we know that numerous factors besides the intention to be creative (Baumeister et al., 2007) can influence levels of creativity. Alcohol increases creativity (Jarosz et al., 2012); sleepiness increases creativity (Wieth & Zacks, 2011); and being in a good or relaxed mood improves creativity (Subramaniam et al., 2009). Direct-current stimulation applied to left prefrontal cortex also increases creativity (Chrysikou et al., 2013), presumably by down-regulating top-down attentional control.[10] And musicians engaged in creative improvisation show lesser activity in dorsolateral prefrontal cortex than do those who are playing a tune they know well (Limb & Braun, 2008). Moreover, particularly creative individuals tend to be lower in what is called "latent inhibition," which is the capacity to screen from awareness stimuli previously experienced as irrelevant to one's task (Carson et al., 2003).

Such data might seem to support a passivity view of creativity, since they show that creativity happens when top-down attentional control is relaxed. But, as previously, the data are equally consistent with an account in terms of bottom-up forms of attention competing to influence the direction of top-down attentional networks in the absence of a strong and active goal, with the top-down network being controlled by momentary decisions of maximal relevance. For example, here is what might happen when someone searches for unusual things one could do with a brick. The intention to be creative leads to a defocusing of attention,

---

[10] Direct-current stimulation, like transcranial magnetic stimulation (TMS), suppresses the level of neural activity in regions to which it is applied.

removing the suppressing effect on remotely associated representations that are activated (albeit only weakly) by the thought of a brick. (On the contrary, it is the obvious and familiar uses of a brick—such as building a wall—that need to be suppressed.) These associated representations are received by the region of ventral parietal cortex that forms part of the bottom-up attentional network. This communicates back and forth with right ventrolateral prefrontal cortex to evaluate their degree of interest. The result is a competition to gain control of the top-down network. This takes place in the medial frontal gyrus and anterior cingulate cortex, issuing in a decision to redirect the top-down network toward one set of representations in particular. The result is that a particular idea pops into the person's conscious mind, seemingly unbidden, thereby enabling a reflective, conscious evaluation of its merits.

Is there evidence to support such an interpretation? There is some. One imaging study of creativity, for example, found a trade-off between frontal and occipital–temporal cortical activity depending on whether the task was mundane (greater frontal) or creative, suggesting lesser top-down control in the latter case (Chrysikou & Thompson-Schill, 2011). Another found increased activity in anterior cingulate cortex in creative conditions (associated with conflict monitoring and decisions about the direction of top-down control), as well as in the medial central gyrus of right prefrontal cortex, which is a component of the bottom-up attentional network, as we noted in Chapter 3.4 (Howard-Jones et al., 2005). Moreover, numerous studies of creativity have found associated activity in ventral parietal cortex, which is another crucial component of the bottom-up attentional network (Bekhtereva et al., 2004; Jung-Beeman et al., 2004; Geake & Hansen, 2005; Subramaniam et al., 2009).

While more evidence would be welcome, it seems that current findings are at least consistent with the active nature of creative idea-generation sketched here. Moreover, since the level of activation of unattended but weakly active neural representations will fluctuate stochastically, the present account can accommodate quite naturally the partly stochastic nature of creative idea-generation (Simonton, 2003). For as one rather than another representation becomes more active, so will it have a greater impact on the competition for control of top-down attention.

In previous work I urged the benefits of a theory of creativity that is action based (Carruthers, 2007, 2011b). Among other things, I argued that known properties of the motor system can help explain the partly stochastic nature of creativity. For at some levels of representation action selection is itself stochastic in nature (Rosenbaum et al., 2001, 2008). I also argued that an action-based account enables human creativity to be situated phylogenetically, as an exaptation of the kinds of protean motor behavior exhibited by many species of animal (especially when escaping from a predator; Driver & Humphries, 1988; Miller, 1997). These properties, I suggested, are inherited by human speech-production systems, issuing in the striking creativity of much overt (and inner) speech. But these suggestions were made before I had come to realize that attention is itself a form of action. The present account can thus inherit all of the advantages of my previous one, but broadened to encompass creative imagery quite generally.

The main point of the present discussion, however, is just that one can provide an active, sensory-based account of creative idea generation that is consistent with (and to some degree supported by) the existing evidence.

5.3. Why mind-wander?

Why do people mind-wander at all? The question can be understood either distally or proximally. Consider the former first. From a functional and evolutionary perspective it might seem puzzling that people's minds should often drift from the here-and-now, meandering across past, future, and merely possible scenarios instead. But only a little reflection is needed to dispel any air of mystery. There are frequently lessons to be acquired from the past that were not learned at the time. Recalling those episodes, thereby making them globally available in working memory, can issue in novel inferences and affective reactions. The results can in turn be stored for future use. Moreover, the value of prospective reasoning has already been emphasized. By entertaining representations of various future actions in working memory, one can predict their likely consequences and respond affectively to them, thereby enabling one to plan (Damasio, 1994; Gilbert & Wilson, 2007). Even merely hypothetical or counterfactual scenarios can give rise to potentially useful information. So the adaptive nature of mind wandering (at least in the absence of any significant current task) should not be in doubt. In Chapter 8 we will consider whether, and to what extent, mind wandering has evolutionary precursors.

Now consider the proximal causes that initiate episodes of mind wandering. In light of the above, it makes sense that there should be a strong disposition to begin mind wandering as soon as one finds oneself without any current task, such as lying in an fMRI scanner while waiting for instructions from an experimenter or (more mundanely) when waiting for a bus. For by having such a disposition, any "down time" of this sort can be put to adaptive use. What in turn grounds this disposition might be that people find mind wandering inherently rewarding (Picciuto, 2011), in addition to any content-related rewards they might experience. (Of course the contents one entertains when mind wandering are often—

but by no means always—experienced as pleasurable. Think, here, especially of fantasy.) It is more puzzling, however, why one should so often mind-wander when engaged in an important task. Why is it often so hard to keep one's attention on one's current task, even when one is highly motivated to do so? And what causes one to shift attention away from that task when one does?

Kurzban et al. (2013) provide a general model in terms of which this issue can be understood. They argue that the experience of intellectual effort is an affective response designed to make one's current activity seem bad, grounded in a cost–benefit analysis of that activity in comparison with what else one could be devoting one's attention to at the time (including mind wandering). They amass an impressive range of evidence in support of their model, while contrasting it favorably with competitors. In effect, the idea is that when one switches attention away from one's current task and initiates an episode of mind wandering, one has taken a *decision* that the latter activity is the better of the two in the circumstances. This decision is not conscious, of course, and people are generally unaware that they have made it, or why. This is why one seems to just *find oneself* mind-wandering, passively, often issuing in conscious regret. But in fact, initiating mind wandering is an action (or is at least action-like), just as are the individual movements of attention that determine the latter's contents. Further confirming the correctness of this account, a very similar model is presented independently by Shenhav et al. (2013). They propose that the computational function of anterior cingulate cortex is to take decisions about the allocation of top-down control mechanisms on the basis of cost–benefit analyses of the various options.

In conclusion, then, a case can be made for saying that all aspects of the stream of consciousness are really active in nature. Not only is this true, most obviously, of inner speech and the mental rehearsal of action generally (for example, in prospection), but it is also true of forms of reflection that seem intuitively to be passive. Even the genesis of creative ideas and seemingly undirected mind wandering result from decisions to redirect top-down attention in the light of cost–benefit judgments or judgments of relevance.

6. Conclusion

This chapter has outlined a sensory-based, working-memory-based account of conscious reflection and the stream of consciousness. On this view one's amodal attitudes operate entirely in the background, helping to determine the contents of working memory and the direction that one's reflections will take. Moreover, the stream of consciousness is thoroughly active in nature, at least to the extent that its momentary contents are under intentional control. This is because it always depends on the direction of attention, and often depends on mental rehearsals of action, both of which are action-like in nature.

Our common-sense belief that reflection is often an active process is thus vindicated. But common sense also maintains that conscious thinking is often *not* active, because thoughts and images enter our minds and interrupt our reflections unbidden, seemingly appearing out of nowhere. According to the view outlined here, this aspect of common-sense belief is mistaken. Ideas that appear seemingly from nowhere are really a result of unconscious decisions that resolve conflicts over the direction of attention, or concerning what actions to rehearse. The difference between the cases that common sense regards as being under our control and those that it maintains are not is simply that in the former cases we think we know *why* we reflect as we do, whereas in the latter cases we don't. This difference is merely epistemic, however, and demonstrates nothing about the real nature of the causal processes that produce the conscious contents in question.

Recall from Chapter 2.3 that philosophers who claim that our amodal attitudes are sometimes active and under intentional control are committed to the view that such attitudes admit of two distinct varieties: a set of action-like attitudes, and a set of passive ones invoked to explain the active status of the former set. As we saw in Chapter 2.3, this commitment gives rise to a number of problems. Work needs to be done to explain why active and passive instances of belief, for instance, should nevertheless be considered as belonging to the same mental-attitude kind; for the functional roles of those two sorts of instance will be quite different. And some sort of complex mental architecture will need to be postulated to explain how some propositional attitudes can participate in the intentional control of others. Since we have no knowledge of such an architecture, this aspect of the stream of consciousness would remain currently unexplained.

The sensory-based model of reflection makes no such commitment, of course, and gives rise to no such problems. It holds that amodal attitudes are never under direct intentional control, whereas the stream of consciousness always is; and the latter is explained in terms of mechanisms that are already known to exist, and about which much is already known. The sensory-based model therefore has greater explanatory adequacy, as well as an attractive simplicity and elegance that the philosophers' account lacks. This amounts to yet another strike against the latter. In addition to all of the direct evidence against the idea of an amodal central workspace and in support of its sensory-based competitor, reviewed over the course of previous chapters, the sensory-based model of reflection is also favored by considerations of simplicity and explanatory adequacy.

7

Reasoning, Working Memory, and Attitudes

The present chapter will consider the nature of the dual systems of reasoning advocated by many psychologists. One goal is to continue the work begun in Chapter 6, developing the sensory-based account of reflection in more detail. A second goal is to further consolidate one of the main claims of Chapter 5. This is that once we have taken account of all the factors that are known to contribute to individual differences in reflective reasoning ability, there is no variance remaining that might be explained by the properties of an amodal attitude workspace. A third goal is to consider two alternative ways in which the dual-systems framework might be thought to provide support for the idea of a global workspace in which all types of attitude can be activated.

1. Dual Systems of Reasoning

Scientists who study human cognition across a range of different domains have increasingly converged on the idea that there are two distinct systems (or types of system) involved. These domains include learning (Berry & Dienes, 1993; Reber, 1993), conditional and probabilistic reasoning (Evans & Over, 1996; Sloman, 1996, 2002; Stanovich, 1999), decision making (Kahneman & Frederick, 2002; Kahneman, 2011), and social cognition of various sorts (Petty & Cacioppo, 1986; Chaiken et al., 1989; Wilson et al., 2000; Lieberman, 2013). Although terminology has differed, many now use the labels "System 1" and "System 2" to mark the intended distinction. System 1 is supposed to be fast and unconscious in its operations, issuing in intuitively compelling answers to learning or reasoning problems in ways that subjects themselves have no access to. System 2, in contrast, is supposed to be slow and conscious in its operations, and is engaged whenever we are induced to tackle reasoning tasks in a reflective manner. Many theorists now accept that System 1 is really a *set* of systems, arranged in parallel, while believing that System 2 is a single serially operating ability.

Note that since System 2 is believed to be the system in which reflective thinking and reasoning take place, the best account of the former will also give us our best theory of the latter. This should provide the sensory-based account of reflection with its strongest test: can it accommodate and explain the dominant scientific account of the nature of reflective thinking?

1.1. *Introducing the two systems*

Throughout the latter half of the last century evidence was mounting that human reasoning performance is subject to systematic errors (Kahneman et al., 1982; Gilovich et al., 2002). People regularly exhibit biases across a range of domains and types of reasoning, and they tend to use "quick and dirty" heuristics rather than employing normatively correct principles of reasoning. While some have argued that these heuristics are computationally frugal and produce results that are sufficiently reliable in many environments to be adaptive (Gigerenzer et al., 1999), there is no disputing the fact that people nevertheless go wrong in predictable ways—sometimes with disastrous consequences. However, there are also a minority of people who tend to get the normatively correct solutions, and who do so systematically across types of task (Stanovich, 1999). It was the study of these individual differences that led to the two-systems framework (in the domain of reasoning, at least).

One factor that distinguishes those who get the normatively correct answers to reasoning problems is that they tend to have higher fluid general intelligence, or *g*. This is not surprising, of course. One might expect that smart people would reason better.[1] But another factor distinguishing those who tend to get the answers right is best characterized as a feature of personality: *reflectiveness*, or "need for cognition" (Stanovich, 1999). People who get the correct answers tend not, as one says, to jump to conclusions. Rather, they answer more slowly than other people (De Neys, 2006a), and engage in significant amounts of conscious reflection before settling on their answer.

Many reasoning tasks can be arranged so that one answer, in particular, leaps immediately to mind. (And on social matters, too, people generally arrive at swift intuitive appraisals of others, or of social situations; Lieberman, 2013.) Those who fail to reflect will then provide this as their answer, often incorrectly. The cognitive and evaluative systems that issue in these intuitions have come to be referred to collectively as "System 1." They operate swiftly outside of conscious

---

[1] Note, however, that given the heavy overlap between fluid *g* and working-memory abilities, discussed in Chapter 5, this is already an indication that variance in working-memory capacities might play a big role in explaining reasoning performance.

awareness, and are largely impervious to top-down influences, at least in the short term. For example, many of the intuitions produced by System 1 survive reflection (somewhat as visual illusions do). Even when one is convinced of their incorrectness, one can continue to feel their tug. Many of the biases produced by System 1 are now well understood, as are the processing heuristics that are employed (Kahneman, 2011).

The reflective system—System 2—in contrast is engaged whenever one pauses to evaluate one's initial intuitive answer, and attempts to think through the problem in a systematic manner. System 2 reasoning processes are conscious and serially ordered. And many understand System 2 to be governed, necessarily, by normatively correct principles. (As we will see, this is a mistake.) Although only some people systematically respond to reasoning tasks in a System 2 manner, it is thought that System 2 reasoning is nevertheless *available* to everyone. In what follows our focus will be on the nature of System 2, in particular. For this appears to be the system in which conscious reflection takes place.

1.2. Properties of the two systems

The sets of properties that have been said to characterize the two systems over the years are quite extensive. In part this is because the two-systems framework has been developed by many different theorists, working in different domains, and with differing theoretical commitments. Everyone agrees that System 1 operations are unconscious, whereas those of System 2 are conscious; and everyone agrees that System 1 processes are high in capacity (perhaps involving parallel processing), whereas System 2 processes are quite limited in capacity and serial in nature. But beyond this, there are a great many additional contrasts that are often said to distinguish the two systems. Most of these only work on the whole, however, or in limited domains.

For example, it is often claimed that System 1 processes are fast and automatic, whereas System 2 processes are slow and controlled (Frankish, 2009). Something of the sort may be generally true. But there are also System 1 processes that are slow and controlled. Consider the phenomenon of "sleeping on it." It is a familiar occurrence in daily life that one's reflective reasoning about some problem has become stuck—one is unable to see a way to a solution. So one lays the problem aside, either literally going to sleep for the night or occupying oneself with other tasks. But then sometimes after an interval the solution suddenly and unexpectedly emerges into consciousness. It is natural to think that one must have continued reasoning about the problem, unconsciously, in the interim. Admittedly, this interpretation is not forced on us. For it may be that the reason one had got stuck with the problem in the first place is that one had adopted an inappropriate mental "set," which framed and constrained one's conscious reflection. What happened during the time when one was asleep or doing other things, then, may be that this initial set was *forgotten*. With that constraint out of the way, one was able to approach the problem afresh, resulting in success.

No doubt this sort of "set shifting" explanation is sometimes appropriate (Schooler & Melcher, 1995). But it cannot explain those cases where a solution emerges fully formed into consciousness without any prior attention to the problem. For if all that happens in the interval following one's previous attempts is that one forgets the initial line of approach to the problem that had led one astray, then one would expect that one would thereafter have to think *reflectively* about the problem once again in order to achieve a solution. But this isn't always what happens. Here, as in the case of creative cognition discussed in Chapter 6.5, bottom-up cortical attentional processes must continue to sift through potential solutions while one's top-down attention is occupied elsewhere, hijacking control of the latter when something appraised as meeting the task demands is found. This can take considerable time. And although the *process* of bottom-up attentional search may not be fully controlled, it is nevertheless goal dependent. And the eventual decision to switch top-down attention to one of the products of that search (thereby causing that content to enter consciousness) *is* controlled.[2]

It has also often been claimed that System 1 is both universal to all humans and largely shared with other animals, whereas System 2 is uniquely human while varying in its properties by culture and individual learning. But in fact some System 1 processes, too, depend upon individual learning. For many cognitive skills can become automatized, moving with practice from System 2 to System 1. The intuitions of a chess Grandmaster, for example, when he glances at a particular layout of the board ("White has a winning position"), should count as System 1. But these are intuitions that few other people in the world will share. Moreover, as we will see in Chapter 8, some System 2 processes (especially those involving prospective reasoning and episodic memory) are likely to be shared with other animals.

Most importantly, it has often been thought that System 1 is associative in its operations (or perhaps heuristic based), whereas System 2 is both rule based and embodies some sort of normative reasoning competence (Sloman, 2002). It is true that System 2 processes are partly guided by explicit rules for reasoning and decision making that have been acquired from one's culture. (Stanovich, 2009,

---

[2] See Bos et al. (2008) for a demonstration that unconscious reasoning processes can be goal dependent.

refers to such rules as "mindware.") Among people who have taken courses in logic or statistics, these rules will be normatively sound. But while it is true that reflection can sometimes involve appeal to valid norms of reasoning, it can also involve the use of heuristics. Some of these can be good and useful, and some can be bad. The "sleep on it" heuristic, which is often consciously and reflectively employed by people in our culture, might be a good example of the first sort. But a moment's thought is sufficient to show that many culturally sanctioned reasoning heuristics can be quite bad. Consider the common practice in many cultures of consulting an oracle (such as the entrails of a newly killed chicken) when making an important decision. It is plain to us that decisions made on this basis will be at chance. And it is equally obvious that people in such a culture would be much better off not reflecting about the decision at all, given that reflection will call to mind the "look at the entrails" heuristic, which is then likely to be followed.

There is also intriguing evidence that at least one form of *intuitive* reasoning embodies a normative reasoning competence. If so, then System 1 processes can be rational, not merely in delivering an optimal or near-optimal output, but also in the processing rules that they employ. The system in question is thought to be engaged whenever one enters into a verbal argument with someone, and is said to be an adaptation arising from an "arms race" in evolutionary history that characterized the relations between communicators and their audiences (Mercier & Sperber, 2011). Besides the evolutionary logic that predicts the existence of such a system, the main line of evidence supporting it consists in an extensive body of work showing that people who fail at paper-and-pencil tests of reasoning do *much* better when evaluating the arguments of other people, or when engaged in debate with others.

Confusingly, Mercier & Sperber themselves describe the argumentation system as a *reflective* one, on the grounds that it is often engaged when we explicitly and consciously evaluate the arguments of others or propose counter-arguments ourselves. This may be so. But since the internal operations of the system are always unconscious it is plain, I think, that it should be classified as an intuitive— System 1—system. For *all* intuitive systems are capable of issuing in conscious outputs, and many may help to guide cycles of conscious reflection. Indeed, when presented with someone's argument, the argumentation system will swiftly and unconsciously generate an intuition about the strength of that argument, together with intuitions about its likely weak spots. This fits the normal characterization of a System 1 system.

It seems, then, that many of the properties that have been said to be distinct-ive of the two systems don't really line up with one another. Some have used this to criticize the two-systems framework as such (Keren & Schul, 2009). But as Evans & Stanovich (2013) point out, all it really does is force us to distinguish between properties that are *definitive* of the two systems and those that may generally, or perhaps only sometimes, hold true of them. There is nothing here to challenge the distinction between intuitive forms of reasoning (which are unconscious and high capacity) and reflective reasoning (which is conscious and limited capacity). Even those who have been among the staunchest critics of the dual-systems framework accept that this distinction is valid (Kruglanski & Gigerenzer, 2011; Kruglanski, 2013).

1.3. System 2 and working memory

We have already noted that System 2 appears to involve the use of working memory. This is because differences in fluid g explain a significant amount of the variance among people in their abilities to solve reasoning tasks, and because there is a heavy overlap between fluid g and working-memory capacity, as we discussed in Chapter 5.4. But other sources of evidence point toward the same conclusion. For example, intuitive, biased forms of responding in reasoning tasks increase when people are put under time pressure, and logical forms of responding decrease (Evans & Curtis-Holmes, 2005). For it is well known that time-pressured responding reduces people's reliance on working-memory resources. More importantly, perhaps, when people engage in reasoning tasks under concurrent working-memory load, this impacts their performance when logical and intuitive responses are in conflict, while having no impact on performance when intuitive methods will suffice (De Neys, 2006a, 2006b). These findings demonstrate that working memory plays a significant causal role, at least, in System 2 reasoning.

The same conclusion is supported by the available neuroimaging evidence. Numerous studies demonstrate executive-system involvement in System 2 reasoning. For example, De Neys et al. (2008) show that while anterior cingulate cortex is active whenever people attempt to answer classic decision-making problems, right ventrolateral prefrontal cortex is especially active only when people are able to inhibit the intuitive response and answer correctly.[3] Similarly,

---

[3] Recall that anterior cingulate is thought to be involved in the detection of conflict (Botvinick et al., 2004; Kerns et al., 2004). It therefore seems that people generally *detect* the conflict between intuitive and normative responses in this study, while only more rarely inhibiting the former and selecting the latter. Recall, too, that right ventrolateral prefrontal cortex forms an important component of the bottom-up attentional network (Corbetta et al., 2008), as well as playing a crucial role in a variety of forms of self-control (Aron et al., 2004; Cohen & Lieberman, 2010).

Tsujii & Watanabe (2009, 2010) show that ventrolateral prefrontal cortex (especially in the right hemisphere) is active in trials in which people are able to overcome an intuitive reasoning bias and answer with the logically correct solution.

More directly, Goel (2008) reviews evidence showing that when people tackle familiar reasoning problems that they can solve in a heuristic-based way, a network involving left temporal regions and left lateral prefrontal cortex is active. When people work on unfamiliar problems that require them to ignore heuristic responses and answer logically, in contrast, bilateral regions of dorsal prefrontal cortex and the parietal lobes are active. The regions involved suggest the distinctive involvement of the top-down attentional network. Since the latter is a signature of working-memory activity, we can conclude that logical responding, in contrast with heuristic responding, makes use of the resources of working memory.

Important confirmation of these findings in the domain of reasoning comes from investigations of the brain regions involved in social cognition. Lieberman (2009) reviews a range of studies in the field of social cognitive neuroscience, particularly concerning the brain networks that are differentially active when people respond intuitively versus reflectively. The intuitive system involves a network of regions including the lateral temporal lobes, orbitofrontal cortex, and the amygdala. The reflective system, in contrast, overlaps heavily with the default network, and includes lateral and dorsal prefrontal cortex, the medial temporal lobes surrounding the hippocampus, and large areas of dorsal and lateral parietal cortex. Roughly speaking, the distinction seems to be between a semantic–evaluative network, on the one hand, and one that involves explicit memories and the resources of working memory, on the other.

Reviewing these and other forms of evidence, two of the leading proponents of the two-systems framework have recently concluded that the distinctive feature of System 2 forms of reasoning, decision making, and social cognition is simply that they make constitutive use of working memory (Evans & Stanovich, 2013). All tasks will likely make *some* use of working memory, of course. For example, working memory will be involved in understanding the task instructions and processing some of the stimulus materials. But when answering in a System 2 manner one intervenes to inhibit an intuitive response and takes time to engage in conscious reflection. It is the latter that constitutively depends on the use of working-memory abilities. So while System 1 comprises a heterogeneous set of processing systems, System 2 has some claim to be considered a natural kind. For it can largely be identified with the working-memory system, which surely qualifies as such.

1.4. The case of the missing variance revisited

While some have concluded that working memory is the system underlying reflective forms of thinking, it is by no means true that variations in working-memory ability alone explain all of the variance among people in reasoning tasks. So there is an opportunity here to address, again, the question discussed in Chapter 5.4. This is whether there is room for an amodal attitudinal workspace to play a role in reasoning tasks, in addition to the sensory-based working-memory system. To answer this question, we need to consider what other sources of variance there are underlying people's reasoning performance.

Stanovich (1999, 2009) argues that variance in reasoning abilities can be fully accounted for in terms of three factors. The first is fluid general intelligence. Smarter people generally do better. But as we saw in Chapter 5.4, variance in fluid *g*, in turn, can be explained by a combination of working-memory capacity and processing speed. So there is nothing here to indicate the involvement of an amodal workspace. The second factor has already been mentioned: it is a disposition to reflect. People who often or habitually reflect before responding do better on tests of reasoning, and are better able to avoid the intuitive (but incorrect) response. Again, there is nothing here to indicate a role for an amodal workspace. For this factor is, in effect, a feature of *personality* rather than a cognitive system of any sort. The third factor underlying variance in reasoning abilities, according to Stanovich, is *mindware*. This comprises well-rehearsed procedures for reasoning, generally acquired through training and repeated practice, together with explicit beliefs about appropriate norms of reasoning, mostly learned as a result of formal education. Once again, there is nothing here to indicate the presence of an amodal workspace in which reasoning can take place. Rather, this factor comprises a body of implicit and explicit *knowledge*.

The argument against an amodal workspace—in which attitudes of all types can be activated consciously and in which reasoning can take place—is thus strengthened still further. For this workspace is supposed to be engaged specifically during conscious reflection. But our best empirically grounded theories of the latter implicate the sensory-based working-memory system together with features of personality as well as implicit and explicit forms of knowledge. While it is now beyond dispute that there is an important distinction between intuitive and reflective forms of reasoning, decision making, and social responding, there is nothing to suggest that the cognitive system underlying conscious reflection is anything other than the sensory-based working-memory system.

2. How System 2 Reasoning Works

Given that the only structure that is distinctive of System 2 processing is the working-memory system, this section will show how working memory can recruit the resources of acquired skills, System 1 systems, and explicit knowledge and memories to issue in System 2 performance. The goal is to show, at least in outline, how the sensory-based theory of reflection can account for this important body of findings.

2.1. Mindware

Consider what happens when people are presented with a task involving probabilistic reasoning, for example. Those who pause to reflect before answering, and who have taken a course in statistics or probability theory, may recall that they possess knowledge relevant to determining the answer. Once this has happened, they may then implement a well-rehearsed body of procedures, perhaps involving paper-and-pencil calculations, to achieve a solution.

At a more fine-grained level, what may happen is that concepts evoked by phrases such as, "How *likely* is it...?" or, "What are the *chances*...?" in the presentation of the task activate episodic memories of having taken a relevant class, or may activate some of the relevant behavioral procedures directly. If the person is habitually disposed to suppress an initial intuitive response and conduct a wider search of memory, then what may ensue is an evaluation of various items of knowledge activated through the bottom-up attentional system, or an evaluation of a number of alternative action schemata. When appraised as sufficiently relevant, one of these may be sufficient to begin implementation of the procedures needed for a solution.

As another example, consider people who are presented with a version of the Wason selection task, requiring them to select the information that they need to evaluate the truth of a conditional statement.[4] Those who have taken courses in propositional logic may recognize at an explicit level that this is what is required of them, perhaps leading them to entertain the question in inner speech, "How does one evaluate a conditional?" This question, when processed by the language comprehension system and understood, may activate various items of knowledge

---

[4] For example, participants might be presented with four cards and told that each has a number on one side and a letter on the other. They are asked to turn over all and only the cards necessary to evaluate the truth of the conditional statement, "If a card has an even number on one side, then it has a vowel on the other." When the cards in question show, "4," "3," "K," and "E," the correct answer is the first and third. Most people answer with just the 4-card, or else the 4-card and the E-card.

that compete for control of the language production process, leading them to rehearse a statement like, "To evaluate a conditional one needs to look for a case where the antecedent is true and the consequent is false." Alternatively, the question may evoke a visual image of the standard truth-table for the material conditional, which is held in working memory and mapped onto the four possibilities they have been given for evaluating the conditional in question.

Notice that among people who have acquired the relevant reasoning mindware, a disposition to pause and reflect—asking oneself additional questions before answering and so on—may significantly raise the chances that one's mindware is brought to bear on the solution to the problem presented. The mere act of pausing before answering will allow time for bottom-up competitive processes to do their work, perhaps leading to a recognition that the initial answer that sprang to mind may not be the best one. Or the act of asking oneself questions may evoke knowledge by way of answer that would otherwise not have made it to the level of consciousness.

Having a reflective disposition is by no means a *necessary* condition for getting the answer right, however. Those who possess relevant mindware that is sufficiently accessible may call it to mind simultaneously with the heuristically based intuitive answer, appraising it as preferable. For example, a trained logician may see immediately what information is needed to evaluate the truth of the conditional in a Wason selection task. Arguably, however, this should then be considered an instance of System 1 rather than System 2 reasoning. For no reflection is needed, and working memory is not constitutively involved. The point made earlier, that System 1 performance can sometimes be normatively correct, is thus further reinforced.

2.2. Multiple contributions

Notice that one of the benefits of reflection is independent of the sorts of mindware skills and explicit knowledge of norms of reasoning that one might have acquired through formal education. For reflection makes it possible for many more System 1 systems to have a chance to contribute to the decision, or to the solution to the problem. Often when one is confronted with a problem there is one particular solution that is especially intuitive or salient. But by pausing, asking oneself, "Am I sure that is right?," or by conducting a search of memory for other similar cases and how they were dealt with, one may activate knowledge into working memory that suggests a better decision or a better solution. In effect, one of the benefits of reflection is that by employing the global workspace one is able to harness the resources of many more System 1 systems. By asking oneself questions, searching for memories, and so on, one can evoke knowledge or procedures that were either not activated at all by the initial presentation of the problem, or were not activated sufficiently strongly to outcompete one's swift intuitive response.

Reflection can also utilize the resources of a single System 1 system on an iterated basis. This is what happens, for example, when one reflectively tries to understand the actions or mental states of another person. Often the output of one's mindreading system is swift and intuitive, of course. One just *sees* someone as attempting to open a door, or *hears* someone as speaking ironically or jokingly. So normal everyday mindreading qualifies as System 1. But one can, if one chooses, reflect to confirm or overturn one's initial intuitive interpretation. (We are especially likely to do this when the stakes are high.) And sometimes people behave in ways that leave one puzzled. In such cases one can frame questions, call to mind memories of similar instances of behavior, imagine oneself in the circumstances of the other person, and so on. Each of these will issue in contents that are received as input by the mindreading faculty, leading it to suggest an interpretation. In this way one may work one's way to a plausible theory for understanding the other person's actions, utilizing the resources of the mindreading faculty on an iterated basis, together with episodic memories and other forms of knowledge that are evoked by reflection.

Notice that at each stage in reflective reasoning of the above sorts, all we need to appeal to are the sensory-based contents of working memory (visual images, inner speech, and so on) together with other factors. These include the set of System 1 systems that receive the contents of working memory as input, as well as forms of implicit and explicit knowledge that are activated associatively by the contents of working memory and evaluated through bottom-up attentional processes, before being inserted into working memory in turn. In order to explain System 2 reasoning there is no need to appeal to the workings of an amodal attitude-containing conscious workspace.

2.3. Prospection

Perhaps the most common form of reflective reasoning occurs during prospection. Often when we are trying to decide what to do (or when we know merely that we *may* need to decide what to do at a later time), we imagine ourselves making each of the available choices while responding affectively to the results (Damasio, 1994; Gilbert & Wilson, 2007). The actions in question are rehearsed, or the outcomes of those actions are imagined. This issues in sensory-based content in working memory that is received and elaborated by a variety of System 1 inferential and predictive systems, issuing in yet further contents in working memory. These contents are also received as input by a suite of evaluative mechanisms, issuing in some degree of arousal, and leading us to see the situations in question as good or bad to some extent.

We know that everyday prospective reasoning falls prey to a variety of biases and fallacies (Gilbert & Wilson, 2007). For example, in prospection we tend to concentrate just on the focal event, forgetting to take into account the surrounding circumstances. In deciding whether or not to attend a concert in town, one may call on memories of the music and of previous concerts, while forgetting about the time spent looking for a parking space and the time spent travelling in heavy traffic. We also fail to take account of how much else will remain the same whatever we decide to do. Hence we predict that winning the lottery would be wonderful, while failing to allow for the fact that one's marriage will still be just as aggravating thereafter, and that one's health will still be just as poor. As a result, this sort of reasoning would not be classified as "System 2" by anyone who thinks that System 2 reasoning is, necessarily, normatively optimal or correct. If one thinks, in contrast (as I do, and as do the central experts in the field), that System 2 reasoning is distinctive only in making constitutive use of the resources of working memory, then prospective reasoning certainly qualifies, despite its frequent failings.

Notice that although prospective reasoning is less than optimal, there are many circumstances in which it is nevertheless more effective than attempting to make the same decision discursively (Wilson et al., 1993; Wilson, 2002). For if one bases a decision entirely on reasons one can articulate, one will be apt to focus just on those factors that are easy to express in words. Moreover, recall from Chapter 6.1 that the evaluative component of prospective reasoning makes essential use of orbitofrontal cortex, and that people's decision making is quite poor when the latter is damaged, despite the fact that they can still reason in a discursive way perfectly normally about the choices that confront them (Damasio, 1994). Rather than attempting to take decisions discursively, a better strategy is to try to correct for some of the biases inherent in prospective reasoning, reminding oneself to imagine the context and consequences of the choices that one faces, as well as the focal events themselves, for example.

3. System 2 Reasoning in Action

We have sketched how System 2 reasoning works, utilizing just the resources of the sensory-based working-memory system together with System 1 systems and stored knowledge. But how does System 2 reasoning have an impact on motivation, memory, and (especially) action? Recall that one thesis of this book is that our amodal attitudes (including decisions) do not figure among the contents of working memory. In that case, since System 2 reasoning takes place in working memory, it can seem mysterious how reflection can have its effects. For instance, we know that decisions cause actions. But how can a sensory-based event such as saying to oneself, "I should turn over this card and that card" (rehearsed by a participant in a Wason selection test) cause the corresponding action?

3.1. Engaging motivational systems

It is easy to see how System 2 processes can issue in new forms of motivation. This is because such processes make constitutive use of the sensory-based working-memory system. And as we saw in Chapter 4, working memory makes its contents globally available, piggybacking on the same attentional mechanisms that result in the global broadcast of perceptual information. In particular, the contents of working memory will be received as input by a suite of evaluative mechanisms that issue in some degree of affect directed at those contents. Just as *seeing* a novel event, or hearing someone describe it, can issue in a new motivational state, so can *imagining* or *thinking of* a novel event (in visual imagery or inner speech). The same kinds of representation will be received by one's evaluative mechanisms in each case. The difference concerns just whether those representations are exogenously or endogenously caused.

Consider how this works in the case of prospection, where one imagines oneself performing an action or experiencing its results. When considering whether or not to accept an offer to relocate to Chicago, one might imagine oneself being in Chicago. As a result, the concept CHICAGO or some set of related concepts will be bound into the content of the image and broadcast along with it, while that content evokes positive or negative emotional valence. Similarly the detailed content of what one imagines—such as the Chicago skyline on a sunny day, or walking in a bitter winter wind—will evoke affective reactions, somewhat as if one were really experiencing such things. The images are likely to be less vivid and determinate than the corresponding perceptions would be, of course, with corresponding reductions in affective reaction. But the processes in question are of essentially the same kind. As a result, being in Chicago seems good or bad to one (or some mixture of the two).

Prospective reasoning about what to say works in a similar manner. When one mentally rehearses making a remark to an imagined audience the result is an auditory image of oneself saying that thing. This is made globally available to a suite of System 1 systems, salient among which is the mindreading system. The latter predicts the likely effects on one's interlocutor, and these, in turn, are added to the contents of working memory. For example, one now sees the person, in imagination, as horrified, or bored, or amused. Depending on one's goals and values, this may be experienced as a good or bad thing, which in turn causes us to experience the making of that remark as a good or bad thing. We are thus motivated to say, or not to say, the original remark through our affective reaction to its simulated effects.

Not all inner speech has an imagined audience, of course. Sometimes it takes the form of inner commentary, or is used for purposes of reasoning. In considering where to go on a winter vacation, for example, the sorts of underlying competitive processes discussed in Chapter 6.4 may lead one to articulate in inner speech, "The sea around Bonaire will still be warm in January." When processed by the language comprehension and mindreading systems, this is heard as expressing a *judgment* with that content. Provided no contrary information is evoked, this will issue in one's acceptance of that content. (See Section 3.2 below.) As a result, one's evaluative systems will respond to that content as if it were true. If one generally enjoys swimming in the ocean, the result is likely to be positive affect directed toward the possibility of being in Bonaire in January.

3.2. Forming new beliefs

It is somewhat less easy to see how System 2 reasoning could issue in new beliefs, on the model sketched here. For how is it that *imagining* oneself doing or saying various things can lead one to form a new belief about what is actually the case in the world? We surely do not systematically confuse fantasy with reality. But it can easily seem as if this must be happening, if new beliefs are to be formed on the basis of what one imagines.

We can make progress with this question by noticing that imagining something need not lead one to believe in that very thing. If imagining P leads one to believe P, then that does seem like it would be confusing fantasy with reality. But frequently when one imagines P, what one actually comes to believe is a conditional of the form, *if P then Q*. For example, when one imagines throwing a rock toward a window, one's imagery (when globally broadcast and processed by a suite of System 1 predictive mechanisms) may become elaborated to include a representation of the window shattering (depending on the represented weight of the rock and the speed of its trajectory). As a result one forms a belief with the content, *if I throw that rock at that window, then it will break.* The same mechanism that leads one to form an expectation of a shattered window when one *sees* a rock hurtling toward it is here co-opted to issue in the conditional belief that the window will shatter if hit by a rock with that sort of momentum. It is such conditional beliefs that play a crucial role in prospective reasoning. If the representation of a broken window issues in some degree of negative affect, then the presence of the conditional belief enables that affective reaction to be transferred to the antecedent of the conditional. Hence the action of throwing the rock will come to seem equally bad.

An account of how one can form new beliefs through discursive reasoning (in inner speech) needs to be somewhat different—although it, too, piggybacks on an existing mechanism for issuing in new beliefs on the basis of perception. In this case the mechanism is one that enables us to form new beliefs from the assertions of other people. When one hears someone say something—for example, "The sea around Bonaire is warm in January"—the sounds in question are processed by the language and mindreading systems, with the result that one hears the person as *asserting* or *telling one* that the sea around Bonaire is warm in January. If one fails to detect any inconsistency with one's own beliefs, and if the informant is appraised as trustworthy, then one will form a new belief with that content.

Now suppose that an episode of discursive reasoning leads one to express the same sentence in inner speech. (Perhaps one has just read that the sea in the Caribbean is warm in January. Glancing at a map, one sees that Bonaire is in the Caribbean. This leads one to say, "The sea around Bonaire is warm in January.") Here, too, the sentence will be heard as asserting that the sea around Bonaire is warm in January. (Alternatively, or in addition, it might be heard as expressing the *judgment* that the sea around Bonaire is warm in January.) If no inconsistencies with one's existing beliefs are detected, and if we assume that one's own assertions (and judgments) are treated as reliable by default, then one will likewise form the belief that the sea around Bonaire is warm in January. In effect, one believes one's own assertions, much as if they were statements from a reliable informant.

3.3. Mental commitments

Others have suggested a more elaborate mechanism through which episodes of inner speech can acquire a belief-like role. (The question whether these really *are* instances of belief will be addressed in Section 4.) Frankish (2004) argues that we often hear ourselves, not merely as *asserting* something in inner or outer speech, but as *committing ourselves* to the truth of what we assert. (See also Moran, 2001; Bilgrami, 2006.) The idea is that an assertion can function in the same sort of way as a promise does, constraining both our overt and covert behavior in the future accordingly. Regarding oneself as committed to the truth of the proposition, *The sea around Bonaire is warm in January*, for example, one will thereafter feel obliged to act as if it were true. If one wants to go somewhere in January where the swimming is warm, one cannot refuse to consider Bonaire without reneging on one's previous commitment.

Notice the contrast between Frankish's (2004) proposal and the one outlined in Section 3.2. According to the latter, hearing oneself as asserting that P causes one (in the absence of any conflict with existing belief) to believe that P. According to the former, hearing oneself as committed to the truth of *P* leads one to feel obliged in future to think and act just as if one believed that P. This requires us to postulate an independent source of motivation, such as a desire to keep one's commitments, or the presence of an evaluative mechanism that leads one to see instances of commitment-keeping as good.

The two proposals are consistent with one another, of course. For one might treat one's own assertions as instances of reliable testimony on some occasions and as commitments on others. And I have no doubt that both are correct, at least sometimes. But a commitment-based account is only really plausible in cases where one makes overt statements in the presence of an audience. When one says something in a public forum one generally feels committed to the truth of what one has said, and will act accordingly. It is much less likely that one will hear one's assertions in *inner* speech as expressing commitments, unless they are made with a special imagined intonation and stress. Nevertheless, an account in the spirit of Frankish's can still apply. For if one hears oneself as *judging* that P, one will thereafter believe that one *has* judged that P (and has not changed one's mind). As a result, one may feel obliged to think and act in the future on the assumption that *P* is true, provided that one wants to be consistent, or provided that one wants to think and behave as one believes a rational agent should.

3.4. Making new decisions

It is easy to see how System 2 reasoning can issue in a new decision (and hence cause action) when the reasoning in question involves prospective imagining. Since such imagining engages motivational systems in something resembling the normal way, as we saw in Section 3.1, it will lead to a new decision in something like the normal way too. For example, suppose one has returned home late at night without one's door key, and is reflecting on what to do. One imagines throwing a stone at a bedroom window to rouse the occupant, but the resulting image of smashed glass leads one to see the action as bad. So one decides not to do it, and casts around for an alternative. Likewise, if imagining oneself to be living in Chicago is seen as good, then this may lead one to accept the offer to relocate (provided that there are no contrary motivations, of course). This is just regular first-order decision making, with decisions resulting from an unopposed motivation to do the thing in question, or from a perception that the thing is better than the alternatives.

It is less obvious how episodes of *discursive* reasoning can issue in novel decisions. For there is nothing here quite corresponding to the mechanisms that lead one to accept other people's testimony (which are then co-opted in inner speech) in the manner discussed in Section 3.2. Admittedly, people sometimes tell one what to do, or exhort one to act, or tell one what one *should* do, which often creates a social motivation of some sort to act accordingly. And *sometimes* inner speech can take this form ("Don't open the fridge!," one tells oneself, "Keep your eyes off the chocolate cake!," "I *should* turn over this card and that one," and so on). In such cases one attempts to influence one's own behavior by simulating the social pressure that other people's exhortations and evaluative statements can create. But it seems implausible that discursive decision making should always take this form. On the contrary, the speech employed in this form of System 2 reasoning can often be neutral in tone. After reflecting on the facts that one will need cash for an evening on the town together with the presence of an empty wallet one might conclude, "So, I will stop at the ATM on the way to the metro." This doesn't seem like a self-directed exhortation, and contains no evaluative concepts. So how does it achieve its effects?

Sometimes, of course, the components of discursive reasoning that appear decision-like may be epiphenomenal with respect to the eventual action. In the case just described, for example, it may be that while saying, "I need cash for the evening" one imagines oneself having to scrounge from one's friends, and feels negative affect as a result. When combined with the image of the nearby ATM this may lead one to see stopping at the latter as good. It may be that this perception leads to an (unconscious) decision to act accordingly, which in turn causes one to *say* (in inner speech), "I will stop at the ATM." Although the latter looks like it plays a decision-like causal role, it does not. Rather, it is caused by the underlying real decision. And it is the latter that causes one's later stopping behavior.

There is also, however, the possibility of appealing here to commitment-like states of the sort discussed in Section 3.3. Suppose that rehearsal in inner speech of the sentence, "I will stop at the ATM" is caused by some sort of competitive interaction among speech-action schemata that does *not* involve a decision to visit the ATM. Nevertheless, if one *hears* that inner sentence as expressing a commitment to visit the ATM or (more plausibly) as expressing a decision to do so, one may thereafter feel obliged to act accordingly. Supposing that one wants to keep one's commitments, or wants to be the sort of strong-willed person who sticks by one's decisions, one may *subsequently* take a decision to stop at the ATM, motivated by just such desires.

Overall, then, the question of how System 2 reasoning has effects on motivation, memory, and decision making may best be answered pluralistically. Sometimes these effects are pretty direct, relying on the global broadcasting qualities of working memory that mimic the effects of perception. But in other cases those effects may be routed through higher-order beliefs and desires. It may be because one *believes* that one has made a decision, for example, and *wants* to be the sort of person who executes one's decisions, that one then goes ahead and decides and acts accordingly. In Section 4 we will focus on this latter sort of possibility, considering whether it enables us to find a place for conscious attitudes of all kinds within the operations of System 2.

4. A Second Mind?

Some theorists maintain that the dual-systems literature warrants us in thinking in terms of two kinds of mind (Frankish, 2004, 2009; Evans, 2010). The present section will examine this suggestion, in order to see whether it provides any support for the idea of an amodal workspace in which conscious attitude-involving reflection can take place.

4.1. An ambiguity

It is important to distinguish between two things that might be meant by saying that System 1 and System 2 constitute two distinct minds (Evans, 2010), or by saying that the addition of System 2 forms of mentality to the basic primate mind amounts to the creation of a new *kind* of mind (Dennett, 1996). On the one hand, such statements can be intended just to emphasize that the two systems have radically different powers, and need to be accounted for using distinct explanatory frameworks. So understood, such claims seem to me to be mostly unobjectionable. For there is no doubt that the powers of the human mind differ very significantly from those of other animals, and that some of these differences are due to the human capacity for System 2 forms of reasoning.[5] If people wish to mark this difference by saying that the human mind differs in *kind* from the minds of nonhuman animals, then I have no principled objection to them doing so—although I think it is more fruitful, myself, to emphasize the continuities.

On the other hand, in claiming that the two systems constitute two minds, some have intended something much more ambitious. The claim is that each system replicates the core functionality of a mind, and contains its own distinctive goals,

---

[5] As we will see in Chapter 8, however, System 2 reasoning comes in degrees, and many other species of animal are capable of it to some extent.

beliefs, reasoning processes, and decisions. Frankish (2004, 2009), in particular, develops such a view. He suggests that the commitments we make at the System 2 level—to want certain things, believe certain things, and decide certain things—constitute novel forms of wanting, believing, and deciding, respectively. For these events are said to possess not only the content but the functional profile of the attitudes in question. Someone who is committed to believing that P will thereafter reason and act in ways that a *P*-believer should; and someone who is committed to having taken a decision to do something will be likely to do that very thing thereafter, just as would someone who had decided to do that thing in the normal manner.

Frankish's view suggests an alternative way of defending the idea of a central workspace in which attitudes of all types can be activated and conscious. He can allow that our critique of the traditional account is essentially correct, while claiming that System 2 attitudes are realized in the controlled use of working memory together with a set of attitudes that exist at the System 1 level. It is by rehearsing in inner speech a sentence such as, "I will stop at the ATM," and by coming to believe of oneself that one has made a commitment to stop to get cash (combined with an underlying motivation to execute one's commitments), that one *constitutes oneself* as deciding to stop on the way to the metro to obtain cash. The event of entertaining the sentence in question is conscious, of course, and that event *is* an event of deciding, on this view. So there are conscious as well as unconscious decisions, contrary to the claims I have been defending in this book. Similar accounts can then be given of conscious judging, conscious wanting, conscious wondering, and so on, establishing the existence of conscious attitudes of all other types.

4.2. System 2 attitudes are not amodal

Let us suppose, for the moment, that System 2 contains attitudes of various familiar types (beliefs, goals, decisions, and so on), in something resembling the way Frankish (2004) suggests. It is important to realize, however, that this would do nothing to vindicate the idea of an *amodal* workspace in which attitudes of all types can be active and conscious. For the attitudes in question are modality specific (generally involving auditory images of sentences in inner speech). Admittedly, the events in question acquire the causal role distinctive of an attitude of some specific type through the work of an underlying set of amodal attitudes, such as the belief that one has taken a decision together with a desire to be the sort of person who stands by one's decisions. But these attitudes do their work unconsciously, and they do not themselves belong to System 2. It is also true that the System 2 events in question will have amodal concepts bound into them, such as the amodal content, *I will stop at the ATM* bound into the content of an episode of inner speech. But the same is also true of perceptual and working-memory contents generally, of course. There is nothing here to suggest that the *attitudes* that figure in System 2 are amodal and not sensory dependent.

If Frankish accepts that System 2 attitudes are tokened in working memory (generally in the form of inner speech) and that working memory is sensory dependent, then he must also accept that those attitudes constitutively involve modality-specific representations. Moreover, they will involve such representations essentially, not accidentally, since the conscious status of the System 2 events depends on attention directed at midlevel sensory areas of the brain together with the resulting global broadcast of sensory-based information. So there is nothing here that can be used to defend the reality of an amodal workspace. A position of this sort might represent a partial victory for common sense, nevertheless. For one can represent some of the core theses that are under attack in this book as involving a conjunction of two claims: first, attitudes of all familiar types can be conscious and globally accessible; second, the attitudes that figure in conscious reflection can be amodal in nature. I deny both. But a Frankish-style account would vindicate the first claim while dropping the second. It is therefore important to consider whether or not there are System 2 attitudes, as Frankish claims. I will argue in Sections 4.3 and 4.4 that there are not.

Notice, however, that a Frankish-style partial vindication of common sense is likely to provide would-be defenders of common sense with pretty thin gruel. For conscious attitudes will only exist in *some* people *some of the time*, on this account. Introspection-sampling studies suggest that some people never engage in inner speech at all, for example (Heavey & Hurlburt, 2008). In that case it seems unlikely that they will ever experience themselves as making a commitment to the truth of a proposition when they reflect. Moreover, it seems quite plausible that many people never hear themselves as making internal commitments when they do engage in inner speech. And while experiencing oneself as making judgments and decisions when engaged in inner speech is surely much more common, it is likely that many people lack the motivations (to be consistent, to be the sort of person who executes one's decisions) that are necessary to transform the events in question into Frankish-style attitudes. In addition, of course, much conscious reflection will in any case involve simpler sorts of attitude-causing activity of the kinds discussed in Section 3, where no appeals to System 2 attitudes need to be made. This is a far cry from the idea of a conscious workspace in which attitudes of all types *regularly* and *routinely* figure in *everyone's* reflections.

4.3. There are no System 2 decisions

I have conceded that people sometimes behave in the sorts of way that Frankish (2004) supposes. Sometimes they hear themselves as making a commitment to the truth of a proposition, and thereafter feel obliged to constrain their thinking and deciding accordingly. And sometimes people hear themselves as taking a decision to do something (in circumstances where the only underlying decision was to rehearse one sentence rather than another), and thereafter are motivated to act accordingly. The question is whether these System 2 events *are* attitudes of the appropriate kind (beliefs and decisions respectively). Elsewhere I have argued at length against this idea (Carruthers, 2011a, 2013b), showing how it fails for a number of different types of attitude in turn. Here I will provide just a sketch of the main point, focusing on the case of alleged System 2 decisions in particular. (Section 4.4 will then provide a similar outline of the argument against System 2 beliefs.)

The argument turns on a seemingly compelling claim about the nature of decisions, discussed in Chapter 2.2. This is that their main functional role is to constrain and ultimately close off the process of practical reasoning (Bratman, 1987, 1999). Decisions that are taken for the here-and-now activate the appropriate motor plans needed to put the decision into effect. And decisions that are taken for the future give rise to a stored intention. This intention, when later activated by situational cues, recruits cognitive and motor resources to implement the decision without one needing to revisit the question of whether or not to act. While practical reasoning may occur in such a case, one's reasoning will concern only *how* to act, or whether to act *now*, not whether to act at all. In fact the central purpose of taking decisions and forming intentions is to *close off* reasoning about whether or not to act.

Now notice that the alleged System 2 decisions lack these essential properties. Suppose that one is looking at a bowl of fruit and reasoning discursively about which item to select. "The apples look good," one says to oneself, "but they are rather large. And the last orange I had was somewhat dried out. So I'll take the pear." Following this, one picks up the pear and begins to eat. The final sentence in this sequence does, indeed, close off the process of discursive, inner-speech-based reasoning; and we may suppose that it does cause the resulting action. But on a Frankish-style account it only does so through an additional stage of (unconscious) practical reasoning. It causes one to *believe* that one has made a decision to eat the pear, and this interacts with one's *goal* of being the sort of person who does what one decides, to issue in an (unconscious) decision to eat the pear. Note that this additional practical reasoning is not merely implementational. It is not reasoning about *how* to eat the pear, but about whether or not to do so. And the resulting decision to eat the pear is surely the real one.

Similar points can be made in cases where one reaches an alleged System 2 decision for the future, as when one concludes an episode of discursive reasoning with, "I will stop at the ATM on the way to the metro." On a Frankish-style account, this statement is heard as expressing a decision and gives rise to a memory that one has done so. When driving toward the metro and seeing the bank where the ATM is located, this memory is activated and interacts with the goal of being the sort of person who executes one's decisions to issue in a decision to stop the car. Again it is the latter, surely, that is the real decision, which takes place unconsciously subsequent to the recall of what one takes to have been an earlier decision. And what that initial System 2 event ("I will stop at the ATM") gives rise to is not a stored intention but an episodic memory of what one *believes* to have been a decision.

Someone might propose an alternative to a Frankish-style account. Consider the simplest case where a (nonverbal) decision to stop at the ATM causes one to articulate in inner speech, "I will stop at the ATM." Why can't one regard the initial decision as having been bound into the content of the verbal performance, thereby constituting them both as one and the same decision? In that case one would not need Frankish's apparatus of higher-order beliefs and goals (believing oneself to have made a decision, and wanting to execute one's decisions) in order to explain how the decision achieves its effects. On the contrary, deciding to stop at the ATM is conscious, and causes one to stop at the ATM when the latter is perceived. Recall from Chapter 4.4 that this account cannot work, however. This is because the sentence in inner speech is a sensory forward model generated from a set of *motor* instructions, while the initiating attitude and its content have been left behind. That sensory forward model then needs to be interpreted by the language and mindreading systems working in concert, leading one to hear oneself *as* deciding to stop at the ATM. Although the latter content *represents* the original decision, there is no good sense in which it includes or contains that decision. So the idea that the System 2 event constitutes a conscious (globally available) decision cannot be defended from this direction either.

4.4. There are no System 2 beliefs

A similar argument can be generated by considering the functional roles of judgments and beliefs, which were discussed in Chapter 2.1. A judgment is an event that gives rise to standing beliefs *immediately*, without further theoretical reasoning about what to believe; and it is likewise immediately available to enter into practical decision making. Likewise a stored belief, when activated, is immediately available to influence decision making. In particular, it is immediately available to influence what one says in answer to a query. If one believes that P and is asked, "P?," the activation of the belief (note: not the belief *that one believes* that P, but the first-order belief that P) will normally cause one (either by default, or when combined with a desire to answer truthfully) to answer, "Yes."[6]

Now consider a case where someone's assertion is *heard as* expressing a belief and subsequently assumes some of the roles of belief (Frankish-style), but where the processes that issue in the initial assertion actually involve no such state. For example, someone in the "free choice" condition of a counter-attitudinal essay-writing experiment of the sort discussed in Chapter 5.2 says after writing the essay, "It wouldn't be bad if tuition were raised next term." This is heard as expressing the *judgment* that it wouldn't be bad for tuition to be raised, and an episodic memory with that content is created. (Note that the memory is second order in nature: it is a memory whose content is *that* one made a judgment of a certain sort.) Since the heard-judgment presents as *not bad* the person's previous action of writing an essay defending higher tuition, the person's affective state returns to normal.

Sometime later the person is asked, "Would it be bad if tuition were raised next term?" This activates both a standing belief that higher tuition *would* be bad and an episodic memory of having judged that raising tuition would *not* be bad. The conflict between these two is, in the circumstances, resolved in favor of the latter (perhaps because it is activated more swiftly), and interacts with the goal of acting consistently with one's previous judgments, leading the person to answer, "No, it wouldn't be bad." Notice that the etiology of this assertion is quite different from what one would expect of a (first-order) belief that raising tuition wouldn't be bad. Rather, a higher-order belief to the effect that one *has* such a belief interacts with the (higher-order) goal of acting consistently with one's beliefs to issue in behavior that looks like it manifests a first-order belief, but doesn't really do so. I conclude, therefore, that the System 2 event of initially saying, "Raising tuition next term would not be bad" doesn't have the right kind of functional role to qualify as a judgment or belief.

Of course in any full discussion of this topic there are moves that can potentially be made in response to these points that need to be replied to, and

---

[6] While cognitive models of speech production standardly begin from a *belief to be expressed* (Levelt, 1989), none that I know of maintains that production of a first-order assertion that P begins from the higher-order belief that one believes that P. *Expressing* a belief in speech does not normally need to start from awareness of oneself *as possessing* such a belief. Rather, it begins from the belief.

it would need to be shown that the argument generalizes to alleged System 2 attitudes of all types. These are tasks that I have undertaken elsewhere (Carruthers, 2011a, 2013b). Here I propose just to take for granted that my critique remains solid when articulated in greater depth and detail. This enables us to conclude that a Frankish-style attempt at a partial vindication of common sense is untenable. The inner speech events that we sometimes experience as expressing commitments, decisions, judgments, and so forth are not, themselves, attitudes of the relevant types. (They are, however, sensorily embedded attitudes of hearing *as*, and this is a kind of sensory-based judgment, of course.) Hence System 2 is not a workspace in which attitudes of all types can be active and conscious.

5. An Extended Mind?

The present section will consider the relationship between the account of System 2 reasoning and decision making defended here, and the claim advanced by some philosophers that the mind extends outside the brain into the surrounding world (Clark & Chalmers, 1998; Clark, 2008). The question arises quite naturally, since many forms of System 2 reasoning that are conducted using working memory alone can equally well be undertaken in the public domain. Arithmetic calculations, for example, can be done in one's head or on paper; and episodes of discursive reasoning can be conducted in inner speech or while "thinking aloud," using overt speech or writing. One can then ask whether these public events should be considered as *parts* of the mental activities in question, and hence as parts of the mind. More importantly for our purposes, we can also ask whether some of these public events can constitute propositional attitudes of various kinds, thus providing a very different sort of vindication of the idea of a non-sensory global attitudinal workspace. This is where we begin.

5.1. Extended attitudes?

Humans in literate cultures use written records of various sorts to enhance and support their memories. Many of us record our future intentions in our calendars (the trips we intend to make, tasks we intend to complete, and so on), as well as our aspirations and long-term goals. And many people keep electronic or written records of factual information (the addresses and phone numbers of friends and contacts, for example). Should these physical records be considered as intentions and memories that exist outside the head? Clark & Chalmers (1998) argue that they should, focusing just on the case of belief, and using an example where someone's *only* access to stored factual information is external.

Clark & Chalmers (1998) consider the case of Otto, who suffers from severe amnesia. Since Otto cannot form new memories internally, in his brain, he carries with him a notebook in which he records salient items of information. When Otto reads of an especially interesting exhibition at the Museum of Modern Art and decides to go, he cannot consult his (internal) memory of the location of the museum, since he has none. But he can look up the same information in his notebook, which guides his subsequent behavior in the way that a memory would. Given that Otto always carries his notebook with him, and that his use of it is smooth and habitual, Clark & Chalmers argue that its entries *are* Otto's beliefs. So Otto's mind is not just in his head, but encompasses the physical notebook as well.

If this conclusion is accepted, and if it generalizes to other, more everyday cases of external notes and records, then we can draw two further conclusions. One is that the external environment contains amodal (perceptible but not constitutively sensory) propositional attitudes of various kinds. The second is that the physical environment forms a sort of globally accessible workspace for cognition. The states within it can become globally available to multiple faculties of the mind (through being perceived, as when Otto reads an entry in his notebook), with the information that they encode thereby becoming conscious. So there is a globally available workspace in which amodal propositional attitudes can be stored.[7]

Clark & Chalmers' (1998) suggestion suffers from essentially the same weakness as the System 2 attitudes proposed by Frankish (2004), which were critiqued in Sections 4.3 and 4.4. While the functional role of an entry in Otto's notebook is broadly similar to that of a memory, on a more fine-grained level it is markedly different.[8] Granted, when Otto wants to know the location of the Museum of Modern Art he consults his notebook, just as an ordinary person might consult her memory; and both forms of search will issue in a sensory-based representation of that location entertained in working memory, which guides decision making quite similarly thereafter. But the processes that are involved in search of the two kinds are quite different.

---

[7] On some views these externally stored attitudes will even qualify as conscious. If a conscious mental state is a mental state that one is *aware of* (Rosenthal, 2005), and one becomes aware of what are actually one's beliefs by reading entries in a notebook, then those entries can count as conscious beliefs.

[8] Recall from Sections 4.3 and 4.4 that while events in System 2 have roles somewhat like those of beliefs and decisions, the manner in which they achieve their effects is quite different, relying on higher-order beliefs about one's attitudes together with higher-order goals such as a desire to execute one's intentions.

When Otto searches his notebook, he needs to execute some overt physical actions to do so. In particular, he has to pick up the notebook and turn the pages to find the correct entry (perhaps using an index or table of contents of some sort). In consequence, he cannot access this information if he is paralyzed, or while his hands are occupied with something else. And in order to activate the information contained in the entry, he must rely on overt perception to do so. In particular, he needs to read the entry, or visually examine a diagram if the information is encoded in map-like form. Hence he cannot access the information contained in his notebook in the dark, or without his reading glasses. When ordinary folk search for a memory, in contrast, they use a combination of conceptual cues and top-down attentional signals to activate the information into working memory. Neither overt action nor external perception are needed. So (and in contrast with Otto's case) memories can be accessed while tying one's shoelaces or while lying in bed in the dark.

On a coarse-grained level the functional roles of notebook entries and memories are similar, then. But when examined more closely those roles differ a good deal. Which level should we use for purposes of individuation? Should we count notebook entries as forms of memory or not? I assume these questions concern, not our superficial pragmatic interests, but rather the psychological kinds that really exist in the world (that is, the psychological kinds that cognitive science should recognize). In that case it is plain that a notebook entry is not a memory. For the means by which Otto and ordinary people access their stored information are quite different. Moreover, in the case of regular memories the nature and functioning of the storage system (long-term memory) is itself a topic of study for cognitive science, whereas the preservation of written entries in notebooks is of interest only to archivists or applied physicists.

This critique of extended attitudes is similar to that provided by Adams & Aizawa (2008). Drawing on what they take to be the commitments of cognitive science generally, they claim that a cognitive state (such as a belief) is a state possessing *underived intentionality* over which computational processes of some sort are defined. A genuine memory of the location of the Museum of Modern Art will be about that place *intrinsically*, not in virtue of anyone's intentions or interpretations. And a genuine memory should also be able to enter *directly* into computational processes of various sorts. An entry in Otto's notebook, in contrast, only represents what it does through the conventions of the English language, or through Otto's interpretive dispositions. And the entry itself doesn't enter into any computations. It is only the representations that Otto derives from it through reading that do that.

Adams & Aizawa's critique amounts to the same as the one I sketched earlier if we assume that cognitive science should only be interested in computational states that possess underived intentionality. I think my own critique goes deeper, however, since it depends on fewer substantive assumptions about cognitive science. Some people think that many of the states studied by cognitive science lack intentional content altogether, for example (Egan, 1995; Ramsey, 2007). And as we noted in Chapter 2.5, radical connectionists deny that cognitive science studies processes that are computational in nature. In contrast, no one thinks that cognitive scientists should be studying the way ink-marks are preserved on paper, or how those marks differentially impact the reflection of light. These are matters for physicists to investigate. All we need to assume, then, is that cognitive states are ones whose natures and interactions can be studied by cognitive scientists using the standard methods of cognitive science (whatever those are). This alone enables us to conclude that the entries in Otto's notebook are not cognitive states (and are therefore not beliefs).

5.2. An extended workspace?

I have argued that there are no propositional attitudes existing outside the head. Someone might concede this, while insisting that cognitive *processes* nevertheless extend beyond the brain (Clark, 2008). For notice that the procedures used in both overt and covert forms of reasoning can be quite similar. Someone who is performing an arithmetic calculation in working memory, for example, may activate the same sequence of motor commands as would be used when physically inscribing the relevant numerals on a piece of paper. Each motor command is used to create a sensory forward model of the result, which when entered into working memory provides a prompt for the next action in a well-rehearsed procedure, just as each physical action using paper creates a perception of the result, and which then provides a prompt for the next action in the procedure. And just as working memory serves as a repository of sensory-based contents that evoke and guide the procedure, so one might think of the physical environment including pencils and paper as doing the same. When one performs a calculation on paper the "workspace" for the process includes the pencil, paper, and the inscriptions thereon. When the calculation is done in working memory alone, in contrast, the process mimics or simulates that overt activity to the same end.

There is no harm in thinking of the surrounding environment as constituting part of the workspace for a cognitive procedure. For those external props, aids, and activities support (and in complex cases make possible) the cognitive processes in question. But it is another matter to claim that the physical and behavioral events that take place in that workspace are themselves cognitive.

Indeed, if we take as our criterion of the cognitive what is a potential object of scientific inquiry for cognitive science, then it is plain that the extended workspace should *not* be counted as a part of cognition. Cognitive scientists need to study the processes that lead from motor intentions to motor actions, of course; and they need to investigate the processes that transform light impacting the retina into perceptual experiences. They also need to investigate how sensory-based contents can evoke stored knowledge and activate and guide behavioral procedures, as well as the manner in which the latter can be activated and used covertly. But cognitive science has no interest in the question how graphite moved across the surface of some paper leaves a set of marks, or in the question how those marks influence the way light is reflected from the surface. Nor is cognitive science interested in how movements of the keys of a computer are transformed into digitally stored information. These are questions for physicists and electronic engineers to answer.

It might be replied that this argument ignores the existence of dynamical-systems approaches to cognition (Beer, 2000). For example, Thelen et al. (2001) offer a dynamical-systems account of the interactions between infants and the detailed properties of their environment in explaining the varied circumstances in which infants will, or will not, perseverate in their reaching and succumb to the *A not B error*.[9] In such models, all of the different variables are regarded as being on a par. No distinction is drawn between internal (putatively cognitive) variables and those that exist in the surrounding environment. This might be thought to provide a reason to treat all as equally cognitive, just as Clark (2008) urges.

In fact, however, dynamical-systems theories are ontologically neutral. They provide abstract mathematical formalisms for studying the behavior over time of any complex interacting system, no matter how ontologically diverse that system is. One can, for example, use dynamical-systems theory to study the interactions among beavers, trees, mud, and water that take place when beavers create dams across streams. The success of such models should not, of course, lead us to think that beavers and mud, or beavers and trees, belong to the same ontological kinds. Likewise, then, when the systems studied involve both mental and physical states. One cannot conclude from the fact that one can model as a dynamical system the way an infant's goals and motor plans interact with features of the physical environment that the latter are themselves cognitive. Nor can one conclude that every aspect of the interaction constitutes a part of the infant's mind.

---

[9] In this paradigm the infant is first repeatedly shown an object being hidden in one location—location A—and allowed to retrieve it. Then the infant is shown the object being placed elsewhere (location B). Many infants nevertheless perseverate, and reach for location A, not B.

It is true, of course, that modern humans have vastly extended the powers of the mind through the invention and use of a variety of external aids. These include books, writing implements, computers, and the internet. Humans interacting with these external objects can achieve far more than anyone could hope to do covertly, using working memory alone. This is, or should be, a truism. But in order to understand how this happens it is not necessary to claim that the mind has become extended into the world. This adds nothing to what we can account for in terms of cycles of *interaction* between our minds and the physical world, where the physical world has been arranged so as to prompt and supplement our mental activity. Moreover, even if we *were* to think of the physical environment as constituting a part of the workspace within which cognitive processes occur, it is not a workspace in which amodal attitudes can be activated. So there is nothing, here, that can be used either to shore up standard models of reflection, or to undermine the sensory-based account.

6. Conclusion

This chapter has shown that there is nothing in the two-systems literature to support the existence of an amodal workspace in which attitudes of all kinds can be activated and conscious. On the contrary, what is distinctive of System 2 processes is just that they make constitutive use of working memory. Moreover, the factors that explain people's variance in reasoning abilities leave no room for any contribution from an amodal workspace. We have also seen that attempts to claim that there are a set of System 2 attitudes constituting of sensory-based events in working memory are unsuccessful, as are attempts to locate such attitudes in overt physical records of one sort or another. More importantly, and in a more positive vein, we have seen how the framework outlined in previous chapters can be put to work in explaining episodes of System 2 reasoning, with amodal attitudes working in the background to manipulate the sensory-based contents of working memory (or to issue in overt actions that have similar effects). In a variety of ways, then, the case for thinking that reflection is sensory based has been strengthened still further, as has the case for denying the existence of any workspace in which attitudes of all types can be activated and conscious.

8

The Evolution of Reflection

This chapter has two goals. The first is to address what is, perhaps, the primary difficulty for the sensory-based account of reflection developed in this book. This is the challenge of explaining *why* reflection should be sensory based. Given that there are amodal attitudes (as I and most others believe), why is the mind nevertheless organized in such a way that those attitudes cannot enter into reflection directly? Why can they only operate behind the scenes, directing and manipulating the sensory-based contents of working memory? My answer to this challenge is an evolutionary one. Evolution is always constrained by pre-existing structures. I will suggest that sensory-based attentional and working-memory systems are an ancient adaptation, placing constraints on later evolutionary developments. This will require us to review some of the evidence of working-memory abilities in nonhuman animals.

The second, subsidiary, goal of this chapter is to offer an additional—evolutionary—argument for the sensory-based account of reflection. Given that reflection utilizes working memory (as does the stream of consciousness more generally), and that working memory is grounded in sensory-based attentional and rehearsal mechanisms of ancient evolutionary ancestry, it would have required the emergence of a whole new kind of global workspace in order for amodal attitudes to be conscious and to figure in our reflections. To the extent this is implausible, to that extent the sensory-based account is further supported.

1. The Central Puzzle

The present section will lay out and develop the main puzzle that this chapter is intended to address: why is it that reflection is sensory based?

1.1. Content versus format

We can engage in reflection about anything under the sun. Indeed, we often reflect about highly abstract matters, such as the state of the economy, the relationships among friends and acquaintances, the existence of God, or the principles of logic and mathematics. Only rarely does reflection concern the sensory properties of things and events. Painters and house decorators sometimes reflect on choices of color, and composers may need to reflect on what timbre of instrument would best carry a musical theme. More prosaically, we sometimes reflect on the colors in a sunset or in a tree's foliage, or on the night-time screeches of a neighbor's cat. But for the most part the properties that are the objects of our reflections are not sensory ones. Why, then, are those reflections constrained to take place in a sensory-based format, such as visual imagery or inner speech? What is the benefit of using sensory-based representations, given that the things represented are only rarely sensory in nature?

One can imagine someone wanting to respond to this challenge by claiming that reflection about abstract matters is a recent cultural phenomenon, perhaps restricted to literate and scientific cultures. For in that case it would not be puzzling that reflection would need to make use of representations that were designed for other purposes. But such a claim is not remotely plausible. On the contrary, humans everywhere and always have reflected about the mental states of others, relationships among group members and kin, relationships of ownership and obligation, together with a panoply of potential deities (Brown, 1991). However, this attempted response to the challenge does get one thing right, as we will see. This is that reflection (construed broadly, to include all inferential processes that make constitutive use of working memory) was not originally designed from scratch for thinking about abstract matters of the sort listed above. Rather, it evolved many millions of years before humans ever walked the Earth, and is an exaptation of systems that evolved initially for perception and perceptually based working memory.

1.2. A design perspective

Another way of articulating the puzzle of the sensory-based character of reflection is to adopt the perspective of a designer or engineer. Supposing one set out to design a mechanism that could engage in intelligent forms of reasoning and problem solving across a variety of domains, how would one do it? The question need not be hypothetical, since there is a branch of cognitive science that attempts to do just this. Designers in the field of artificial intelligence have developed a number of architectures for intelligent domain-general reasoning. Two of the most prominent frameworks are Soar models of unified cognition (Newell, 1990; Young & Lewis, 1999) and ACT-R accounts (Anderson, 1993; Lovett et al., 1999). Neither of these requires the representations employed within the architecture to be sensory based. (Nor, to the best of my knowledge, do any others.) Given that no one designing a reflective reasoning system would constrain it to be sensory based, the obvious question is why evolution nevertheless did so.

Two points are worth emphasizing here, however. The first is that most artificial intelligence frameworks were not created with the goal of explaining the fine-grained details of human performance. (Had the designers pursued such a goal, they would arguably have made their systems sensory based, given the evidence of the sensory-based nature of human working memory discussed in Chapter 4.) Rather, the goal was partly philosophical and partly practical. One aim was to demonstrate that a machine *could* be intelligent. Another was to create intelligent machines that could be put to work on our behalf. These aims enabled designers to abstract away from the messy details of human performance and the constraints imposed by human biology.

The second point to emphasize is that while artificial reasoning mechanisms do not *require* the representations employed within them to be sensory based, neither do they exclude such a possibility. Both Soar and ACT-R, for example, are neutral on the question of the representational format of the representations they use. So versions of these architectures *could* be designed to employ sensory-based representations. The sensory-based account of reflection is therefore *consistent* with these models, even if it receives no support from them. It remains the case, however, that when viewed from the perspective of artificial intelligence, the sensory-based nature of reflection seems like an arbitrary constraint.

1.3. Constraints on design

Imagine that humans had, from time immemorial, lived in circumstances where possession of a third hand would have been beneficial. Imagine that many of the tasks that form an essential part of human life-history could only be performed with three hands, requiring the cooperation of two or more people. (Suppose that in these circumstances a lone human could not survive for more than a few days.) The absence of a third hand would then have seemed almost like a disability, and it would have been natural to wonder why natural selection had failed to provide us with what we need. But in this case the answer would have been straightforward. Bilateral symmetry is an ancient adaptation associated with deeply embedded principles of embryology, and is almost as old as animal life itself (Finnerty et al., 2004). Indeed, evolution could not even have provided humans with *four* hands rather than two (together with two legs), given that the four-limb body plan is so deeply ingrained in all amphibians, reptiles, birds, and mammals.

I will suggest that the brain design enabling the global broadcast of attended sensory information is almost equally ancient, being common at least to all birds and mammals, and perhaps to all vertebrates. The use of these attentional networks to sustain and manipulate information in working memory is likewise quite ancient. When reflection on abstract matters started to figure as an important aspect of human life-history, therefore (or perhaps earlier, among primates more generally), there was little option but to co-opt these ancient attentional networks for the task. Evolving a global workspace in which amodal attitudes of all types could be activated and conscious may well have been as difficult as evolving a third hand or a novel pair of limbs. It would have required an entirely new pattern of cortical organization, which would have needed, in turn, a very different trajectory of neurogenesis in the developing embryo and fetus.

If this argument is to be successful, then it must be true that the basic organization of the nervous system is highly conserved across animals, just as the skeletal system is. And indeed this is the case (Striedter, 2004; Geary, 2005; Swanson, 2012). The organization of the nervous system into forebrain (cortex in mammals), midbrain, hindbrain, and spinal cord is common to all vertebrates, and is discernable early in embryogenesis. Moreover, the long-distance wiring maps of the brain and the forebrain are highly conserved across vertebrates as well, as are many specific subsystems within each of the main components (Salas et al., 2003).

It is also possible to make a general argument that we should *expect* attentional networks to be among the highly conserved features of vertebrate nervous systems. (In Section 2 we will see that this expectation is fulfilled.) This is because all but the very simplest animals confront essentially the same problem; namely, that there is more information potentially available in the world around them and detectable by their sensory systems than they could possibly hope to make use of. Indeed, there is much more information actually impacting an organism's sensory systems at any given moment than could possibly be processed, let alone responded to. All animals therefore confront the problem of informational selection: how to select for processing the information that is most relevant to their fitness in the circumstances. This is the problem that attentional systems are designed to solve. By selecting some information for widespread processing from among the much larger extent available, these systems insure that the organism confronts its most pressing problems and that motivational, inferential, and decision-making systems respond to them in a coordinated manner. Indeed, this is the main benefit of having the brain organization that I have described as "the centered mind." A global broadcasting architecture solves the coordination problem for brains that are inundated with information while being composed of multiple specialized subsystems, as all brains are (Carruthers, 2006). We should therefore expect this architecture to be highly conserved across vertebrate species.

2. The Age of Attention

This section will argue that the prediction made at the end of Section 1.3 is fulfilled. Key components of the brain systems for both overt and covert attention are widespread among vertebrates, and are present in birds and mammals at least. In later sections we will discuss behavioral evidence suggesting that members of these groups make use of the covert attentional system for purposes of remembering and reasoning, thereby engaging in simple forms of reflection.

2.1. Conserved networks

Attentional mechanisms are strongly conserved among primates at least, involving homologous cortical and subcortical networks. These include a top-down system in the cortex, linking dorsolateral prefrontal cortex, the frontal eye-fields, and the intraparietal sulcus, as well as a bottom-up subcortical system linking structures such as the amygdala, thalamus, and (especially) the superior colliculus. Indeed, much of what we know about attentional systems in humans was learned initially from work done with monkeys (Goldman-Rakic et al., 1990; Goldman-Rakic, 1995; Luck et al., 1997; Baluch & Itti, 2011). The top-down attentional system plays the same boosting-while-suppressing role that it does in humans (described in Chapter 3.4), modulating activity not only in sensory cortices but also in the superior colliculus. And the bottom-up system plays the same role in grabbing attention and causing the animal to orient toward surprising, novel, or highly salient stimuli, modulated by the animal's ongoing needs and goals.

Homologs of key components of these networks are present in all vertebrates. Specifically, in birds and fish the optic tectum is a homolog of the superior colliculus, and plays the same role in orienting behavior and in the control of bottom-up attention (Luiten, 1981; Gruberg et al., 2006; Knudsen, 2011). Indeed, the same microcircuits in the two structures control the boosting-while-suppressing role of attention on neural responses, modulated by both bottom-up and top-down signals (Mysore & Knudsen, 2013). Moreover, the forebrains of birds, at least, contain a homolog of the frontal eye-fields, called the arcopallial gaze fields, or AGF (Winkowski & Knudsen, 2007, 2008). These modulate neural activity in the optic tectum as well as in sensory areas, and the mechanism through which this modulation operates has now been successfully modeled (Lai et al., 2011).

While important components of the attentional networks present in humans and other mammals are present in all vertebrates, it is not yet known whether other components of the cortical network likewise have homologs in the forebrains of birds and fish. (These would include dorsolateral prefrontal cortex and the intraparietal sulcus, as well as the bottom-up cortical network linking right ventral parietal cortex with right ventrolateral prefrontal cortex and the anterior cingulate.) Nor is it known how the functions of these networks have become elaborated over the course of evolution. But at a neurophysiological level, at least, we can conclude that attentional networks are ancient structures, highly conserved over evolutionary timescales.

2.2. Covert attention in birds

The frontal eye-fields in humans and other mammals play a central role in the control of eye movements, and the superior colliculus is crucial for an animal to display an orienting response to a novel or salient stimulus. Hence this network is important for the control of overt attention. While it has been known for many years that the frontal eye-fields in primates play an important role in covert forms of attention as well (just as they do in humans), the role of the superior colliculus has often been thought to be restricted to control of the overt orienting response. But knowledge of the modulating role that signals from the frontal eye-fields play in the superior colliculus would lead one to predict that the latter is also influenced by covert forms of attention. This has now been demonstrated behaviorally in monkeys (Lovejoy & Krauzlis, 2010). The task required the animals to ignore distractor stimuli while attending covertly to a cued location that would inform them where to orient next. Innervation of the superior colliculus disrupted performance in this task, but only when distractor stimuli were present. Hence it was covert attention that was disrupted, not overt orientation and eye movements.

We know, too, that the homolog of the frontal eye-fields in birds is involved in the control of both overt and covert forms of attention. Application of a strong electrical stimulus to a component of this forebrain region causes the bird to orient toward the corresponding region of space, thus engaging in a shift in overt attention. But application of a weak electrical stimulus leads to the neural and behavioral enhancements that are characteristic of a shift in covert attention (Winkowski & Knudsen, 2007, 2008). Specifically, when stimulated for a specific region of visual space, the neural responses to stimuli emanating from that region are enhanced in the optic tectum, and the bird is also more successful at noticing and discriminating those stimuli.

Since attention is necessary to evoke and sustain episodic memories in humans (as we saw in Chapter 4.1), and since the interplay between these networks performs such an important role in both prospective and retrospective forms of reflective reasoning, it is worth noting that episodic memory networks, too, are highly conserved across species. (Behavioral evidence of episodic memory in birds will be discussed in Section 3.) In humans the hippocampus, together with parahippocampal structures on the inside of the temporal lobe, play an essential role in the formation and retrieval of episodic memories (as well as in prospection). Allen & Fortin (2013) review evidence for the presence of these structures across species. They conclude that the hippocampus itself is homologous in all mammals and birds, and may be present in vertebrates generally. The parahippocampal system is homologous in all mammals, but is replaced in birds by a closely analogous set of structures. Moreover, just as the hippocampus receives direct signals from the prefrontal cortex in mammals, so does it receive signals from the analogous region of the avian forebrain, called the nidopallium caudolaterale.

2.3. Brain plasticity?

I have been arguing that the mechanisms responsible for the global broadcast of attended representations in the brain are of ancient ancestry and are highly conserved across vertebrate species. So when humans (and perhaps other primates) began to reason about abstract, non-perceptible states and properties they were constrained to use this ancient sensory-based system to do so. But this argument only works if one cannot easily evolve a new network. What would have been needed would have been one with similar boosting-while-suppressing properties to the attentional network, which would likewise result in the global broadcast of targeted representations. But it would be focused on semantic and decision-making networks in the frontal, parietal, and temporal lobes, rather than on midlevel sensory regions of cortex. In addition, an objector might say that the evidence of cortical plasticity that has accumulated in recent decades counts against the picture of a fixed rigid brain architecture. If brains can be plastic in response to injury or training, then surely they can be equally flexible over evolutionary timescales?

Let me first address the question of cortical plasticity. We know that regions of cortex devoted to processing input from, say, a particular finger can expand or contract in response to training, or to injury that results in loss of input (Buonomano & Merzenich, 1998). But the mechanism involved seems to be invasion of new synapses from nearby regions of cortex. This is very different from the new long-range cortical connections that would be required to build a new kind of attentional system and a global workspace in which amodal attitudes can be activated.

We also know that regions of cortex can acquire wholly new processing properties in response to novel input. Thus the left fusiform gyrus in the temporal lobe, which in illiterate people is a face-processing area, becomes the visual word-form area in people who have learned to read (Dehaene, 2009). Even more dramatically, regions of left visual cortex become specialized for language processing in people who are congenitally blind (Bedny et al., 2011).[1] The explanation for these changes is thought to be that regions of cortex that have specific computational properties, as well as the right kinds of long-range connections to realize a new function, can acquire novel content-processing properties in response to new forms of input (Dehaene, 2004; Anderson, 2010). Plainly, however, this is not the sort of plasticity that would be needed for the creation of an amodal attentional system. For the latter would require a new long-range network to be built, not just the use of existing regions to process novel forms of content.

Admittedly, we do know that long-range functional connections can be strengthened as a result of training. This is presumably what happens to the top-down attentional system in people who improve their fluid g as a result of working-memory training (Jaeggi et al., 2008, 2011). And there is direct evidence of increased long-range connectivity in people who have learned to read. The result is a strengthening of the arcuate fasciculus, which is a pathway linking the visual word-form area with regions of the brain subserving semantic and phonological processes (Thiebaut de Schotten et al., 2014). But the increases measured in this study reflect white-matter volume, which varies with the extent of myelination of the long-range fibers in question. So the improved functional connectivity may result from increasing myelination of existing neurons, rather than from the growth of new ones. Indeed, we lack any model of how new long-range connections could be grown as a result of learning. For these connections are created early in development, with the axons growing along genetically specified chemical gradients while brain regions are still differentiating from one another (Huber et al., 2003).

What is known about brain plasticity does nothing to undermine the idea that long-range brain networks are highly conserved across species, then. But this doesn't really address the point that the networks necessary to support an amodal global workspace might have evolved at some point in the primate or hominin

---

[1] Intriguingly, if attentional systems directed at midlevel visual areas remain functional in congenitally blind people, then it may be that non-sensory syntactic or semantic information can be globally broadcast in such people in the absence of any sensory basis. For the neural activity in such areas that can be boosted or suppressed by the direction of attention carries linguistic, not visual, content. This would then be a counter-example to the claim of this book that all working-memory contents are sensory based. But this would hardly be a victory for amodal models of reflective thinking, either. That congenitally blind people may be capable of certain kinds of amodal reflection says nothing whatever about the rest of us.

line, with these networks now existing alongside the strongly conserved sensory-based ones. But consider how complex this new system would have had to be. Not only would a new form of attentional system have needed to be created, targeted at many different cortical sites that realize amodal attitudes of various sorts, but numerous connections would need to have been built from each of these sites to the brain regions needed for the global availability of attended amodal representations. These would include regions for forming new memories, for generating affective reactions, for drawing inferences of various sorts, for reporting in speech, and for decision making. While all this is no doubt possible in principle, it is far from clear that network-wide changes of this magnitude can be created out of nothing over the course of merely a few million years. Indeed, given the highly conservative nature of the evolution of brain architecture in general (Swanson, 2012), it seems somewhat unlikely.

There is an important dialectical point to be made here, however. This is that I do not need to provide a positive demonstration that an amodal workspace *could not* have evolved. For we have already reviewed numerous sources of evidence over previous chapters suggesting that it has not, in fact, done so. Our task in this chapter is rather to provide a plausible *explanation* for the sensory-based character of reflection, which otherwise seems so unsuited for the amodal purposes for which reflection is often now used. (This explanation will at the same time provide a positive reason for believing that reflection is sensory based, since this is what one might then expect on evolutionary grounds alone.) For this, I just need to show that the sensory-based working-memory system is of ancient ancestry, and that it would not have been easy for evolution to create a new system for amodal use. I take it that both points are now on the way to being established. The upshot is that it should be easy to understand how humans had little option but to co-opt the sensory-based system inherited from their primate ancestors. This would need to be employed for reflection about unobservable as well as observable properties.[2]

3. Episodic Memory and Prospection in Birds

Section 2 discussed neurological evidence that the brain systems exist in birds that are necessary for simple forms of reflection (including episodic memory and prospection). The present section will discuss behavioral evidence suggesting that

---

[2] Moreover, the same constraint might well iterate further back into the evolutionary past. For even if other creatures, likewise, use their sensory-based working-memory systems for reflective reasoning about unobservable properties, it may be that they, too, had no option but to do so given the ancestral designs *they* inherited.

these networks are, indeed, used for such purposes, thus enabling them to deal adaptively with perceptible features of their environment. Most of the evidence derives from work done with corvids (rooks, crows, and jays), together with parrots and cockatoos. It is not known whether members of these species are unusual in employing for purposes of reflection the brain networks that all birds share, or whether other avian species might perform similarly in some circumstances.[3]

3.1. What, where, and when

Some have suggested that "mental time-travel" (or the capacity to re-experience the past and imagine the future) is a uniquely human ability (Suddendorf & Corballis, 1997, 2007). Critics of this view have mostly shied away from the question of animal consciousness, as well as from the question whether animals can represent *themselves* in the past and future. They have focused on animals' capacities to represent the *what*, *where*, and *when* properties of events. But in fact, given the shared brain architecture discussed in Section 2, if it can be shown that animals recall what happened, where, and when, and that they can use this information to guide their overall behavior, then it would be reasonable to conclude that these representations are globally broadcast as a result of top-down attentional signals, just as human episodic memories are. Hence they will qualify as conscious in at least the access-conscious sense we have been employing in this book. (The question of *self*-consciousness is another matter, however, and is one that I won't address here.)

Across a series of studies Clayton and colleagues have investigated the memory abilities of scrub jays, demonstrating the birds' flexible use of *what*, *where*, and *when* components (Clayton & Dickinson, 1999; Clayton et al., 2001, 2003, 2005). Many birds cache food for later consumption, and it is well known that their memory for the locations of their caches can be remarkable (Bednekoff & Balda, 1997). But in the absence of experimentation one cannot tell whether they also recall *what* they have cached, and *when* they did so. This is what Clayton and colleagues have been able to demonstrate, using a variety of controls to rule out simpler associationist explanations of their data. They have been able to show, moreover, that the memories in question are flexibly available in the service of behavior, interacting appropriately with newly acquired beliefs and goals.

One of the basic findings is as follows (Clayton et al., 2003). Naïve scrub jays were given the opportunity to cache both peanuts and dead crickets in two separate locations, repeating the process on successive days for three days. On

---

[3] Note that there will be many differences among species that could influence performance in any given test, such as variations in neophilia and neophobia (Auersperg et al., 2011).

the fourth day they were allowed, when hungry, to retrieve their caches from the first day. One group of birds found both forms of food in good condition, whereas the other group found that the crickets had degraded in the interval. This experience was repeated on the fifth day with the caches created on the second day. Then on the sixth day the birds were allowed to access the cache locations used on the third day, which had actually been emptied of all caches by the experimenters. The question was where the birds would look who had learned that crickets degrade after a three-day interval. In fact these birds all went initially to the location where they had cached peanuts, and while they thereafter searched in both locations, they spent far more time looking for peanuts than crickets. The control group, in contrast (who expected that the crickets would still be fresh), searched initially in the cricket-cache locations, and spent most of their time searching for crickets. (This is what one would expect, since scrub jays greatly prefer crickets to peanuts.) Moreover, the switch in behavior was specific to the three-day interval. When given a test just one day after caching (when the decay-group would have had no reason to think that the crickets would yet have decayed), both groups searched preferentially for crickets.

In order to explain the behavior of birds in these and related experiments, we need to suppose that they have memories specifying *what* they cached, *where* they cached it, and *when* they did so. And these memories must be centrally available, interacting with their goals and other beliefs to determine appropriate forms of action. So their memories are at least episodic *like*. Admittedly, it does not yet follow that the birds' access to these memories takes the form of re-experiencing the process of initial caching, as a human episodic memory would. But given the commonalities in the brain mechanisms involved, and given that human memories are formed when the hippocampus binds together sensory representations that are active during the original event, it is reasonable to expect that the same will be true of birds as well. This expectation will be further strengthened if it can be shown that birds show future-oriented behavior of the sort that would be guided by prospective reasoning in humans. For the latter involves a sort of *pre*-experiencing of potential future actions and their consequences, as we have seen in previous chapters.

3.2. Avian prospection

Corvids are known to be remarkable problem-solvers, fashioning tools out of sticks or pieces of wire to retrieve food, for example (Weir et al., 2002; Weir & Kacelnik, 2006). In the case of the experiments just cited, the birds involved were New Caledonian crows, who use sticks as tools in the wild, and for whom a disposition to do so seems to be innately channeled (Kenward et al., 2005). But similar behavior has also been found in rooks, who do not use tools in the wild (Bird & Emery, 2009a). So it seems that the cognitive capacities underlying this behavior involve general-purpose reasoning abilities of some sort, rather than a domain-specific adaptation. This is *consistent* with the use of prospection, but of course it does not demonstrate it. Nevertheless, we can at least conclude that corvids (and cockatoos; see Auersperg et al., 2013) are quite adept at discerning the physical affordances of things, and of adapting their behavior accordingly.

What we would like is evidence of some capacity to "think ahead" beyond immediately perceptible physical affordances. Just such evidence is provided by Bird & Emery (2009a), who presented rooks with a problem whose solution would require two separate actions: using a large stone to drop down a transparent tube to open a trap-door to obtain a small stone, which could then be dropped down another (narrower) tube to open a door to obtain food. All of the components necessary for success were visible throughout, but the birds were offered a choice between using the first stone to get a stone of similar size (which would be too large to insert into the apparatus to get the food), or using it to get a smaller stone. All the birds solved this problem on the first trial. In order to solve it, they had to be able to perceive the size-affordances of the various stones, for sure. But it is hard to see how one could get to a solution (without using trial and error) unless one *imagined* attempting to drop the available stone down the various tubes, predicted the results, and then imagined what one could do from there.

The rooks who participated in the experiment just described were later presented with an even more challenging task (Bird & Emery, 2009b). They were shown a pile of stones next to a tall Perspex tube containing water, in which some food floated on a platform. The water level was too low for the birds to reach their beaks into the container to get the food. A solution required realizing that by dropping a series of stones into the container one could raise the water level far enough to bring the food within reach. Two of the birds solved this task on the first trial, and the remaining two birds solved it on the second trial. Although these birds had previously used stones to obtain a reward, the setup here was quite different, and required multiple stones to be dropped in sequence to raise the water level sufficiently. The birds made no attempt to reach the food after dropping the first stone, but immediately went to retrieve another. This suggests that they had envisaged, in advance, the sequence of actions that they needed to perform. Note that when employed with apes and human children, experiments of this sort have been regarded as tests of imaginative insight (Hanus et al., 2011). It is reasonable, then, to reach the same conclusion in the case of the rooks.

Even more remarkably, Taylor et al. (2010) show that crows can solve a *three*-step problem. The birds were presented with a setup containing the following components: some food visible in a Perspex container, but too far from the entrance to be reached either by beak or with a short stick; a short stick hanging on a piece of string from a branch; and a long stick behind the bars of a cage, but too deep within the cage for the birds to reach by beak. A solution would require pulling up the string to get the short stick, using the short stick to get the long stick, and then using the long stick to get the meat. The birds had previously been given experience with some (but only some) of the components of the task. Specifically, they had experienced: (1) using a long stick to extract meat from a container, (2) getting a long stick from behind some bars with their beaks and using it to get meat from a container, (3) using a stick that was too short to get the meat in a container, and (4) pulling up a string on which some meat was attached. None had pulled up a string to obtain a stick, and none had used a stick to obtain another stick from behind some bars.

All four birds had solved this task by the fourth trial, and two solved it on their first trial. One of these two birds inspected the setup for a full 110 seconds before acting, and then completed the entire sequence smoothly and without hesitation. The other of the two inspected the setup for forty-three seconds, then pulled up and dropped the string. He then inspected the setup for a further forty seconds before executing the entire three-step sequence. It is hard to see what either bird could have been doing during these pauses that would have led to a solution except engaging in something closely resembling human prospection. We can presume that they mentally rehearsed some of the actions suggested by the visible affordances of the setup, foresaw the consequences, and held those in working memory while rehearsing other actions, until all three of the necessary components were in place, and were in the correct order.

In the experiments described thus far, the potential rewards were visible throughout. The problem for the birds was to figure out a means to get them. But there are also data showing that corvids can plan for *future* need. For example, Raby et al. (2007) show that jays can plan for tomorrow's breakfast. The jays were housed in a cage consisting of three adjoining compartments, which could be separated from one another. Each evening they were fed in the central compartment with the doors to the other compartments left open, but each morning they were confined to one of the two adjoining compartments, either to the left or right on alternating days. In one of these compartments there was always food available at breakfast, but in the other the birds had to remain hungry for two hours until released into the central compartment. For six days the birds followed this alternating cycle (with the order counterbalanced across birds), and during this time the food they had available to eat in the central compartment at night was powdered pine-nuts, which cannot be cached. Then for the first time they were provided with whole nuts in the evening. As a result, the birds cached some of the nuts, and did so much more in the compartment where no food had been available to them in the morning. The birds were able to foresee that they *would* be hungry in that compartment in future, and acted to assuage that future hunger. (A further experiment ruled out a simpler disposition to cache in places associated with hunger.)

Correia et al. (2007) were able to demonstrate the same point using a different paradigm.[4] The experiments utilized the phenomenon of *specific satiety*. This is the fact (familiar to all of us) that an animal that has fed to satiety on a specific type of food is no longer willing to eat more of that food, but will nevertheless eat a different food. (Think of a chocolate dessert after a large steak entrée.) Correia et al. first showed that the specific satiety effect extends to caching behavior. That is, birds who have fed to satiety on food A will preferentially cache food B when allowed to cache either A or B. Then the experimenters presented the birds with the following sequence: feeding to satiety on food A; ten minutes to cache either food A or food B; a delay of thirty minutes followed by feeding to satiety on food B; followed by a ten-minute opportunity to recover caches made at the second stage. (Birds in the control condition were fed to satiety on food A both times.) While all the birds initially cached food B at the second stage (the food that had not been devalued by satiety), those in the switched condition changed their strategy on the second trial, and thereafter cached food A, apparently foreseeing that this was the food that they *would* want at the final stage of the trial (when they would already have been eating food B).

Each of the experiments described above contained numerous control conditions designed to rule out alternative, deflationary explanations. When taken together with the findings outlined in Section 2 (that birds share the brain-networks necessary to engage in episodic memory and prospection of the future) the resulting data provide powerful reasons for thinking that the use of an attention-based working-memory system for purposes of episodic-like remembering and prospective reasoning is widespread in the animal kingdom.

4. Working Memory in Mammals

In Section 2 we noted that important components, at least, of attentional and episodic memory networks are homologous across mammalian species. The

---

[4] This demonstration was later extended to a distinct species of jay, while adding a separate set of control conditions (Cheke & Clayton, 2012).

present section will review behavioral evidence suggesting that mammals do, indeed, possess working-memory systems not unlike our own and that apes, at least, make use of those systems for purposes of prospective reasoning. Section 5 will then address the question of the differences in working-memory abilities between humans and other animals.

4.1. *Different forms of memory revisited*

Before we begin our discussion of the evidence of working memory in mammals, it is important to revisit the distinctions drawn in Chapter 1.3 between working memory and two other forms of memory with which it is sometimes conflated. One is sensory short-term memory, which can retain information in sensory cortices for around two seconds in the absence of attention. The contents of working memory, in contrast, are attention-dependent and conscious, and can be held in an active state for as long as attention is directed at them.

Some experimental results with animals that have been thought to support the existence of working-memory capacities are in fact best interpreted as tests of sensory short-term memory. Thus consider the finding that chimpanzees and baboons can reliably recall a random sequence of spatial positions up to a limit of five to six items (or in the case of one animal, nine items) (Kawai & Matsuzawa, 2000; Inoue & Matsuzawa, 2007, 2009; Fagot & Lillo, 2011). The temporal delays in these experiments are of the order of fractions of a second, with the animals' response to the entire sequence generally being executed very swiftly over a period of around two seconds. So while these tasks *might* involve working memory, the data can be accounted for in terms of sensory short-term memory alone.

The other contrast is with a form of long-term memory that is sometimes called in the human literature "long-term working memory" (Ericsson & Kintsch, 1995). These are representations that are no longer among the active contents of working memory (having fallen out of the focus of attention), but which remain readily *accessible* to working-memory processes. Sometimes these representations have been recently activated from long-term memory, but sometimes they concern stimuli that were previously encoded into working memory but will be forgotten within a period of minutes. In this context it is important to note that numerous comparative studies of animals, such as those that use the radial-arm maze with rodents, employ the *term* "working memory," when it is really a form of long-term memory that is being measured. For the timescales involved, as well as the number of items that can be recalled, far exceed human working-memory abilities. Indeed, some writers are quite explicit that working memory in such studies should be defined as memory that is used *within a testing session* (often lasting for minutes or hours) but not typically between testing sessions (such as the next day) (Dudchenko, 2004; Shettleworth, 2010).

As we noted in Chapter 1.3, working memory can be distinguished empirically from all forms of long-term memory through its sensitivity to attentional interference. Information sustained in working memory will be lost if subjects are distracted and turn their attention fully to other matters. Long-term memories, in contrast, will merely decay at the normal rate in such circumstances. Kawai & Matsuzawa (2000), for example, note that on some occasions the test chimpanzee who was about to recall a sequence of spatial positions was interrupted for a few seconds by a loud disturbance in a neighboring cage, but was nevertheless able to complete the sequence correctly thereafter. Although the authors suggest that this behavior manifests the operation of working memory, in fact it is unlikely. Undiminished performance following sustained and full distraction is an indication that long-term memory is involved.

4.2. Working memory and g in mice

In Chapter 5.3 we noted that working-memory abilities in humans depend heavily on capacities to resist interference from competing stimuli and competing memories. We also noted that they are tightly correlated with differences in fluid general intelligence, or g. Both factors have been explored in a series of experimental studies with mice.

The first study identified a general-intelligence factor that explains about 40 percent of variance across a range of dissimilar learning tasks (Matzel et al., 2003). Moreover, while this g-factor is not significantly correlated with measures of simple working-memory retention, it is strongly correlated with performance in a more complex working-memory task, in which the animals have to resist interference from competing memories (Kolata et al., 2005). In both cases the animals were first trained on two visually distinct radial-arm mazes located in the same room. In the test of working-memory retention, the animals were confined to the central compartment of one of the mazes for a fixed interval of sixty or ninety seconds having made their first four correct choices before being allowed to complete their search. In the test of working-memory interference, in contrast, the animals were removed from the first maze having made three correct choices and placed in the second maze; after three correct choices there, they were returned to the first maze until they had made another three correct choices, and so on. The fact that performance on the interference working-memory test but not the retention working-memory test correlates with a measure of g in mice provides confirming evidence that mice and humans have homologous working-memory mechanisms.

One might question whether this and other experiments conducted in the same lab are genuinely measuring active working memory rather than long-term working memory. For how are we to know that the mice kept a representation of the arms already visited active in the focus of attention? Indeed, in experiments with rats using the eight-arm radial maze, rats typically show near-perfect performance on the final four arms of the maze following delays of a number of *hours* after visiting the first four arms, enabling us to be quite confident that long-term memory is involved (Shettleworth, 2010). On reflection, however, we can be sure that active working memory is also used. So while the tests might not be suitable for measuring working-memory *span* (since both short-term and long-term memory are involved), they can enable us to draw conclusions about the relationship between working memory and *g*.

The reason why interrupted search in a radial-arm maze involves inter-actions between short-term and long-term working memory is as follows. When commencing search following an interruption, the animal will need to access long-term representations of the four arms previously visited, holding those active in working memory long enough to select a fifth. And thereafter, for the final three choices, the animal will need to use spatial retrieval cues to access a long-term memory of each of the arms initially visited while keeping active in working memory the immediately previous selections, and while orienting itself appropriately to make another choice. In addition, in the interference condition of the experiments described earlier (in which the mice are switched back and forth between two mazes) irrelevant memories will need to be suppressed, requiring the mice to pay careful online attention to the cues that individuate the arms of the two mazes. At the very least we can be confident that this task will place significant demands on the animals' use of selective attention, which is at the core of human working-memory abilities, as we saw in Chapter 4.[5]

A subsequent study of correlations between working-memory abilities and *g* in mice attempted to pull apart the components of working memory still further (Kolata et al., 2007). It involved tests of working-memory retention *time*, work-ing-memory retention *capacity*, as well as capacities for selective attention. The first measured the temporal limits of the animals' capacity to recall which of the two arms in a T-maze they had previously visited. The test of working-memory

---

[5] Moreover, recall from Chapter 5.3 that some of the research on human working memory suggests that attentional control and efficient access to long-term memory are two distinct compo-nents of human working-memory abilities, while also making separate contributions to fluid *g* (Unsworth & Spillers, 2010).

capacity used a non-spatial version of the radial-arm maze, in which cues attached to baited cups at the end of each arm were randomly shuffled following each choice, in such a way that the mice would need to keep in mind the cues (and which ones they had already selected) without relying on spatial position. Finally, the test of selective attention used two distinct discrimination tasks (one involving shapes and the other involving odors) which had initially been learned in separate contexts. At test, the animals were then presented with all cues of both kinds in one or other of the two contexts, so that they would need to ignore one set of cues on which they had previously been trained in favor of the other. The results of this experiment were that retention time did not correlate with g at all, working-memory capacity correlated moderately with g, whereas selective attention was strongly correlated with g. This, too, is what one might have predicted from what we know about human working memory.

Perhaps the most impressive set of results from this series of studies with mice is the finding that working-memory training improves g, just as it can do in humans (Light et al., 2010). In the first of these experiments animals who received training using two alternating radial-arm mazes scored significantly higher than controls on subsequent tests of general learning abilities, while also scoring higher on a test of selective attention. The second experiment then showed that it is the attentional component of working-memory training specifically that leads to an improvement in g. This experiment used three groups of mice. One group received training in two alternating and visually similar radial-arm mazes located within the same room, which would require the mice to attend to minor differences in cues provided by spatial context to discriminate the arms of the two mazes. A second group also received training on two alternating radial-arm mazes, but this time located in separate rooms, thus placing fewer attentional demands on the animals. The third group was a control, and received no working-memory training. The finding was that the attentionally demanding group showed the greatest increase in g, while the second group also displayed significant improvement relative to controls.

Taken together, this series of findings with mice suggests that working-memory abilities in this species are heavily dependent on attentional capacities (just as they are in humans), and that mice not only have a simple capacity to retain salient information beyond the temporal window of sensory short-term memory, but that they (like humans) can do so in the face of interference, and can manipulate that information in the service of a goal. This set of findings provides further confirmation, therefore, that core working-memory abilities are homologous across mammals.

4.3. Future planning in apes

We turn now to evidence of the use of working memory for purposes of future planning. One set of studies has carefully documented the behavior of an alpha male chimpanzee in an open-plan zoo (Osvath, 2009; Osvath & Karvonen, 2011). The male initially collected and stored piles of stones early in the morning, to throw at zoo visitors later in the day as part of an aggressive threat-display. When the zoo keepers responded by removing his stashes before the zoo opened each day to prevent this, he proved quite adept at concealing his stashes, and at manufacturing projectiles afterward by breaking off pieces of brittle concrete from the walls in his enclosure. Note that at the times when he collected and concealed his stashes he was in a calm state, in the absence of the stimuli (human visitors) that would later provoke his rage. Such behavior in a human would likely be caused by imagining the later presence of the audience and mental rehearsal of the actions involved in grasping and throwing projectiles, issuing in a positive affective response which would in turn motivate the collection of some stones. It is reasonable to assume that similar processes took place in the mind of the chimpanzee.

Experimental data with chimpanzees point toward similar conclusions. In one experiment, chimpanzees not only selected and carried with them to their sleeping quarters a tool that they would need the next day to access a desired reward, but they remembered to bring it back with them on their return (Mulcahy & Call, 2004). In a conceptual replication of this experiment by another lab, chimpanzees again selected a tool needed to retrieve a later reward, and remembered to bring the tool with them when returning (Osvath & Osvath, 2008). Moreover, the animals were able to resist a smaller current reward (a grape), choosing instead the tool that would get them a more valued reward later (a container of juice). In addition, when presented with a number of unfamiliar objects (while being prevented from handling them) they reliably selected and took with them the one best suited to obtain the future reward. Note that humans would solve a task of this sort by mentally rehearsing some actions directed toward the juice-container involving the various objects, noting which ones could be successful.

In Section 3.2 we discussed how rooks can solve the floating-reward problem, by dropping stones into a tube containing water to raise the reward high enough to be reached. Replicating and extending a study by Mendes et al. (2007), Hanus et al. (2011) presented essentially the same task to apes and human children. (The main differences were that the tube was initially dry in some conditions, and that in all conditions accessing the reward required the participants to spit water into the tube to make the peanut rise to the top.) Some of the apes, and some of the six-year-old children, were able to solve this task. (None of the four-year-old children did so.) Moreover, some of the apes who failed seemed to have figured out what was necessary to succeed, but they had trouble transporting water in their mouths from the nearby bucket and spitting it accurately enough into the tube. After a few attempts, they lost interest. It is hard to imagine how one could solve this problem except by mentally rehearsing some of the actions open to one in the circumstances, envisaging and evaluating the likely consequences.

Moreover, Völter & Call (2014) review a variety of forms of evidence of advance planning in apes before describing their own experiments involving both apes and human children. Participants were presented with a vertical maze, in which a reward positioned on the top level had to be moved down through two more levels before it could be accessed at the bottom. At each level the reward could be directed left or right, with different alternatives having been visibly closed off by the experimenters before the start of the trial. On some trials participants would need to plan two steps ahead in order to succeed. The apes mostly succeeded in this task, and performed about as well as five-year-old children. (At any rate the younger ones did: older apes showed a marked decline in their working-memory abilities in this experiment, just as happens in older humans.) Moreover, their failures tended not to result from failures of advance planning (as did those of the children), but rather from difficulties in suppressing prepotent motor responses. That is, having moved the reward to the left on one level, say, there was a tendency to repeat that action at the next level, even if the correct choice was a move to the right.

This body of evidence from captive chimpanzees is fully consistent with what we know of the behavior of chimpanzees in the wild (Janmaat et al., 2014). For example, chimpanzees in the Congo regularly harvest termites from both above-ground and subterranean nests, each of which requires a distinct set of tools. The subterranean nests, in particular, require a sharp, stout puncturing stick, which is always made from the branches of a particular species of tree. The chimpanzees never arrived at the site of a subterranean nest without bringing such a stick with them, unless one had previously been left at the site. And this was true even though the nearest appropriate tree was tens of meters away in the forest, from which point the nest site could not be seen (Sanz et al., 2004). Such behavior in humans would involve imagining the target together with mental rehearsal of the actions needed to acquire it, which would both remind and motivate one to deviate from one's path to find an appropriate species of tree.

It seems that apes, like humans and corvids, make use of their working-memory systems for purposes of advance planning. Note that all of the examples of such planning considered so far have involved observable states and properties. It is unlikely, however, that planning in nonhuman animals is restricted to such properties. This is because of evidence that chimpanzees, at least, are capable of reasoning flexibly about the mental states of competitors (Fletcher & Carruthers, 2013). If chimpanzees can plan their route to some food in such a way as to avoid being seen or heard by a competitor, for example (Melis et al., 2006), then their working-memory contents must include sensorily embedded mental-state concepts, just as human reasoning often does. This means that while it can still be true, as I claim, that the sensory-based working-memory system was designed initially for perceiving, recalling, and reasoning about observable features of the world, it would be an over-simplification to claim that the use of this system by all nonhuman animals is entirely confined to such properties.[6]

5. Evolutionary Developments across Species?

Very little is known for sure about evolutionary developments in working-memory capacities across species (Carruthers, 2013c). Given the tight connection between working-memory abilities and fluid g, however, and given how smart humans are in comparison to most other animals, one might expect to find significant differences. The present section will provide a brief review of the main possibilities.

5.1. Simple retention capacities

Some have claimed that nonhuman apes have a working-memory limit of two items, in contrast with the human limit of three to four chunks of information

---

[6] Recall from Chapter 2.4 that many animals can engage in inferences involving amodal representations. However, many of these representations (although amodal) are representations of observable objects or properties, such as an individual conspecific, a type of action, or the numerosity of a set. This is by no means true of all amodal representations employed by nonhuman animals, however. For example, a dominance hierarchy cannot be observed, and neither can the large-scale spatial layout of a territory. Knowledge of these things must be constructed over time from multiple observations. It is an open question, though, whether the inferences that baboons draw concerning dominance hierarchies take place in working memory. (I assume that the map-like inferences made by bees when navigating do not.) They might rather be System 1 inferences of a domain-specific sort, involving mechanisms that are innate or innately channeled, and whose operations are unreflective and unconscious. The data from chimpanzees, in contrast, suggest that these animals engage in flexible forms of System 2 planning that are sensitive to the mental states of other agents, indicating that these animals, like humans, can engage in conscious reflection about unobservables.

(Read, 2008). But this claim is based on a questionable analysis of the working-memory requirements of various tasks that apes cannot solve, and assumes that failure does not result from other sources, such as lack of understanding of physical forces and their effects. In contrast, experimental work with animals suggests that their working-memory limits may fall within the human range. Consider, for example, a test of serial recall of position conducted with a macaque monkey, modeled on tests that have been employed with humans (Botvinick et al., 2009). The retention interval required in this test was about four seconds for the first item in the sequence, increasing to eleven seconds for the fourth, which places it squarely in the domain of working memory. The monkey was successful in recalling the first three items in a sequence, but was at chance with the fourth.[7]

It should be stressed, however, that the work on human working memory demonstrating that it has a capacity limit of three to four chunks (rather than Miller's famous seven ± two) has focused on the pure memory-sustaining function of working memory (Cowan, 2001). Great care has been taken to exclude other strategies for maintaining representations in working memory, such as covert mental rehearsal and informational chunking, which can extend its overall capacity still further. In the serial-recall test just described, in contrast, the monkey may have used mental rehearsals of its planned movements to support its working memory of the sequence of positions, thereby extending its pure memory-sustaining limits. This would be consistent with a claimed working-memory limit of one to two items.

Other data suggesting that animals have working-memory retention capacities in the human range are not so easily critiqued, however. For example, using paradigms that have previously been employed with human infants, it has been shown that monkeys can track three to four items of food placed sequentially into one of two opaque containers (where those items remain out of sight for a period of at least a few seconds). The monkeys reliably distinguish between containers that hold two versus three items, and also three versus four items, but not three versus five items (Hauser et al., 2000).[8] Similar tests have been conducted with horses, showing that they can distinguish between a bucket into which two apples have been placed and one containing three apples, while failing to distinguish

---

[7] The experiment also demonstrated a very similar profile of recency, latency, and other effects commonly found with humans, further confirming the suggestion that both species employ an homologous working-memory mechanism.

[8] One might wonder why these data do not demonstrate that monkeys have a working-memory limit of seven (three items in one container and four in another) rather than four. The answer is that comparisons *between* containers benefit from chunking, and don't just reflect raw retention limits.

between buckets containing four apples and six apples respectively (Uller & Lewis, 2009).

In such experiments it seems unlikely that the animals could benefit from chunking, since all of the items are of the same type. And it is likewise unclear how nonverbal forms of behavioral rehearsal could assist with the task (especially in the case of horses, whose repertoire of actions differs so widely from that of the human demonstrator). So the limit of three to four items revealed here seems most likely to reflect pure working-memory retention capacity. But until comparative psychologists employ direct tests of simple working-memory retention abilities that can be conducted in parallel with adult humans, children, and members of various other species of animal, we will not be able to know for sure.

5.2. Attentional control and mental manipulation

It would not be especially surprising if it turns out that pure working-memory retention abilities are similar across mammalian species, despite the intuitive differences in intelligence between them. For we know that the simple retention component of working memory is not a reliable predictor of fluid g in humans (nor is it stable within a single individual across separate occasions of testing). Rather, only complex span tasks and so-called "n-back" tasks lead to stable results over time and are reliable predictors of g (Engle, 2010). What we should expect, then, is that humans will excel at working-memory tasks that place the greatest weight on capacities for attentional control and the mental manipulation of representations. While this suggestion is certainly consistent with the advantage that humans are said to enjoy over other animals in executive function abilities, there have been no systematic comparative investigations of the question.

What we can say with some confidence, however, is that humans will be the only creatures that sometimes constrain the ways in which they employ their working-memory abilities in accordance with socially acquired rules of reasoning (in the manner discussed in Chapter 7). While many animals employ System 2 reasoning in the broad sense that their reasoning makes constitutive use of working memory (as we have seen in Sections 3 and 4 of this chapter), none will reason in accordance with explicit norms that have been learned from others in their group. As a result, there will be many specific types of reflection that are unique to humans. Also as a result, human reasoning abilities display a cultural "ratchet effect," as each generation uses the reasoning procedures acquired from the surrounding culture to further refine and improve those procedures. These can then be transmitted to others in turn. The result is that we now have logic, mathematics, and scientific method.

5.3. Conceptual chunking and inner speech

There are other ways in which one can be confident that human working-memory abilities differ systematically from those of other animals. One is that humans are surely unique in the extent to which their working-memory processes benefit from conceptual chunking of information, resulting from a vastly greater conceptual repertoire. It is well known that when various items can be brought together under a single concept this makes them much easier to remember. This is even true of human infants. In the absence of any grouping cues, fourteen-month-old infants can keep track of only three objects at once. However, they significantly exceed this limit when given conceptual, linguistic, or spatial cues enabling them to parse a larger array into smaller units (Feigenson & Halberda, 2008). Since no one doubts that human concepts (many of which are, of course, acquired through linguistic communication) greatly outnumber those available to other animals, we can be confident that humans are unique in the extent to which (and the flexibility with which) their reflections benefit from chunking.

Moreover, while other animals, like humans, can mentally rehearse actions for purposes of reasoning (as we have seen in Sections 3 and 4), there is an entire *class* of actions that can only be rehearsed by humans. These are speech actions, since humans are uniquely capable of speech. Mental rehearsal of speech actions gives rise to inner speech, which occupies a good deal of the conscious mental lives of many people. This point now merges with the one made in Section 5.2, that humans are unique in using explicit norms of reasoning to constrain their reflections. For many of these norms concern linguistically expressed propositions.

5.4. Chronic mind wandering?

Even if the working-memory capacities of animals were comparable to those of humans in all major respects, it may nevertheless be the case that animals only make use of them when confronted with specific practical, learning, or reasoning problems. Humans, in contrast, make frequent use of working memory in ways that are irrelevant to any current task, thereby constituting the default network (Buckner et al., 2008; Spreng et al., 2009). Even when one is not confronted with a task one's mind will be occupied with fantasies, episodic memories, imagined social situations, imagined conversations, snatches of song, and so on, all of which rely heavily on working memory. Indeed, even when humans *are* engaged in a task they are apt to begin mind wandering, during which working memory is populated with representations unrelated to the task demands (Mason et al., 2007).

There is little comparative data bearing directly on this question. But the suggestion that humans may be unique in how *much* they make use of working memory is at least consistent with the vastly greater extent of human creativity, innovation, and long-term planning. For much of the time that humans spend mind wandering is occupied with reviewing and exploring future scenarios and anticipating future problems or successes. Moreover, there is evidence that mind wandering is significantly correlated with creativity, involving, as it does, defocused attention combined with executive control and selection (Baird et al., 2012). It has also been suggested that the uniquely human disposition to engage in pretend play in childhood is an adaptation for increased creativity in adulthood, encouraging us to use working memory for purposes of creative scenario-building (Picciuto & Carruthers, 2014).

Data suggesting that chronic mind wandering may *not* be uniquely human, however, come from a study comparing default-network activity in humans and chimpanzees (Rilling et al., 2007). Similar regions of the brain displayed greater activity at rest in both species, including medial prefrontal cortex and posterior cingulate cortex, suggesting that chimpanzees, too, spend much of their time ruminating when not engaged in other tasks. These data need to be treated with caution, however, because default-mode networks overlapping those of humans have now been found in both monkeys and rodents under conditions of general anesthesia (Vincent et al., 2007; Lu et al., 2012). So default-mode activity does not entail conscious mind wandering of the sort that would implicate the resources of working memory. Rather, the explanation for these findings may be that the main components of the default network (especially medial regions of both prefrontal and parietal cortex) are important connecting *hubs* in the neural architecture of the brain, serving to link together other more-modular regions (Sporns, 2011). As such they will generally exhibit greater neural activity than the regions they connect, just as airports that serve as major hubs show greater flight activity than others. In humans we know that these default-network hubs play an important role in mind wandering. But it does not follow that any animal with similar brain connectivity will also make use of its working memory when at rest to replay the past and explore the future to anything like the extent that we do.

It seems, then, that at present there is no real evidence to counter the suggestion that humans are unique in making frequent use of working memory for purposes of rumination and mind wandering. Yet this suggestion is supported (albeit weakly) by a theoretical inference from differences in long-term planning and creativity.

Note, however, that none of the likely differences between humans and other animals discussed in this section are suggestive of architectural differences between the species. Rather, those differences concern the extent to which humans can exert executive control over the contents of working memory (including capacities to enforce compliance with explicit norms of reasoning), the extent to which humans engage in conceptual chunking, differences in behavioral repertoire that underlie our unique capacity for inner speech, and perhaps differences in the extent to which we engage in stimulus-independent thought at all. Such differences reflect merely different modes of *use* of the same sensory-based working-memory system that we share with other animals.

6. Conclusion

The primary goal of this chapter has been to answer a puzzle: why is it that human reflection is sensory based, given that so much of what we reflect *about* is abstract and unobservable? The answer, I have suggested, is that human reflection makes use of the same sensory-based working-memory system that we share with other animals. Not only do all birds and mammals possess at least important components of this system, but some birds and some mammals make use of it, as we do, for reflecting about the past and future. The system is of ancient ancestry, making use of even earlier-emerging sensory attentional mechanisms, and it evolved initially for reasoning about the perceptible properties of things. It is reasonable to suggest that the evolution of this key component of human cognition was constrained by pre-existing architectures, just as the evolution of the human body-plan was constrained by the symmetrical four-limbed architecture that we share with all other vertebrates.

Another goal of this chapter has been to use the same set of comparative data to construct a further—evolutionary—argument in support of the sensory-based account of reflection and the stream of consciousness. Since many other animals are capable of using top-down attentional signals and mental rehearsals of action to reason in an off-line reflective manner about perceptible features of their environment, one should predict that human capacities for reflection would somehow utilize the same shared sensory-based mechanisms. For it is rare for evolution to build a whole new set of mechanisms from scratch, of the sort that would be necessary to support an amodal attitudinal workspace for reflection. Even in advance of any experimental investigation of human working-memory abilities, therefore, one might have predicted that they would turn out to be sensory based. Since that is just what we seem to find, our credence in those findings is strengthened still further.

9

Conclusion

The Conscious Mind as Marionette

This brief concluding chapter will summarize the case against an amodal work-space in which propositional attitudes of all types can be activated and conscious, while reminding us of the explanatory virtues of the competing sensory-based account. Some implications for philosophy will then be sketched, and questions for future consideration raised.

1. Against the Intuitive View

Our intuitive view (widely endorsed among philosophers) is that thoughts of all types can become activated and conscious when we reflect, entering into processes of reasoning and decision making with other such thoughts. (See Chapter 1.1.) I have suggested, in contrast, that reflection is always sensory based, and that our amodal attitudes are only ever active behind the scenes, influencing and controlling the sensory-based contents of working memory.

One part of the case against the intuitive view is an absence-of-evidence argument. There is ample evidence that the working-memory system is sensory based, utilizing the top-down attentional network (often in conjunction with mental rehearsals of action) to issue in the global broadcast of sensory-based representations. (See Chapters 3 and 4.) There is also ample evidence that conscious reflection often utilizes the sensory-based working-memory system, involving inner speech, for example, or visually imagined future actions. Moreover, there is good reason to think that these sensory-based representations are not epiphenomenal with respect to our reflections and the behavior that results, but play important causal roles in each. (See Chapters 5 and 6.) So we can take it as solidly established that reflection is *often* sensory based. In contrast, there is no substantial evidence that reflection ever contains, among its contents, conscious activations of amodal attitudes. Nor is there any evidence of the attentional or other networks that would enable such attitudes to become globally available (and thus access-conscious). Hence the most reasonable, best warranted conclusion to draw is that reflection is *always* sensory based.

It should be emphasized that little or no evidential weight can be placed on the fact that we find it highly *intuitive* to believe that amodal attitudes such as goals, decisions, and intentions are often conscious. For the intuition in question, albeit natural, can be explained away. This can be done in a way that is independently motivated, by appealing to people's implicit assumption that their thoughts are transparently available to them. (See Chapter 1.1 and Carruthers, 2011a.) This assumption leads us to feel that we are directly aware of our attitudes while we manipulate sensory-based contents in working memory, resulting from the interpretive work of the mindreading faculty. Moreover, the introspection-sampling data suggesting that people are sometimes aware of entertaining purely propositional (non-sensory) thoughts (Heavey & Hurlburt, 2008) can likewise be given an alternative—and equally convincing—explanation. (See Chapter 1.1 and Carruthers, 2011a.) So there is no real evidence here with which to support the case for a workspace in which amodal propositional attitudes can be activated and conscious.

Moreover, as we will be reminded in Section 2, the sensory-based account can provide at least an outline of an explanation of the ways in which reflection and the stream of consciousness are created and controlled, appealing to known mechanisms and processes. In contrast, the amodal-attitude account is incapable of *explaining* how reflection takes place. For to offer such an explanation one would need to appeal to known mechanisms of one sort or another. But as already noted above, we know of no mechanisms that can result in the global broadcast of amodal attitudes. This provides us with another argument against the amodal-workspace view. For whenever there is competition among theories of some domain, the theory that *can* offer an explanation of the domain always trumps a theory that needs to appeal to as-yet-unknown mechanisms to do so (other things being equal, of course). This is our situation here: the sensory-based view can explain how reflection takes place in terms of known mechanisms, whereas the amodal-attitude account cannot.

A related argument from *simplicity* supports the same conclusion. Everyone should be committed to sensory-based forms of reflection and the stream of consciousness anyway. For no one denies that sometimes our reflections involve sensory images of one sort or another. Yet there is no convincing evidence of an amodal reflective system, as we have seen. So it is simpler to suppose that sensory-based reflection is the only kind of reflection that there is. Since one should not postulate additional systems or structures without necessity, one should not believe in an amodal attitude workspace. The fact that we find such a workspace *intuitive* is not a reason for adding additional components to our cognitive models, especially since this intuition is explicable in light of our everyday assumption that minds are transparent to themselves. (See Chapter 1.1 and Carruthers, 2011a.)

Although there is no *direct* evidence supporting the existence of an amodal workspace in which reflection can take place, there might nevertheless be *indirect* evidence. In particular, if there were things that reflection can do that the sensory-based working-memory system is incapable of doing, then that might provide some reason for believing in the existence of a propositional-attitude workspace. If logical reasoning, for example, could not be performed in sensory-based format, then that might force us to accept an amodal workspace by default. There is no reason to suppose that there are any such limits on what a working-memory system can do, however. (See Chapters 5, 6, and 7.) So the conclusion of the absence-of-evidence, absence-of-explanation, and simplicity-based arguments can stand: the most reasonable conclusion is that reflection is always sensory based.

Another part of the case against the intuitive view consists of a number of failures-of-prediction argument. (See Chapter 5.) If the human mind contains an amodal workspace in which attitudes of all types can be consciously activated and figure in our reflections, then a variety of predictions can be made. Two are especially important. One is that self-knowledge of our currently activated attitudes (or at least their contents) should be direct and non-interpretive. But the evidence suggests that this is not the case. (See Chapter 5.2 and Carruthers, 2011a.) Another prediction is that if the human mind contains such an amodal workspace, then the properties of that system should make a significant contribution to our general intelligence. In that case we should need to appeal to differences among people in the properties of the amodal reflective system in order to account for some portion of their variance in fluid general intelligence. But this seems not to be the case, either. Rather, variations in fluid g can be fully accounted for in terms of some combination of variance in sensory-based working-memory ability, speed of processing, and perhaps associative learning. (See Chapter 5.4.)

The final part of the case against the intuitive view picks up on a less-central (but nevertheless widely endorsed) aspect of the account. This is the claim that amodal attitudes such as judgments and decisions are sometimes forms of action, and are under direct intentional control. The result is that we are required to postulate two fundamentally different kinds of propositional attitude: those that are active and controlled, and those that are passive and do the controlling (Arpaly & Schroeder, 2012; Kornblith, 2012). As we saw in Chapter 2.3, this is not only conceptually problematic, but requires us to postulate a set of unknown mechanisms to make active control of attitudes possible. In contrast, the sensory-based account of reflection maintains that all attitudes share the same passive nature, whereas the contents of working memory (the contents of reflection and the stream of consciousness) are always actively controlled. (See Chapter 6.) The sensory-based view therefore provides a simpler, more cohesive account of the nature of our amodal attitudes, while nevertheless accommodating our belief that reflection is a controlled active process.

In sum: (1) there is no substantial evidence of the existence of an amodal attitude workspace; (2) belief in such a workspace leaves us unable to explain how reflection takes place, whereas the sensory-based account can provide such an explanation, appealing to known mechanisms; (3) it is simpler to think that all reflection is sensory based than to maintain that some is sensory based (as everyone accepts) while some involves conscious amodal attitudes; (4) the hypothesis of an amodal workspace makes at least two clear predictions that we have good reason to think are false; and (5) the hypothesis of an amodal workspace provides an account of the active nature of conscious reflection that is in various ways problematic. Collectively then, we have good reason to reject the intuitive view.

2. The Positive Picture

The sensory-based account accepts that there are, indeed, a number of types of amodal attitude, including goals, non-sensory judgments, decisions, and intentions. But it claims that these attitudes cannot, themselves, figure consciously among the contents of reflection. Rather, they are active in the background, motivating the shifts of attention and mental rehearsals of action that generate the sensory-based contents of reflection and the stream of consciousness. Put differently, amodal attitudes belong within the executive component of the working-memory system, rather than among the globally broadcast contents of that system. Amodal attitudes are never conscious, therefore (in the access-conscious sense, at least). For only the sensory-based contents of working memory are made globally accessible. The only propositional attitudes that are ever conscious are sensorily dependent ones such as episodic memories and sensorily embedded judgments (seeing *as*, hearing *as*, imagining *as*, and so forth).

This is not to say, however, that amodal *concepts* and *propositions* are never consciously accessible. On the contrary, amodal concepts are routinely bound into the sensory-based contents of perception and working memory, and are globally broadcast as components of the object-files or event-files to which they belong. The result is generally a sensorily embedded event of seeing *as*, hearing *as*, or imagining *as*. For example, a sentence in inner speech might be experienced as expressing a decision to stop by the ATM on the way to the metro. This is then a sensorily embedded judgment with the content, *I have decided to stop at the ATM on the way to the metro*. The result is an amodal proposition that is bound into the sensory content of an imagined (mentally rehearsed) sentence as its meaning. But the event of hearing *as* is not an amodal attitude. Even less is it an amodal decision to stop by the ATM on the way to the metro. The latter event (supposing that it occurred, and that the sentence in inner speech didn't have some more complex etiology) was the *cause* of the event that figured consciously in reflection. It did not itself do so. (See Chapters 6 and 7.) Nor does the sensorily embedded judgment that one has made a new decision ever come to *constitute* such a decision, even though one might constrain one's future behavior to be consistent with it. (See Chapter 7.4.)

The sensory-based account builds on our knowledge of the relationship between attention and the global broadcasting of sensory-involving representations, as well as of the neural mechanisms that underlie each. (See Chapter 3.) This knowledge coheres quite nicely with the account of working memory that has emerged out of numerous scientific labs over the last twenty years. This is that working memory depends on top-down attentional signals directed at midlevel sensory regions of the brain, enabling memories and other representations to be sustained and manipulated in a global workspace. (See Chapter 4.) We also know that mentally rehearsed actions will issue in sensory forward models of the likely consequences of those actions, which can also be globally broadcast when attended to. (See Chapter 4.4, as well as Chapter 6.3 and Chapter 6.4.) As a result, among the contents of working memory will often be episodes of inner speech together with visual and other representations of potential actions. Since there is extensive evidence supporting each of its main components, we can conclude that the sensory-based model of reflection is built on solid scientific foundations.

According to the sensory-based account, not only is reflection always active (or at least action-like) in nature, but so is the stream of consciousness more generally. (See Chapter 6.) This is because the two main determinants of the contents of working memory (attention and the mental rehearsal of action) are themselves action-like, in that they are controlled by executive decision-making processes. Even seemingly passive forms of mind wandering (where one finds oneself entertaining a given content, one knows not why) are really active in nature. In such cases the competition for attentional resources induced by bottom-up forms of attention results in a *decision* to redirect the spotlight of top-down attention onto the representations in question, thereby rendering them conscious. Our belief that reflection is often an active process is thus preserved, while the intuition that much of the stream of consciousness is passive in nature is explained away.[1]

The sensory-based model is also consistent with, while receiving additional support from, contemporary accounts of System 2 forms of reflective reasoning and decision making. Indeed, it has the resources to explain many aspects of those accounts. (See Chapter 7.) In particular, it can explain how culturally acquired norms of reasoning can come to control some instances of System 2 reasoning. Such norms can be stored in the form of well-rehearsed action schemata that can be evoked by the task instructions or features of the context. (Think, here, of many familiar arithmetic procedures.) Or they can be stored as explicit beliefs about standards of reasoning that can be activated into working memory by top-down attention and used to guide appropriate sequences of mentally rehearsed action thereafter.

Finally, the sensory-based model has the resources to explain *why* conscious reflection should be sensory based, despite the fact that many of our thoughts concern abstract non-sensory properties of one sort or another. (See Chapter 8.) For there is reason to think that the sensory-based working-memory system is an ancient adaptation, and that both birds and nonhuman mammals use it for episodic recollection and for purposes of prospective reasoning about observable properties and events. When humans began to evolve, it is likely that they were constrained to make use of this pre-existing sensory-based system, just as they were constrained to be bilaterally symmetrical and to have just four limbs.

In sum, the sensory-based account can explain many known properties of reflection and the stream of consciousness, while appealing to known mechanisms and well-understood cognitive processes. It coheres well with surrounding scientific theories while being strongly supported by an inference to the best explanation of the available data.

3. Implications for Philosophy and Future Questions

This section will describe and briefly discuss some potential implications of the sensory-based account of reflection. It will also mention some questions for future research.

---

[1] The explanation is that we conflate our lack of *knowledge* of the decisions that determine the contents of the stream of consciousness with contents that are not actually determined by decisions at all.

3.1. The thoughts of nonhuman animals

As we noted in Chapter 1.2, many philosophers have denied that animals are capable of genuine thought. Instead animals are, at best, said to be capable only of *proto*-thoughts (Dummett, 1991; Brandom, 1994; McDowell, 1994; Bermúdez, 2003; Hurley, 2006). In large part these claims have been driven by beliefs about the distinctive *inferential promiscuity* enjoyed by human propositional attitudes. Philosophers have thought that in principle any one of our attitudes can enter into inferences with any other attitude, and can do so in indefinitely flexible ways. Expressed in terms that are more friendly to cognitive science, the belief is that humans (and only humans) possess a central cognitive workspace in which any of our attitudes can be activated and conscious, thereby making them available to interact with any other activated attitudes.

The sensory-based account of reflection, of course, maintains that there is no such workspace. Indeed, it claims that there are no differences in *kind* between the attitudes of humans and other animals. Both employ structured amodal representational states that guide and motivate both action and attention. (See Chapter 2.4.) The main differences are just that humans are capable of manipulating the sensory-based contents of working memory in more flexible, creative, and culture-specific ways, and that only humans, of course, are capable of entertaining sentences of inner speech. While the *powers* of the human mind may be very different from those of other animals, the underlying cognitive architecture is shared, as are capacities for amodal thought.

There are some respects in which the human mind is unique, no doubt, and in Chapter 8 we discussed some of them. We are unique in being capable of mentally rehearsing, not just actions, but *speech* actions; we are probably unique in the extent to which we can exert executive control over the working-memory system; and we may be unique in making chronic and creative use of that system. But none of this warrants claiming that our minds differ in *kind* from the minds of nonhuman animals. Admittedly, being capable of inner speech may make a qualitative difference to what our minds are able to achieve, especially when embedded within a culture (such as our own) that encourages the acquisition of valid norms of reasoning to which conscious sequences of reflection can be made to conform. But this is a difference in the *use* that we make of a working-memory system that we share with other animals, rather than a whole other kind of mind.

3.2. The generality constraint

Many philosophers have endorsed a related constraint on what it takes to possess genuine *concepts*, one that is likely to exclude nonhuman animals from qualifying. In particular, many have claimed that it is essential to concepts that they should be freely combinable with one another to issue in novel thoughts, hypotheses, or suppositions. Evans (1982) was the first to propose this famous "generality constraint" on concept-possession, which has been widely endorsed by philosophers since (Peacocke, 1992; Camp, 2004; Beck, 2012). The constraint is that each of the concepts possessed by a subject must be capable of combining with all others of appropriate form or adicity to issue in novel thoughts. Hence if one possesses the concepts F and a needed to entertain the thought Fa, and one can also combine the concepts G and b in the thought Gb, then one must likewise be capable of entertaining the thoughts Fb and Ga.

I have criticized the generality constraint at length elsewhere (Carruthers, 2009b). In brief, I argue that it conflates together two things that should be kept separate. One is a genuine structural constraint on concepts, namely that they should be capable of combining with *some* other concepts to give rise to compositionally structured thoughts. For it is essential to concepts that they should be the building blocks of thought. The other is a distinctively human ability to *freely* combine concepts with *all* other concepts of appropriate form. This may reflect only greatly increased capacities for *creative* concept-combination and *creative* thought. Since there are no good reasons for insisting that creatures must be capable of creative thought in order to be capable of thought at all, nor are there good reasons for insisting that genuine concepts must satisfy the generality constraint.

Given the sensory-based account of reflection, however, it is a moot question whether even *human* concepts satisfy the generality constraint directly, or whether the capacity for free combination of concepts piggybacks on our linguistic capacity for free combination of *words*. Which of these views is correct may depend on the best account of creative language production. On one account, concepts are always combined together first into a thought-to-be-expressed (Levelt, 1989). If true, then this would vindicate the claim that human concepts are freely co-combinable directly. For if a sentence expresses a novel metaphor, say, then it would follow that the corresponding novel combination of concepts must first have occurred in thought. On an alternative view, however, when we think creatively it is *words* that are brought together in novel combinations, with the speech gestures that would produce those combinations of words being evaluated swiftly for relevance by bottom-up competitive processes prior to articulation aloud or in inner speech (Dennett, 1991; Carruthers, 2011b; Lind et al., 2014). On this account, creative concept combination would be a causal product of creative word combination, rather than taking place directly. Given that speech production probably happens in parallel, however, with choices of semantics, syntax, and phonology taking place simultaneously—or at least interactively (Nozari et al., 2011)—it may be that the truth is a complicated mixture of both views. This is a topic for future research.

3.3. *Personal versus subpersonal attitudes*

Philosophers commonly distinguish between personal-level attitudes, which are the attitudes of the whole person, and subpersonal attitudes, which are the attitudes of some part or subsystem within the person (Davies, 2000; Hornsby, 2000). This raises the question, of course, of what it *is* for an attitude to be possessed by the whole person, rather than a part. Consider an unconscious decision to redirect attention toward the sound of one's own name at a party, for example. Is this a personal-level decision or not? On the one hand, if the sensory-based model of reflection is correct, then *all* decisions are unconscious, resulting from competitive interactions among goals, desires, information, and/or action plans. (See Chapters 6 and 7.) But on the other hand, the decision in question is one that the person is unaware of having taken, and neither is it taken for reasons that are conscious. All that one is aware of is the sudden sound of one's own name, resulting from an unconscious decision to shift attention. If this latter consideration is taken to show that the decision is not a personal one, then it will follow that *there are no* personal-level decisions. Similar considerations can then be used to establish that there are no personal-level goals, intentions, or amodal judgments either.

Although the sensory-based account leaves no room for a distinction between conscious and unconscious amodal attitudes (rather, all are unconscious), a related distinction can still be drawn. This may provide philosophers with at least some of what they want. In particular, one can distinguish between attitudes that are formed as a result of one's conscious reflections and those that are caused by unconscious processes (Levy, 2014). Although attitudes that result from conscious reflection are still unconscious ones (albeit ones that subjects often know to exist, resulting from mindreading-based interpretation of the sensory-based contents of reflection), they are nevertheless ones whose formation the entire person has contributed to. Asking oneself in inner speech, "What should I decide?," for example, issues in a globally broadcast request for information, thereby allowing all the different consumer subsystems that receive such broadcasts a chance to contribute an answer. There is a good sense, then, in which attitudes that are formed as a result of conscious reflection are owned by the whole person, in a way that a decision to redirect attention to the sound of one's own name is not. On this view, then, personal and subpersonal attitudes would be attitudes of the very same kind, but differing in etiology. Personal attitudes would be (unconscious) attitudes that are caused by conscious reflection whereas sub-personal attitudes are not.

3.4. Rational agency

We noted in Chapter 1.2 that numerous philosophers have developed a conception of agency, or of rational agency, that requires one's attitudes and actions to be appropriately sensitive to *reasons* (McDowell, 1994; Brandom, 1994, 2000; Korsgaard, 1996, 2009). If reasons, in turn, are thought to require conscious attitudes—either because reasons *are* conscious attitudes, or because reasons are features of the world accessible to us through conscious attitudes—then it follows from the arguments of this book that there is no such thing as conscious agency. It will be important for philosophers working in this tradition, therefore, to consider whether they can make do with the thinner notion of a personal-level attitude outlined in Section 3.3. That is, such philosophers need to ask themselves whether the purposes for which a concept of rational agency is needed really require sensitivity to conscious *attitudes*, or whether it could be enough that one is sensitive to processes of conscious (sensory-based) *reflection*. This, too, is a topic for future research.

Philosophers belonging to this and other traditions who think that the formation and deployment of attitudes is sometimes under our direct control confront a similar dilemma. Either it turns out that they are flat-out wrong because (according to the sensory-based account) our attitudes are never under our direct control, or the philosophical purposes subserved by their claims don't really require *direct* control over attitudes, and it would be sufficient that we can influence our attitudes *in*directly, by engaging in conscious forms of sensory-based reflection that *are* under direct control.

Sensorily embedded attitudes can figure consciously in reflection, of course (as we have often noted), but their doing so is not constitutively active. Rather, they are caused by unconscious mental actions, and of course no one will deny that we can have *indirect* control over our attitudes. For example, the tokening of a sentence in inner speech is caused by the decision to rehearse the motor-plan in question. But the resulting sensorily embedded judgment (such as hearing oneself as deciding to stop at the ATM) is caused by comprehension processes getting to work on the sensory forward model of the rehearsed action. So the resulting sensorily embedded judgment is no more active than is hearing someone *else* say that they will stop at the ATM. In each case we have a passively formed judgment that is caused by a prior action (in the one case, one's own, in the other case, the action of someone else).

What *is* true, of course, is that humans have the capacity for rational, norm-governed control *of reflection*. Since reflection is an active process, generated by shifts of attention and mental rehearsals of action, it is under intentional control. And since humans are capable of acquiring true beliefs about rational norms, they are capable of controlling their reflections in accordance with those norms, provided they recall them and are motivated to do so.[2] But the fact that reflection can be under direct rational control does not entail, of course, that any *attitudes* are under such control. And the latter is false if the sensory-based account of reflection is true.

3.5. Moral responsibility

Some accounts of moral responsibility assume that actions for which we are responsible are those that issue from conscious attitudes and conscious decisions (King & Carruthers, 2012). Given the correctness of the sensory-based model defended in this book, such accounts, too, face a dilemma: either they are false, or there is no such thing as moral responsibility. Assuming that the latter option is unacceptable, where does that leave us? Would we then have no way of accommodating the sorts of considerations that motivate such views? For example, would we have no way of distinguishing between actions that result from so-called "implicit attitudes" (Greenwald et al., 2002) and those that result from conscious reflection? Imagine someone who has an implicit bias against black people of which he is unaware. When reviewing applicants for a job, this leads him to pass over a well-qualified black applicant in favor of a white candidate who is somewhat less qualified. It is disputable whether or not he is blameworthy for doing so. What is surely *not* disputable, however, is that he is much *less* blameworthy than someone who thinks to himself, "I don't want a black person working for me" while reviewing the materials, leading him to reject the person's application.

This distinction can be accommodated, however, by drawing on the point made in Section 3.3. This is that a decision that results from conscious reflection about the (alleged) de-merits of black people is one that the entire person has an opportunity to contribute to. It therefore reflects, in some sense, his entire self (Levy, 2014). In contrast, where the decision results unknowingly from an unconscious bias, it is only this bias that the decision reflects. All of the person's other goals and values might pull in the contrary direction, in such a way that,

---

[2] How much human reflection *actually* takes place in accordance with rational norms is another matter entirely, of course. In fact, we know from the literature on dual systems of reasoning that the proportion will be small or negligible in most cases.

had his attention been drawn to the difference in qualifications between the two candidates as well as his own implicit bias, he would immediately have selected the black candidate.

3.6. Other issues

The belief that there are conscious as well as unconscious thoughts may have influenced debates in a number of other areas of philosophy. For example, those discussing freedom of the will might assume that free decisions are ones that are conscious and under our control. Any such discussions will need to be revisited if the sensory-based account is correct. I won't presume to guess the outcome of such re-examinations. But it should be plain that, since some version of the amodal workspace account is quite widely accepted, much new thinking may need to be done. Indeed, since for many people the amodal model has the status of a background *assumption*, rather than a clearly articulated explicit doctrine, it may require some work even to figure out *which* philosophical theories may need to be re-examined. I propose to leave this work to others. My goal in this book has been to develop the sensory-based account of reflection in enough detail to show that it is well established, while demonstrating that there is no such thing as an amodal workspace in which attitudes of all types can be activated and conscious. Figuring out the further philosophical implications of the account is something I am happy to leave to others.

3.7. Remaining questions for science

In addition to some of the questions for future philosophical research mentioned earlier in this section, there are (of course) numerous scientific issues remaining. We need a much better understanding of the manner in which top-down attentional signals can result in the global broadcasting of targeted information, and of how these signals can be guided by concepts and goals to activate representations endogenously. We also need to know much more about the bottom-up attentional networks, and how they interact with both standing valuational systems and current goals to determine the relevance of the various representations received. And then we need to understand how the top-down and bottom-up attention networks interact, as well as the contributions made by the component parts of each. Moreover, we need to understand how decisions are taken to direct top-down attention and to select actions to be rehearsed, at both cognitive and neural levels of description. Once all this knowledge is in place, only then will we have a firm grip on the nature and causal determinants of conscious reflection and the stream of consciousness.

4. Conclusion

The science of working memory has a great deal to teach us about the nature of human thought. For the contents of working memory are not only conscious but sensory based, and it seems that there are no non-sensory systems that can likewise contain endogenously caused conscious states. So conscious thought, too, is constrained to be sensory based. This result is consistent with sensori-motor and empiricist theories of thought, of course, of the sort defended by Barsalou (1999) and Prinz (2002). But a better view is that there are many forms of amodal—non-sensory-based—thought, which remain unconscious (and which function within the executive component of the working-memory system, among other roles). Moreover, amodal concepts can be bound into the sensory-based contents of working memory, issuing in sensorily embedded attitudes of hearing *as*, imagining *as*, and so on. What is true is just that even the most abstract of our conscious reflections are constrained to have a sensory-based format.

Building on scientific accounts of the working-memory system, and weaving these together with a range of related findings in cognitive science, I have tried to show that one can construct at least the outline of a theory of how both the stream of consciousness in general, and conscious reflection in particular, are produced. No doubt there are many details remaining to be added, and much that may need to be corrected. But I hope that at least the overall framework of the theory of conscious thought that I have provided will survive the test of time, and will be deepened and corroborated by further scientific scrutiny.

References

Acton, G. & Schroeder, D. (2001). Sensory discrimination as related to general intelligence. *Intelligence*, 29, 263–71.

Adams, F. & Aizawa, K. (2008). *The Bounds of Cognition*. Blackwell.

Addis, D., Wong, A., & Schacter, D. (2007). Remembering the past and imagining the future: Common and distinct neural substrates during event construction and elaboration. *Neuropsychologia*, 45, 1363–77.

Allen, T. & Fortin, N. (2013). The evolution of episodic memory. *Proceedings of the National Academy of Sciences*, 110, 10379–86.

Amodio, D. & Devine, P. (2006). Stereotyping and evaluation in implicit race bias: Evidence for independent constructs and unique effects on behavior. *Journal of Personality and Social Psychology*, 91, 652–61.

Anderson, J. (1993). *Rules of the Mind*. Erlbaum.

Anderson, M. (2010). Neural reuse: A fundamental organizational principle of the brain. *Behavioral and Brain Sciences*, 33, 245–66.

Andrews-Hanna, J., Smallwood, J., & Spreng, R.N. (2014). The default network and self-generated thought: Component processes, dynamic control, and clinical relevance. *Annals of the New York Academy of Sciences*, 1316, 29–52.

Anscombe, E. (1957). *Intention*. Blackwell.

Aron, A., Robbins, T., & Poldrack, R. (2004). Inhibition and the right inferior frontal cortex. *Trends in Cognitive Sciences*, 8, 170–7.

Arpaly, N. & Schroeder, T. (2012). Deliberation and acting for reasons. *Philosophical Review*, 121, 209–39.

Auersperg, A., Kacelnik, A., & von Bayern, A. (2013). Explorative learning and functional inferences on a five-step means–means–end problem in Goffin's cockatoos (*Cacatua goffini*). *PLoS One*, 8, e68979.

Auersperg, A., von Bayern, A., Gajdon, G., Huber, L., & Kacelnik, A. (2011). Flexibility in problem solving and tool use of Kea and New Caledonian Crows in a multi access box paradigm. *PLoS One*, 6, e20231.

Awh, E. & Jonides, J. (2001). Overlapping mechanisms of attention and spatial working memory. *Trends in Cognitive Sciences*, 5, 119–26.

Baars, B. (1988). *A Cognitive Theory of Consciousness*. Cambridge University Press.

Baddeley, A. (1986). *Working Memory*. Oxford University Press.

Baddeley, A. & Hitch, G. (1974). Working memory. In G. Bower (ed.), *The Psychology of Learning and Motivation*, vol. 8, Academic Press.

Baillargeon, R., He, Z., Setoh, P., Scott, R., & Yang, D. (2014). The development of false-belief understanding and why it matters. In M. Banaji & S. Gelman (eds.), *The Development of Social Cognition*, Erlbaum.

Baird, B., Smallwood, J., Mrazek, M., Kam, J., Franklin, M., & Schooler, J. (2012). Inspired by distraction: Mind wandering facilitates creative incubation. *Psychological Science*, 23, 1117–22.

Balci, F., Freestone, D., & Gallistel, C.R. (2009). Risk assessment in man and mouse. *Proceedings of the National Academy of Sciences*, 106, 2459–63.

Baluch, F. & Itti, L. (2011). Mechanisms of top–down attention. *Trends in Neurosciences*, 34, 210–24.

Bargh, J., Gollwitzer, P., Lee Chai, A., Barndollar, K., & Trötschel, R. (2001). The automated will: Nonconscious activation and pursuit of behavioral goals. *Journal of Personality and Social Psychology*, 81, 1014–27.

Barrett, C. (2005). Enzymatic computation and cognitive modularity. *Mind & Language*, 20, 259–87.

Barrett, L. (1998). Discrete emotions or dimensions? The role of valence focus and arousal focus. *Cognition and Emotion*, 12, 579–99.

Barrett, L. & Bar, M. (2009). See it with feeling: Affective predictions during object perception. *Philosophical Transactions of the Royal Society B*, 364, 1325–34.

Barsalou, L. (1999). Perceptual symbol systems. *Behavioral and Brain Sciences*, 22, 577–660.

Barth, H., Kanwisher, N., & Spelke, E. (2003). The construction of large number representations in adults. *Cognition*, 86, 201–21.

Bartolomeo, P. & Chokron, S. (2002). Orienting of attention in left unilateral neglect. *Neuroscience and Biobehavioral Reviews*, 26, 217–34.

Baumeister, R., Schmeichel, B., DeWall, C., & Vohs, K. (2007). Is the conscious self a help, an hindrance, or an irrelevance to the creative process? In A. Columbus (ed.), *Advances in Psychology Research*, vol. 53, Nova Science Publishers.

Bayne, T. & Montague, M. (eds.) (2011). *Cognitive Phenomenology*. Oxford University Press.

Beck, D., Muggleton, N., Walsh, V., & Lavie, N. (2006). Right parietal cortex plays a critical role in change blindness. *Cerebral Cortex*, 16, 712–17.

Beck, J. (2012). The Generality Constraint and the structure of thought. *Mind*, 121, 563–600.

Bednekoff, P. & Balda, R. (1997). Clark's nutcracker spatial memory: Many errors might not be due to forgetting. *Animal Behavior*, 54, 691–8.

Bedny, M. & Caramazza, A. (2011). Perception, action, and word meanings in the human brain: The case from action verbs. *Annals of the New York Academy of Sciences*, 1224, 81–95.

Bedny, M., Caramazza, A., Pascual-Leone, A., & Saxe, R. (2012). Typical neural representations of action verbs develop without vision. *Cerebral Cortex*, 22, 286–93.

Bedny, M., Pascual-Leone, A., Dodell-Feder, D., Fedorenko, E., & Saxe, R. (2011). Language processing in the occipital cortex of congenitally blind adults. *Proceedings of the National Academy of Sciences*, 108, 4429–34.

Beer, R. (2000). Dynamical approaches to cognitive science. *Trends in Cognitive Sciences*, 4, 91–9.

Bekhtereva, N., Korotkov, A., Pakhomov, S., Roudas, M., Starchenko, M., & Medvedev, S. (2004). Pet study of brain maintenance of verbal creative activity. *International Journal of Psychophysiology*, 53, 11–20.

Bekinschtein, T., Dehaene, S., Rohaut, B., Tadel, F., Cohen, L., & Naccache, L. (2009). Neural signature of the conscious processing of auditory regularities. *Proceedings of the National Academy of Sciences*, 106, 1672–7.

Benton, S., Kraft, R., Glover, J., & Plake, B. (1984). Cognitive capacity differences among writers. *Journal of Educational Psychology*, 76, 820–34.

Berkeley, G. (1710). *A Treatise Concerning the Principles of Human Knowledge*. London: Rhames and Pepyat.

Bermúdez, J. (2003). *Thinking without Words*. Oxford University Press.

Berridge, K. & Kringelbach, M. (2008). Affective neuroscience of pleasure: reward in humans and animals. *Psychopharmacology*, 199, 457–80.

Berry, D. & Dienes, Z. (1993). *Implicit learning*. Erlbaum.

Berryhill, M. (2012). Insights from neuropsychology: Pinpointing the role of the posterior parietal cortex in episodic and working memory. *Frontiers in Integrative Neuroscience*, 6, 1–12.

Berryhill, M., Chein, J., & Olsen, I. (2011). At the intersection of attention and memory: The mechanistic role of the posterior parietal lobe in working memory. *Neuropsychologia*, 49, 1306–15.

Berryhill, M., Phuong, L., Picasso, L., Cabeza, R., & Olson, I. (2007). Parietal lobe and episodic memory: Bilateral damage causes impaired free recall of autobiographical memory. *The Journal of Neuroscience*, 27, 14415–23.

Bickel, W., Yi, R., Landes, R., Hill, P., & Baxter, C. (2011). Remember the future: Working memory training decreases delay discounting among stimulant addicts. *Biological Psychiatry*, 69, 260–5.

Bilgrami, A. (2006). *Self-Knowledge and Resentment*. Harvard University Press.

Binder, J., Westbury, C., McKiernan, K., Possing, E., & Medler, D. (2005). Distinct brain systems for processing concrete and abstract concepts. *Journal of Cognitive Neuroscience*, 17:6, 1–13.

Bird, C. & Emery, N. (2009a). Insightful problem solving and creative tool modification by captive nontool-using rooks. *Proceedings of the National Academy of Sciences*, 106, 10370–5.

Bird, C. & Emery, N. (2009b). Rooks use stones to raise the water level to reach a floating worm. *Current Biology*, 19, 1410–14.

Bisley, J. (2011). The neural basis of visual attention. *Journal of Physiology*, 589, 49–57.

Blakemore, S-J., Frith, C., & Wolpert, D. (2001). The cerebellum is involved in predicting the sensory consequences of action. *Neuroreport*, 12, 1879–85.

Block, N. (1986). Advertisement for a semantics for psychology. *Midwest Studies in Philosophy*, 10, 615–78.

Block, N. (1995). A confusion about the function of consciousness. *Behavioral and Brain Sciences*, 18, 227–47.

Block, N. (2002). The harder problem of consciousness. *The Journal of Philosophy*, 99, 1–35.

Block, N. (2013). The grain of vision and the grain of attention. *Thought*, 1, 170–84.

Boghossian, P. (2003). The normativity of content. *Philosophical Issues*, 13, 31–45.

Boly, M., Balteau, E., Schnakers, C., Degueldre, C., Moonen, G., Luxen, A., Phillips, C., Peigneux, P., Maquet, P., & Laureys, S. (2007). Baseline brain activity fluctuations predict somatosensory perception in humans. *Proceedings of the National Academy of Sciences*, 104, 12187–92.

Bos, M., Dijksterhuis, A., & van Baaren, R. (2008). On the goal-dependency of unconscious thought. *Journal of Experimental Social Psychology*, 44, 1114–20.

Botterill, G. & Carruthers, P. (1999). *The Philosophy of Psychology*. Cambridge University Press.

Botvinick, G., Cohen, J., & Carter, C. (2004). Conflict monitoring and anterior cingulate cortex: An update. *Trends in Cognitive Sciences*, 8, 539–46.

Botvinick, G., Wang, J., Cowan, E., Roy, S., Bastianen, C., Mayo, P., & Houk, J. (2009). An analysis of immediate serial recall performance in a macaque. *Animal Cognition*, 12, 671–8.

Brandom, R. (1994). *Making it Explicit*. Harvard University Press.

Brandom, R. (2000). *Articulating Reasons*. Harvard University Press.

Bratman, M. (1987). *Intentions, Plans, and Practical Reason*. Harvard University Press.

Bratman, M. (1999). *Faces of Intention*. Cambridge University Press.

Brehmer, Y., Westerberg, H., & Bäckman, L. (2012). Working-memory training in younger and older adults: Training gains, transfer, and maintenance. *Frontiers in Human Neuroscience*, 6, 63.

Bressan, P. & Pizzighello, S. (2008). The attentional cost of inattentional blindness. *Cognition*, 106, 370–83.

Brewer, B. (1999). *Perception and Reason*. Oxford University Press.

Bridge, H., Harrold, S., Holmes, E., Stokes, M., & Kennard, C. (2012). Vivid visual mental imagery in the absence of the primary visual cortex. *Journal of Neurology*, 259, 1062–70.

Broadway, J. & Engle, R. (2010). Validating running memory span: Measurement of working memory capacity and links with fluid intelligence. *Behavior Research Methods*, 42, 563–70.

Brown, D. (1991). *Human Universals*. McGraw-Hill.

Buchsbaum, B., Greer, S., Chang, W-L., & Berman, K. (2005). Meta-analysis of neuroimaging studies of the Wisconsin Card-Sorting Task and component processes. *Human Brain Mapping*, 25, 35–45.

Buckner, R. (2010). The role of the hippocampus in prediction and imagination. *Annual Review of Psychology*, 61, 27–48.

Buckner, R., Andrews-Hanna, J., & Schacter, D. (2008). The brain's default network: Anatomy, function, and relevance to disease. *Annals of the New York Academy of Sciences*, 1124, 1–38.

Buonomano, D. & Merzenich, M. (1998). Cortical plasticity: From synapses to maps. *Annual Review of Neuroscience*, 21, 149–86.

Burge, T. (1996). Our entitlement to self-knowledge. *Proceedings of the Aristotelian Society*, 96, 91–116.

Burgess, G., Gray, J., Conway, A., & Braver, T. (2011). Neural mechanisms of interference control underlie the relationship between fluid intelligence and working memory span. *Journal of Experimental Psychology: General*, 140, 674–92.

Buttelmann, D., Carpenter, M., & Tomasello, M. (2009). Eighteen-month-old infants show false belief understanding in an active helping paradigm. *Cognition*, 112, 337–42.

Butterfill, S. & Apperly, I. (2013). How to build a minimal theory of mind. *Mind & Language*, 28, 606–37.

Cabeza, R. (2008). Role of parietal regions in episodic memory retrieval: The dual attentional processes hypothesis. *Neuropsychologia*, 46, 1813–27.

Cabeza, R., Ciaramelli, E., & Moscovitch, M. (2012). Cognitive contributions of the ventral parietal cortex: An integrative theoretical account. *Trends in Cognitive Sciences*, 16, 338–52.

Cabeza, R., Mazuz, Y., Stokes, J., Kragel, J., Woldorff, M., Ciaramelli, E., Olson, I., & Moscovich, M. (2010). Overlapping parietal activity in memory and perception: Evidence for the attention to memory model. *Journal of Cognitive Neuroscience*, 23, 3209–17.

Camp, E. (2004). The generality constraint, nonsense, and categorical restrictions. *Philosophical Quarterly*, 54, 209–31.

Camp, E. (2009). A language of Baboon thought? In R. Lurz (ed.), *The Philosophy of Animal Minds*, Cambridge University Press.

Campana, G., Cowey, A., & Walsh, V. (2002). Priming of motion direction and area V5/MT: A test of perceptual memory. *Cerebral Cortex*, 12, 663–9.

Capon, A., Handley, S., & Dennis, I. (2003). Working memory and reasoning: An individual differences perspective. *Thinking and Reasoning*, 9, 203–44.

Carrasco, M. & McElree, B. (2001). Covert attention accelerates the rate of visual information processing. *Proceedings of the National Academy of Sciences*, 98, 5363–7.

Carrasco, M., Ling, S., & Read, S. (2004). Attention alters appearance. *Nature Neuroscience*, 7, 308–13.

Carruthers, P. (2000). *Phenomenal Consciousness*. Cambridge University Press.

Carruthers, P. (2005). *Consciousness*. Oxford University Press.

Carruthers, P. (2006). *The Architecture of the Mind*. Oxford University Press.

Carruthers, P. (2007). The creative-action theory of creativity. In P. Carruthers, S. Laurence, & S. Stich (eds.), *The Innate Mind: Volume 3: Foundations and the Future*, Oxford University Press.

Carruthers, P. (2009a). Action-awareness and the active mind. *Philosophical Papers*, 38, 133–56.

Carruthers, P. (2009b). Invertebrate concepts confront the generality constraint (and win). In R. Lurz (ed.), *The Philosophy of Animal Minds*, Cambridge University Press.

Carruthers, P. (2011a). *The Opacity of Mind*. Oxford University Press.

Carruthers, P. (2011b). Creative action in mind. *Philosophical Psychology*, 24, 347–61.

Carruthers, P. (2013a). Mindreading in infancy. *Mind & Language*, 28, 141–72.

Carruthers, P. (2013b). On knowing your own beliefs. In N. Nottelmann (ed.), *New Essays on Belief*, Palgrave MacMillan.

Carruthers, P. (2013c). Evolution of working memory. *Proceedings of the National Academy of Sciences*, 110, 10371–8.

Carson, S., Peterson, J., & Higgins, D. (2003). Decreased latent inhibition is associated with increased creative achievement in high-functioning individuals. *Journal of Personality and Social Psychology*, 85, 499–506.

Centerbar, D. & Clore, G. (2006). Do approach–avoidance actions create attitudes? *Psychological Science*, 17, 22–9.

Chaiken, S., Liberman, A., & Eagly, A. (1989). Heuristic and systematic processing within and beyond the persuasion context. In J. Uleman & J. Bargh (eds.), *Unintended Thought*, Guilford Press.

Chalmers, D. (1996). *The Conscious Mind*. Oxford University Press.

Chalmers, D. (1997). Availability: The cognitive basis of experience. *Behavioral and Brain Sciences*, 20, 148–9.

Chein, J. & Morrison, A. (2010). Expanding the mind's workspace: Training and transfer effects with a complex working memory span task. *Psychonomic Bulletin & Review*, 17, 193–9.

Cheke, L. & Clayton, N. (2012). Eurasian jays (*Garrulus glandarius*) overcome their current desires to anticipate two distinct needs and plan for them appropriately. *Biology Letters*, 8, 171–5.

Cheney, D. & Seyfarth, R. (2007). *Baboon Metaphysics*. University of Chicago Press.

Christoff, K. (2012). Undirected thought: Neural determinants and correlates. *Brain Research*, 1428, 51–9.

Christoff, K., Gordon, A., Smallwood, J., Smith, R., & Schooler, J. (2009). Experience sampling during fMRI reveals default network and executive system contributions to mind wandering. *Proceedings of the National Academy of Sciences*, 106, 8719–24.

Chrysikou, E. & Thompson-Schill, S. (2011). Dissociable brain states linked to common and creative object use. *Human Brain Mapping*, 32, 665–75.

Chrysikou, E., Hamilton, R., Coslett, H., Datta, A., Bikson, M., & Thompson-Schill, S. (2013). Noninvasive transcranial direct current stimulation over the left prefrontal cortex facilitates cognitive flexibility in tool use. *Cognitive Neuroscience*, 4, 81–9.

Chun, M., Golomb, J., & Turk-Browne, N. (2011). A taxonomy of external and internal attention. *Annual Review of Psychology*, 62, 73–101.

Churchland, P.M. (1979). Eliminative materialism and the propositional attitudes. *Journal of Philosophy*, 78, 67–90.

Churchland, P.M. (1993). State-space semantics and meaning holism. *Philosophy and Phenomenological Research*, 53, 667–72.

Churchland, P.M. (2012). *Plato's Camera: How the Physical Brain Captures a Landscape of Abstract Universals*. MIT Press.

Cialdini, R. & Petty, R. (1981). Anticipatory opinion effects. In R. Petty, T. Ostrom, & T. Brock (eds.), *Cognitive Responses in Persuasion*, Erlbaum.

Ciaramelli, E., Grady, C., & Moscovitch, M. (2008). Top–down and bottom–up attention to memory: A hypothesis (AtoM) on the role of the posterior parietal cortex in memory retrieval. *Neuropsychologia*, 46, 1828–51.

Clark, A. (2008). *Supersizing the Mind*. Oxford University Press.

Clark, A. & Chalmers, D. (1998). The extended mind. *Analysis*, 58, 7–19.

Clay, O., Edwards, J., Ross, L., Okonkwo, O., Wadley, V., Roth, D., & Ball, K. (2009). Visual function and cognitive speed of processing mediate age-related decline in memory span and fluid intelligence. *Journal of Aging Health*, 21, 547–66.

Clayton, N. & Dickinson, A. (1999). Scrub-jays (*Aphelocoma coerulescens*) remember the relative time of caching as well as the location and content of their caches. *Journal of Comparative Psychology*, 113, 403–16.

Clayton, N., Dally, J., Gilbert, J., & Dickinson, A. (2005). Food caching by western scrub-jays (*Aphelocoma californica*) is sensitive to the conditions at recovery. *Journal of Experimental Psychology: Animal Behavior Processes*, 31, 115–24.

Clayton, N., Yu, K., & Dickinson, A. (2001). Scrub jays (*Aphelocoma coerulescens*) form integrated memories of the multiple features of caching episodes. *Journal of Experimental Psychology: Animal Behavior Processes*, 27, 17–29.

Clayton, N., Yu, K., & Dickinson, A. (2003). Interacting cache memories: Evidence for flexible memory use by western scrub-jays (*Aphelocoma californica*). *Journal of Experimental Psychology: Animal Behavior Processes*, 29, 14–22.

Cohen, J. & Lieberman, M. (2010). The common neural basis of exerting self-control in multiple domains. In Y. Trope, R. Hassin, & K. Ochsner (eds.), *Self-Control*, Oxford University Press.

Cohen, M., Alvarez, G., & Nakayama, K. (2011). Natural-scene perception requires attention. *Psychological Science*, 22, 1165–72.

Colom, R., Abad, F., Quiroga, A., Shih, P., & Flores-Mendoza, C. (2008). Working memory and intelligence are highly related constructs, but why? *Intelligence*, 36, 584–606.

Colom, R., Quiroga, Á., Shih, P., Martínez, K., Burgaleta, M., Martínez-Molina, A., Román, F., Requena, L., & Ramírez, I. (2010). Improvement in working memory is not related to increased intelligence scores. *Intelligence*, 38, 497–505.

Colom, R., Rebollo, I., Palacios, A., Juan-Espinosa, M., & Kyllonen, P. (2004). Working memory is (almost) perfectly predicted by *g*. *Intelligence*, 32, 277–96.

Conway, A., Kane, M., & Engle, R. (2003). Working memory capacity and its relation to general intelligence. *Trends in Cognitive Sciences*, 7, 547–52.

Cools, R., Gibbs, S., Miyakawa, A., Jagust, W., & D'Esposito, M. (2008). Working memory capacity predicts dopamine synthesis capacity in the human striatum. *The Journal of Neuroscience*, 28, 1208–12.

Corbetta, M. & Shulman, G. (2002). Control of goal-directed and stimulus-driven attention in the brain. *Nature Reviews Neuroscience*, 3, 201–15.

Corbetta, M., Patel, G., & Shulman, G. (2008). The reorienting system of the human brain: From environment to theory of mind. *Neuron*, 58, 306–24.

Correia, S., Dickinson, A., & Clayton, N. (2007). Western scrub-jays anticipate future needs independently of their current motivational state. *Current Biology*, 17, 856–61.

Cowan, N. (1988). Evolving conceptions of memory storage, selective attention, and their mutual constraints within the human information processing system. *Psychological Bulletin*, 104, 163–91.

Cowan, N. (1995). *Attention and Memory*. Oxford University Press.

Cowan, N. (2001). The magical number 4 in short-term memory: A reconsideration of mental storage capacity. *Behavioral and Brain Sciences*, 24, 87–185.

Cowan, N., Elliott, E., Saults, J.S., Morey, C., Mattox, S., Hismjatullina, A., & Conway, A. (2005). On the capacity of attention: Its estimation and its role in working memory and cognitive aptitudes. *Cognitive Psychology*, 51, 42–100.

Cowan, N., Li, D., Moffitt, A., Becker, T., Martin, E., Saults, S., & Christ, S. (2011). A neural region of abstract working memory. *Journal of Cognitive Neuroscience*, 23, 2852–63.

Coyle, T., Pillow, D., Snyder, A., & Kochunov, P. (2011). Processing speed mediates the development of general intelligence (*g*) in adolescence. *Psychological Science*, 22, 1265–9.

Crick, F. & Koch, C. (1990). Towards a neurobiological theory of consciousness. *Seminars in the Neurosciences*, 2, 263–75.

Crick, F. & Koch, C. (2003). A framework for consciousness. *Nature Neuroscience*, 6, 119–26.

Cristescu, T., Devlin, J., & Nobre, A. (2006). Orienting attention to semantic categories. *NeuroImage*, 33, 1178–87.

Curtis, C. (2006). Prefrontal and parietal contributions to spatial working memory. *Neuroscience*, 139, 173–80.

D'Esposito, M. (2007). From cognitive to neural models of working memory. *Philosophical Transactions of the Royal Society B*, 362, 761–72.

Dade, L., Zatorre, R., Evans, A., & Jones-Gottman, M. (2001). Working memory in another dimension: functional imaging of human olfactory working memory. *Neuroimage*, 14, 650–60.

Damasio, A. (1994). *Descartes' Error*. Papermac.

Daneman, M. & Carpenter, P. (1980). Individual differences in working memory and reading. *Journal of Verbal Learning and Verbal Behavior*, 19, 450–66.

Daneman, M. & Carpenter, P. (1983). Individual differences in integrating information between and within sentences. *Journal of Experimental Psychology: Learning, Memory, and Cognition*, 9, 561–84.

Daneman, M. & Green, I. (1986). Individual differences in comprehending and producing words in context. *Journal of Memory and Language*, 25, 1–18.

Daselaar, S., Porat, Y., Huijbers, W., & Pennartz, C. (2010). Modality-specific and modality-independent components of the human imagery system. *NeuroImage*, 52, 677–85.

Davies, M. (1991). Concepts, connectionism, and the language of thought. In W. Ramsey, S. Stich, & D. Rumelhart (eds.), *Philosophy and Connectionist Theory*, Erlbaum.

Davies, M. (1998). Language, thought, and the language of thought (Aunty's own argument revisited). In P. Carruthers & J. Boucher (eds.), *Language and Thought*, Cambridge University Press.

Davies, M. (2000). Interaction without reduction: The relationship between personal and sub-personal levels of description. *Mind & Society*, 2, 87–105.

De Brigard, F. (2012). The role of attention in conscious recollection. *Frontiers in Psychology*, vol. 3, article 29.

De Neys, W. (2006a). Automatic–heuristic and executive–analytic processing during reasoning: Chronometric and dual-task considerations. *Quarterly Journal of Experimental Psychology*, 59, 1070–100.

De Neys, W. (2006b). Dual processing in reasoning: Two systems but one reasoner. *Psychological Science*, 17, 428–33.

De Neys, W., Vartanian, O., & Goel, V. (2008). Smarter than we think: When our brains detect that we are biased. *Psychological Science*, 19, 483–9.

Deary, I., Bell, P., Bell, A., Campbell, M., & Fazal, N. (2004). Sensory discrimination and intelligence: Testing Spearman's other hypothesis. *American Journal of Psychology*, 117, 1–18.

Deary, I., Penke, L., & Johnson, W. (2010). The neuroscience of human intelligence differences. *Nature Reviews Neuroscience*, 11, 201–11.

Dehaene, S. (1997). *The Number Sense*. Penguin Press.

Dehaene, S. (2004). Evolution of human cortical circuits for reading and arithmetic: The "neuronal recycling" hypothesis. In S. Dehaene, J. Duhamel, M. Hauser, & G. Rizzolatti (eds.), *From Monkey Brain to Human Brain*, MIT Press.

Dehaene, S. (2009). *Reading in the Brain*. Penguin Press.

Dehaene, S. & Changeux, J-P. (2011). Experimental and theoretical approaches to conscious processing. *Neuron*, 70, 200–27.

Dehaene, S., Changeux, J-P., Naccache, L., Sackur, J., & Sergent, C. (2006). Conscious, preconscious, and subliminal processing: A testable taxonomy. *Trends in Cognitive Sciences*, 10, 204–11.

Dehaene, S., Naccache, L., Le Clec'H, G., Koechlin, E., Mueller, Mi., Dehaene-Lambertz, G., van de Moortele, P-F., & Le Bihan, D. (1998). Imaging unconscious semantic priming. *Nature*, 395, 597–600.

Del Cul, A., Baillet, S., & Dehaene, S. (2007). Brain dynamics underlying the nonlinear threshold for access to consciousness. *PLoS Biology*, 5:10, e260.

Demetriou, A., Spandoudis, G., Shayer, M., Mouyi, A., Kazi, S., & Platsidou, M. (2013). Cycles in speed–working memory–G relations: Towards a developmental–differential theory of the mind. *Intelligence*, 41, 34–50.

Dennett, D. (1978). Towards a computational theory of consciousness. In D. Dennett, *Brainstorms*, Harvester Press.

Dennett, D. (1991). *Consciousness Explained*. Penguin Press.

Dennett, D. (1996). *Kinds of Minds*. Basic Books.

Dennett, D. (2001). Are we explaining consciousness yet? *Cognition*, 79, 221–37.

Diekhof, E., Biedermann, F., Ruebsamen, R., & Gruber, O. (2009). Top-down and bottom-up modulation of brain structures involved in auditory discrimination. *Brain Research*, 1297, 118–23.

Dijksterhuis, A. & Aarts, H. (2010). Goals, attention, and (un)consciousness. *Annual Review of Psychology*, 61, 467–90.

Dijksterhuis, A., Bos, M., Nordgren, L., & van Baaren, R. (2006). On making the right choice: The deliberation-without-attention effect. *Science*, 311, 1005–7.

Dretske, F. (1979). Simple seeing. In D. Gustafson & B. Tapscott (eds.), *Body, Mind, and Method*, Reidel.

Dretske, F. (1988). *Explaining Behavior*. MIT Press.

Dretske, F. (1995). *Naturalizing the Mind*. MIT Press.

Driver, P. & Humphries, N. (1988). *Protean Behavior: The Biology of Unpredictability*. Oxford University Press.

Dudchenko, P. (2004). An overview of the tasks used to test working memory in rodents. *Neuroscience and Biobehavioral Reviews*, 28, 699–709.

Dummett, M. (1991). *Frege and Other Philosophers*. Oxford University Press.

Edelman, G. (2003). Naturalizing consciousness: A theoretical framework. *Proceedings of the National Academy of Sciences*, 100, 5520–4.

Egan, F. (1995). Computation and content. *Philosophical Review*, 104, 181–203.

Eichenbaum, H., Sauvage, M., Fortin, N., Komorowski, R., & Lipton, P. (2012). Towards a functional organization of episodic memory in the medial temporal lobe. *Neuroscience and Biobehavioral Reviews*, 36, 1597–608.

Ellamil, M., Dobson, C., Beeman, M., & Christoff, K. (2012). Evaluative and generative modes of thought during the creative process. *NeuroImage*, 59, 1783–94.

Elliot, A. & Devine, P. (1994). On the motivational nature of cognitive dissonance: Dissonance as psychological discomfort. *Journal of Personality and Social Psychology*, 67, 382–94.

Engle, R. (2002). Working memory capacity as executive attention. *Current Directions in Psychological Science*, 11, 19–23.

Engle, R. (2010). Role of working-memory capacity in cognitive control. *Current Anthropology*, 51, S17–S26.

Engle, R., Carullo, J., & Collins, K. (1991). Individual differences in working memory for comprehension and following directions. *Journal of Educational Research*, 84, 253–62.

Engle, R., Tuholksi, S., Laughlin, J., & Conway, A. (1999). Working memory, short-term memory, and fluid general intelligence: A latent-variable approach. *Journal of Experimental Psychology: General*, 128, 309–31.

Ericsson, A. & Kintsch, W. (1995). Long-term working memory. *Psychological Review*, 102, 211–45.

Ericsson, A. & Simon, H. (1993). *Protocol Analysis: Verbal Reports as Data*. Revised edition, MIT Press.

Evans, G. (1982). *The Varieties of Reference*. Oxford University Press.

Evans, J. (2010). *Thinking Twice: Two Minds in One Brain*. Oxford University Press.

Evans, J. & Curtis-Holmes, J. (2005). Rapid responding increases belief bias: Evidence for the dual-process theory of reasoning. *Thinking & Reasoning*, 11, 382–9.

Evans, J. & Over, D. (1996). *Rationality and Reasoning*. Psychology Press.

Evans, J. & Stanovich, K. (2013). Dual-process theories of higher cognition: Advancing the debate. *Perspectives on Psychological Science*, 8, 223–41.

Fagot, J. & Lillo, C. (2011). A comparative study of working memory: Immediate serial spatial recall in baboons and humans. *Neuropsychologia*, 49, 3870–80.

Farroni, T., Johnson, M., Menon, E., Zulian, L., Faraguna, D., & Csibra, G. (2005). Newborns' preference for face-relevant stimuli: Effect of contrast polarity. *Proceedings of the National Academy of Sciences*, 102, 17245–50.

Feigenson, L. & Halberda, J. (2008). Conceptual knowledge increases infants' memory capacity. *Proceedings of the National Academy of Sciences*, 105, 9926–30.

Festinger, L. (1957). *A Theory of Cognitive Dissonance*. Stanford University Press.

Field, H. (1977). Logic, meaning, and conceptual role. *Journal of Philosophy*, 74, 379–409.

Finke, R. (1995). Creative realism. In S. Smith, T. Ward, & R. Finke (eds.), *The Creative Cognition Approach*, Cambridge University Press.

Finke, R., Ward, T., & Smith, S. (1992). *Creative Cognition*. MIT Press.

Finnerty, J., Pang, K., Burton, P., Paulson, D., & Martindale, M. (2004). Origins of bilateral symmetry: *Hox* and *Dpp* expression in a sea anemone. *Science*, 304, 1335–7.

Fiske, S. & Taylor, S. (2008). *Social Cognition: From Brains to Behavior*. McGraw Hill.

Fletcher, L. & Carruthers, P. (2013). Behavior-reading versus mentalizing in animals. In J. Metcalfe & H. Terrace (eds.), *Agency and Joint Attention*, Oxford University Press.

Fodor, J. (1975). *The Language of Thought*. Harvard University Press.

Fodor, J. (1983). *The Modularity of Mind*. MIT Press.

Fodor, J. (1990). *A Theory of Content and Other Essays*. MIT Press.

Fodor, J. & McLaughlin, B. (1990). Connectionism and the problem of systematicity. *Cognition*, 35, 183–204.

Fodor, J. & Pylyshyn, Z. (1988). Connectionism and cognitive architecture. *Cognition*, 28, 3–71.

Franconeri, S., Alvarez, G., & Cavanagh, P. (2013). Flexible cognitive resources: Competitive content maps for attention and memory. *Trends in Cognitive Sciences*, 17, 134–41.

Frankish, K. (2004). *Mind and Supermind*. Cambridge University Press.

Frankish, K. (2009). Systems and levels. In J. Evans & K. Frankish (eds.), *In Two Minds*, Oxford University Press.

Frith, C., Blakemore, S-J., & Wolpert, D. (2000). Abnormalities in the awareness and control of action. *Philosophical Transactions of the Royal Society of London: B*, 355, 1771–88.

Frith, U. & Frith, C. (2003). Development and neurophysiology of mentalizing. *Philosophical Transactions of the Royal Society of London B: Biological Sciences*, 358, 459–73.

Gallistel, R., Mark, T., King, A., & Lantham, P. (2001). The rat approximates an ideal detector of rates of reward. *Journal of Experimental Psychology: Animal Behavior Processes*, 27, 354–72.

Ganis, G., Keenan, J., Kosslyn, S., & Pascual-Leone, A. (2000). Transcranian magnetic stimulation of primary motor cortex affects mental rotation. *Cerebral Cortex*, 10, 175–80.

Gathercole, S. (1994). Neuropsychology and working memory: A review. *Neuropsychology*, 8, 494–505.

Gazzaley, A. & Nobre, A. (2012). Top–down modulation: Bridging selective attention and working memory. *Trends in Cognitive Sciences*, 16, 129–35.

Gazzaley, A., Cooney, J., McEvoy, K., Knight, R., & D'Esposito, M. (2005). Top-down enhancement and suppression of the magnitude and speed of neural activity. *Journal of Cognitive Neuroscience*, 17, 507–17.

Geake, J. & Hansen, P. (2005). Neural correlates of intelligence as revealed by fMRI of fluid analogies. *NeuroImage*, 26, 555–64.

Geary, D. (2005). *The Origin of Mind*. American Psychological Association.

Gigerenzer, G., Todd, P., & the ABC Research Group (1999). *Simple Heuristics that Make Us Smart*. Oxford University Press.

Gilbert, D. & Wilson, T. (2007). Prospection: Experiencing the future. *Science*, 317, 1351–4.

Gilovich, T., Griffin, D., & Kahneman, D. (eds.) (2002). *Heuristics and Biases*. Cambridge University Press.

Giurfa, M., Zhang, S., Jenett, A., Menzel, R., & Srinivasan, M. (2001). The concepts of "sameness" and "difference" in an insect. *Nature*, 410, 930–3.

Glüer, K. & Wikforss, Å. (2009). Against content normativity. *Mind*, 118, 31–70.

Goel, V. (2008). Anatomy of deductive reasoning. *Trends in Cognitive Sciences*, 11, 435–41.

Goldenberg, G., Müllbacher, W., & Nowak, A. (1995). Imagery without perception: A case study of anosognosia for cortical blindness. *Neuropsychologia*, 33, 1373–82.

Goldin-Meadow, S. (2005). *Hearing Gesture: How our Hands Help us Think*. Harvard University Press.

Goldman, A. (2006). *Simulating Minds.* Oxford University Press.

Goldman-Rakic, P. (1995). Cellular basis of working memory. *Neuron,* 14, 477–85.

Goldman-Rakic, P., Funahashi, S., & Bruce, C. (1990). Neocortical memory circuits. *Quarterly Journal of Quantitative Biology,* 55, 1025–38.

Goldstone, R. (1994). Influences of categorization on perceptual discrimination. *Journal of Experimental Psychology: General,* 123, 178–200.

Goldstone, R., Lippa, Y., & Shiffrin, R. (2001). Altering object representations through category learning. *Cognition,* 78, 27–43.

Gollwitzer, P. & Sheeran, P. (2006). Implementation intentions and goal achievement: A meta-analysis of effects and processes. *Advances in Experimental Social Psychology,* 38, 69–119.

Gray, J. & Thompson, P. (2004). Neurobiology of intelligence: Science and ethics. *Nature Reviews Neuroscience,* 5, 471–82.

Greenwald, A., Banaji, M., Rudman, L., Farnham, S., Nosek, B., & Mellott, D. (2002). A unified theory of implicit attitudes, stereotypes, self-esteem, and self-concept. *Psychological Review,* 109, 3–25.

Gruberg, E., Dudkin, E., Wang, Y., Marin, G., Salas, C., Sentis, E., Letelier, J., Mpodozis, J., Malpeli, J., Cui, H., Ma, R., Northmore, D., & Udin, S. (2006). Influencing and interpreting visual input: the role of a visual feedback system. *Journal of Neuroscience,* 26, 10368–71.

Grush, R. (2004). The emulation theory of representation: Motor control, imagery, and perception. *Behavioral and Brain Sciences,* 27, 377–442.

Halberda, J., Mazzocco, M., & Feigenson, L. (2008). Individual differences in nonverbal number acuity correlate with maths achievement. *Nature,* 455, 665–9.

Hanus, D., Mendes, N., Tennie, C., & Call, J. (2011). Comparing the performances of apes (*Gorilla gorilla, pan troglodytes, Pongo pymaeus*) and human children (*Homo sapiens*) in the floating peanut task. *PLoS One,* 6, e19555.

Harris, J., Miniussi, C., Harris, I., & Diamond, M. (2002). Transient storage of a tactile memory trace in primary somatosensory cortex. *Journal of Neuroscience,* 22, 8720–5.

Hassabis, D., Kumaran, D., & Maguire, E. (2007). Using imagination to understand the neural basis of episodic memory. *The Journal of Neuroscience,* 27, 14365–74.

Hassin, R. (2013). Yes it can: On the functional abilities of the human unconscious. *Perspectives on Psychological Science,* 8, 195–207.

Hassin, R., Bargh, J., Engell, A., & McCulloch, K. (2009). Implicit working memory. *Consciousness and Cognition,* 18, 665–78.

Hauser, M., Carey, S., Hauser, L. (2000). Spontaneous number representation in semi-free-ranging rhesus monkeys. *Proceedings of the Royal Society of London B: Biological Sciences,* 267, 829–33.

Heavey, C. & Hurlburt, R. (2008). The phenomena of inner experience. *Consciousness and Cognition,* 17, 798–810.

Herwig, U., Abler, B., Schönfeldt-Lecuona, C., Wunderlich, A., Grothe, J., Spitzer, M., & Walter, H. (2003). Verbal storage in a premotor–parietal network: Evidence from fMRI-guided magnetic stimulation. *NeuroImage,* 20, 1032–41.

Hickok, G. & Poeppel, D. (2007). The cortical organization of speech processing. *Nature Reviews Neuroscience,* 8, 393–402.

Hills, T. (2006). Animal foraging and the evolution of goal-directed cognition. *Cognitive Science*, 30, 3–41.

Hills, T. & Dukas, R. (2012). The evolution of cognitive search. In P. Todd, T. Hills, & T. Robbins (eds.), *Cognitive Search: Evolution, Algorithms, and the Brain*, MIT Press.

Hills, T., Jones, M., & Todd, P. (2012). Optimal foraging in semantic memory. *Psychological Review*, 119, 431–40.

Hornsby, J. (2000). Personal and sub-personal: A defense of Dennett's early distinction. *Philosophical Explorations*, 3, 6–24.

Horton, W. & Keysar, B. (1996). When do speakers take into account common ground? *Cognition*, 59, 91–117.

Howard-Jones, P., Blakemore, S-J., Samuel, E., Summers, I., & Claxton, G. (2005). Semantic divergence and creative story generation: An fMRI investigation. *Cognitive Brain Research*, 25, 240–50.

Huang, J. & Bargh, J. (2014). The selfish goal: Autonomously operating motivational structures as the proximate cause of human judgment and behavior. *Behavioral and Brain Sciences*, 37, 121–35.

Huber, A., Kolodkin, A., Ginty, D., & Cloutier, J-F. (2003). Signaling at the growth cone: Ligand-receptor complexes and the control of axon growth and guidance. *Annual Review of Neuroscience*, 26, 509–63.

Hurlburt, R. (2009). Unsymbolized thinking, sensory awareness, and mindreading. *Behavioral and Brain Sciences*, 32, 149–50.

Hurlburt, R. & Akhter, S. (2008). Unsymbolized thinking. *Consciousness and Cognition*, 17, 1364–74.

Hurley, S. (2006). Making sense of animals. In S. Hurley & M. Nudds (eds.), *Rational Animals?* Oxford University Press.

Hutchinson, J., Uncapher, M., & Wagner, A. (2009). Posterior parietal cortex and episodic retrieval: Convergent and divergent effects of attention and memory. *Learning and Memory*, 16, 343–56.

Ikkai, A., McCollough, A., & Vogel, E. (2010). Contralateral delay activity provides a neural measure of the number of representations in working memory. *Journal of Neurophysiology*, 103, 1963–8.

Inoue, S. & Matsuzawa, T. (2007). Working memory of numerals in chimpanzees. *Current Biology*, 17, R1004–R1005.

Inoue, S. & Matsuzawa, T. (2009). Acquisition and memory of sequence order in young and adult chimpanzees (*Pan troglodytes*). *Animal Cognition*, 12, S59–S69.

Izard, V., Sann, C., Spelke, E., & Streri, A. (2009). Newborn infants perceive abstract numbers. *Proceedings of the National Academy of Sciences*, 106, 10382–5.

Jackendoff, R. (2007). *Language, Consciousness, Culture: Essays on Mental Structure*. MIT Press.

Jackendoff, R. (2012). *A User's Guide to Thought and Meaning*. Oxford University Press.

Jaeggi, S., Buschkuehl, M., Jonides, J., & Perrig, W. (2008). Improving fluid intelligence with training on working memory. *Proceedings of the National Academy of Sciences*, 105, 6829–33.

Jaeggi, S., Buschkuehl, M., Jonides, J., & Shah, P. (2011). Short- and long-term benefits of cognitive training. *Proceedings of the National Academy of Sciences*, 108, 10081–6.

Jaeggi, S., Buschkuehl, M., Shah, P., & Jonides, J. (2014). The role of individual differences in cognitive training and transfer. *Memory and Cognition*, 42, 464–80.

Jaeggi, S., Studer-Luethi, B., Buschkuehl, M., Su, Y-F., Jonides, J., & Perrig, W. (2010). The relationship between n-back performance and matrix reasoning—implications for training and transfer. *Intelligence*, 38, 625–35.

Janmaat, K., Polansky, L., Dagui Ban, S., & Boesch, C. (2014). Wild chimpanzees plan their breakfast time, type, and location. *Proceedings of the National Academy of Sciences*, 111, 16343–8.

Jarosz, A., Colflesh, G., & Wiley, J. (2012). Uncorking the muse: Alcohol intoxication facilitates creative problem solving. *Consciousness and Cognition*, 21, 487–93.

Jaušovec, N. & Jaušovec, K. (2012). Working memory training: Improving intelligence—changing brain activity. *Brain and Cognition*, 79, 96–106.

Jeannerod, M. (2006). *Motor Cognition*. Oxford University Press.

Jensen, O., Kaiser, J., & Lachaux, J-P. (2007). Human gamma-frequency oscillations associated with attention and memory. *Trends in Neurosciences*, 30, 317–24.

Ji, L., Peng, K., & Nisbett, R. (2000). Culture, control, and perception of relationships in the environment. *Journal of Personality and Social Psychology*, 78, 943–55.

Jones, S., Pritchett, D., Stufflebeam, S., Hamalainen, M., & Moore, C. (2007). Neural correlates of tactile detection: A combined magnetoencephalography and biophysically based computational modeling study. *Journal of Neuroscience*, 27, 10751–64.

Jonides, J., Lewis, R., Nee, D., Lustig, C., Berman, M., & Moore, K. (2008). The mind and brain of short-term memory. *Annual Review of Psychology*, 59, 193–224.

Jordan, K., MacLean, E., & Brannon, E. (2008). Monkeys match and tally quantities across senses. *Cognition*, 108, 617–25.

Jung, R. & Haier, R. (2007). The Parieto-Frontal Integration Theory (PFIT) of intelligence: Converging neuroimaging evidence. *Behavioral and Brain Sciences*, 30, 135–54.

Jung-Beeman, M., Bowden, E., Haberman, J., Frymiare, J., Arambel-Liu, S., Greenblatt, R., Reber, P., & Kounios, J. (2004). Neural activity when people solve verbal problems with insight. *PLoS Biology*, 2, 500–10.

Kaas, J. (1997). Topographic maps are fundamental to sensory processing. *Brain Research Bulletin*, 44, 107–12.

Kahneman, D. (2011). *Thinking, Fast and Slow*. Farrar, Straus, and Grioux.

Kahneman, D. & Frederick, S. (2002). Representativeness revisited: Attribute substitution in intuitive judgment. In T. Gilovich, D. Griffin, & D. Kahneman (eds.), *Heuristics and Biases*, Cambridge University Press.

Kahneman, D. & Triesman, A. (1984). Changing views of attention and automaticity. In R. Parasuraman & D. Davies (eds.), *Varieties of Attention*, Academic Press.

Kahneman, D., Slovic, P., & Tversky, A. (eds.) (1982). *Judgment Under Uncertainty: Heuristics and Biases*. Cambridge University Press.

Kahneman, D., Triesman, A., & Gibbs, B. (1992). The reviewing of object files: Object specific integration of information. *Cognitive Psychology*, 24, 175–219.

Kanai, R., Muggleton, N., & Walsh, V. (2008). TMS over the intraparietal sulcus induces perceptual fading. *Journal of Neurophysiology*, 100, 3343–50.

Kane, M. & Engle, R. (2003). Working-memory capacity and the control of attention: The contributions of goal neglect, response competition, and task set to Stroop interference. *Journal of Experimental Psychology: General*, 132, 47–70.

Kane, M., Bleckley, M.K., Conway, A., & Engle, R. (2001). A controlled-attention view of working memory capacity. *Journal of Experimental Psychology: General*, 130, 169–83.

Kane, M., Brown, L., McVay, J., Silvia, P., Myin-Germeys, I., & Kwapil, T. (2007). For whom the mind wanders and when: An experience-sampling study of working memory and executive control in daily life. *Psychological Science*, 18, 614–21.

Kane, M., Hambrick, D., & Conway, A. (2005). Working memory capacity and fluid intelligence are strongly related constructs. *Psychological Bulletin*, 131, 66–71.

Kane, M., Hambrick, D., Tuholski, S., Wilhelm, O., Payne, T., & Engle, R. (2004). The generality of working memory capacity: A latent-variable approach to verbal and visuospatial memory span and reasoning. *Journal of Experimental Psychology: General*, 133, 189–217.

Kastner, S. & Pinsk, M. (2004). Visual attention as a multilevel selection process. *Cognitive, Affective, and Behavioral Neuroscience*, 4, 483–500.

Kaufman, S., DeYoung, C., Gray, J., Brown, J., & Mackintosh, N. (2009). Associative learning predicts intelligence above and beyond working memory and processing speed. *Intelligence*, 37, 374–82.

Kawai, N. & Matsuzawa, T. (2000). Numerical memory span in a chimpanzee. *Nature*, 403, 39.

Kawato, M., Kuroda, T., Imamizu, H., Nakano, E., Miyauchi, S., & Yoshioka, T. (2003). Internal forward models in the cerebellum: fMRI study on grip force and load force coupling. *Progress in Brain Research*, 142, 171–88.

Kelly, A., Uddin, L., Biswal, B., Castellanos, F., & Milham, M. (2008). Competition between functional brain networks mediates behavioral variability. *NeuroImage*, 39, 527–37.

Kentridge, R., Nijboer, T., & Heywood, C. (2008). Attended but unseen: Visual attention is not sufficient for visual awareness. *Neuropsychologia*, 46, 864–9.

Kenward, B., Weir, A., Rutz, C., & Kacelnik, A. (2005). Tool manufacture by naïve juvenile crows. *Nature*, 433, 121.

Keren, G. & Schul, Y. (2009). Two is not always better than one: A critical evaluation of two-system theories. *Perspectives on Psychological Science*, 4, 533–50.

Kerns, J., Cohen, J., MacDonald, A., Cho, R., Stenger, V., & Carter, C. (2004). Anterior cingulate conflict monitoring and adjustments of control. *Science*, 303, 1023–6.

Kidd, C., Piantadosi, S., & Aslin, R. (2012). The Goldilocks Effect: Human infants allocate attention to visual sequences that are neither too simple nor too complex. *PLoS ONE*, 7, e36399.

Kiewra, K. & Benton, S. (1988). The relationship between information processing ability and notetaking. *Contemporary Educational Psychology*, 13, 33–44.

Kim, H. & Cabeza, R. (2007). Trusting our memories: Dissociating the neural correlates of confidence in veridical vs. illusory memories. *Journal of Neuroscience*, 27, 12190–7.

King, J. & Just, M. (1991). Individual differences in syntactic processing: The role of working memory. *Journal of Memory and Language*, 30, 580–602.

King, M. & Carruthers, P. (2012). Moral responsibility and consciousness. *Journal of Moral Philosophy*, 9, 200–28.

Klingberg, T. (2010). Training and plasticity of working memory. *Trends in Cognitive Sciences*, 14, 317–24.

Knudsen, B. & Liszkowski, U. (2012). 18-month-olds predict specific action mistakes through attribution of false belief, not ignorance, and intervene accordingly. *Infancy*, 17, 672–91.

Knudsen, E. (2007). Fundamental components of attention. *Annual Review of Neuroscience*, 30, 57–78.

Knudsen, E. (2011). Control from below: The role of a midbrain network in spatial attention. *European Journal of Neuroscience*, 33, 1961–72.

Koch, C. & Tsuchiya, N. (2007). Attention and consciousness: Two distinct brain processes. *Trends in Cognitive Sciences*, 11, 16–22.

Koch, C., Oliveri, M., Torriero, S., Carlesimo, G., Turriziani, P., & Caltagirone, C. (2005). rTMS evidence of different delay and decision processes in a fronto-parietal neuronal network activated during spatial working memory. *NeuroImage*, 24, 34–9.

Kolata, S., Light, K., Grossman, H., Hale, G., & Matzel, L. (2007). Selective attention is a primary determinant of the relationship between working memory and general learning ability in outbred mice. *Learning and Memory*, 14, 22–8.

Kolata, S., Light, K., Townsend, D., Hale, G., Grossman, H., & Matzel, L. (2005). Variations in working memory capacity predict individual differences in general learning abilities among genetically diverse mice. *Neurobiology of Learning and Memory*, 84, 241–6.

Kornblith, H. (2012). *On Reflection*. Oxford University Press.

Korsgaard, C. (1996). *Sources of Normativity*. Cambridge University Press.

Korsgaard, C. (2009). The activity of reason. *Proceedings and Addresses of the American Philosophical Association*, 83, 27–47.

Kosslyn, S. (1994). *Image and Brain*. MIT Press.

Kosslyn, S., Thompson, W., & Ganis, G. (2006). *The Case for Mental Imagery*. Oxford University Press.

Kosslyn, S., Téglás, E., & Endress, A. (2010). The social sense: Susceptibility to others' beliefs in human infants and adults. *Science*, 330, 1830–4.

Kroesbergen, E., Van Luit, J., Van Lieshout, E. Van Loosbroek, E., & Van de Rijt, B. (2009). Individual differences in early numeracy: The role of executive functions and subitizing. *Journal of Psychoeducational Assessment*, 27, 226–36.

Kruglanski, A. (2013). Only one? The default interventionist perspective as a unimodel—Commentary on Evans & Stanovich (2013). *Perspectives on Psychological Science*, 8, 242–7.

Kruglanski, A. & Gigerenzer, G. (2011). Intuitive and deliberate judgments are based on common principles. *Psychological Review*, 118, 97–109.

Kunda, Z. (1999). *Social Cognition*. MIT Press.

Kundu, B., Sutterer, D., Emrich, S., & Postle, B. (2013). Strengthened effective connectivity underlies transfer of working memory training to tests of short-term memory and attention. *The Journal of Neuroscience*, 33, 8705–15.

Kurzban, R. (2011). *Why Everyone (Else) is a Hypocrite*. Princeton University Press.

Kurzban, R., Duckworth, A., Kable, J., & Myers, J. (2013). An opportunity cost model of subjective effort and task performance. *Behavioral and Brain Sciences*, 36, 661–79.

Kyllonen, P. & Christal, R. (1990). Reasoning ability is (little more than) working-memory capacity?! *Intelligence*, 14, 389–433.

Lai, D., Brandt, S., Luksch, H., & Wessel, R. (2011). Recurrent antitopographic inhibition mediates competitive stimulus selection in an attention network. *Journal of Neurophysiology*, 105, 793–805.

Lamme, V. (2003). Why visual awareness and attention are different. *Trends in Cognitive Sciences*, 7, 12–18.

Landman, R., Spekreijse, H., & Lamme, V. (2003). Large capacity storage of integrated objects before change blindness. *Vision Research*, 43, 149–64.

Lau, H. & Passingham, R. (2007). Unconscious activation of the cognitive control system in the human prefrontal cortex. *Journal of Neuroscience*, 27, 5805–11.

Lepsien, J. & Nobre, A. (2006). Cognitive control of attention in the human brain: Insights from orienting attention to mental representations. *Brain Research*, 1105, 20–31.

Lepsien, J., Thornton, I., & Nobre, A. (2011). Modulation of working-memory maintenance by directed attention. *Neuropsychologia*, 49, 1569–77.

Leslie, S-J., Khemlani, S., & Glucksberg, S. (2011). All ducks lay eggs: The generic overgeneralization effect. *Journal of Memory and Language*, 65, 887–900.

Levelt, W. (1983). Monitoring and self-repair in speech. *Cognition*, 14, 41–104.

Levelt, W. (1989). *Speaking: From Intention to Articulation*. MIT Press.

Levine, D., Warach, J., & Farah, M. (1985). Two visual systems in mental imagery: Dissociation of "what" and "where" in imagery disorders due to bilateral posterior cerebral lesions. *Neurology*, 35, 1010–18.

Levy, N. (2014). *Consciousness and Moral Responsibility*. Oxford University Press.

Levy, R. & Goldman-Rakic, P. (2000). Segregation of working memory functions within the dorsolateral prefrontal cortex. *Experimental Brain Research*, 133, 23–32.

Lewis, D. (1970). How to define theoretical terms. *The Journal of Philosophy*, 67, 427–46.

Lewis-Peacock, J., Drysdale, A., Oberauer, K., & Postle, B. (2012). Neural evidence for a distinction between short-term memory and the focus of attention. *Journal of Cognitive Neuroscience*, 24, 61–79.

Lhermitte, F. (1983). "Utilization behavior" and its relation to lesions of the frontal lobes. *Brain*, 106, 237–55.

Lhermitte, F. (1986). Human autonomy and the frontal lobes. II. Patient behavior in complex and social situations: the "environmental dependency syndrome." *Annals of Neurology*, 19, 335–43.

Li, D., Christ, S., & Cowan, N. (2014). Domain-general and domain-specific functional networks in working memory. *NeuroImage*, 102, 646–56.

Lieberman, M. (2009). What zombies can't do: A social cognitive neuroscience approach to the irreducibility of reflective consciousness. In J. Evans & K. Frankish (eds.), *In Two Minds*, Oxford University Press.

Lieberman, M. (2013). *Social: Why our brains are wired to connect*. Crown Publishers.

Light, K., Kolata, S., Wass, C., Denman-Brice, A., Zagalsky, R., & Matzel, L. (2010). Working memory training promotes general cognitive abilities in genetically heterogeneous mice. *Current Biology*, 20, 777–82.

Limb, C. & Braun, A. (2008). Neural substrates of spontaneous musical performance: An fMRI study of jazz improvisation. *PLoS ONE*, 3(2), e1679.

Lind, A., Hall, L., Breidegard, B., Balkenius, C., & Johansson, P. (2014). Speakers' acceptance of real-time speech exchange indicates that we use auditory feedback to specify the meaning of what we say. *Psychological Science*, 25, 1198–205.

Lisman, J. & Sternberg, E. (2013). Habit and nonhabit systems for unconscious and conscious behavior: Implications for multitasking. *Journal of Cognitive Neuroscience*, 25, 273–83.

Loar, B. (1981). *Mind and meaning*. Cambridge University Press.

Lovejoy, L. & Krauzlis, R. (2010). Inactivation of primate superior colliculus impairs covert selection of signals for perceptual judgments. *Nature Neuroscience*, 13, 261–7.

Lovett, M., Reder, L., & Lebiere, C. (1999). Modeling working memory in a unified architecture: An ACT-R perspective. In A. Miyake & P. Shah (eds.), *Models of Working Memory*, Cambridge University Press.

Lu, H., Zou, Q., Gu, H., Raichle, M., Stein, E., & Yang, Y. (2012). Rat brains also have a default mode network. *Proceedings of the National Academy of Sciences*, 109, 3979–84.

Luck, S., Chelazzi, L., Hillyard, S., & Desimone, R. (1997). Neural mechanisms of spatial selective attention in areas V1, V2, and V4 of Macaque visual cortex. *Journal of Neurophysiology*, 77, 24–42.

Luiten, P. (1981). Afferent and efferent connections of the optic tectum in the carp (*Cyprinus carpio L.*). *Brain Research*, 220, 51–65.

Luo, Y. (2011). Do 10-month-old infants understand others' false beliefs? *Cognition*, 121, 289–98.

Lupyan, G. (2012). Linguistically modulated perception and cognition: The label-feedback hypothesis. *Frontiers in Psychology*, 3:54.

Lupyan, G. & Spivey, M. (2010a). Redundant spoken labels facilitate perception of multiple items. *Attention, Perception, and Psychophysics*, 72, 2236–53.

Lupyan, G. & Spivey, M. (2010b). Making the invisible visible: Auditory cues facilitate visual object detection. *PLoS ONE*, 5, e11452.

MacDonald, M., Just, M., & Carpenter, P. (1992). Working memory constraints on the processing of syntactic ambiguity. *Cognitive Psychology*, 24, 56–98.

Mack, A. & Rock, I. (1998). *Inattentional Blindness*. MIT Press.

Mahon, B. & Caramazza, A. (2008). A critical look at the embodied cognition hypothesis and a new proposal for grounding conceptual content. *Journal of Physiology—Paris*, 102, 59–70.

Marcus, G. (2001). *The Algebraic Mind*. MIT Press.

Marien, H., Custers, R., Hassin, R., & Aarts, H. (2012). Unconscious goal activation and the hijacking of the executive function. *Journal of Personality and Social Psychology*, 103, 399–415.

Martin, A. (2007). The representation of object concepts in the brain. *Annual Review of Psychology*, 58, 25–45.

Mason, M., Norton, N., Van Horn, J., Wegner, D., Grafton, S., & Macrae, C. (2007). Wandering minds: The default network and stimulus-independent thought. *Science*, 315, 393–5.

Masuda, T. & Nisbett, R. (2001). Attending holistically vs analytically: Comparing the context sensitivity of Japanese and Americans. *Journal of Personality and Social Psychology*, 81, 922–34.

Matzel, L., Han, Y., Grossman, H., Karnik, M., Patel, D., Scott, N., Specht, S., & Gandhi, C. (2003). Individual differences in the expression of a "general" learning ability in mice. *Journal of Neuroscience*, 23, 6423–33.

Mayer, J., Bittner, R., Nikolić, D., Bledowski, C., Goebel, R., & Linden, D. (2007). Common neural substrates for visual working memory and attention. *NeuroImage*, 36, 441–53.

Mayes, A. & Roberts, N. (2002). Theories of episodic memory. In A. Baddeley, M. Conway, & J. Aggleton (eds.), *Episodic Memory*, Oxford University Press.

Mazoyer, B., Zago, L., Mellet, E., Bricogne, S., Etard, O., Houdé, O., Crivello, F., Joliot, M., Petit, L., & Tzourio-Mazoyer, N. (2001). Cortical networks for working memory and executive functions sustain the conscious resting state in man. *Brain Research Bulletin*, 54, 287–98.

McCormick, P. (1997). Orienting attention without awareness. *Journal of Experimental Psychology: Human Perception and Performance*, 23, 168–80.

McDowell, J. (1994). *Mind and World*. Harvard University Press.

McGinn, C. (1982). The structure of content. In A. Woodfield (ed.), *Thought and Object*, Oxford University Press.

McVay, J. & Kane, M. (2009). Conducting the train of thought: Working memory capacity, goal neglect, and mind wandering in an executive-control task. *Journal of Experimental Psychology: Learning, Memory, and Cognition*, 35, 196–204.

Mechelli, A., Price, C., Friston, K., & Ishai, A. (2004). Where bottom–up meets top–down: Neuronal interactions during perception and imagery. *Cerebral Cortex*, 14, 1256–65.

Meister, I., Wienemann, M., Buelte, D., Grünewald, C., Sparing, R., & Dambeck, N. (2006). Hemiextinction induced by transcranial magnetic stimulation over the right temporo-parietal junction. *Neuroscience*, 142, 119–23.

Melis, A., Call, J., & Tomasello, M. (2006). Chimpanzees (*Pan troglodytes*) conceal visual and auditory information from others. *Journal of Comparative Psychology*, 120, 154–62.

Melnick, M., Harison, B., Park, S., Bennetto, L., & Tadin, D. (2013). A strong interactive link between sensory discriminations and intelligence. *Current Biology*, 23, 1013–17.

Mendes, N., Hanus, D., & Call, J. (2007). Raising the level: Orangutans use water as a tool. *Biology Letters*, 3, 453–5.

Menon, V. (2011). Large-scale brain networks and psychopathology: A unifying triple network model. *Trends in Cognitive Sciences*, 15, 483–506.

Menzel, R. & Giurfa, M. (2006). Dimensions of cognition in an insect, the honeybee. *Behavioral and Cognitive Neuroscience Reviews*, 5, 24–40.

Menzel, R., Greggers, U., Smith, A., Berger, S., Brandt, R., Brunke, S., Bundrock, G., Hülse, S., Plümpe, T., Schaupp, F., Schüttler, E., Stach, S., Stindt, J., Stollhoff, N., & Watzl, S. (2005). Honey bees navigate according to a map-like spatial memory. *Proceedings of the National Academy of Sciences*, 102, 3040–5.

Menzel, R., Kirbach, A., Haass, W-D., Fisher, B., Fuchs, J., Koblofsky, M., Lehmann, K., Reiter, L., Meyer, H., Nguyen, H., Jones, S., Norton, P., & Greggers, U. (2011). A common frame of reference for learned and communicated vectors in honeybee navigation. *Current Biology*, 21, 645–50.

Mercier, H. & Sperber, D. (2011). Why do humans reason? Arguments for an argumentative theory. *Behavioral and Brain Sciences*, 34, 57–74.

Mesulam, M. (1999). Spatial attention and neglect: parietal, frontal and cingulate contributions to the mental representation and attentional targeting of salient extrapersonal events. *Philosophical Transactions of the Royal Society B*, 354, 1325–46.

Metcalfe, J. & Mischel, W. (1999). A hot/cool-system analysis of delay of gratification: Dynamics of willpower. *Psychological Review*, 106, 3–19.

Meyer, C., Hagmann-von Arx, P., Lemola, S., & Grob, A. (2010). Correspondence between the general ability to discriminate sensory stimuli and general intelligence. *Journal of Individual Differences*, 31, 46–56.

Mikels, J., Reuter-Lorenz, P., Beyer, J., & Fredrickson, B. (2008). Emotion and working memory: Evidence for domain-specific processes for affective maintenance. *Emotion*, 8, 256–66.

Miller, G. (1997). Protean primates: The evolution of adaptive unpredictability in competition and courtship. In R. Byrne & A. Whiten (eds.), *Machiavellian Intelligence II*, Cambridge University Press.

Millikan, R. (1984). *Language, Thought, and Other Biological Categories*. MIT Press.

Milner, D. & Goodale, M. (1995). *The Visual Brain in Action*. Oxford University Press.

Mischel, H. & Mischel, W. (1983). The development of children's knowledge of self-control strategies. *Child Development*, 54, 603–19.

Miyake, A., Friedman, N., Emerson, M., Witzki, A., Howerter, A., & Wager, T. (2000). The unity and diversity of executive functions and their contributions to complex "frontal lobe" tasks: A latent variable analysis. *Cognitive Psychology*, 41, 49–100.

Mo, L., Xu, G., Kay, P., & Tan, L-H. (2011). Electrophysiological evidence for the left-lateralized effect of language on preattentive categorical perception of color. *Proceedings of the National Academy of Sciences*, 108, 14026–30.

Mole, C. (2010). *Attention is Cognitive Unison*. Oxford University Press.

Monchi, O., Petrides, M., Petre, V., Worsley, K., & Dagher, A. (2001). Wisconsin card sorting revisited: Distinct neural circuits participating in different stages of the task identified by event-related functional magnetic resonance imaging. *The Journal of Neuroscience*, 21, 7733–41.

Moore, D. & Johnson, S. (2011). Mental rotation of dynamic, three-dimensional stimuli by 3-month-old infants. *Infancy*, 16, 435–45.

Moran, R. (2001). *Authority and Estrangement*. Princeton University Press.

Moro, V., Berlucchi, G., Lerch, J., Tomaiuolo, F., & Aglioti, S. (2008). Selective deficit in mental visual imagery with intact primary visual cortex and visual perception. *Cortex*, 44, 109–18.

Moskowitz, G. (2005). *Social Cognition: Understanding Self and Others*. Guilford Press.

Mottaghy, F. (2006). Interfering with working memory in humans. *Neuroscience*, 139, 85–90.

Mottaghy, F., Döring, T., Müller-Gärtner, H-W., Töpper, R., & Krause, B. (2002). Bilateral parieto-frontal network for verbal working memory: An interference approach using repetitive transcranial magnetic stimulation (rTMS). *European Journal of Neuroscience*, 16, 1627–32.

Mulcahy, N. & Call, J. (2004). Apes save tools for future use. *Science*, 312, 1038–40.

Müller, N. & Knight, R. (2006). The functional neuroanatomy of working memory: Contributions of human brain lesion studies. *Neuroscience*, 139, 51–8.

Mysore, S. & Knudsen, E. (2013). A shared inhibitory circuit for both exogenous and endogenous control of stimulus selection. *Nature Neuroscience*, 16, 473–8.

Nee, D., Brown, J., Askren, M., Berman, M., Demiralp, E., Krawitz, A., & Jonides, J. (2013). A meta-analysis of executive components of working memory. *Cerebral Cortex*, 23, 264–82.

Negri, G., Rumiati, R., Zadini, A., Ukmar, M., Mahon, B., & Caramazza, A. (2007). What is the role of motor simulation in action and object recognition? Evidence from apraxia. *Cognitive Neuropsychology*, 24, 795–816.

Newell, A. (1990). *Unified Theories of Cognition*. Harvard University Press.

Nichols, S. & Stich, S. (2003). *Mindreading*. Oxford University Press.

Nisbett, R. (2003). *The Geography of Thought*. The Free Press.

Nisbett, R. (2009). *Intelligence and How to Get It*. Norton & Company.

Novick, J., Trueswell, J., & Thompson-Schill, S. (2010). Broca's area and language processing: Evidence for the cognitive control connection. *Language and Linguistics Compass*, 4, 906–24.

Nozari, N., Dell, G., & Schwartz, M. (2011). Is comprehension necessary for error detection? A conflict-based account of monitoring in speech production. *Cognitive Psychology*, 63, 1–33.

O'Brien, L. & Soteriou, M. (eds.) (2009). *Mental Action*. Oxford University Press.

Oliveri, M., Turriziani, P., Carlesimo, G., Koch, G., Tomaiuolo, F., Panella, M., & Caltagirone, C. (2001). Parietal-frontal interactions in visual-object and visual-spatial working memory: Evidence from transcranial magnetic stimulation. *Cerebral Cortex*, 11, 606–18.

Onishi, K. & Baillargeon, R. (2005). Do 15-month-olds understand false beliefs? *Science*, 308, 255–8.

Oppenheim, G. & Dell, G. (2010). Motor movement matters: The flexible abstractness of inner speech. *Memory & Cognition*, 38, 1147–60.

Ormrod, J. & Cochran, K. (1988). Relationship of verbal ability and working memory to spelling achievement and learning to spell. *Reading Research and Instruction*, 28, 33–43.

Osvath, M. (2009). Spontaneous planning for future stone throwing by a male chimpanzee. *Current Biology*, 19, R190–R191.

Osvath, M. & Karvonen, E. (2011). Spontaneous innovation for future deception in a male chimpanzee. *PLoS One*, 7, e36782.

Osvath, M. & Osvath, H. (2008). Chimpanzee and orangutan forethought: Self-control and pre-experience in the face of future tool use. *Animal Cognition*, 11, 661–74.

Oyserman, D. & Lee, S. (2008). Does culture influence what and how we think? Effects of priming individualism and collectivism. *Psychological Bulletin*, 134, 311–42.

Palmer, S. (1999). *Vision Science*. MIT Press.

Papineau, D. (1987). *Reality and Representation*. Blackwell.

Pasternak, T. & Greenlee, M. (2005). Working memory in primate sensory systems. *Nature Reviews Neuroscience*, 6, 97–107.

Paulesu, E., Frith, C., & Frackowiak, R. (1993). The neural correlates of the verbal component of working memory. *Nature*, 362, 342–5.

Peacocke, C. (1992). *A Study of Concepts*. MIT Press.

Peacocke, C. (2008). *Truly Understood*. Oxford University Press.

Perner, J. (2010). Who took the cog out of cognitive science? Mentalism in an era of anti-cognitivism. In P. Frensch & R. Schwarzer (eds.), *Cognition and Neuropsychology: Volume 1*, Psychology Press.

Pessoa, L. (2013). *The Cognitive-Emotional Brain*. MIT Press.

Pessoa, L. & Ungerleider, L. (2004). Neural correlates of change detection and change blindness in a working memory task. *Cerebral Cortex*, 14, 511–20.

Petty, R. & Cacioppo, J. (1986). The elaboration likelihood model of persuasion. In L. Berkowitz (ed.), *Advances in Experimental Social Psychology* (vol. 19), Academic Press.

Pfurtscheller, G. & Neuper, C. (1997). Motor imagery activates primary sensorimotor area in humans. *Neuroscience Letters*, 239, 65–8.

Picciuto, E. (2011). The pleasures of suppositions. *Philosophical Psychology*, 22, 487–503.

Picciuto, E. & Carruthers, P. (2014). The origins of creativity. In E. Paul & S. Kaufman (eds.), *The Philosophy of Creativity*, Oxford University Press.

Pietroski, P. (2010). Concepts, meanings, and truth: First nature, second nature and hard work. *Mind and Language*, 25, 247–78.

Pinsk, M., Doniger, G., & Kastner, S. (2004). Push-pull mechanism of selective attention in human extrastriate cortex. *Journal of Neurophysiology*, 92, 622–9.

Pitt, D. (2004). The phenomenology of cognition. *Philosophy and Phenomenological Research*, 59, 1–36.

Posner, M. & Gilbert, C. (1999). Attention and primary visual cortex. *Proceedings of the National Academy of Sciences*, 96, 2585–7.

Postle, B. (2006). Working memory as an emergent property of the mind and brain. *Neuroscience*, 139, 23–38.

Postle, B., Ferrarelli, F., Hamidi, M., Feredoes, E., Massimini, M., Peterson, M., Alexander, A., & Tononi, G. (2006). Repetitive transcranial magnetic stimulation dissociates working memory manipulation from retention functions in the prefrontal, but not posterior parietal, cortex. *Journal of Cognitive Neuroscience*, 18, 1712–22.

Poulin-Dubois, D. & Chow, V. (2009). The effect of a looker's past reliability on infants' reasoning about beliefs. *Developmental Psychology*, 45, 1576–82.

Povinelli, D. and Vonk, J. (2004). We don't need a microscope to explore the chimpanzee's mind. *Mind and Language*, 19, 1–28.

Prabhakaran, V., Smith, J.A., Desmond, J., Glover, G., & Gabrieli, J. (1997). Neural substrates of fluid reasoning: An fMRI study of neocortical activation during performance of the Raven's Progressive Matrices Test. *Cognitive Psychology*, 33, 43–63.

Prinz, J. (2002). *Furnishing the Mind*. MIT Press.

Prinz, J. (2012). *The Conscious Brain*. Oxford University Press.

Pylyshyn, Z. (2003). *Seeing and Visualizing*. MIT Press.

Raby, C., Alexis, D., Dickinson, A., & Clayton, N. (2007). Planning for the future by western scrub-jays. *Nature*, 445, 919–21.

Raghubar, K., Barnes, M., & Hecht, S. (2010). Working memory and mathematics: A review of developmental, individual difference, and cognitive approaches. *Learning and Individual Differences*, 20, 110–22.

Raichle, M., MacLeod, A., Snyder, A., Powers, W., Gusnard, D., & Shulman, G. (2001). A default mode of brain function. *Proceedings of the National Academy of Sciences*, 98, 676–82.

Ramsey, W. (2007). *Representation Reconsidered*. Cambridge University Press.

Read, D. (2008). Working memory: A cognitive limit to non-human primate recursive thinking prior to hominid evolution? *Evolutionary Psychology*, 6, 676–714.

Reber, A. (1993). *Implicit Learning and Tacit Knowledge*. Oxford University Press.

Reddy, L., Tsuchiya, N., & Serre, T. (2010). Reading the mind's eye: Decoding category information during mental imagery. *Neuroimage*, 50, 818–25.

Redick, T., Shipstead, Z., Harrison, T., Hicks, K., Fried, D., Hambrick, D., Kane, M., & Engle, R. (2012a). No evidence of intelligence improvement after working memory training: A randomized, placebo-controlled study. *Journal of Experimental Psychology: General*, 142, 359–79.

Redick, T., Unsworth, N., Kelly, A., & Engle, R. (2012b). Faster, smarter? Working memory capacity and perceptual speed in relation to fluid intelligence. *Journal of Cognitive Psychology*, 24, 844–54.

Rensink, R., O'Regan, J., & Clark, J. (1997). To see or not to see: The need for attention to perceive changes in scenes. *Psychological Science*, 8, 368–73.

Reuter, F., Del Cul, A., Audoin, B., Malikova, I., Naccache, L., Ranjeva, J.P., Lyon-Caen, O., Ali Cherif, A., Cohen, L., Dehaene, S., & Pelletier, J. (2007). Intact subliminal processing and delayed conscious access in multiple sclerosis. *Neuropsychologia*, 45, 2683–91.

Reuter, F., Del Cul, A., Malikova, I., Naccache, L., Confort-Gouny, S., Cohen, L., Cheriff, A., Cozzone, P., Pelletier, J., Ranjeva, J., Dehaene, S., & Audoin, B. (2009). White matter damage impairs access to consciousness in multiple sclerosis. *Neuroimage*, 44, 590–9.

Rey, G. (2013). We are not all "self-blind": A defense of a modest introspectionism. *Mind & Language*, 28, 259–85.

Reynolds, J. & Chelazzi, L. (2004). Attentional modulation of visual processing. *Annual Reviews Neuroscience*, 27, 611–47.

Richter, W., Somorjat, R., Summers, R., Jarnasz, N., Menon, R., Gati, J., Georgopoulos, A., Tegeler, C., Ugerbil, K., & Kim, S. (2000). Motor area activity during mental rotation studied by time-resolved single-trial fMRI. *Journal of Cognitive Neuroscience*, 12, 310–20.

Rilling, J., Barks, S., Parr, L., Preuss, T., Faber, T., Pagnoni, G., Bremner, D., & Votaw, J. (2007). A comparison of resting-state brain activity in humans and chimpanzees. *Proceedings of the National Academy of Sciences*, 104, 17146–51.

Riquimaroux, H., Gaioni, S., & Suga, N. (1991). Cortical computational maps control auditory perception. *Science*, 251, 565–8.

Robertson, I., Tegner, R., Tham, K., Lo, A., & Nimmo-smith, I. (1995). Sustained attention training for unilateral neglect: Theoretical and rehabilitation implications. *Journal of Clinical and Experimental Neuropsychology*, 17, 416–30.

Rolls, E. (1999). *The Brain and Emotion*. Oxford University Press.

Rosenbaum, D. (2010). *Human Motor Control* (second edition). Academic Press.

Rosenbaum, D., Meulenbroek, R., Vaughan, J., & Jansen, C. (2001). Posture-based motion planning. *Psychological Review*, 108, 709–34.

Rosenbaum, D., Vaughan, J., Meulenbroek, R., Jax, S., & Cohen, R. (2008). Smart moves: The psychology of everyday perceptual-motor acts. In E. Morsella, J. Bargh, & P. Gollwitzer (eds.), *Oxford Handbook of Human Action*, Oxford University Press.

Rosenthal, D. (2005). *Consciousness and Mind*. Oxford University Press.

Rottschy, C., Langner, R., Dogan, I., Reetz, K., Laird, A., Schulz, J., Fox, P., & Eickhoff, S. (2012). Modelling neural correlates of working memory: A coordinate-based meta-analysis. *NeuroImage*, 60, 830–46.

Rumelhart, D. & McClelland, J. (1986). *Parallel Distributed Processing*. MIT Press.

Russell, J. (1980). A circumplex model of affect. *Journal of Personality and Social Psychology*, 39, 1161–78.

Sadaghiani, S., Hesselmann, G., & Kleinschmidt, A. (2009). Distributed and antagonistic contributions of ongoing activity fluctuations to auditory stimulus detection. *Journal of Neuroscience*, 29, 13410–17.

Salas, C., Broglio, C., & Rodriguez, F. (2003). Evolution of forebrain and spatial cognition in vertebrates: Conservation across diversity. *Brain, Behavior and Evolution*, 62, 72–82.

Sanz, C., Morgan, D., & Gulick, S. (2004). New insights into chimpanzees, tools, and termites from the Congo basin. *American Naturalist*, 164, 567–81.

Saults, J. & Cowan, N. (2007). A central capacity limit to the simultaneous storage of visual and auditory arrays in working memory. *Journal of Experimental Psychology: General*, 136, 663–84.

Saxe, R. (2009). Theory of mind (neural basis). In W. Banks (ed.), *Encyclopedia of Consciousness*, MIT Press.

Saxe, R., Whitfield-Gabrieli, S., Pelphrey, K., & Scholz, J. (2009). Brain regions for perceiving and reasoning about other people in school-aged children. *Child Development*, 80, 1197–209.

Schacter, D. (2001). *The Seven Sins of Memory*. Houghton & Mifflin.

Schacter, D., Addis, D., & Buckner, R. (2007). Remembering the past to imagine the future: The prospective brain. *Nature Reviews Neuroscience*, 8, 657–61.

Schönwiesner, M., Novitski, N., Pakarinen, S., Carlson, S., Tervaniemi, M., & Näätänen, R. (2007). Heschl's gyrus, posterior superior temporal gyrus, and mid-ventrolateral prefrontal cortex have different roles in the detection of acoustic changes. *Journal of Neuophysiology*, 97, 2075–82.

Schooler, J. & Melcher, J. (1995). The ineffability of insight. In S. Smith, T. Ward, & R. Finke (eds.), *The Creative Cognition Approach*, MIT Press.

Schooler, J., Ohlsson, S., & Brooks, K. (1993). Thoughts beyond words: When language overshadows insight. *Journal of Experimental Psychology: General*, 122, 166–83.

Schretlen, D., Pearlson, G., Anthony, J., Aylward, E., Augustine, A., Davis, A., & Barta, P. (2000). Elucidating the contributions of processing speed, executive ability, and frontal lobe volume to normal age-related differences in fluid intelligence. *Journal of the International Neuropsychological Society*, 6, 52–61.

Scott, M., Yeung, H., Gick, B., & Werker, J. (2013). Inner speech captures the perception of external speech. *Journal of the Acoustic Society of America*, 133, 286–92.

Scott, R. & Baillargeon, R. (2009). Which penguin is this? Attributing false beliefs about object identity at 18 months. *Child Development*, 80, 1172–96.

Scott, R., Baillargeon, R., Song, H., & Leslie, A. (2010). Attributing false beliefs about non-obvious properties at 18 months. *Cognitive Psychology*, 63.

Searle, J. (1983). *Intentionality*. Cambridge University Press.

Serences, J., Ester, E., Vogel, E., & Awh, E. (2009). Stimulus-specific delay activity in human primary visual cortex. *Psychological Science*, 20, 207–14.

Sergent, C. & Dehaene, S. (2004). Is consciousness a gradual phenomenon? Evidence for an all-or-none bifurcation during the attentional blink. *Psychological Science*, 15, 1656–74.

Sergent, C., Baillet, S., & Dehaene, S. (2005). Timing of the brain events underlying access to consciousness during the attentional blink. *Nature Neuroscience*, 8, 1391–400.

Sergent, C., Wyart, V., Babo-Rebelo, M., Cohen, L., Naccache, L., & Tallon-Baudry, C. (2013). Cueing attention after the stimulus is gone can retrospectively trigger conscious perception. *Current Biology*, 23, 150–5.

Sestieri, C., Shulman, G., & Corbetta, M. (2010). Attention to memory and the environment: Functional specialization and dynamic competition in human posterior parietal cortex. *The Journal of Neuroscience*, 30, 8445–56.

Shamosh, N., & Gray, J. (2008). Delay discounting and intelligence: A meta-analysis. *Intelligence*, 38, 289–305.

Shamosh, N., DeYoung, C., Green, A., Reis, D., Johnson, M., Conway, A., Engle, R., Braver, T., & Gray, J. (2009). Individual differences in delay discounting: Relation to intelligence, working memory, and anterior prefrontal cortex. *Psychological Science*, 19, 904–11.

Shenhav, A., Botvinick, M., & Cohen, J. (2013). The expected value of control: An integrative theory of anterior cingulate cortex function. *Neuron*, 79, 217–40.

Shergill, S., Bullmore, E., Brammer, M., Williams, S., Murray, R., & McGuire, P. (2001). A functional study of auditory verbal imagery. *Psychological Medicine*, 31, 241–53.

Shettleworth, S. (2010). *Cognition, Evolution, and Behavior*. Second Edition. Oxford University Press.

Shintel, H. & Keysar, B. (2009). Less is more: A minimalist account of joint action in communication. *Topics in Cognitive Science*, 1, 260–73.

Shipstead, Z., Lindsey, D., Marshall, R., & Engle, R. (2014). The mechanisms of working memory capacity: Primary memory, secondary memory, and attention control. *Journal of Memory and Language*, 72, 116–41.

Shipstead, Z., Redick, T., & Engle, R. (2010). Does working memory training generalize? *Psychologica Belgica*, 50, 245–76.

Shipstead, Z., Redick, T., Hicks, K., & Engle, R. (2012). The scope and control of attention as separate aspects of working memory. *Memory*, 20, 608–28.

Shomstein, S. & Yantis, S. (2006). Parietal cortex mediates voluntary control of spatial and nonspatial auditory attention. *Journal of Neuroscience*, 26, 435–9.

Shuler, M. & Bear, M. (2006). Neurons in the primary visual cortex respond differently to a flash of light after it has been paired with a reward, unexpectedly showing that cognitive information is coded at this level in the cortex. *Science*, 311, 1606–9.

Siewert, C. (1998). *The Significance of Consciousness*. Princeton University Press.

Simon, L., Greenberg, J., & Brehm, J. (1995). Trivialization: The forgotten mode of dissonance reduction. *Journal of Personality and Social Psychology*, 68, 247–60.

Simons, D. & Levin, D. (1997). Change blindness. *Trends in Cognitive Sciences*, 1, 261–7.

Simonton, D. (2003). Scientific creativity as constrained stochastic behavior. *Psychological Bulletin*, 129, 475–94.

Sligte, I., Scholte, H.S., & Lamme, V. (2008). Are there multiple visual short-term memory stores? *PLoS ONE*, 3, e1699.

Sloman, S. (1996). The empirical case for two systems of reasoning. *Psychological Bulletin*, 119, 3–22.

Sloman, S. (2002). Two systems of reasoning. In T. Gilovich, D. Griffin, & D. Kahneman (eds.), *Heuristics and Biases*, Cambridge University Press.

Smallwood, J., Brown, K., Baird, B., & Schooler, J. (2011). Cooperation between the default mode network and the frontal–parietal network in the production of an internal train of thought. *Brain Research*, 1428, 60–70.

Smolensky, P. (1991). Connectionism, constituency, and the language of thought. In B. Loewer and G. Rey (eds.), *Meaning in Mind*, Blackwell.

Smolensky, P. (1995). Constituent structure and the explanation of an integrated connectionist/symbolic cognitive architecture. In C. MacDonald and G. MacDonald (eds.), *Connectionism*, Blackwell.

Smolensky, P. & Legendre, G. (2006). *The Harmonic Mind* (2 volumes). MIT Press.

Song, H. & Baillargeon, R. (2008). Infants' reasoning about others' false perceptions. *Developmental Psychology*, 44, 1789–95.

Song, H., Onishi, K., Baillargeon, R., & Fisher, C. (2008). Can an actor's false belief be corrected by an appropriate communication? Psychological reasoning in 18.5-month-old infants. *Cognition*, 109, 295–315.

Soto, D., Mäntylä, T., & Silvanto, J. (2011). Working memory without consciousness. *Current Biology*, 21, R912.

Southgate, V. & Vernetti, A. (2014). Belief-based action prediction in preverbal infants. *Cognition*, 130, 1–10.

Southgate, V., Chevallier, C., & Csibra, G. (2010). Seventeen-month-olds appeal to false beliefs to interpret others' referential communication. *Developmental Science*, 13, 907–12.

Southgate, V., Senju, A., & Csibra, G. (2007). Action anticipation through attribution of false belief by 2-year-olds. *Psychological Science*, 18, 587–92.

Sperber, D. & Wilson, D. (1995). *Relevance: Communication and Cognition*. Second Edition. Blackwell.

Sperling, G. (1960). The information available in brief visual presentations. *Psychological Monographs: General and Applied*, 74, 1–29.

Sporns, O. (2011). *Networks of the Brain*. MIT Press.

Spreng, R., Mar, R., & Kim, A. (2009). The common neural basis of autobiographical memory, prospection, navigation, theory of mind, and the default mode: A quantitative meta-analysis. *Journal of Cognitive Neuroscience*, 21, 489–510.

Sreenivasan, K., Sambhara, D., & Jha, A. (2011). Working memory templates are maintained as feature-specific perceptual codes. *Journal of Neurophysiology*, 106, 115–21.

Stalnaker, R. (2002). Common ground. *Linguistics and Philosophy*, 25, 701–21.

Stanovich, K. (1999). *Who is Rational? Studies of Individual Differences in Reasoning.* Lawrence Erlbaum.

Stanovich, K. (2009). *What Intelligence Tests Miss: The Psychology of Rational Thought.* Yale University Press.

Stephens, D. & Krebs, J. (1987). *Foraging Theory.* Princeton University Press.

Stippich, C., Ochmann, H., & Sartor, K. (2002). Somatotopic mapping of the human primary sensorimotor cortex during motor imagery and motor execution by functional magnetic resonance imaging. *Neuroscience Letters,* 331, 50–4.

Störmer, V., McDonald, J., & Hillyard, S. (2009). Cross-modal cueing of attention alters appearance and early cortical processing of visual stimuli. *Proceedings of the National Academy of Sciences,* 106, 22456–61.

Strawson, G. (1994). *Mental Reality.* MIT Press.

Striedter, G. (2004). *Principles of Brain Evolution.* Sinauer Associates.

Subramaniam, K., Kounios, J., Parrish, T., & Jung-Beeman, M. (2009). A brain mechanism for facilitation of insight by positive affect. *Journal of Cognitive Neuroscience,* 21, 415–32.

Suddendorf, T. & Corballis, M. (1997). Mental time travel and the evolution of the human mind. *Genetic, Social and General Psychology Monographs,* 123, 133–67.

Suddendorf, T. & Corballis, M. (2007). The evolution of foresight: What is mental time travel, and is it unique to humans? *Behavioral and Brain Sciences,* 30, 299–316.

Suddendorf, T., Addis, D., & Corballis, M. (2009). Mental time travel and the shaping of the human mind. *Philosophical Transactions of the Royal Society B: Biological Sciences,* 364, 1317–24.

Sugita, Y. (2008). Face perception in monkeys reared with no exposure to faces. *Proceedings of the National Academy of Sciences,* 105, 394–8.

Summerfield, J., Hassabis, D., & Maguire, E. (2010). Differential engagement of brain regions within a "core" network during scene construction. *Neuropsychologia,* 48, 1501–9.

Surian, L., Caldi, S., & Sperber, D. (2007). Attribution of beliefs by 13-month-old infants. *Psychological Science,* 18, 580–6.

Süß, H-M., Oberauer, K., Wittmann, W., Wilhelm, O., & Schulze, R. (2002). Working-memory capacity explains reasoning ability—and a little bit more. *Intelligence,* 30, 261–88.

Swanson, L. (2012). *Brain Architecture.* (Second Edition.) Oxford University Press.

Szameitat, A., Shen, S., & Sterr, A. (2007). Motor imagery of complex everyday movements. An fMRI study. *NeuroImage,* 34, 702–13.

Tang, C., Eaves, E., Ng, J., Carpenter, D., Mai, X., Schroeder, D., Condon, C., Colom, R., & Haier, R. (2010). Brain networks for working memory and factors of intelligence assessed in males and females with fMRI and DTI. *Intelligence,* 38, 293–303.

Tangney, J., Baumeister, R., & Boone, A. (2004). High self-control predicts good adjustment, less pathology, better grades, and interpersonal success. *Journal of Personality,* 72, 271–324.

Taylor, A., Elliffe, D., Hunt, G., & Gray, R. (2010). Complex cognition and behavioral innovation in New Caledonian crows. *Proceedings of the Royal Society B: Biological Sciences,* 277, 2637–43.

Thelen, E., Schöner, G., Scheier, C., & Smith, L. (2001). The dynamics of embodiment: A field theory of infant perseverative reaching. *Behavioral and Brain Sciences*, 24, 1–34.

Thiebaut de Schotten, M., Cohen, L., Amemiya, E., Braga, L., & Dehaene, S. (2014). Learning to read improves the structure of the arcuate fasciculus. *Cerebral Cortex*, 24, 989–95.

Thierry, G., Athanasopoulos, P., Wiggett, A., Dering, B., & Kuipers, J-R. (2009). Unconscious effects of language-specific terminology on preattentive color perception. *Proceedings of the National Academy of Sciences*, 106, 4567–70.

Thompson-Schill, S. (2013). Data presented at the University of Maryland Cognitive Science Colloquium, September 2013.

Tian, X. & Poeppel, D. (2012). Mental imagery of speech: Linking motor and perceptual systems through internal simulation and estimation. *Frontiers in Human Neuroscience*, 6, 314.

Todd, J. & Marois, R. (2004). Capacity limit of visual short-term memory in human posterior parietal cortex. *Nature*, 428, 751–4.

Todd, J., Fougnie, D., & Marois, R. (2005). Visual short-term memory load suppresses temporo-parietal junction activity and induces inattentional blindness. *Psychological Science*, 16, 965–72.

Tononi, G. (2008). Consciousness as integrated information: A provisional manifesto. *Biology Bulletin*, 215, 216–42.

Tononi, G. & Koch, C. (2008). The neural correlates of consciousness: An update. *Annals of the New York Academy of Sciences*, 1124, 239–61.

Träuble, B., Marinovic, V., & Pauen, S. (2010). Early theory of mind competencies: Do infants understand others' beliefs? *Infancy*, 15, 434–44.

Treue, S. & Maunsell, J. (1996). Attentional modulation of visual motion processing in cortical areas MT and MST. *Nature*, 382, 539–41.

Tsujii, T. & Watanabe, S. (2009). Neural correlates of dual-task effect on belief-bias syllogistic reasoning: A near-infrared spectroscopy study. *Brain Research*, 1287, 118–25.

Tsujii, T. & Watanabe, S. (2010). Neural correlates of belief-bias reasoning under time pressure: A near-infrared spectroscopy study. *NeuroImage*, 50, 1320–6.

Tulving, E. (2002). Episodic memory: From mind to brain. *Annual Review of Psychology*, 53, 1–25.

Tulving, E. & Markowitsch, H. (1998). Episodic and declarative memory: Role of the hippocampus. *Hippocampus*, 8, 198–204.

Tye, M. (1995). *Ten Problems of Consciousness*. MIT Press.

Tye, M. (2000). *Consciousness, Color, and Content*. MIT Press.

Uddin, L., Supekar, K., Amin, H., Rykhlevskaia, E., Nguyen, D., Greicius, M., and Menon, V. (2010). Dissociable connectivity within human angular gyrus and intraparietal sulcus: Evidence from functional and structural connectivity. *Cerebral Cortex*, 20, 2636–46.

Uller, C. & Lewis, J. (2009). Horses select the greater of two quantities in small numerical contrasts. *Animal Cognition*, 12, 733–8.

Ungerleider, L. & Mishkin, M. (1982). Two cortical visual systems. In D. Ingle, M. Goodale, & R. Mansfield (eds.), *Analysis of Visual Behavior*, MIT Press.

Unsworth, N. & Engle, R. (2007). The nature of individual differences in working memory capacity: Active maintenance in primary memory and controlled search from secondary memory. *Psychological Review*, 114, 104–32.

Unsworth, N. & Spillers, G. (2010). Working memory capacity: Attention control, secondary memory, or both? A direct test of the dual-component model. *Journal of Memory and Language*, 62, 392–406.

Van Boxtel, J., Tsuchiya, N., & Koch, C. (2010). Consciousness and attention: On sufficiency and necessity. *Frontiers in Psychology*, 1, article 217.

van der Wel, R., Sebanz, N., & Knoblich, G. (2014). Do people automatically track others' beliefs? Evidence from a continuous measure. *Cognition*, 130, 128–33.

Vargha-Khadem, F., Gadian, D., Watkins, K., Connelly, A., Van Paesschen, W., & Mishkin, M. (1997). Differential effects of early hippocampal pathology on episodic and semantic memory. *Science*, 277, 376–80.

Veillet, B. & Carruthers, P. (2011). The case against cognitive phenomenology. In T. Bayne & M. Montague (eds.), *Cognitive Phenomenology*, Oxford University Press.

Vetter, P. & Newen, A. (2014). Varieties of cognitive penetration in visual perception. *Consciousness and Cognition*, 27, 62–75.

Vetter, P., Smith, F., & Muckli, L. (2014). Decoding sound and imagery content in early visual cortex. *Current Biology*, 24, 1256–62.

Vincent, J., Patel, G., Fox, M., Snyder, A., Baker, J., Van Essen, D., Zempel, J., Snyder, L., Corbetta, M., & Raichle, M. (2007). Intrinsic functional architecture in the anaesthetized monkey brain. *Nature*, 447, 83–6.

Vincent, J., Snyder, A., Fox, M., Shannon, B., Andrews, J., Raichle, M., & Buckner, R. (2006). Coherent spontaneous activity identifies a hippocampal–parietal memory network. *Journal of Neurophysiology*, 96, 3517–31.

Vingerhoets, G., de Lange, F., Vandemaele, P., Deblaere, K., & Achten, E. (2002). Motor imagery in mental rotation: An fMRI study. *NeuroImage*, 17, 1623–33.

Voisin, J., Bidet-Caulet, A., Bertrand, O., & Fonlupt, P. (2006). Listening in silence activates auditory areas: A functional magnetic resonance imaging study. *Journal of Neuroscience*, 26, 273–8.

Völter, C. & Call, J. (2014). Younger apes and human children plan their moves in a maze task. *Cognition*, 130, 186–203.

Vuilleumier, P. (2005). How brains beware: Neural mechanisms of emotional attention. *Trends in Cognitive Sciences*, 9, 585–94.

Vuontela, V., Rama, P., Raninen, A., Aronen, H., & Carlson, S. (1999). Selective interference reveals dissociation between memory for location and color. *Neuroreport*, 10, 2235–40.

Wagner, A., Shannon, B., Kahn, I., & Buckner, R. (2005). Parietal lobe contributions to episodic memory retrieval. *Trends in Cognitive Sciences*, 9, 445–53.

Wallis, J., Anderson, K., & Miller, E. (2001). Single neurons in prefrontal cortex encode abstract rules. *Nature*, 411, 953–6.

Ward, T., Smith, S., & Finke, R. (1999). Creative cognition. In R. Sternberg (ed.), *Handbook of Creativity*, Cambridge University Press.

Wegner, D. & Wheatley, T. (1999). Apparent mental causation: Sources of the experience of the will. *American Psychologist*, 54, 480–91.

Weir, A. & Kacelnik, A. (2006). A New Caledonian crow (*Corvus moneduloides*) creatively re-designs tools by bending or unbending aluminium strips. *Animal Cognition*, 9, 317–34.

Weir, A., Chappell, J., & Kacelnik, A. (2002). Shaping of hooks in New Caledonian Crows. *Science*, 297, 981.

Wexler, M., Kosslyn, S., & Berthoz, A. (1998). Motor processes in mental rotation. *Cognition*, 68, 77–94.

Wheeler, M., Peterson, S., & Buckner, R. (2000). Memory's echo: Vivid remembering reactivates sensory-specific cortex. *Proceedings of the National Academy of Sciences*, 97, 11125–9.

Wieth, M. & Zacks, R. (2011). Time of day effects on problem solving: When the non-optimal is optimal. *Thinking & Reasoning*, 17, 387–401.

Williams, B. (1973). Deciding to believe. In his *Problems of the Self.* Cambridge University Press.

Wilson, M. & Fox, G. (2007). Working memory for language is not special: Evidence for an articulatory loop for novel stimuli. *Psychonomic Bulletin & Review*, 14, 470–3.

Wilson, T. (2002). *Strangers to Ourselves.* Harvard University Press.

Wilson, T., Lindsey, S., & Schooler, T. (2000). A model of dual attitudes. *Psychological Review*, 107, 101–26.

Wilson, T., Schooler, J., Hodges, S., Klaaren, K., & LaFleur, S. (1993). Introspecting about reasons can reduce post-choice satisfaction. *Personality and Social Psychology Bulletin*, 19, 331–9.

Winawer, J., Witthoft, N., Frank, M., Wu, L., Wade, A., & Boroditsky, L. (2007). Russian blues reveal effects of language on color discrimination. *Proceedings of the National Academy of Sciences*, 104, 7780–5.

Winkowski, D. & Knudsen, E. (2007). Top-down control of multimodal sensitivity in the Barn Owl optic tectum. *Journal of Neuroscience*, 27, 13279–91.

Winkowski, D. & Knudsen, E. (2008). Distinct mechanisms for the top-down control of neural gain and sensitivity in the Owl optic tectum. *Neuron*, 60, 698–708.

Wolpert, D. & Ghahramani, Z. (2000). Computational principles of movement neuroscience. *Nature Neuroscience*, 3, 1212–17.

Wolpert, D. & Kawato, M. (1998). Multiple paired forward and inverse models for motor control. *Neural Networks*, 11, 1317–29.

Wu, C., Weissman, D., Roberts, K., & Woldorff, M. (2007). The neural circuitry underlying the executive control of spatial attention. *Brain Research*, 1134, 189–98.

Wu, W. (2011). Confronting many-many problems: Attention and agentive control. *Nous*, 45, 50–76.

Yeo, B.T., Krienen, F., Sepulcre, J., Sabuncu, M., Lashkari, D., Hollinshead, M., Roffman, J., Smoller, J., Zöllei, L., Polimeni, J., Fischl, B., Liu, H., & Buckner, R. (2011). The organization of human cerebral cortex estimated by intrinsic functional connectivity. *Journal of Neurophysiology*, 106, 1125–65.

Yott, J. & Poulin-Dubois, D. (2012). Breaking the rules: Do infants have a true understanding of false belief? *British Journal of Developmental Psychology*, 30, 156–71.

Young, R. & Lewis, R. (1999). The Soar cognitive architecture and human working memory. In A. Miyake & P. Shah (eds.), *Models of Working Memory*, Cambridge University Press.

Zanto, T., Rubens, M., Thangavel, A., & Gazzaley, A. (2011). Causal role of the prefrontal cortex in top–down modulation of visual processing and working memory. *Nature Neuroscience*, 14, 656–61.

Index of Names

Index of Subjects